LEARNING
Computer Applications
Projects & Exercises
3rd Edition

Lisa A. Bucki

PEARSON

Prentice
Hall
DDC

Appendix B

❖ Database Planning Worksheet

Notes

To ensure that your database includes all the information you need, take the time to plan out what fields it will include, what field names to use, and what type of data each field will hold. If needed, you can even specify the field size (width) in characters. (For some field types, like Date/Time fields, you can't change the field size.) Make as many copies of this planning worksheet as you need.

Database Planning Worksheet			
Database Information			
Student Name:			
Date:			
Database Purpose:			
File Name:			
Field Information			
Description	Name	Data Type	Size (Width)

Vice President and Publisher: Natalie E. Anderson
Executive Editor: Jennifer Frew
Manufacturing Buyer: Natacha St. Hill Moore
Technical Editor: Joyce Nielsen
Cover Designer: Amy Capuano
Composition: Shu Chen
Manager, Print Production: Christy Mahon
Printer/Binder: Quebecor World Book Services/Dubuque
Cover Printer: Phoenix Color Corporation

Credits and acknowledgements borrowed from other sources and reproduced, with permission, in this textbook are as follows:

Microsoft, Windows, PowerPoint, Outlook, FrontPage, Visual Basic, MSN, The Microsoft Network, and/or other Microsoft products referenced herein are either trademarks or registered trademarks of Microsoft Corporation in the U.S.A. and other countries. This book is not sponsored or endorsed by or affiliated with Microsoft Corporation.

10 9 8 7 6 5 4 3
ISBN 0-13-185600-6

	A	B	C	D	E	F	G
1							
2							
3							
4							
5							
6							
7							
8							
9							
10							
11							
12							
13							
14							
15							
16							
17							
18							
19							
20							

Table of Contents

Appendix A

❖ Spreadsheet Grid

Notes

You can use the spreadsheet grid on the following page to plan out where you want rows and columns of entries to go in your spreadsheet. For example, should you enter the sales figures for a single product across a row, or down a column? What labels do you need, and where should they go? Where do you want to put your formulas? Should you add labels to identify what each formula calculates? Make as many copies of this grid as you need.

IV. Desktop Publishing

V. Spreadsheet

VI. Database

VII. Presentation Graphics

Quiz Break 8

Circle the correct answer to each of the questions below:

T	F	1. You can use text from your word processor to create a slide show.
T	F	2. You must create a table before you paste spreadsheet data into your word processor or presentation graphics program.
T	F	3. In some instances, you can link information between files from different applications.
T	F	4. Most word processors do not let you use database data for a mail merge.
T	F	5. Having a title in the first cell of a spreadsheet usually interferes when you try to import the spreadsheet into a database.
T	F	6. Hyperlinks only work for Web pages.
T	F	7. You can use various applications to save information in Web format, and even edit the Web information.
T	F	8. Using quotation marks can help make a Web search more specific.
T	F	9. E-mail disappears immediately after you read it.
T	F	10. PIM stands for Processing Incoming Mail.
T	F	11. You can sort your to-do list.
T	F	12. Your PIM enables you to track appointments.

Circle the correct answer to each of the questions below:

1. URL is:
   A. The command button that you use for underlining text.
   B. An acronym for Uniform Resource Locator.
   C. A Web page address.
   D. Both B and C.

2. To send e-mail, you can:
   A. E-mail a file from an application.
   B. E-mail from your PIM or e-mail program.
   C. Send an e-mail without a file from an application.
   D. All of the above.

3. You use the following command to link information between applications:
   A. Insert | New Link.
   B. Link | Paste Copy.
   C. Edit | Paste Special
   D. Edit | Link.

4. You can set reminders for:
   A. Tasks.
   B. Appointments.
   C. E-mails.
   D. A and B only

5. You use a theme to:
   A. Start a presentation before importing word processor text.
   B. Format Web page information in a word processor.
   C. Format an e-mail message.
   D. Identify similar tasks or appointments.

VIII. Integration & Communications on CD 💿

IX. APPENDIXES

X. Index

9. Wait a few minutes, then send and receive messages again. You should receive an assignment request from your designated classmate.
10. Choose to accept the assignment, then send a return message to your classmate.
11. Wait a few minutes, then send and receive messages again.

12. If prompted to verify the accepted assignment, do so.
   ✓ In Outlook 2003, *if you receive a message about a declined task, open the message in its own window, then choose Actions | Return to Task List.*
13. Close the PIM and disconnect from the Internet if you've finished working.

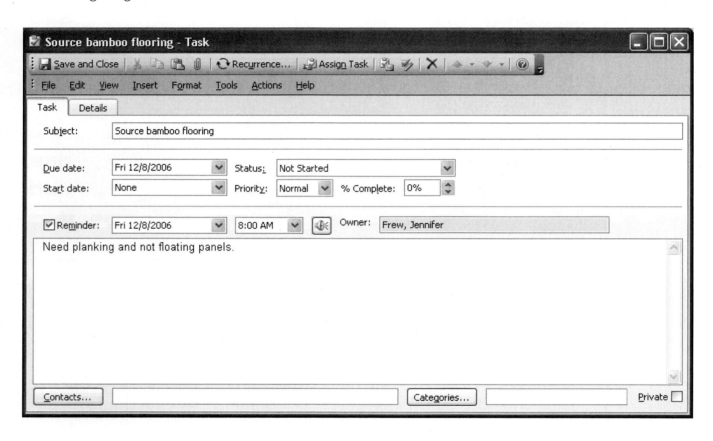

Introduction

When you need to practice the computer skills you've learned in class, spend some time with a computer and this book, **Learning Computer Applications: Projects and Exercises, 3rd Edition**. It offers word processing, desktop publishing, spreadsheet, database, presentation graphics, integration, and Internet exercises geared to help you feel more confident completing essential tasks.

Within each section, early exercises reinforce basic skills. Working through those earlier exercises prepares you for the later exercises, which present intermediate-level challenges.

How We've Organized the Book

Learning Computer Applications: Projects and Exercises, 3rd Edition divides information into eight main sections:

- **Introduction to Computers and Applications**. Reviews basic features of personal computers and applications, as well as Windows and Macintosh software.

- **File Management**. Discusses working with files and folders.

- **Word Processing**. Presents exercises for creating and editing documents.

- **Desktop Publishing**. Offers exercises for applying formatting to word processing documents to make the documents more readable and attractive. (Lesson 14 covers Publisher, which is a Microsoft Office application for Windows only.)

- **Spreadsheet**. Gives you exercises for creating spreadsheets to organize and calculate data.

- **Database**. Provides exercises so you can practice organizing lengthy lists of information.

- **Presentation Graphics**. Contains exercises to hone your skills in developing effective on-screen presentations.

- **Integration and Communications**. Includes exercises for both using various applications together and using applications in conjunction with the Internet. Also includes exercises on task and time management.

All sections—but the first two—group exercises by topic into lessons. Every exercise stands alone, so you can use the section and lesson names to find exercises you most need, and then work through those exercises in any order.

Exercise 34

❖ Assign a Task to Someone Else

Notes

Today's PIMs increasingly include features to help **work groups** (teams of people) to work together more effectively. Specifically, many PIM programs now include the capability for you to ask another person to handle a particular task. This process generates an e-mail message to the other person and makes that person the task's **owner** (responsible party) in the PIM. That person can either **accept** (agree to take on) or **decline** (not agree to take on) the assignment in the return message to you. (If the person declines the task, you can then assign it to a new owner.) Once a task has been accepted, you can typically request progress updates via e-mail, as well.

You want to delegate one of your tasks to a junior associate at Design Architects, LLC. Try assigning a task now.

Vocabulary

work group   owner   accept   decline

Directions

1. Start the PIM (e-mail) program, if needed.

   ✓ *This exercise requires that the PIM or e-mail program be properly configured and that you be able to connect to the Internet.*

2. Display a view that includes the task list or taskpad. This may be the tasks view, the calendar view, or either view, depending on your PIM program.

3. Start a new task using the method that enables you to add more task details.

4. Enter **Source bamboo flooring** as the task subject (name), and specify a due date of a week from today.

5. Enter **Need planking and not floating panels.** in the notes area of the task window or dialog box. The task should now resemble the illustration on the following page.

6. Choose the button or option for assigning the task.

7. Enter a classmate's e-mail address (buddy up with another student, as indicated by your instructor) in the To: or Recipient: text box, then send the message.

   ✓ *If you see a message that the task reminder will be turned off, click OK or the equivalent to accept that change.*

   ✓ *Your PIM typically sends the message to your e-mail outbox first.*

8. Switch to your e-mail program if needed, connect to the Internet if needed, then send and receive messages.

   ✓ *Refer to exercises in the previous lesson if you want to practice sending and receiving e-mail.*

In addition, the CD that comes with this book includes a **GLOSSARY** of important computer and software terms you need to understand, work with, and talk about, including terms about the Internet and World Wide Web.

The focus of this book is on applying computer skills—not on keyboarding. This way students can focus on the tasks essential to the exercise's objective rather than on typing or data entry. As a result, many of the exercises are designed to be created with the provided data files. Some data files may contain formatting that may not be evident in the exercise illustration. If you choose to have the students create the exercises from scratch, have them work to match the illustrations. Encourage students to apply their critical thinking skills as they create the various documents.

Support Material

A complete instructor support package is available with all the tools teachers need:

- Annotated teacher's edition includes entire student book with teacher notes, course curriculum guide, and lesson plans. Includes solution file CD-ROM (ISBN: 0-13-185706-1)

- Test bank with pre- and post-assessment tests, mid-term exams, and final exams. (ISBN: 0-13-185708-8)

- Printouts of exercise solutions with solution file CD-ROM. (ISBN: 0-13-185707-X)

- Solution file CD-ROM. (ISBN: 0-13-185709-6)

- Procedure booklets that cover all of the skills necessary to complete each exercise. (Microsoft Office XP, ISBN: 0-13-185710-X; Microsoft Office 2003, ISBN: 0-13-185713-4)

Working with Files and Disks

As you work through the exercises in this book, you'll be creating, opening, and saving files. Keep the following instructions in mind as you do so:

- Unless the book instructs otherwise, use the default settings for text size, margin size, and so on when you're creating a file. If someone has changed the default software settings for the computer you're using, your exercise files may not look the same as those shown in this book. In addition, the appearance of your files may look different if the system is set to a screen resolution other than 800 x 600. If any of these differences confuse you, ask your instructor for help.

- Many exercises instruct you to open a file from the CD-ROM that comes with this book. The files are organized into particular folders on the CD-ROM. Or, your instructor may have copied the files to a particular folder or network location. Ask your instructor if you need help finding the exercise files.

Exercise 33

❖ Respond to Reminders

Notes

You saw in earlier exercises that you can control reminder settings for both tasks and appointments. When you have a reminder or alert set, a reminder message appears on-screen to alert you to the upcoming task deadline or appointment. (Generally, your PIM software has to be running for the reminders to appear.) You also can include an alert sound to make the reminder more obvious. Once the reminder message appears on-screen, you generally have the option to **postpone** the reminder for some period of time or to **dismiss** the reminder assuming you don't need to see it again.

Your boss at Design Architects LLC asked you to join him in the conference room in 10 minutes. Set up a reminder for that new event, and dismiss the reminder once you've read it.

Vocabulary

postpone   dismiss

Directions

1. Start the PIM (e-mail) program, if needed.
2. Display the calendar in its current day view.
3. Create a new appointment scheduled to start less than 10 minutes in the future. Name the appointment **CR Reminder**.
4. Set a reminder for **5 minutes** (or less) before the appointment.
5. Change the reminder sound to another sound available on your system.

   ✓ *In most Windows versions, you can find additional .WAV sound files in the \Windows\Media folder.*

6. Finish creating the appointment.

7. When the reminder appears on-screen, postpone the reminder for another 5 minutes.

   ✓ *In Outlook, you use the Snooze feature to postpone the reminder.*

   ✓ *If you choose to open the item, that means that the appointment details will appear on-screen in a window or dialog box, so that you can review the details. This is useful to do if you've typed in particular notes about the appointment, such as appointment location information.*

8. When the reminder reappears, dismiss it.
9. Close the PIM if you've finished working.

- The Directory of Files at the beginning of each section lists the exercise file (from the CD-ROM) you'll need to open to complete each exercise. A "None" listing means that the exercise requires you to create a new file from scratch rather than opening an exercise file.

- All the exercises instruct you to save the files you create or to save the exercise files under a new name. Ask your instructor for the name of the hard disk or network folder to which you should save your files.

A Word about the Examples

Certain illustrations are based on templates that do not follow traditional business communications spacing. You may choose to have your class modify documents to adhere to traditional business communications formats. For example, if a letter does not call for reference initials, you may ask your students to add them on their own. Also refer to the annotated teacher's edition for additional information on how to modify exercises to match traditional business communications formats.

In the vast majority of cases, the information in the exercise examples is purely fictional. The examples are not intended to provide advice—career, business, legal, or otherwise. Nor do we intend the exercise examples to convey facts or information to use in decision-making. The examples are illustrative only.

All terms mentioned in this book that are known to be trademarks or service marks are appropriately capitalized. Use of a term in this book should not be regarded as affecting the validity of any trademark or service mark.

What's on the CD

We've included on the CD:

- **Data files for many of the exercises**. This way students don't have to type lengthy documents from scratch.

- **Glossary**. The glossary covers hundreds of the most important computer terms you need to understand and use, including terms about the Internet and World Wide Web.

- **Touch 'N' Type Keyboarding course**. This course was designed for those who would like to learn to type in the shortest possible period of time. The keyboarding skill-building drills are also ideal for those who wish to practice and improve their keyboarding. The exercises can be printed out, copied, and distributed to students. The files have been prepared in Adobe Acrobat format. You must have Adobe Reader installed on your computer in order to open the files. Visit www.adobe.com for a free download.

- **Computer Literacy Basics**. These exercises include information on computer care, computer basics, and a brief history of computers. The exercises in this section are Windows-specific. You must have Adobe Reader installed on your computer in order open the files.

Exercise 32

❖ View and Print Your Appointments

Notes

Most PIMs also give you a great deal of flexibility in viewing your upcoming calendar. You can view the schedule for the current day, or for a particular date, week, or month. Further, you can print any view of your upcoming schedule, so you'll have the pertinent information with you even when you're away from your computer.

  ✓ *Some of the leading PIM programs, such as Outlook, also can synchronize information with palm and handheld computers, giving you another method for keeping your task, schedule, and contact information with you.*

You want to review your appointments so that you honor all your commitments to Design Architects. View your calendar in various ways now, and print a hard copy so you can take your schedule with you.

Vocabulary

No new vocabulary in this exercise.

Directions

1. Start the PIM (e-mail) program, if needed.

  ✓ *This exercise requires the appointment entries made in Exercise 31, so complete that exercise now if you haven't already done so.*

2. Go to **November 10, 2006**.
3. Scroll to later dates to confirm the weekly meetings on Fridays.
4. Return to **November 10, 2006**.
5. Print the calendar in current day view, label the printout with your name and the exercise number, and provide the printout to your instructor if required.

6. Change to the weekly calendar view.

  ✓ *Outlook 2003 also includes a work week view that shows Monday through Friday only.*

7. Display the print preview for this view.
8. Review how the preview looks and then close the print preview.
9. Change to the monthly calendar view.
10. Review how the preview looks and then close the print preview.
11. Return to the current day view.
12. Close the PIM if you've finished working.

To access the files from Windows:

1. Put the CD in your CD-ROM drive.
2. Open Windows Explorer. (Right-click on the **Start** button ![start] and click **Explore**.)
3. Select the CD-ROM drive letter from the All Folders pane of the Explorer window.

To copy the data files:

a. Click to select the **Data Files** folder in the Contents of (CD-ROM drive letter) pane of the Explorer window.

b. Drag the folder onto the letter of the drive to which you wish to copy the data files (usually **C:**) in the All Folders pane of the Explorer Window.

To access the Glossary:

- Leave the Glossary files on the CD and open, view, and print them from the CD. These files are in a folder called **Glossary**.
- Copy the files to your hard drive using Windows Explorer. Once on your hard drive you can open, view, and print the files. These files are in a folder called **Glossary**.

  ✓ *You must have Adobe Reader installed on your computer in order to open the files.*

To access the Keyboarding Course:

- Leave the Keyboarding Course files on the CD and open, view, and print them from the CD. These files are in a folder called **Keyboarding**.
- Copy some or all of them to your hard drive using Windows Explorer. Once on your hard drive you can open, view, and print the files. These files are in a folder called **Keyboarding**.

  ✓ *You must have Adobe Reader installed on your computer in order to open the files.*

To access the Computer Literacy Basics files:

- Leave the Computer Literacy files on the CD and open, view, and print them from the CD. The Computer Literacy files are located in the **Literacy** folder.
- Copy some or all of the exercises to your hard drive using Windows Explorer. Once on your hard drive you can open, view, and print the files. The Computer Literacy files are located in the **Literacy** folder.

  ✓ *You must have Adobe Reader installed on your computer in order to open the files.*

Illustration 2

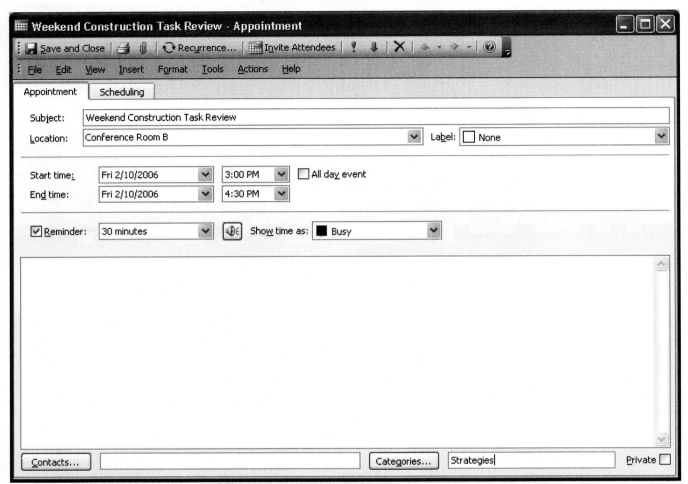

To access the files from a Mac:

1. Insert the CD in your CD-ROM drive. The **CD-ROM** icon will appear on your desktop.
2. Double-click the **CD-ROM** icon .

To copy data files on to a hard drive:

1. Double-click the **Data Files** folder.
2. Double-click your **Hard Disk** icon Macintosh .
3. Locate the folder or create a new folder where you want to store your files.
4. Drag the **Data Files** folder to the folder on your hard drive. A copy will be created and you can put the original away for back-up.

To access the Keyboarding Course:

- Leave the Keyboarding Course files on the CD and open, view, and print them from the CD. These files are in a folder called **Keyboarding**.
- Drag some or all of the exercises to your hard drive. Once on your hard drive you can open, view, and print the files. These files are in a folder called **Keyboarding**.

  ✓ *You must have Adobe Reader installed on your computer in order to open the files.*

To access the Glossary:

- Leave the Glossary files on the CD and open, view, and print them from the CD. These files are in a folder called **Glossary**.
- Drag the files to your hard drive. Once on your hard drive you can open, view, and print the files. These files are in a folder called **Glossary**.

  ✓ *You must have Adobe Reader installed on your computer in order to open the files.*

Illustration 1

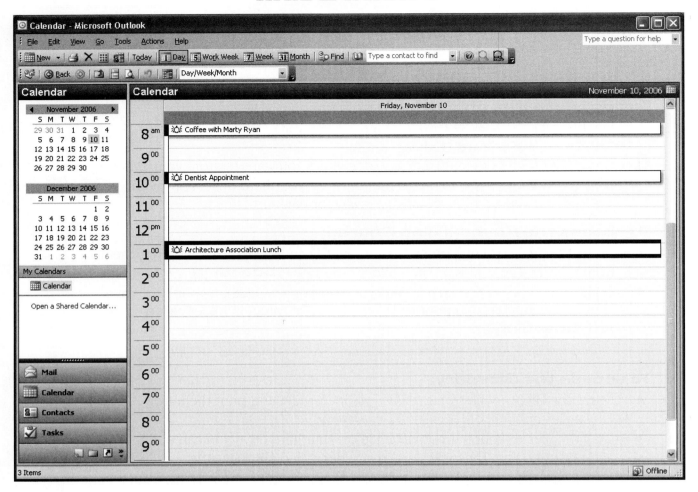

Introduction

Introduction to Computers and Applications

Exercise 31

❖ Add an Appointment

Notes

Beyond a simple list of tasks, most personal information manager (PIM) software enables you to keep track of your upcoming **appointments**, whether a class, a meeting, a doctor's appointment, or an all-day event. Using the reminders feature along with your appointments helps keep you on time for your commitments. In addition, you can set up a **recurring appointment**, which automatically repeats an appointment in your schedule, so that you don't have to calculate each appointment date and time.

Add an appointment with one of your architecture clients in this exercise.

Vocabulary

appointment   recurring appointment

Directions

1. Start the PIM (e-mail) program, if needed.
2. Display the calendar in its current day view.
   - ✓ *In most PIMs, the current day view appears by default when you switch to the calendar.*
3. Go to the date **November 10, 2006**.
4. Use the quick method to add the new appointments shown in Illustration 1 on the following page.
   - ✓ *The quick method usually involves clicking a blank time in the calendar, typing the task name, and then pressing Enter.*
5. Start a new appointment at **3:00** using the method that enables you to add more appointment details.
   - ✓ *To display a dialog box that enables you to create a new appointment and enter more details about it, you generally can double-click a blank time in the calendar, choose a command like File|New|Appointment, or use the New button on a toolbar or command bar.*

6. Specify the appointment subject (name), location, end time, reminder, and category information as shown in Illustration 2 on page 552.
   - ✓ *As with tasks, you can generally sort or view appointments by category.*
   - ✓ *To delete a task or assignment in a view, you can typically right-click on it and then click Delete.*
7. Set the appointment up as a recurring (repeating) appointment taking place for five consecutive Fridays (that is, every week for five weeks).
8. Finish adding the appointment.
9. You can then close the PIM if you've finished working.

Introduction

According to Computer Industry Almanac, the number of personal computers (PCs) in use in the United States surpassed 200 million during the year 2002. PCs have become almost as commonplace as televisions in the home and as commonplace as telephones in the workplace. Because most employers want all employees to be comfortable using a computer, it's important for you to get the most out of your computer classes in high school, college, and vocational school.

To work effectively with your computer, you need to understand the computer's parts and the kinds of software you use on the computer. This section provides a review of that information, as well as reviewing key operations you'll need to perform with the Windows or Macintosh operating system—the software that enables you and other software programs to work with the computer. Finally, you'll learn what programs today have in common.

Computer Basics

The typical new computer system today offers extras like speakers for playing audio, drives that burn CD-Rs or DVD-Rs for file backup and sharing, and other "peripherals"—including those that can simply be "plugged and played" with simple USB and FireWire connectors (explained later in this section). While computers consist of numerous parts, you don't need to know about all of them, unless you plan to repair your own PC. The components in a basic business computer system have been consistent for years, so you only really need to know about these key components:

- **System Unit.** This metal case houses the internal components of the computer. Wide and flat desktop system units sit horizontally on a desk or table. Tall and narrow tower and minitower system units can sit vertically on the floor, leaving desktop space free. Notebook computers—portable computers that fold open and close like a clamshell—use a smaller system unit case that integrates other components of the system, like the keyboard. Some desktop computers even feature a compact, all-in-one design that combines the system unit and monitor to save space on your desk.

- **Central Processing Unit (CPU) and Motherboard.** The CPU provides the brainpower for the PC, executing commands, performing calculations, and sometimes routing information between the various parts of the system. The CPU plugs into the motherboard, a board that holds the internal circuitry for the computer and slots where other components plug in. The CPU's speed and capabilities serve as the single greatest factor for determining the overall system's speed and power. Some of the fastest new systems today offer the Intel Pentium 4 CPU, which operates at speeds up to 3.2 GHz (gigahertz). Advanced Micro Devices (AMD) offers a 2.2 GHz Athlon XP 3200 processor that is also used in faster Windows-based systems. (AMD also offers even faster 64-bit CPUs for use in high-end environments and networks.) Some Windows-based PCs use the lower-priced but full-featured Intel Celeron processor. Notebooks typically use a Mobile Celeron, Centrino, or power-conserving Pentium Mobile (Pentium M) from Intel. The latest Macintosh systems use the PowerPC G5 processor, but the iBook and PowerBook

Illustration 2

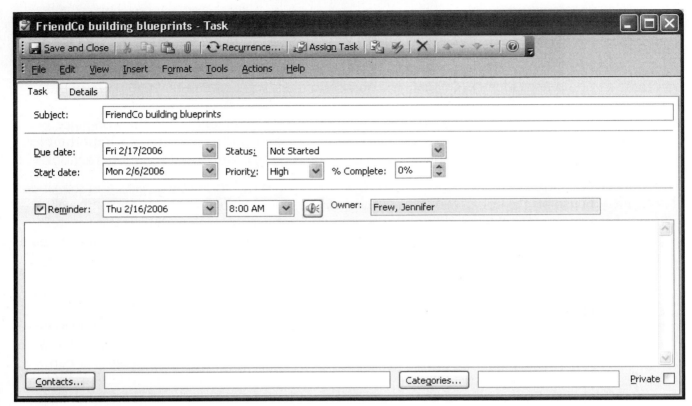

notebooks and desktop eMac and iMac models still use the older PowerPC G4 processor. Most systems also include a cache as part of the CPU. The cache holds data that the CPU needs frequently, reducing the time it takes for the CPU to retrieve that data.

■ **Random Access Memory (RAM).** RAM holds information temporarily within the system. For this reason, it's commonly called the system's "working memory." For example, as you're typing a new file, the PC stores what you type in RAM until you save the file. If you close a new file or turn off the system without saving the file, the system clears the file contents out of RAM, so the information is not preserved for later reuse. The PC's RAM contributes to how quickly the system runs, but more importantly affects how many programs and files you can open at a time. For example, a system with 256 megabytes (or 256M) of RAM can have more programs open than a system with 128M of RAM. Many systems shipping today have a full gigabyte (1G) of RAM.

✓ *The difference between RAM (memory) and storage (disk space) often trips up beginners. RAM stores information temporarily. When you turn off the system, everything in RAM gets erased. Disks store information semi-permanently. After you save a file to a disk, the file remains there until you remove or delete it.*

✓ *Different system manufacturers now use slightly different types of RAM, such as SDRAM or PC2100 DDR RAM. If you ever want to add RAM into a system you own, be sure to buy the correct kind of RAM.*

■ **Hard Disk.** The hard disk, actually composed of several platters of magnetic storage material stored within a mechanism called the *hard disk drive*, holds the computer's system files, other programs, and the files that you create. You can divide the available storage space on the hard disk into folders. You create a folder, give it the name you want, and then save your files in it. When you install a new program, the installation program automatically creates folders to hold the program files. Obviously, the larger the hard disk a system has, the more files and programs it can hold. New systems today hold 40G (and up) worth of information, with each gigabyte representing more than a billion characters.

■ **Floppy or Other Removable Disk Drive.** In addition to the hard disk drive, most systems offer at least one other disk drive. Traditionally, this second disk drive has been a floppy disk drive into which you can insert and remove 3½" floppy disks. Today, some systems include drives and readers using other removable disk formats, like the popular Iomega Zip drive or slots for various types of device storage such as the CompactFlash, SecureDigital, and SmartMedia commonly used by digital cameras. (You also can buy a reader for digital media that connects to your computer if the reading slots aren't built in.) When you insert any type of removable disk or media into the drive or slot, you can open files from it or save files to it. A 3½" floppy holds about 1.44 megabytes of information, or well more than a million characters.

✓ *Never remove a floppy or removable disk from the disk drive or slot while the drive light is lit. That light means that the drive is still spinning the disk. Pulling the disk out while it's spinning can damage the files on the disk.*

■ **Display.** A computer's display really consists of two parts. The TV-like monitor shows program information, as well as information you type or choices you make. Many users opt for the increasingly-popular LCD flat panel monitors. These monitors use less power and desk space, a tradeoff for the fact that they still cost a bit more than traditional CRD (cathode ray tube) style monitors. Either type of monitor actually connects to a receptacle on the back of the video card,

7. Create a Client category in the master list of categories and assign it to the task.

   ✓ **Categories** *help you identify related tasks or tasks that pertain to a particular overall activity. Generally, you use a command or button to display the available categories, and then click to check (select) those that you want to assign. You can typically then use the View menu to choose a view that organizes tasks according to category.*

   ✓ *If you see a Recurrence button (or a similarly-named button), you can use it to set up a repeating task.*

   ✓ *A task (or appointment) window or dialog box typically includes a large text box where you can type notes, such as details about the task or instructions for finding the appointment location.*

8. Finish adding the task.
9. Sort the tasks by due date. Typically, you can sort the task list by clicking on a column heading in the list.
10. Resort the tasks by due date (from earliest date to latest).

    ✓ *You may have to click twice on a column to get the right sort order.*

11. Click to check the first and third tasks to mark them as completed.
12. Print the task list, label the printout with your name and the exercise number, and provide the printout to your instructor if required. You can then close the PIM if you've finished working.

Illustration 1

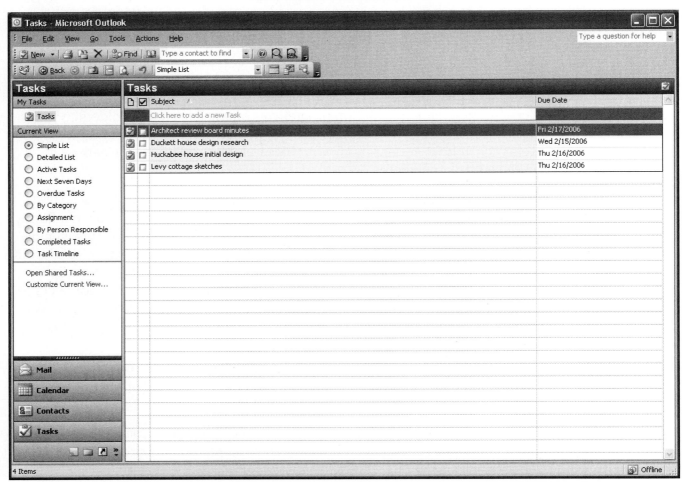

the second part of the computer's display. The video card plugs into a receptacle on the motherboard within the system unit. The video card controls how many colors the monitor can display. It also controls the screen resolution. Higher resolution means that the system can fit more information on the screen. So, a system displaying at 1,280 × 1,024 shows more than one displaying at 1,024 × 768. (The numbers represent the number of pixels—display dots—shown horizontally and vertically.) Note that a video card includes its own RAM (memory). If you plan to play highly graphical games or work with video or graphics programs, choose a fast video card with as much memory as possible; top cards feature 256M. Some video cards even enable a computer to receive and play TV programming, but this capability might distract a user from the work at hand.

- **Keyboard.** You use the keyboard as your primary means of giving the computer input. You can choose commands with the keyboard or type in information. Computer keyboards include a number of special keys, including the F-keys or function keys. F-keys typically appear in a row above the alphanumeric keys. You can sometimes use the F-keys as shortcut keys (either alone or along with another key) for performing a command. You can use the Ctrl and Alt commands similarly, for performing commands. Computer keyboards also include keys like Insert and Delete, which you can use to make changes to information. The Home, End, Page Up, Page Down, and arrow keys enable you to move around in a file. And an extra numeric keyboard at the right side of some keyboards makes it more convenient to enter numbers.

- **Mouse.** This hand-sized device rolls on your desk and connects to the system via a tail like cable. Rolling the mouse moves an on-screen pointer in the corresponding direction. Then, you can press a button on the mouse to select what's underneath the pointer. Pressing and releasing the left mouse button once quickly is called *clicking*. Pressing and releasing the left mouse button twice quickly is called double-clicking. Pressing and releasing the right mouse button once is called *right-clicking*. Some mice are cordless while others use optical technology in place of the rolling mouse ball, and nearly all newer mice for Windows-based systems feature a scroll wheel in between the buttons to make navigation actions like scrolling a document faster and easier.

- **CD-ROM or DVD-ROM, CD-R/CD-RW, and DVD-R/DVD-RW Drives.** Most systems today offer a CD-ROM (Compact Disc-Read Only Memory) drive. This type of drive reads a CD-ROM disc, a disc that's just under 5" in diameter and made of plastics and other materials. Some systems instead have a DVD-ROM drive. DVD-ROMs (Digital Versatile Disc-Read Only Memory or Digital Video Disk-Read Only Memory) can store more information (17G or more) than CD-ROMs, so they're typically used to store movie and game content. These drives use a laser to read information stored on the disc inserted into the drive. Today's desktop systems also typically include a CD-R (CD-Recordable) or DVD-R (DVD-Recordable) drive, which not only read discs but also record material on special CD-R or DVD-R discs. These drives have become popular for system backups or storing music files. CD-RW (CD-Rewritable) drives can write to CD-R discs as well as CD-RW discs, which allow the drive to write and then erase and rewrite data. Likewise, DVD-R drives write to DVD-R discs and rewritable DVD-RW discs.

- **Modem, Network Interface, and Other Connections.** A modem enables your computer to communicate over telephone lines. (A special type of modem, called a *cable modem*, enables a system to communicate at higher speeds over TV cable lines. Another high-speed connection uses a DSL *modem* and special telephone line capabilities.) The computer can use the modem to send information and receive information. Similarly, a Network Interface Card (NIC)

Exercise 30

❖ Track Your To-Dos

Notes

The professional versions of the major software suites offer a special type of program called a **personal information manager (PIM)**. PIMs help you to manage your schedule. With a PIM, you can track a list of tasks, sort and prioritize tasks, and check tasks when you complete the work.

  ✓ *In Microsoft Office, Outlook provides PIM features as well as e-mail management. In the WordPerfect Suite, CorelCENTRAL provides e-mail and PIM features. Even if your operating system and office suite software don't include a PIM, you can purchase PIM software for a relatively modest cost.*

You are an architect with Design Architects, LLC. You have a number of projects, so you want to create a to-do list. Add and manage some to do list tasks now.

Vocabulary

personal information manager (PIM)	task task list (to-do list)	taskpad reminder	category

Directions

1. Start the PIM (e-mail) program, if needed.
2. Display a view that includes the **task** list or taskpad. This may be the tasks view, the calendar view, or another view, depending on your PIM program.
3. Use the quick method to add the new tasks shown in Illustration 1 on the following page.

  ✓ *The quick method usually involves clicking a blank line in the **task list** or **taskpad**, typing the task name, and then pressing Enter. If the quick method in your PIM enables you to include a task deadline, press Tab after you type the task name, enter the deadline, and then press Enter.*

4. Start a new task using the method that enables you to add more task details.

  ✓ *To display a dialog box that enables you to create a new task and enter more details about it, you generally can double-click a blank line in the task list, choose a command like File | New | Task, or use the New button on a toolbar or command bar.*

5. Enter the task subject (name), date information, and priority as shown in Illustration 2 on page 549.
6. Adjust the **reminder** settings to receive a reminder a day before the due date.

enables your computer to connect to a LAN (local area network) via network cabling or a wireless network. When connected to a network, a computer can share files and messages with other computers also connected to the network. Most systems today have at least one of these communications devices, but some have both. Systems today also feature several types of ports for connecting devices such as printers, scanners, cameras, and auxiliary drives. In addition to the traditional serial and parallel ports, most systems include at least two USB (Universal Serial Bus) ports. USB ports enable you to connect up to 127 devices in a sequence called a *daisy chain*. The latest type of USB connection, as USB 2.0 connection, can transfer data at a fast 480 Mbps (480 million bits per second), as opposed to 12 Mbps for the older USB 1.1 standard. (You can still connect an older USB device to a faster USB 2.0 port, however.) A still faster type of port called a FireWire (IEEE 1394) port is becoming popular for external hard disk and digital video camera connections. FireWire ports can transfer data at rates between 400 and 800 Mbps. Both types of connections enable you to hot plug a device (plug it in after the system is running without restarting).

- **Operating System Software.** Each of the computer parts listed above is a piece of **hardware**—the physical machinery and parts of the computer. In contrast, **software** consists of programming instructions that enable the computer to work and enable you to communicate with the computer. Every computer must have **operating system software**, which essentially **operates** the hardware. For example, the operating system software helps move information into and out of the CPU. If you're using this book, chances are your system uses a form of the Windows operating system software. (For more about Windows, see "Understanding Features of Windows and Windows Applications" on page 8.) Macintosh (Mac) computer systems use the Mac OS X 10.3 Panther operating system, or perhaps an older version of Mac OS X or the even older Mac OS 9.x operating system. Without operating system software, a PC can't run.

Types of Applications

The terms "program," "software," and "application" mean the same thing. They refer to the programming instructions that run your computer or that are used to perform a particular operation. Over time, applications have evolved into a number of categories based on what you do with them. Understanding what each category of software does helps in choosing the right program to use when a job is to be performed.

Most computers come with the required operating system software, as well as a few other programs. This book covers the most-used application categories:

- **Word Processor.** Use word processing programs to create documents such as a letter, memo, or report. Your work can be checked and fixed on-screen before printing it. Word processors include spelling and grammar checkers to help catch errors and a thesaurus to suggest alternate words. Word processors also enable applying fancy formatting to documents. The styling of letters can be changed, borders added, or graphics inserted. These formatting features previously were only available in special programs called *desktop publishing programs*. Desktop publishing programs make it possible for anyone—not just graphic artists—to produce professional publications like color ads, newsletters, brochures, and so forth. Current word

Integration and Communications

Lesson 31
Manage Your Time

Exercises 30-34

- ❖ Build a to-do list
- ❖ Track and print your appointments
- ❖ Work with an appointment reminder
- ❖ Make a task assignment

processors offer a number of "desktop publishing" features, so this book includes coverage about "desktop publishing" using a word processor. Most word processors (and some other applications) also enable you to publish information as a Web page.

- **Spreadsheet.** Spreadsheet (or worksheet) programs organize the words and numbers entered in a grid of rows and columns. Each cell (the intersection of a row and column) in a spreadsheet holds a single entry. Formulas can be entered in other cells to perform calculations on number entries. Spreadsheets also offer functions—prewritten formulas that help create more complicated calculations. If you want your numbers to be neat, want to ensure accurate calculations, or want to test different calculations, use a spreadsheet program.

- **Database.** A database file holds a list of information. Address book lists, membership lists, product catalog lists, and the like are examples of lists that could be entered into a database. You break each entry or *record*—in the database down into similar parts called fields. For a product catalog database, each product entry is a record. The product name, description, item number, price, color, and quantity in stock are separate fields. When creating your database file, enter the records into a grid called a *table* that resembles a spreadsheet. Then you can sort the list or find desired records. Attractive reports can be created for subtotaling, displaying, and printing selected information from the list.

- **Presentation Graphics.** With a presentation graphics program, you can create and organize slides or pages of information. Then, display the presentation on your computer page by page as you talk. Or, print the pages for your audience. Each page can include a colorful background, text, graphics, and charts. You can add sounds and animations, and even set up the pages to display automatically in sequence. By incorporating text, charts, graphics, and more, a presentation graphics program helps a message have more impact and be more memorable to the audience.

- **Internet (Web Browsing and E-Mail).** A network of computer networks covering the earth forms the Internet. With the Internet and Internet e-mail software, e-mail messages can be sent that arrive the same hour, if not the same minute. With Internet Web browser software, you can view graphical, informative Web pages stored all over the world. There are other types of Internet software and ways to work on the Internet, but e-mail and the Web are most popular by far. However, instant messaging programs, which enable you to type and send real-time messages and share files, have emerged as a fast-growing category, with millions of users already chatting away. And users typically use FTP programs to store files on and retrieve them from special servers (FTP servers) connected to the Internet. Note that to connect to the Internet, your computer also must have a modem and an account with an Internet Service Provider (ISP), or must be connected to a network that provides Internet access.

While we won't be covering them in this book, sooner or later you'll encounter other types of computer software that deserve discussion:

- **Games.** Computers can be tools for fun as well as work. Whether you're hip to kickboxing, flying, working puzzles, solving mysteries, testing your trivia knowledge, or some other kind of mindless fun, there is a game program that can occupy you for hours.

Illustration 2

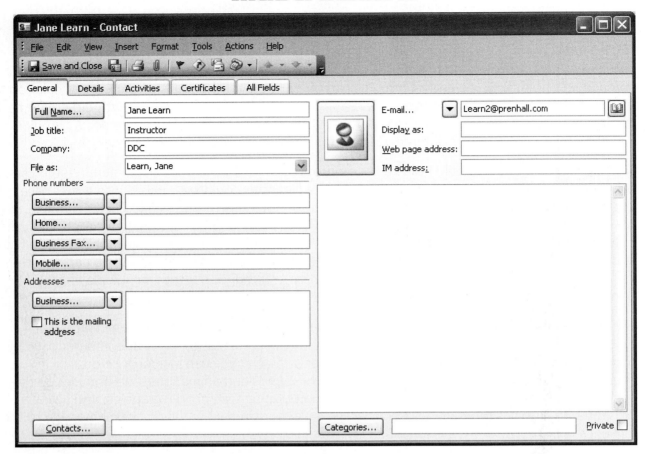

Illustration 3

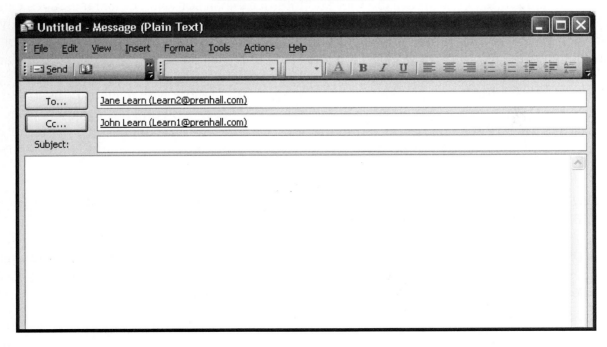

- **Utilities.** Utility programs help maintain your computer. Your operating system software typically offers some utility programs, but you can purchase separate programs to handle nearly any other system maintenance need. For example, virus-checker programs check your files for computer viruses (programs that can damage your system or files) and then remove any viruses found. A backup utility makes a special copy of important files, creating a spare in case the original becomes damaged.

  ✓ *Many games and utilities, in particular, are distributed over the Internet as* **shareware programs**. *Upon installing and regularly using the shareware, a small fee needs to be paid to the program's author. In contrast,* **freeware programs** *are truly free. Copy them, give them to friends, and have fun. Just remember that it's never fair or legal to copy a program that's not freeware.*

- **Accounting.** If you want to print checks using your computer, need help keeping your checkbook accurate, or would like to create and follow a budget, try a personal accounting program. More powerful accounting programs can keep track of income and expenses for home businesses and small businesses.

- **Graphics and Desktop Publishing.** Graphics programs enable creating and working with graphic images, or picture files. Some graphics programs enable drawing and editing images. For example, use a graphics program to create a logo for your newsletter or flyer. Other graphics programs enable organizing and displaying images you've downloaded, created, or shot with a digital camera. Desktop publishing programs provide more features for creating professional publications with text and graphics. Entry-level desktop publishing programs offer helpful templates to help the user position text and graphics and choose design elements, while high-end programs offer sophisticated features for indexing a publication, managing document color, and more.

- **Video, Audio, and Other Media Software.** Computer hardware manufacturers have been releasing an increasing number of tools that enable you to use your computer to capture and edit video and audio (sound and music). Use special software programs along with that hardware to put together your final production. For example, you can splice together video clips, then add sound. Some types of media software enable composing your own songs.

- **Project and Time Management.** Project management programs help you keep track of all the tasks, people, and other resources needed to complete a complicated project. The software can help estimate how long a project will take and how much it will cost. The software can be used to track your process toward completing the project as compared with your original plan. Time management programs work on a more individual scale, enabling you to track your to-dos, appointments, contacts, and notes. Many e-mail programs have at least some time-management features built in.

- **Other.** New software concepts emerge all the time. Software can be found for creating greeting cards, learning a new language, learning to play guitar, and more.

Illustration 1

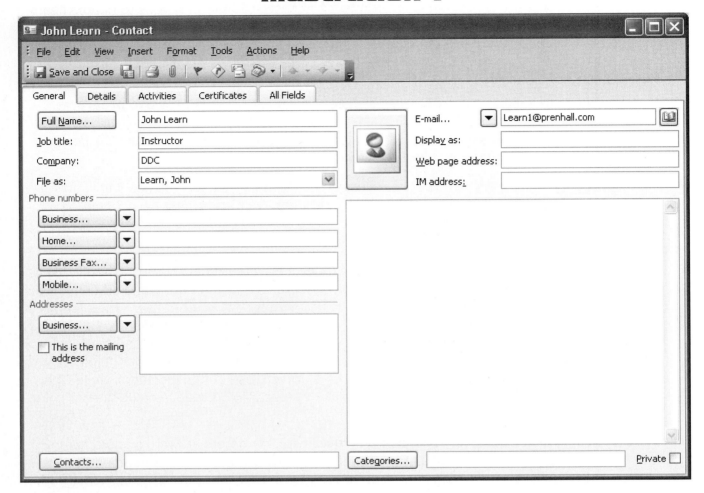

Understanding Features of Windows & Windows Applications

Tens of millions of computers now use some version of the Microsoft Windows operating system: Windows 95, Windows 98, Windows 2000, Windows Millennium Edition (Me) Windows XP, Windows NT, or Windows NT Workstation. For most basic operations, all these versions work the same.

Windows applications run "on top of" Windows. Windows lends these applications a consistent look and consistent way of operating. The illustration below shows you the key features of the latest version of Windows (XP), described next:

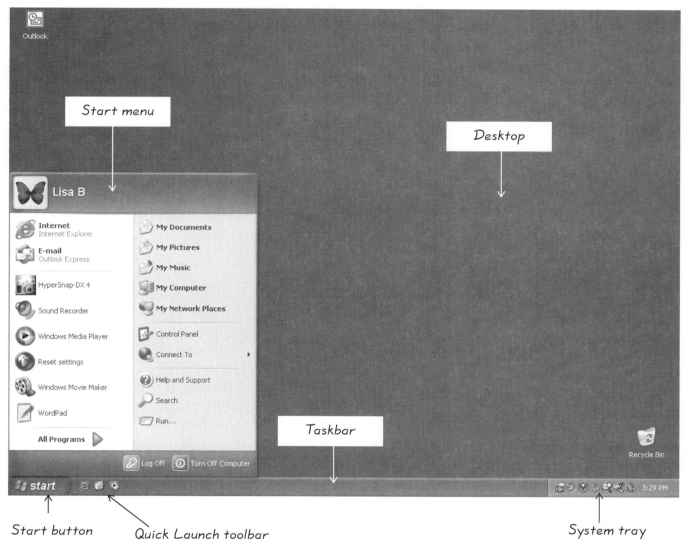

✓ The illustration shows Windows XP Home Edition. Other Windows versions may look a little different, but those versions offer the same features described next.

Exercise 29

❖ Work with E-Mail Addresses

Notes

If you sent multiple messages from earlier exercises to the same recipient, you may have noticed that your e-mail program remembered the address for you and helped you make the entry. But your e-mail program and operating system offer an even better way for storing and reusing e-mail addresses, especially in instances where you need to address a message to multiple recipients. This feature is commonly called an **address book**, and it stores the list of your key contacts. This exercise gives you an opportunity to practice saving and using address book entries.

You need to send e-mail to some new contacts. Add those contacts to your address book and create the e-mail now.

Vocabulary

address book

Directions

1. Start your e-mail program.
   - ✓ *You may be prompted to connect to the Internet. If that happens, connect now to complete this exercise.*
2. Use the command or button for displaying the address book feature in your e-mail program.
   - ✓ *If you're using Outlook, you also should make sure that Contacts is selected in the Show Names From The drop-down list.*
3. Choose the button or command for adding a new contact, and then verify that you want to create a single new contact rather than a group or list if prompted to do so.
4. Enter new contact information as shown in Illustration 1 on the following page.
   - ✓ *Of course, when you enter real-world contact information, you would include addresses, phone numbers, and any other relevant details about each contact.*
5. Save and close the new contact.
6. Choose the button or command for adding a new contact, and then verify that you want to create a single new contact rather than a group or list if prompted to do so.
7. Enter new contact information as shown in Illustration 2 on page 545.
8. Close the new contact, and then close the address book window.
9. Start a new e-mail message.
10. Use the To: or Recipient: button to open the address book list.
11. Add **Jane Learn** as the primary recipient, then add **John Learn** to the Cc: list.
12. Close the address book list. Your message should resemble the example in Illustration 3 on page 545.
13. Close the e-mail message without sending it.
14. Close your e-mail program.

- **Desktop.** The Windows desktop holds everything seen in Windows. When you open a program, it appears in its own window on top of the desktop.

- **Taskbar.** The taskbar by default runs along the bottom of the desktop. After you open an application, a button for that application appears on the taskbar. Click on the taskbar button for an application to make that application current (or active) so that you can work with it. In addition, the taskbar may show a button for files that you open in certain applications; you can then click on a particular button to make the file it represents current or active.

- **Start Button and Start Menu.** Click the Start button at the left end of the taskbar to display the Start menu. The Start menu holds commands (and folders holding commands) for starting programs and accessing Windows features.

  ✓ *Windows 98, 2000, Me, and XP offer extra buttons to the right of the Start button in a special area called the Quick Launch toolbar. (Windows 95 does not offer the Quick Launch toolbar.) In Windows XP, the Quick Launch toolbar may be off; to display it, right-click the taskbar, point to Toolbars in the menu that appears, and then click Quick Launch in the submenu.*

- **System Tray.** The system tray area at the right end of the taskbar displays time and (generally) a volume icon. It also may include icons for such programs as a virus checker, power monitor, volume control, and other programs that typically run automatically in the background when your computer is on. Windows XP also has a preference that will hide tray icons for inactive programs. If this feature is turned on (right-click the taskbar, click Properties, and check Hide inactive icons on the Taskbar tab of the Taskbar and Start Menu Properties dialog box), an arrow button will appear to indicate that icons are hidden. Click on the double-arrow button to expand the tray so that you can see the icons.

After you use the Start menu to start a program, the program opens in its own program or application window (see the next illustration of Microsoft Office Word 2003).

Illustration 2

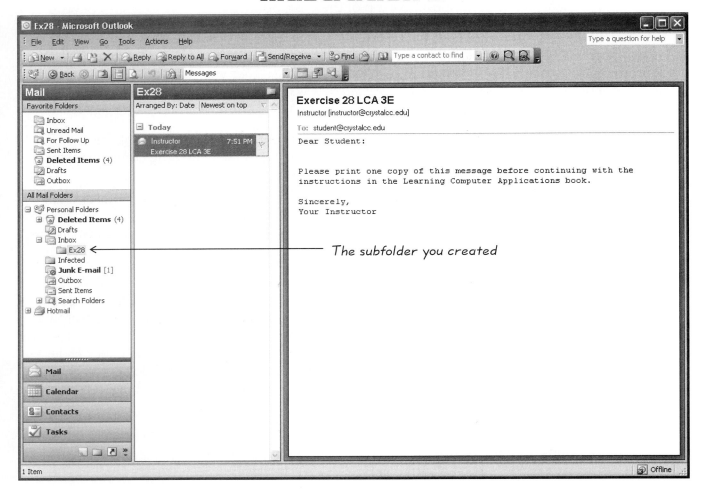

The subfolder you created

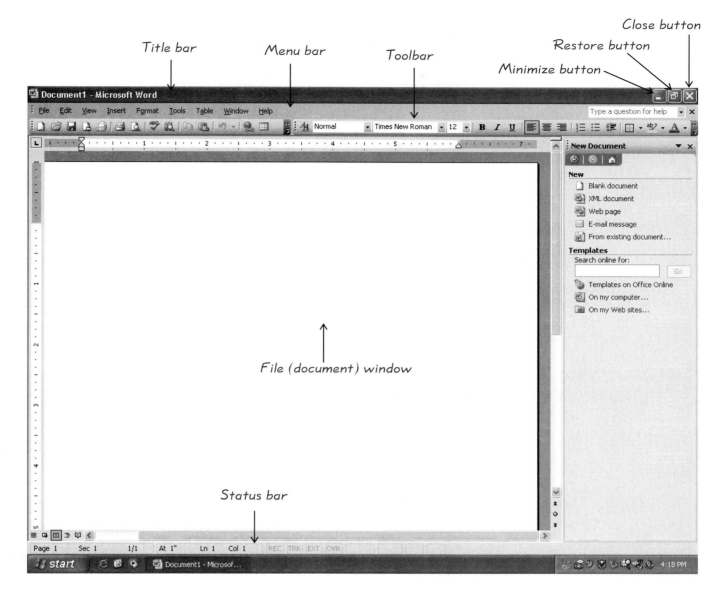

Title bar

Menu bar

Toolbar

Minimize button

Restore button

Close button

File (document) window

Status bar

All Windows applications have these common elements that can be used to navigate and work with the program:

- **Title Bar.** The title bar displays the name of the program and the file that's currently open. If the application window appears at less than full-screen size, drag the title bar to move the application window on-screen.

   ✓ *To drag with the mouse, point to the item to drag, press and hold the left mouse button, move the mouse until the item appears in the location you want, then release the mouse button.*

- **Minimize Button.** Click this button to reduce the application window to a button on the taskbar. The application remains open. Minimizing it just temporarily moves it out of your way. Click the taskbar button to resume working with the application. Also, note that in some cases, you'll see a Minimize button for the file window. Clicking it minimizes the file window to an icon. Click the icon or use the Window menu to redisplay the file.

7. Create a folder named **Ex28** as a subfolder of your inbox. (Do not create any shortcut buttons or icons for the folder.) Your folder list should then resemble Illustration 2 on the following page.

   ✓ *Creating a subfolder typically involves right-clicking on the inbox folder in the folder list, clicking a command such as New Folder, then using the dialog box that appears to specify the subfolder name and location.*

8. Move the **Exercise 28 LCA 3E** message to the new subfolder.

   ✓ *Most e-mail applications enable you to use the drag and drop technique to file your messages.*

   ✓ *To delete a message, you typically can right-click it and then click Delete.*

9. Display the contents of the **Ex28** subfolder. You should see the **Exercise 28 LCA 3E** message stored there.

10. Disconnect from the Internet, if needed, and close your e-mail program.

Illustration 1

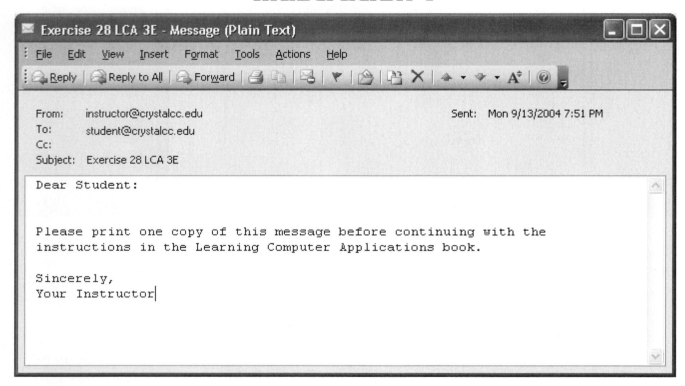

- **Restore Button.** Clicking this button reduces the application window to less than full size, without closing the window. When the window has been reduced, drag the window via its title bar, or drag a window border to resize the window. The Restore button changes to the Maximize button after reducing the window. Clicking the Maximize button restores the window to full-screen size.

- **Close Button.** Click a window's Close button to close the window. Closing an application window shuts down the application.

- **Menu Bar.** The menu bar lists the names of the menus offered in the application. Click a menu name to open that menu and then click the command you want to choose. Press the Alt key plus the underlined letter in the menu name to open the menu, and then press the underlined letter in the command name to select it. Some commands have an ellipsis (...) beside the command name. Choosing such a command displays a dialog box, where you choose options. Commands with a triangle beside them display a submenu of additional command choices. Other commands turn on or off; when such a command is active, a check mark appears to the left of its name.

  ✓ *Right-clicking an item or selection within a file displays a shortcut menu of commands. This saves the time it would take to search through the menus for the command needed.*

- **Toolbar.** Most applications offer some type of toolbar or button bar below the menu bar. Some have more than one—and others allow for two toolbars to appear on one row. Click a button on this bar to perform a command, like applying bold formatting to text that you have selected.

- **File or Document Window.** The file or document window holds the contents of the file you're creating or changing.

  ✓ *The fastest way to make a selection in an application is to drag over the information you want to select.*

- **Status Bar.** The status bar gives information about the file you're working with, such as how many pages it contains. In some applications, the status bar may also enable turning features on or off or applying formatting.

Finally, let's review key features of a dialog box (see the following illustrations). Windows applications use consistent controls (types of choices or options), so once you learn to use a dialog box in one application, you can use a dialog box in another application.

Exercise 28

❖ Read, Print, and File Your E-Mail

Notes

Once you become an active e-mail sender, you'll likely start receiving e-mail from a variety of sources. Many users now even have both home and business e-mail addresses to keep personal correspondence confidential and to avoid receiving business messages at home. Before you know it, messages will pile up in the inbox folder in your e-mail program.

Leading e-mail programs enable you to create folders to organize related messages, just as you'd create a folder on the system hard disk to store related files. Learn here how to read, print, and file a message, as well as tips about other methods for dealing with messages.

Spend some time organizing your personal e-mail messages in this exercise. Your instructor will send an example message so that you'll have at least one to work with.

Vocabulary

No new vocabulary in this exercise.

Directions

1. Start your e-mail program.

   ✓ *You may be prompted to connect to the Internet. If that happens, connect now to complete this exercise.*

2. Use the command or button for sending and receiving e-mail in your e-mail program. (If you haven't connected to the Internet previously and see a prompt to do so, click on Connect or the equivalent command.) The e-mail program connects to the Internet, sends any e-mail messages from the outbox, and receives any incoming e-mail messages.

3. Display the contents of your inbox folder.

4. Open the message from your instructor in its own window. The message title is **Exercise 28 LCA 3E**. The message should look like Illustration 1 on the following page.

   ✓ *Use the Reply button to create a message that replies to the sender of the selected message. The Reply All button creates a message addressed to the sender and all recipients of a message that you've received.*

5. Print one copy of the message and submit the printout to your instructor, if required. (Be sure to write your name and class information at the top of the printout, if needed.)

6. Close the message window.

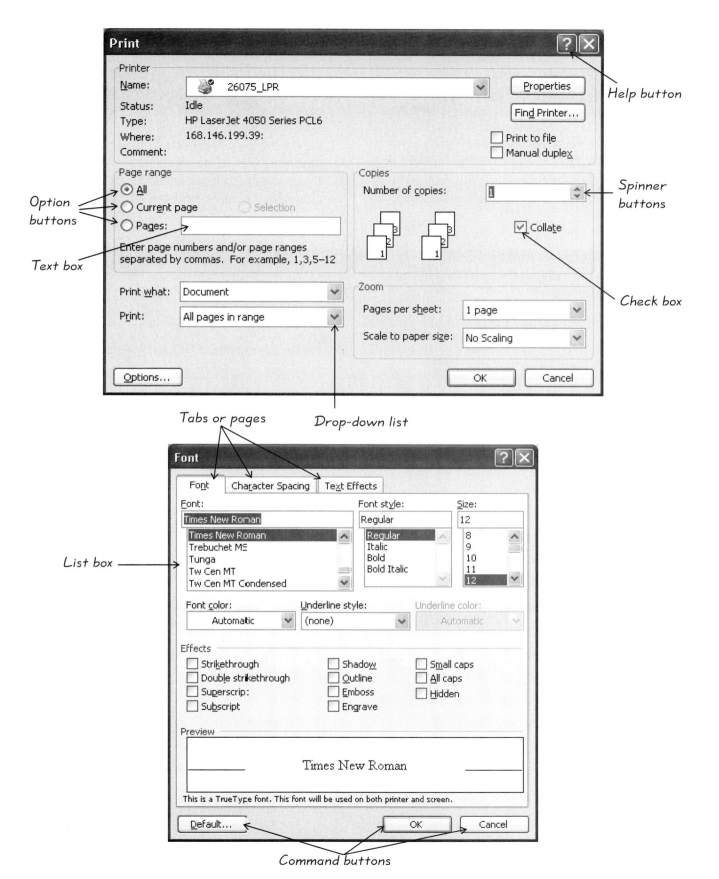

9. Add a request for a delivery receipt to the message. At this point, your message should look like the illustration below.

✓ A ***delivery receipt*** *is a return message notifying you when the message has been delivered to the recipient's e-mail inbox. To receive a message verifying that the recipient has opened the message, include a* ***read receipt***.

10. Send the message to your e-mail Outbox. Generally, you can click the Send button to do this.

11. Use the command or button for sending and receiving e-mail in your e-mail program. (If you haven't connected to the Internet previously and see a prompt to do so, click on Connect or the equivalent command.) The e-mail program connects to the Internet, sends the e-mail message, and receives any incoming e-mail messages.

12. Disconnect from the Internet, if needed, and close your e-mail program.

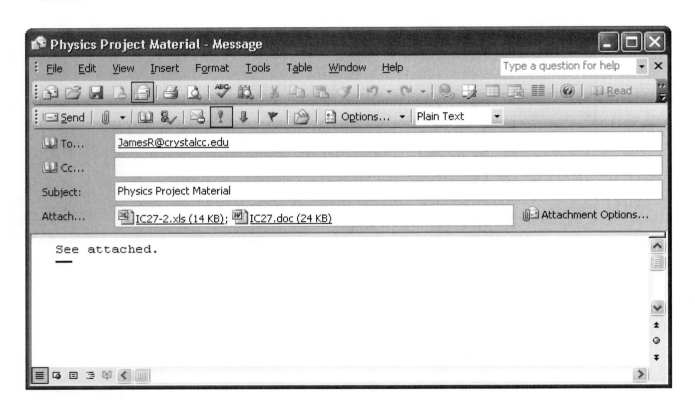

Here are the most common types of controls you'll find in Windows dialog boxes, and how to use each:

- **Help Button.** Click this button and then click any choice in the dialog box to learn about the choice.

- **Text Box.** Type information into a text box. For example, a text box might call for you to type in your name or a file name.

- **Check Box.** Click a check box to place a check in it and turn that checked feature on. Click the check box again to remove the check mark and turn the checked feature off.

- **Option Button.** Round option buttons appear in groups. Click the empty circle beside the option you want to choose. The circle becomes black. Click another option button to choose it, instead.

- **Drop-down List.** Click the arrow at the right end of a drop-down list to open the list and then click your choice in the list.

- **Spinner Buttons.** Click the spinner button with the up arrow on it to increase the value shown in the accompanying text box. Click the spinner button with the down arrow on it to decrease the value in the accompanying text box.

- **Command Button.** Click a command button to display another dialog box, select a command, or close the dialog box and execute your choices. Most dialog boxes have an OK button that allows closing the box and applying your choices. Click the Cancel button to close the dialog box without applying choices.

- **List Box.** A list box presents a list of choices. Use the scroll bar beside the list box to scroll through the choices and then click your choice.
    - ✓ *To move slowly with a scroll bar, click the arrow at either end of the bar. To move more quickly, click on the scroll bar, above or below the large box that appears on the scroll bar or drag the scroll box.*

- **Tabs or Pages.** Many dialog boxes need to give you more options than can fit in a single box. So, dialog boxes group similar options or options that work together on a separate tab or page in the dialog box. To view another set of options in the dialog box, click a tab in the dialog box.

Understanding Features of Macintosh & Macintosh Applications

Tens of millions of computers now use some version of the Apple Macintosh operating system. The most recent version of the Mac OS (Macintosh Operating System) is Mac OS X version 10.3 Panther, which replaced earlier Mac OS X versions and Mac OS 9.x (or version 9) close behind. (This section concentrates primarily on Mac OS X operations. Many operations work just the same in Mac OS 9.x, however.)

Exercise 27

❖ E-Mail from Your E-Mail Program

Notes

While e-mailing from a software application may be convenient, most of the time you'll be working directly in your e-mail program to compose and send e-mail messages. Early e-mail programs offered very simple features. You could address the message, enter some plain text, attach a file, and send the message. E-mail programs have evolved significantly in the last few years. Many e-mail programs now enable you to apply attractive formatting to message text, assign a message priority, request a receipt when the message has been read, attach multiple files to the message, flag a message for follow-up attention, add a category to identify the message, and even use and read the .HTML (Web page) format for messages.

Share the physics information again, but this time from your e-mail program.

Vocabulary

priority   delivery receipt   read receipt

Directions

1. Start your e-mail program.

   ✓ *You may be prompted to connect to the Internet. If that happens, connect now to complete this exercise.*

2. Choose the command (usually found on a submenu of the File menu) or button for creating a new e-mail message. The new message window will appear.

3. If needed, change to the Plain Text format for the message. This message format removes formatting from the message contents.

4. Enter your classmate's or your instructor's e-mail address in the To: or Recipient: text box, where you address the message.

   ✓ *Exercise 29 will show you how to save e-mail addresses and re-use them later. Typically, if you want to enter multiple recipients, you can type a*

comma or semicolon after each e-mail address, then type the next address.

5. Enter **Physics Project Material** in the Subject: or Re: text box, where you place the subject of your e-mail message.

6. Enter **See attached** in the message body area and apply the desired formatting.

7. Insert the **IC27** and **IC27-2** files as attachments to the message.

8. Assign the High or Highest **priority** (importance) setting for the message.

   ✓ *In some e-mail programs, you use an Options command to find additional message settings such as the priority (importance) and receipt settings. For example, you use the View|Options command to find these choices in the latest version of Outlook.*

Macintosh applications run "on top of" Mac OS, which lends these applications a consistent look and consistent way of operating. The illustration below shows you the key features of Mac OS itself, described next:

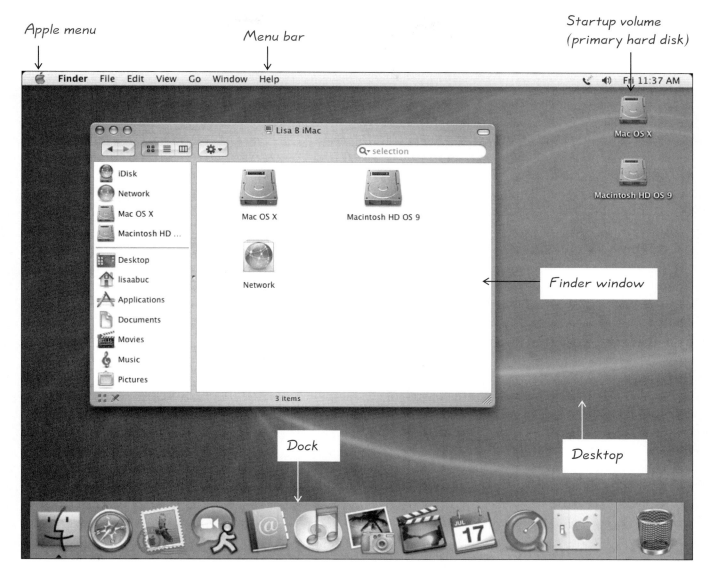

✓ *The illustration shows Mac OS X version 10.3 Panther. Other versions may look a little different, but they all offer the same features described next.*

- **Apple Menu.** Click on the Apple icon at the far-left end of the menu bar to open the Apple menu. This menu contains commands and shortcuts called aliases for starting applications and opening files you've used recently. It also enables you to access Mac OS system features such as the Control Panels (Mac OS 9.x) or System Preferences (Mac OS X) that you can use to change system settings.

- **Desktop.** The Mac OS desktop displays everything on your computer from hard disk to file servers to floppy disks to CD-ROMs. When you open a program, it appears in its own window on top of the desktop. You can open as many windows and applications as you have available RAM.

Illustration 2

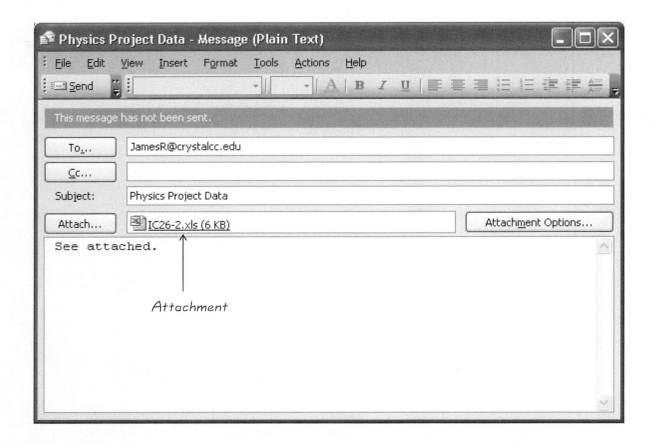

- **Menu Bar.** The menu bar runs along the top of the desktop. After you open an application or use the Dock to make it the active (current) application, the menu bar changes to offer the commands for that application. After the Apple icon, which denotes the Apple menu, the first three items on the left are almost always the application (program name), File, and Edit menus. The item on the far right is the Finder or Applications menu.

- **Dock.** The Dock appears at the bottom of the desktop by default and holds icons for starting applications. A triangle appears below the icon for any active application. Click the icon of an open application on the Dock to make the application the current or active application. You can customize the Dock by dragging any application's startup icon to the Dock, thus adding a startup icon for that application to the Dock. Instead of a Dock, Mac OS 9.x displays a control strip that enables you to access operating system features, such as changing the display resolution. Click a button on the control strip, and then click the desired command or setting in the menu that appears.

- **Finder Window.** Click the Finder icon at the far left to return to the Finder or Mac desktop. To open any file or application, you simply double-click its icon on the desktop or in a file (Finder) window. Alternatively, you can Control-click the item and view all the options available. Clicking on any file window makes its application active, so that you can work with the file in the application. Clicking a folder window or any spot on the desktop activates the Finder. The Finder is synonymous with the desktop, because you must use the Finder menu to switch between applications or use the Finder (desktop) itself to work with files and folders.

  ✓ *Mac OS 9.x and Mac OS X offer contextual menus that you access by pressing the Control key and then right-clicking on any window, folder, or icon. The contextual menu will display the options available for that particular item.*

- **Startup Volume (Primary Hard Disk).** The icon in the upper-right corner of the Desktop is usually the hard disk containing your start up system software. Double-click this icon to open a window displaying the contents of the hard disk. As with Windows, on the Macintosh you organize files in folders. One key default folder, called the *System Folder*, must be intact and must contain a System file and the Finder or your computer will not operate.

  You can view the contents of any folder as an alphanumeric list, as icons, or as buttons. In the button view, you can activate any file, folder, or application with a single click. In the other views, if you click or double-click a file, the application that you used to create the file opens and displays the file.

- **Control Strip or Dock.** Mac OS X features the Dock at the bottom of the screen rather than the Control Strip. You can use the Dock to start applications, switch between documents, and access System Preferences.

  After you open a file or an application, it appears in its own window (see the illustration on the next page). Resize any window by dragging the lower right-hand corner.

box or window for creating an e-mail message. In many cases, the message subject will be filled in for you. Typically, the message uses the name of the document file as the message subject.

5. Enter a classmate's or your instructor's e-mail address in the To: or Recipient: text box, where you address the message.
6. Edit the subject to read **Physics Project Outline**.
7. Enter **See attached** in the message body area. Your message should now resemble Illustration 1.
8. Click the button for sending the message to your e-mail program outbox. (It's usually the Send button.)
9. Start your spreadsheet program.
10. Open the **IC26-2** file.

11. Repeat steps 3-8, entering **Physics Project Data** as the message subject (replacing the default subject provided) and **See attached** as the message body. Illustration 2 on the following page shows you an example of what this message might look like.
12. Start your e-mail program.
13. Use the command or button for sending and receiving e-mail in your e-mail program. (If prompted, choose to connect to the Internet.) The e-mail program connects to the Internet, sends the e-mail messages you created in your word processing and spreadsheet programs, and receives any incoming e-mail messages.
14. Disconnect from the Internet, if needed, and close your e-mail program.
15. Close the word processing and spreadsheet applications without saving changes to your document or spreadsheet file.

Illustration 1

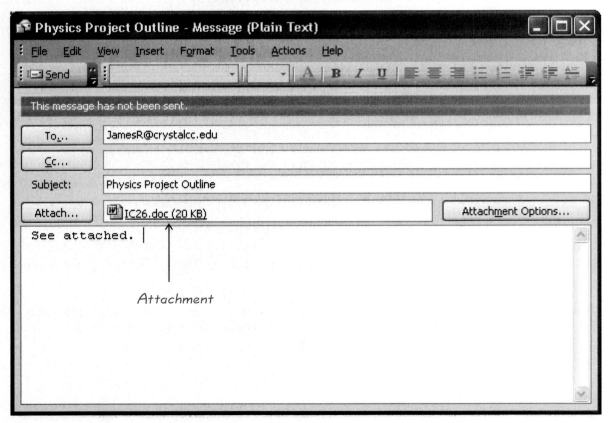

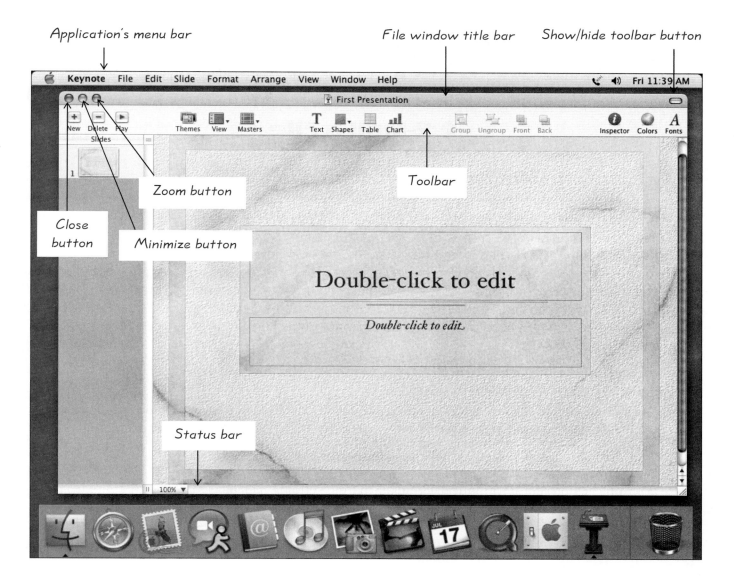

All applications have these common elements that can be used to navigate and work with the program:

- **Title Bar.** The title bar displays the name of the file that is currently open. If a file appears slightly off screen, drag the title bar or any edge to move it on-screen.

  ✓ *To drag with the mouse, point to the item to drag, press and hold the mouse button, move the mouse until the item appears in the location you want, then release the mouse button.*

- **Menu Bar.** The menu bar lists the names of the menus offered in the active application. Click a menu name to open that menu, and then click the command you want to choose. Command shortcut keys appear to the right of many items on the menus. Press these key combinations to choose the command without having to use a menu. Some commands have an ellipsis (...) beside the command name. Choosing such a command displays a sheet, dialog box, or window where you choose options. Commands with a triangle beside them display a submenu of

Exercise 26

❖ E-Mail a File

Notes

As you work with friends and colleagues to complete school and business projects, you may need to send files via e-mail. You could start your e-mail program, create a message, and add the file to send as a **file attachment**. However, this method requires that you remember the name and storage location of the file to send. Instead, you can take a more direct approach. After you finish and save a file in your application (word processing, spreadsheet, database, or presentation graphics), you can create an e-mail message and attach the open file, then send the message with file attachment to your e-mail program. In applications from some software publishers, you can choose to send all or part of the file.

Practice sending an e-mail message with a file attachment from your word processing and presentation graphics programs in this exercise.

✓ *Some of the Microsoft Office applications combine change tracking (revision marking) with sending a file as an attachment. When you use the command for this feature—File | Send To | Mail Recipient (for Review)—the file arrives in the recipient's inbox with the track changes feature enabled. Then, when a recipient returns his or her copy of the file, you'll be prompted to merge those changes into your original copy of the file.*

Share your physics project information with classmates, sending files as e-mail attachments from within your applications.

Vocabulary

file attachment

Directions

1. Start your word processing program.
2. Open the **IC26** file. This is the file you will e-mail as an attachment.
3. Choose the command (usually found on a submenu of the File menu) or button for sending the file as an attachment to an e-mail message.

   ✓ *This command is different from the command you'd use to send an e-mail message alone from your application.*

✓ *The steps for e-mailing attachments from within an application may vary from application to application, particularly if you want to send only a selection from the file. If you have trouble e-mailing a file as an attachment, consult online help or your instructor.*

4. If you have to specify whether to send a message alone or to send all or part of the file, choose the option for sending the file as an attachment. The program will display a dialog

additional command choices. Other commands toggle on or off; when such a command is active, a check mark appears to the left of its name.

- **Close button.** Click a window's red Close button in the upper-left corner to close the window. To quit an application, go to the File menu and choose Quit. Alternatively, you can press the Command+Q. Mac OS 9.x has a Close box rather than a close button.

- **Zoom button.** If you drag a window's lower-right corner to resize the window, you can click this green button (Mac OS X) to return the window to its previous size.

- **Minimize button.** Click this yellow button in the upper-left corner of any window to reduce the window to an icon on the Dock. The file or application remains open. Minimizing it just temporarily moves that window out of your way. Click the Dock icon to return the window to its previous size. Mac OS 9.x instead has a collapse box in the upper-right hand corner of the window; click it to reduce the window to a floating title bar or re-expand the window.

- **Toolbar.** Most applications offer some type of toolbar or button bar below the menu bar. Click a button on this bar to perform a command, like applying bold formatting to text that you have selected. To hide and redisplay the toolbar, click on the oval show/hide toolbar button, which will appear on the toolbar or the application title bar.

- **File Window.** The file window or document window holds the contents of the file you are creating or changing. The mouse pointer changes to a new icon as you move it in and out of the window.
  - ✓ *The fastest way to make a selection in an application is to drag over the information you want to select.*
  - ✓ *Control+click an item or selection within a file displays a shortcut menu of commands. This can save the time it takes to search through the menus for the command you need.*

- **Status Bar.** The status bar gives information about the file you're working with, such as how many pages it contains. In some applications, the status bar also may enable turning features on or off, or applying formatting.

Finally, let's review key features of a sheet or dialog box in the following illustrations. (In Mac OS X, a sheet drops down from the title bar of a window.) Mac applications use consistent controls (types of choices or options), so once you learn to use a dialog box in one application, you can use a dialog box in another application.

Illustration 2

Click to send message to
your e-mail program outbox.

Subject

Recipient's e-mail address

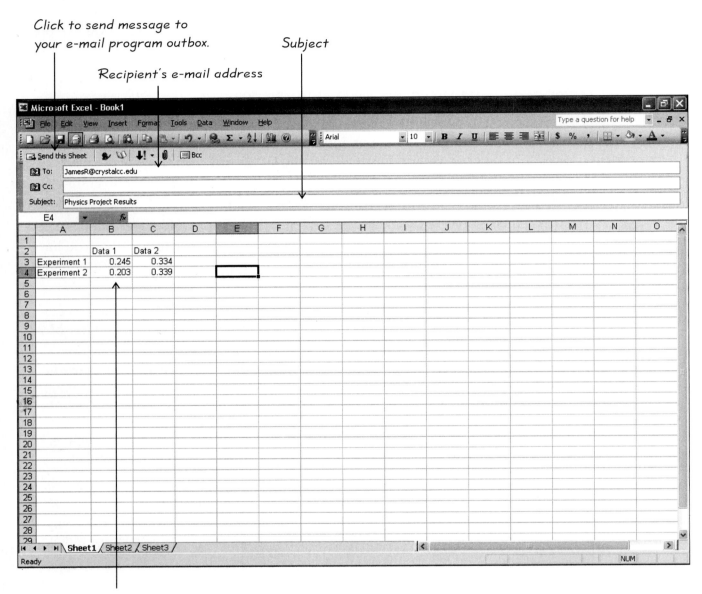

Message body

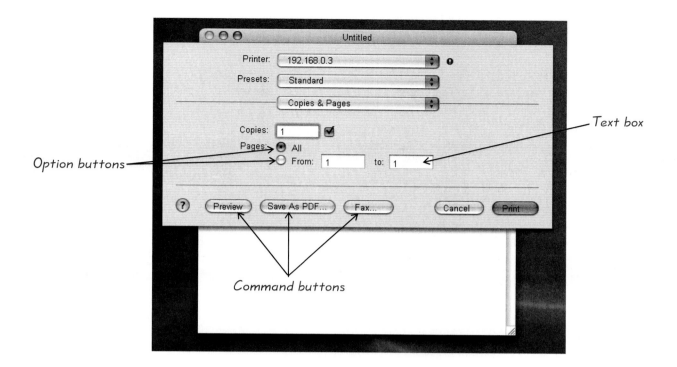

Option buttons

Text box

Command buttons

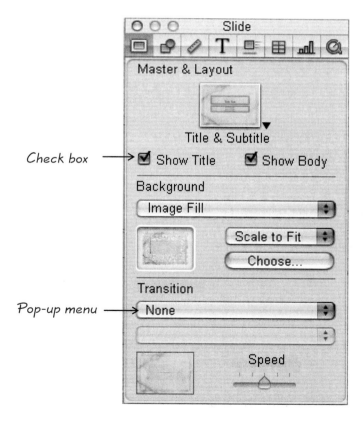

Check box

Pop-up menu

Illustration 1

Click to send message to your e-mail program outbox.

Recipient's e-mail address

Subject

Message body

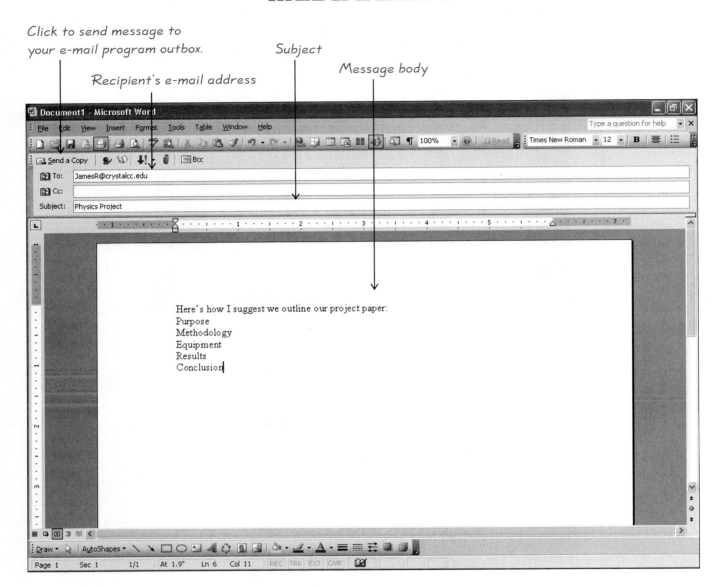

Here are the most common types of controls you'll find in Mac OS dialog boxes, and how to use each:

- **Text Box.** Type information into a text box. For example, a text box might call for you to type in your name or a file name. If a text box is highlighted, you merely start typing to enter information. Or click in an open box and type.

- **Check Box.** Click a check box to place a check in it and turn that checked feature on. Click the check box again to remove the check mark and turn the checked feature off.

- **Option Button.** Round option buttons often appear in groups. Click the empty circle beside the option you want to choose. The circle becomes black. Click another option button to choose it, instead.

- **Pop-Up Menu.** Click the double-arrow button at the right end of a pop-up menu or click the menu box itself to open the menu, then click your choice in the menu.

- **Command Button.** Click a command button to display another dialog box, select a command, or close the dialog box and execute your choices. Most dialog boxes have an OK button that allows closing the box and applying your choices. Click the Cancel button to close the dialog box without applying choices. If a button has a double outline, it is the default and can be chosen by pressing the Enter key.

- **List Box.** A list box presents a list of choices, as shown in the Windows dialog box illustration presented earlier. Use the scroll bar beside the list box to scroll through the choices, and then click your choice.

  ✓ *To move slowly with a scroll bar, click the arrow at either end of the bar. To move more quickly, click on the scroll bar, above or below the slider that appears on the scroll bar. You also can drag the slider up or down.*

- **Tabs or Pages.** Unlike the dialog boxes just shown, many dialog boxes need to give you more options than can fit in a single box. So, dialog boxes group similar options or options that work together on a separate tab or page in the dialog box. (The tabs resemble those in a Windows dialog box as shown earlier.) To view another set of options in the dialog box, click a tab in the dialog box.

Using the Office Help Pane

Microsoft Office still dominates the application software market. The Microsoft Office 2003 applications all feature a task pane that you can hide and display at the right side of the application window. You can use this task pane for fast access to key actions like creating a new file. One such key action is getting help about the application you're using. When you get stuck in an Office application, use the Help pane to find the steps you need. To display the Help pane, first open the task pane by choosing Task Pane from the View menu (Ctrl+F1). Then, click on the Other Task Panes button at the top of the task pane, and click Help in the menu that appears, as shown in the following illustration.

5. Enter **Physics Project** in the Subject: or Re: text box, where you place the subject of your e-mail message.

6. Enter the text that follows in the message body area and apply the appropriate formatting. Illustration 1 on the following page shows you an example of what this message might look like.

   Here's how I suggest we outline our project paper:
   Purpose
   Methodology
   Equipment
   Results
   Conclusion

   ✓ *In the 2003 versions of the Microsoft Office applications, the message "body" area is the blank document, the first blank slide in the presentation, or other blank area. The message recipient may need to scroll down to see the body of the message.*

   ✓ *Office XP messages may include an Introduction text box that you can use to include teaser text or the first few lines of the document to give your message recipients more information.*

7. Click the button for sending the message to your e-mail program outbox. (It's usually the Send button or a similarly-named button.) In some cases, you'll be prompted to connect to the Internet to send the message. You can cancel that connection for now.

8. Start your spreadsheet program. (Close the task pane, if it appears.)

9. Choose to send a message including the contents of the current worksheet (which you'll enter shortly).

10. Address the message to a fellow student and enter **Physics Project Results** as the message subject.

11. Make the spreadsheet entries shown in Illustration 2 on page 534 as the message body. (If you can't use the spreadsheet itself, make the entries as text in the message body.)

12. Click the button for sending the message to your e-mail program outbox. (It's usually the Send button or a similarly-named button.) In some cases, you'll be prompted to connect to the Internet to send the message. You can cancel that connection for now.

    ✓ *When e-mailing from some programs, you can use such additional options as routing a message to a list of recipients or adding voting buttons to an e-mail message.*

13. Start your e-mail program.

14. Use the command or button for sending and receiving e-mail in your e-mail program. (If prompted, choose to connect to the Internet.) The e-mail program connects to the Internet, sends the e-mail messages you created in your word processing and spreadsheet programs, and receives any incoming e-mail messages.

15. Disconnect from the Internet, if needed, and close your e-mail program.

16. Close the word processing and spreadsheet applications without saving changes to your blank document or spreadsheet file.

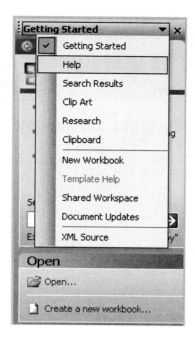

Once the Help pane appears, you can type the topic you need help about into the Search for text box, and then click the green Start searching button (or press Enter) to search for both Office help installed on your computer and help online (assuming your computer has an Internet connection). Or, you can click on one of the other links in the pane to get related information from the Internet.

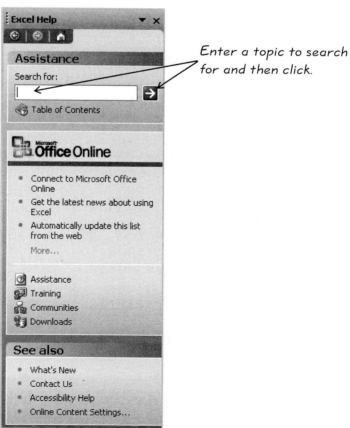

Enter a topic to search for and then click.

Exercise 25

❖ E-Mail from an Application

Notes

Many of the leading applications also enable you to send **e-mail** (electronic mail) messages from the application. The application enables you to prepare the message and then transfer it to your e-mail program **outbox**, from which you can send the message. Note that leading word processing, spreadsheet, and presentation graphics programs offer this feature, but your database program may not.

Your physics instructor has assigned a project in which groups of students must work as a team. Practice e-mailing project information from your word processing and spreadsheet programs.

Vocabulary

e-mail   outbox

Directions

1. Start your word processing program. A new, blank document should open. (Close the task pane, if it appears.)

   ✓ *You must have an Internet connection to complete this exercise (as well as Exercises 26 through 28) and the e-mail program must be set up for your use.*

2. Choose the command (usually found on a submenu of the File menu) or button for sending an e-mail message.

   ✓ *The steps for e-mailing from an application may vary from application to application. If you have trouble with this exercise, consult online help or your instructor.*

   ✓ *In Word 2003, you also can click the E-mail Message choice in the New list of the New Document task pane to start a new e-mail message.*

3. If you have to specify whether to send a message alone or to send all or part of a file, choose the option for sending a message alone. The program will display a dialog box or window for creating an e-mail message (or will alter the appearance of the application window so you can enter message information right in the application).

   ✓ *Typically, in spreadsheet and presentation graphics applications, you only have the option of sending all or part of the current file as the message or an attachment. For example, from Excel 2003, you can use the current worksheet as the body of the message (a process that automatically converts those entries to nicely-aligned text in the message body) or attach the entire workbook file to a message.*

4. Enter a classmate's or your instructor's e-mail address in the To: or Recipient: text box, where you address the message.

The Help pane will display the list of matching help topics, as shown below. You can click a topic to open a separate Help window with the topic information. Or, you can use the top drop-down list in the Search area at the bottom to search a more specific location, such as Offline Help.

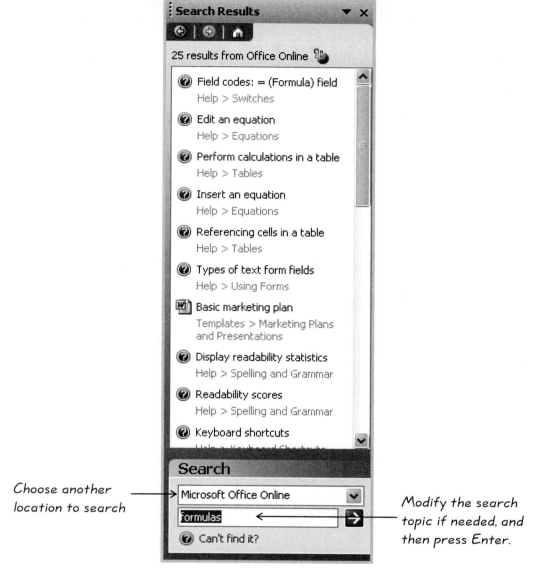

Choose another location to search →

Modify the search topic if needed, and then press Enter.

If you're using applications that aren't from the Office suite, you can still get help by using your program's Help menu. Open the Help menu, and then choose the desired Help command.

Lesson 30
Manage Your E-Mail

Exercises 25–29

❖ **E-mail from an application**
❖ **E-mail a file**
❖ **E-mail from your e-mail program**
❖ **Work with your e-mail**
❖ **Work with your address book**

Lesson 1
Exercises 1-5

Lesson 1
Manage Your Files

7. Using either the bar of Web tools in your word processing or presentation graphics program or your Web browser, go to www.download.com.
8. Search for **games** downloads.
9. Browse through the available files, then download at least one small file.

   ✓ *Check with your instructor before downloading the file. Your instructor may have you delete the file without installing it first.*

✓ *Generally, you click a series of links and respond to online prompts to complete the download. As this process varies from Web site to Web site, consult your instructor if you get stuck at any particular point.*

10. Switch to the word processing or presentation graphics program, if needed, and hide the Web toolbar.
11. Close the application and Web browser, and disconnect from the Internet when prompted.

Search for clip art.

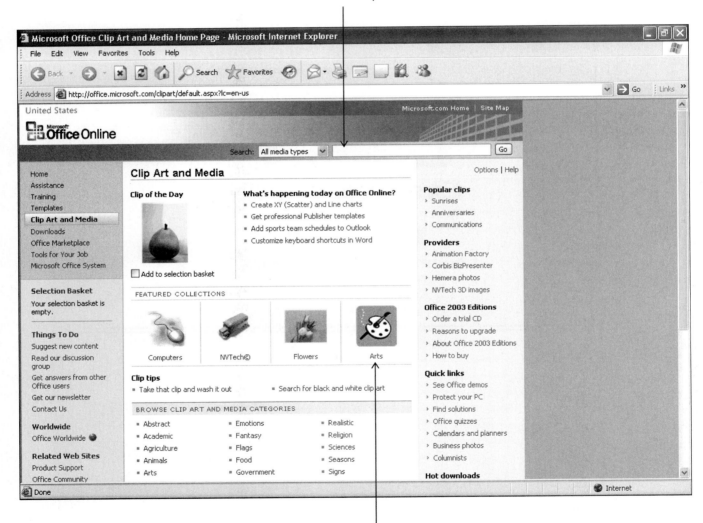

Browse for files to download.

Directory of Files

Exercise	File Name	Page
1	None	—
2	FM02, FM02-2	28
3	FM03, FM03-2	30
4	None	—
5	None	—

Exercise 24

❖ Download Files and Clip Art

Notes

A software publisher typically offers a lot of extras to encourage you to remain loyal to its product line. As such, most software publisher Web sites offer a variety of downloads, and some download functionality may be built right into the program. In addition, many third party sites like www.tucows.com, www.download.com, and www.macaddict.com offer links to freeware and **shareware** (programs distributed on the honor system, where you send a small fee to the software developer if you plan to continue using the software) programs, decorative graphics, and more. In this exercise, you'll explore some download possibilities.

You are tackling some personal projects on the weekend. You want to find a new piece of clip art to create a greeting card, and a shareware game to play when you're bored. Find both of those downloads now.

Vocabulary

shareware

Directions

1. Start your word processing or presentation graphics program. A new, blank file should open.

   ✓ *You must have an Internet connection to complete this exercise.*

2. Start the process for inserting clip art.
3. Click on the link or button that searches for new clips online. (In Microsoft Office 2003 applications, this is Clip art on Office Online, although you also can search for clip art directly from the Clip Art task pane.)

4. If you see a prompt asking whether to connect to the Internet, click the appropriate button to do so. After connecting, your system should open your Web browser application. The Web browser will display a page where you can download or search for clips, as shown in the illustration on the following page.

   ✓ *In some cases, you may have to click on a button to accept licensing terms.*

5. Search for **butterfly** clips.
6. Browse around until you find one interesting clip or graphic, then download it.

File Management

Lesson 1
Manage Your Files

Exercises 1-5

- ❖ **Explore Your Desktop**
- ❖ **Work with Folders**
- ❖ **Work with Files**
- ❖ **Find Files**

5. Enter **"butterfly species"** in the search text box and then click on the Search (or equivalent) button or link. (The illustration below shows a search entry.) The search engine displays a page of links to matching pages.

✓ *Generally, you include quotes around a phrase to tell the search engine to look for that exact phrase or all the words in the phrase. Of course, various search engines have their own specific methods for making such entries, but most offer a help link so that you can learn how to construct your entries for a more effective search.*

6. Click a link and review one of the matching Web pages.
7. Click on the Back button in the browser toolbar. The browser returns to the search results list.
8. Switch to the spreadsheet program, if needed, and hide the Web toolbar.
9. Close the spreadsheet application and Web browser, and disconnect from the Internet when prompted.

Type search word or phrase here and press Enter.

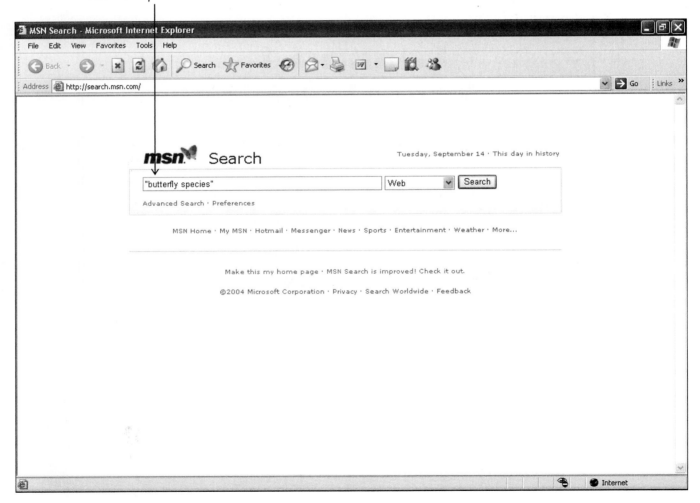

Exercise 1

❖ Get Started with Your Desktop

Notes

Whether you're working with a version of Windows or with the Mac OS, your interaction with your PC starts on the **desktop**. After you start the system, the desktop appears automatically. You use the desktop to work with the **applications (programs)** and files on your system. **Icons**—or small pictures—represent the applications and files on the desktop.

You also use the **Start menu** from the **taskbar** across the bottom of the Windows desktop to access folders and start programs. Use the buttons that appear on the taskbar to switch between applications. On a Mac with Mac OS X, the **Dock** enables you to start and switch between open programs. You also can start applications from the **Applications folder** or any other folder on your Mac.

You just started a new job and have been given a computer previously used by another employee. In this exercise, you will explore the contents of the computer.

Vocabulary

desktop	Start menu	Applications folder	Close button
applications (programs)	taskbar	My Computer	
icon	Dock	hard disk	

Directions

1. Start the computer system, if needed.
2. Open the **My Computer** window, and then choose the drive C: icon in the My Computer window. Or, choose the icon for the primary **hard disk** (often Macintosh HD).

   ✓ *In either Mac or Windows, you double-click by default to choose an icon. However, recent versions of Windows can be set up to use a Web-like style, so that you single-click to choose an icon. You may find that the Windows system you're using has been set up with the single-click style.*

3. Move the window showing the hard disk contents by dragging the window title bar.
4. Open the *User's* Documents or My Documents (Windows), or Documents (Mac), folder on the hard disk.

   ✓ *To open a folder, choose its icon.*

   ✓ *The default User's Documents (Windows XP) or My Documents folder appears on most Windows systems. The Documents folder appears by default on most Macs. If you don't find the appropriate folder on the system you're using, open another folder as indicated by your instructor.*

Exercise 23

❖ Perform a Search

Notes

The Web techniques explored so far assume that you have some idea of the Web information that you want to view. With millions of Web pages online (and more being added every day), it's not possible to know where every page you might need is located. To identify a Web page holding information you might need, you can take advantage of a search engine. A **search engine** catalogs the content on Web pages based on key words and other tags. You enter the word or phrase to search for, run the search, and the search engine returns a list of links to Web pages that include the applicable word or phrase. From there, you can browse the matching pages as needed.

You can start a search from within your Web browser, or (in some cases) using the Web tools in your application. This exercise lets you practice with an example search.

You want to learn more about butterfly species for your Entomology course. Search for that information now.

Vocabulary

Search engine

Directions

1. Start your spreadsheet program. A new, blank spreadsheet file should open.

   ✓ *You must have an Internet connection to complete this exercise.*

2. Display the toolbar or bar of icons that holds Web tools in your application.

3. Click on the button for starting a Web search.

   ✓ *If you're already working in your Web browser, you can click on the Search button in the browser toolbar. In most cases, a pane or search engine page then appears so that you can perform the search.*

4. If you see a prompt asking whether to connect to the Internet, click the appropriate button to do so. After connecting, your system should open your Web browser application. The Web browser will display the search Web page.

   ✓ *Many search engines also enable you to search by browsing category links.*

   ✓ *You also can go to many search locations by typing in the search site or search engine URL. Other Web sites that provide or include a search engine are www.yahoo.com, www.lycos.com, www.google.com, and www.dogpile.com, among others.*

5. Close the folder window by clicking the **Close button**. Also close the My Computer window if you're working in Windows and it's still open.

   ✓ *In the most recent version of Mac OS X, you can choose Go | Applications to open the default folder for most installed applications.*

6. Open the Start menu (Windows). In Mac OS X, you can simply use the Dock; for an older Mac OS, open the Apple menu.

7. Start a program or utility—Word, Excel, or Notepad in Windows; or Address Book, iCal, one of the AppleWorks programs, or TextEdit in Mac OS X.

8. Start another program or utility.

9. Use the taskbar or Dock to switch between programs. (Use the Finder menu if you're working with an older Mac OS.)

10. Close the open programs.

✓ *In most Windows programs, you choose File | Exit to close the program. In most Mac programs, you choose File | Quit Program Name to quit the program. Note that shorthand like "File | Exit" means that you should open the File menu by clicking on it, and then click on the Exit command. Some commands appear on a submenu, such as the View | Arrange Icons by submenu in a My Computer window in Windows. In such cases, the book uses shorthand like "View | Arrange Icons by | Type," which means to click on the menu name (View), point to or drag the mouse over the submenu name (Arrange Icons), and then click on the command name (Type) in the submenu.*

✓ *The Windows Start menu contains the command for shutting down the system. On the Mac, you'll find the command for shutting down on the Apple menu (Mac OS X) or Special menu in the Finder menu bar.*

5. Enter **www.smithsonian.org/about** in the address bar text box and press Enter. The Web browser displays another page from the Smithsonian Web site.
6. Click on the Back button in the browser toolbar. The browser backs up to the first Web page displayed.
7. Click on the Forward button in the browser toolbar. The browser returns to the Web page displayed in Step 5.
8. Switch to the word processing program, if needed, and hide the Web toolbar.
9. Close the word processing application and Web browser, and disconnect from the Internet when prompted.

Type URL here and press Enter.

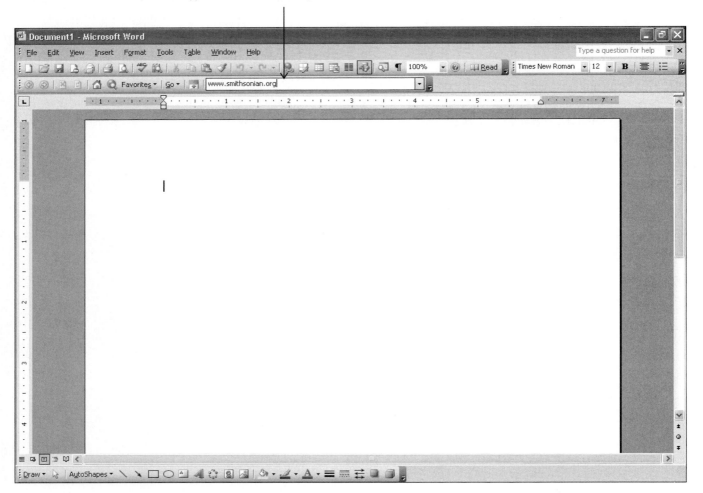

Exercise 2

❖ Make a Folder ❖ Copy Files

Notes

You store files in **folders** that you create on your system's hard disk (or even on a floppy disk or other removable disk). Just as placing papers in labeled manila folders makes it easier to find documents when you need them, placing your files in folders makes it easier to find those files. Choosing (or selecting) a folder's icon opens that folder in a window on the desktop. You can place folders within folders to further control where files are stored.

Once you've saved a file on a disk, you can **copy** the file to another disk or folder. You might copy the file to make a protective **backup** copy that will be available if something goes wrong with the original file. Or, you might copy the file to provide the copy to a coworker. You can copy a file as many times as is needed.

In this exercise, you create a folder to hold the files for the projects you'll be handling as part of your new job. You'll also copy some files that the boss has given you for the first project.

Vocabulary

folder   copy   backup   drag and drop

Directions

1. Open the window for your system's hard disk.

   ✓ In Windows XP, this means Choose My Computer from the Start menu, and then choosing the icon for disk C:. In Mac OS X, you have to change to your Home folder, as the operating system doesn't give users permission to add folders to the root of the hard disk. Choose Go|Home from the Finder toolbar to open your Home folder.

2. Create a new folder.

   ✓ In Windows, you can right-click in the folder window, point to New on the shortcut menu, then click Folder. On the Mac, Control+click the folder window, then click New Folder in the contextual menu.

3. Type **Work Projects** as the folder name, then press Enter.

4. Open the **Work Projects** folder.

5. Navigate to the folder that holds the exercise files for this book using My Computer, Windows Explorer, or the Mac Finder. Make sure that you can see both folder windows on the desktop.

   ✓ Consult your instructor if you need to find out the name of the folder holding the files for this book.

   ✓ If your version of Windows is set up to use only one window rather than a separate window for each disk and folder, choose My Computer again to open a second folder window, then navigate from there. On the Mac, you can double-click the grayed-out hard disk icon to activate the hard disk window for navigation.

Exercise 22

❖ Browse Around

Notes

In Exercise 20, you practiced some basic Web navigation by clicking on links to move between pages. That technique works well if you know which links you need to click to display the information that you need. This exercise enables you to work with some additional techniques for navigating the Web with your browser, such as using a Web page's Internet address or URL (Uniform Resource Locator) or using the Back and Forward buttons in the browser.

To display a Web page, you enter its **URL** (Uniform Resource Locator) or Web address in your Web browser software or in the Web toolbar available in some applications. A URL looks like http://www.prenhall.com—the address for the DDC parent company's Web site. Once you've displayed a Web page, you can use the Back button to return to the prior page. After you've done that, you can use the Forward button to return to the page from which you backed up.

Your U.S. History teacher has asked you to write a report about your choice of topic concerning the western United States. Visit the Smithsonian Institution Web site to research potential topics now.

Vocabulary

URL   Back button   Forward button

Directions

1. Start your word processing program. A new, blank document should open.

   ✓ You must have an Internet connection to complete this exercise.

2. Display the toolbar or bar of icons that holds Web tools in your application.

3. Using the tool that enables you to display a particular Web page, go to **www.smithsonian.org**. (The illustration on the following page shows how to do this.) You usually have to type the URL into an address text box, and then press Enter.

   ✓ If you're already working in your Web browser, you would simply enter the URL in the address text box near the top of the browser, and then press Enter.

4. If you see a prompt asking whether to connect to the Internet, click the appropriate button to do so. After connecting, your system should open your Web browser application. The Web browser will display the main Web site page.

   ✓ When you're entering a URL in your Web browser or a toolbar to go to a Web page, you can usually leave off the "http://" prefix.

6. Select (highlight) the **FM02** file icon. In Windows, either click the file once (when the desktop is set to double-click style) or point to the file icon with the mouse to highlight it. On the Mac, click the file icon once.

7. Press and hold the Ctrl key (Windows) or Option key (Mac), then drag the **FM02** file icon from the folder for the book files to the **Work Projects** folder window, then release the mouse button.

   ✓ *This method is called **drag and drop**.*

   ✓ *In Windows, you also can click the Copy button on the folder window toolbar or right-click the file icon and then click Copy. Select the window for the folder to which you want to copy the file, then click the Paste button on the folder window or right-click in the folder window and click Paste. On the Mac, you can choose File|Duplicate to make a copy of the file and then drag the duplicate icon into the destination window.*

8. Close the **Work Projects** folder window.

9. Insert a floppy disk into the disk drive or into a removable drive.

   ✓ *If you're working on a Mac that doesn't have a floppy or removable disk drive, simply copy the second file to the Work Projects folder.*

10. Open a window for the floppy disk. In Windows, you can select the disk icon from the My Computer window. On the Mac, an icon for the disk appears on the desktop, so you can choose that icon.

11. Go back to the folder window for the exercise files for this book. Make sure you can see both the exercise file folder window and the window for the floppy or removable disk.

12. Select (highlight) the **FM02-2** file icon.

13. Drag the **FM02-2** file icon from the folder for the book files to the window for the floppy or removable disk, then release the mouse button.

   ✓ *Note that in this instance, you don't have to press a key while dragging. That's because when you're copying between separate disks, the drag and drop method automatically copies the file. When you drag a file between folders on the same disk, the drag and drop method automatically moves the file, unless you press a key to tell it otherwise.*

14. Close the open folder and disk windows.

   ✓ *Windows XP and Mac OS X both work easily with CD-R burners for creating backup copies of files. Simply insert a blank CD-R, and you will be prompted to open a folder window for the CD-R (Windows) or the CD-R icon will appear on the desktop where you choose it to open a window for it. Simply copy files to the folder window as usual, then choose the Write these files to CD link (Windows) or Burn Disc icon or File|Burn Disc command (Mac) to burn the files to the CD-R disc.*

Exercise 21

❖ Use the Research Task Pane

Notes

If you are working in the Microsoft Office 2003 suite of applications, you may be familiar with using the various task panes. (To display an alternate task pane, click the Other Task Panes button at the top of the task pane, and then click the name of the desired task pane.) The **Research task pane** enables you to perform a search of one or more reference resources to find more information about a topic from the Web. You can use this task pane to research any topic without leaving your Microsoft Office application.

Your Psychology instructor has asked you to write a paper about Jung. Start your research from the Research task pane in Word.

Vocabulary

Research task pane

Directions

1. Start your word processing program. A new, blank document should open.

   ✓ *You must have an Internet connection to complete this exercise.*

2. Display the Research task pane.
3. Type **Jung** in the Search for text box.
4. Choose to search research sites (All Research Sites), and click the green Start searching arrow beside it. The Research task pane will display a list of results.

   ✓ *To limit the search to specific online resources, open the drop-down list that has the All Reference Books entry, and choose the specific resource to search.*

5. If you see a prompt asking whether to connect to the Internet, click the appropriate button to do so.

   ✓ *In applications from recent versions of the Microsoft Office suite, the first time you display Web help you may have to click on a link for your region of the world in the Web page that appears.*

6. Click the Next link in the upper-left corner of the task pane results to view later results within the same results group.
7. Scroll down the results list in the pane, until you see the next results group, which is collapsed and has a plus sign beside its name.
8. Continue browsing the results list until you see an article of interest.
9. Click on an article link to open the article in your Web browser.
10. Print one copy of the article if requested by your instructor.
11. Close the Web browser and word processing application, and disconnect from the Internet if prompted.

Exercise 3

❖ Move Files and Folders
❖ Rename Files and Folders

Notes

By moving your files and folders as needed (rather than always copying information), you can keep your hard disk well organized without creating clutter. Moving files and folders works a lot like copying files. You can use the easy drag-and-drop method to make the moves.

In the more recent versions of the Windows and Mac operating systems, you can give your folders and files **long file names**. A long file name can include spaces and capital letters, as in *My Botany Notes* or *9-15 Letter to Mom*. Using a long file name that's highly descriptive helps you find a particular file when you need it.

In this exercise, you'll continue organizing information on your new computer at work by moving a file and renaming a file or folder to use a long file name.

Vocabulary

long file names

Directions

1. Open the window for your system's hard disk. In Mac OS X, navigate to your Home folder.
2. Open the **User's Documents** or **My Documents** folder (Windows) or **Documents** folder (Mac) in another window.
3. Drag the **Work Projects** folder from the hard disk folder window to the **User's Documents**, **My Documents,** or **Documents** folder window, then release the mouse button.

   ✓ *Note that in this instance, you don't have to press a key while dragging. That's because when you're dragging between locations on the same disk, the drag and drop method automatically moves the file or folder.*

4. Open the **Work Projects** folder.
5. Navigate to the folder that holds the exercise files for this book. Make sure that you can see both folder windows on the desktop.

   ✓ *Consult your instructor if you need to find out the name of the folder holding the files for this book.*

   ✓ *If your version of Windows is set up to use only one window rather than a separate window for each disk and folder, choose the My Computer icon again to open a second folder window, then navigate from there. On the Mac, you can double-click the grayed-out hard disk icon to activate the hard disk window for navigation.*

5. Choose the command for getting help on the Web about your spreadsheet program or software suite.
6. The Web browser should reappear, and display the Web page. (In some cases, though, this may be the same page as the one you displayed from your word processing program.)
7. Click on a link for a category of help. (See the illustration below for an example.)
8. Click on a help topic in the subsequent Web page that appears. You can then scroll to read help about the topic.
9. If the Help page offers a search feature, click on any button needed to display it.
10. Type **printing** in the Search text box, then press the Go button (or applicable button) on the Web page to start the search.
11. Click on one of the links in the search results to display the help information.
12. Close the Web browser, word processing, and spreadsheet applications, and disconnect from the Internet if prompted.

Click a topic link.

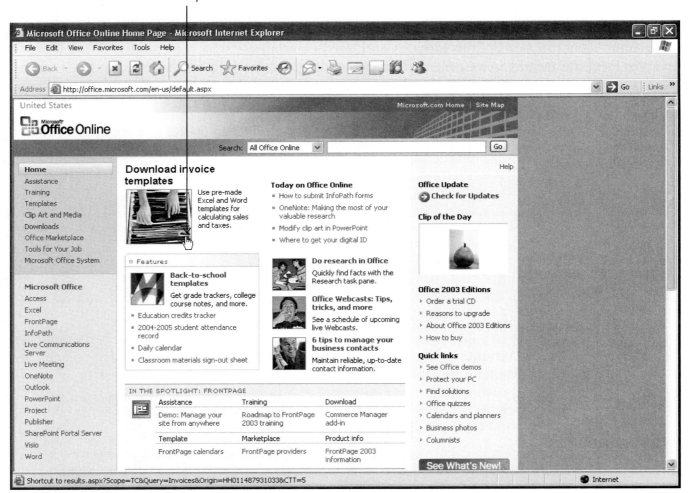

6. Copy the **FM03** and **FM03-2** files from the folder that holds the exercise files for this book to the **Work Projects** folder.

7. Close the folder that holds the exercise files for this book.

8. Insert a floppy disk into the disk drive or into a removable drive.

   ✓ *If you're working on a Mac that doesn't have a floppy or removable disk drive, simply move the second file to the folder of your choice.*

9. Open a window for the floppy disk. In Windows, you can select the disk icon from the My Computer window. On the Mac, an icon for the disk appears on the desktop, so you can choose that icon.

10. Go back to the **Work Projects** folder window. Make sure you can see both the **Work Projects** folder window and the window for the floppy or removable disk.

11. Select (highlight) the **FM03-2** file icon.

12. Press and hold the right mouse button (Windows) or single mouse button (Mac), then drag the **FM03-2** file icon from the **Work Projects** folder to the window for the floppy or removable disk. Release the mouse button. When the shortcut menu appears in windows, click the Move Here choice to finish moving the file.

   ✓ *Note that on the Mac, dragging to another disk always copies the file. You then need to go back and delete the original file. The next exercise describes how to delete files.*

   ✓ *In Windows, you also can click the Cut button on the folder window toolbar or right-click the file icon and then click Cut. Select the window for the folder to which you want to copy the file, then click the Paste button on the folder window or right-click in the folder window and click Paste.*

13. Move the file back from the floppy disk to the **Work Projects** folder.

14. Display the **Work Projects** folder window.

15. In Windows, right-click the **FM03** file icon, then click Rename in the shortcut menu. On the Mac, simply click on the file name at the bottom of the **FM03** file icon.

16. Type **MM Mission Statement** as the file name, then press Enter.

   ✓ *If your Windows installation is displaying file name extensions, you have to be a bit more careful when you rename the file. Drag over the file name to select it (but not the period and the three-letter extension), type the new file name, and press Enter.*

17. Close the **Work Projects** folder window.

18. Go to the window that holds the icon for the **Work Projects** folder.

19. In Windows, right-click the **Work Projects** folder icon, then click Rename in the shortcut menu. On the Mac, simply click on the folder name at the bottom of the **Work Projects** folder icon.

20. Type *Student Name* **Work Projects** as the folder name, substituting your name for *Student Name*, then press Enter.

21. Change the folder name back to **Work Projects**.

22. Close the open folder and disk windows.

Exercise 20

❖ Find Application Help on the Web

Notes

Millions of people on the planet use the **Internet** and **World Wide Web (Web)**, connecting via a computer modem and phone line, high speed connection (cable, DSL, satellite), or network connection. The Web is a collection of online sites (divided into **Web pages**) that display information in a graphical format, including images, sounds, or animations.

Top applications in other categories (word processing, spreadsheet, presentation graphics, and database) now offer commands and tools that launch your **Web browser** (software for displaying Web pages) and then display a Web page to help you with your application, or to connect to the Web location of your choice. Use this exercise to explore the Web help capabilities in your other desktop applications, using your word processing and spreadsheet programs.

You've used your word processing program and spreadsheet for a while, but you want to learn more tips and tricks for working with those programs. Go online to explore the available help.

Vocabulary

Internet   World Wide Web (Web)   Web page   Web browser (browser)

Directions

1. Start your word processing program. A new, blank document should open.

   ✓ *You must have an Internet connection to complete this exercise.*

2. Choose the command for getting help on the Web about your word processing program or software suite (usually found on the Help menu). (If your word processing program offers several commands for getting help on the Web, pick the command of your choice.)

   ✓ *Rather than having different commands for help about word processing, spreadsheets, and so on, your software programs may just allow you to connect to the software publisher's Web site,*

   where you can browse to find more specific help about your application.

3. If you see a prompt asking whether to connect to the Internet, click the appropriate button to do so. After connecting, your system should open your Web browser application. The Web browser will display the help Web page.

   ✓ *In applications from recent versions of the Microsoft Office suite, the first time you display Web help you may have to click on a link for your region of the world in the Web page that appears.*

4. Close the Web browser, and start your spreadsheet program.

Exercise 4

❖ Delete Files and Folders
❖ Restore Files and Folders

Notes

Deleting a file or folder moves it to a temporary holding area called the **Recycle Bin** (Windows) or **Trash** (Mac). If you need to get the file or folder back, you can **restore** it from the Recycle Bin or Trash. While this gives you great protection for your files, the files in the Recycle Bin or Trash do consume hard disk space. Because of this, you do need to periodically **empty** the Recycle Bin or Trash; however, emptying the Recycle Bin or Trash permanently deletes files, so be careful when you take this step.

Your new boss has cautioned you that the pace moves quickly at your company, so you need to be well organized. You've decided to take a few minutes to practice deleting and restoring files, so that you can keep your files and folders streamlined.

Vocabulary

Recycle Bin   Trash   restore   empty

Directions

1. Open the **Work Projects** folder that you used in the last exercise.
2. Select any of the files in the folder.
3. Delete the file (Windows) or move it to the Recycle Bin (Windows) or Trash (Mac).

   ✓ *In Windows, you can simply press the Delete key to start deleting the selected file(s) and folder(s), then click Yes when prompted to confirm the deletion. Or, right-click the selection and click Delete. On the Mac, Control+click the selection, then click Move to Trash in the contextual menu. In either operating system, you can drag a selection and drop it onto the Recycle Bin or Trash icon to delete the selected item(s).*

4. Select the remaining files in the folder.

   ✓ *You can use similar techniques to select multiple files or folders in Windows or on a Mac. Select the first icon with the mouse, press and hold the Control key (Windows) or Shift key (Mac), and click to select additional icons. To select everything in the current folder, choose Edit | Select All from the folder window menu (Windows) or Mac desktop menu bar.*

5. Delete those files.
6. Close the **Work Projects** folder window.
7. Select the icon for the **Work Projects** folder.
8. Delete the folder.

Intergration and Communications

Lesson 29
Work on the Web

Exercises 20-24

❖ **Find help and information on the Web**

❖ **Research a topic**

❖ **Practice with your browser**

❖ **Search for information on the Web**

❖ **Download extras from the Web**

9. Open the Recycle Bin or Trash by double-clicking its icon on the desktop.
10. Restore the **Work Projects** folder to the hard disk.

   ✓ *Start by selecting the folder(s) or file(s) to restore in the Recycle Bin or Trash window. Then, in Windows, you can click the Restore link or chose File | Restore in the Recycle Bin window. For both the Mac and Windows, you can drag and drop the selected items to the appropriate disk or folder to restore them.*

11. Restore the **FM02**, and **MM Mission Statement** files to the **Work Projects** folder.
12. Empty the Recycle Bin or Trash. This should permanently delete the **FM03-2** file.

   ✓ *In Windows, choose File | Empty Recycle Bin, and then click Yes to confirm the deletion. On the Mac, choose Finder | Empty Trash or Special | Empty Trash, and then click on OK.*

13. Close the Recycle Bin or Trash window.

Exercise 19

❖ Critical Thinking

Notes

In this exercise, practice your new Web skills.

You want to add some additional pricing information to the Light Natural Beeswax Candles Web site. Set up those Web pages, including a link, now.

Vocabulary

No new vocabulary in this exercise.

Directions

1. Start your word processing program.
2. Open the **IC19** file.
3. Switch to the Web layout view, and apply the theme of your choice.
4. Download an appropriate piece of clip art from the Web, and insert it where desired in the document.
5. Save the file as a Web page (HTML) file with the name **BEEPR**.
6. Start your spreadsheet program.
7. Open the **IC19-2** file.
8. Save the range A1:D11 as a Web page (HTML) file with the name **BEEPR2**.
9. Close the open file and the spreadsheet program.
10. Switch back to the word processing program, if needed.
11. In the **BEEPR** HTML file, select the text that reads **Click here for current pricing**.
12. Add a hyperlink to the **BEEPR2** Web page file that you saved in step 8.
13. Save your changes to the **BEEPR** file.
14. Use the new link to launch your Web browser program and open the linked file.
    - ✓ *For extra practice, you could work in blank files in your applications, create links to your favorite Web sites, and click the links to display those Web sites.*
15. Close the open files and applications.

Exercise 5

❖ Finding Lost Files

Notes

With today's hard disks averaging dozens of gigabytes in size and with many computers now being connected to a network, it can be very easy to lose track of where you may have saved a file. Fortunately, both the Windows and Mac operating systems offer a tool for finding lost files. In Windows, this feature is called the **Search** or **Find feature**. On a Mac equipped with the most recent version of Mac OS X, you can use the **Find** feature; in older Mac operating systems, you use **Sherlock** to find files. This exercise gives you a little practice with finding a file.

A co-worker at your new job has just shown you how to find files, so you practice now on your own system.

Vocabulary

Windows Search (Find) feature   Sherlock   wildcard characters
Mac Find feature

Directions

1. Start the Find, Search, or Sherlock feature.

   ✓ In Windows 98 or 2000, *click the Start button, point to Find, and then click Files or Folders. In Windows XP, click Start, then click Search. On the Mac, choose File | Find from the Finder menu bar or double-click the Sherlock icon.*

2. Search the hard disk for files that contain **help** in the file name.

   ✓ *Choose the hard disk as the search location, choose the option(s) for searching by file name, type **help** in the appropriate text box, then run the find.*

   ✓ *In Windows XP, the Search Companion in the left pane of the Search Results window will lead you through the search. Click the All Files and Folders choice to get started in this instance.*

3. Select one of the found files, and then review what folder on the disk holds the file.

4. View the properties or file information.

   ✓ *In Windows Find, choose File | Properties in the Find window. On the Mac, choose File | Get Info from the Finder menu.*

5. Search the hard disk (or the disk that holds the exercise files for this book) for the files for this lesson, which all begin with the characters **FM0**.

   ✓ *In Windows and the Mac, you can use an advanced or custom find to locate files of a particular type. In Windows, you also can use **wildcard characters** such as the asterisk (*), which represents a group of characters. For example, to find all the Word document (.DOC) files on the disk, you would enter ***.doc** as the file name for the find.*

6. Close the Search, Find, or Sherlock window.

Exercise 18

❖ Save a Word or Excel Document in XML

Notes

Like HTML, **XML** is a standardized markup language. Whereas HTML facilitates consistent data display, XML was designed to facilitate easier data exchange between widely differing programs. (XML is capable of even more, but further discussion is beyond the scope of this book.) More applications are enabling data to be saved as an XML file, for exchange and manipulation in other programs, notably Word 2003 and Excel 2003 from the Office 2003 Professional suite. This process works best for lists of information.

You have some mobile phone subscriber data for Mobile A Networks in both word processing and spreadsheet files. Save those files as XML files now.

Vocabulary

XML

Directions

1. Start your word processing program.
2. Open the **IC18** file.
3. Start the process for saving the file as an XML document.
   - ✓ Use the File|Save As command, and choose XML Document (*.xml) from the Save as type drop-down list.
4. Save the file as **MOBXML**. The application title bar will show you that the document has been saved as XML, but its on-screen appearance won't change.
5. Close the document and the word processing program.
6. Start your spreadsheet program.
7. Open the **IC18-2** file.
8. Start the process for saving the file as an XML file.
9. Save the file as **MOBXML2**. Again, the application title bar will indicate that the file has been saved as XML, but its on-screen appearance won't change.
10. Close the spreadsheet program.

Quiz Break 1

Circle the correct answer to each of the questions below:

T	F	1. The Operating System (OS) is the name of a new computer brand.
T	F	2. Both the Windows and Macintosh Operating Systems have a desktop.
T	F	3. When you open a folder, it appears in a window.
T	F	4. You can create a folder within a folder.
T	F	5. Use the Close button to close a folder window.
T	F	6. Drag and drop always copies the selected file(s) or folder(s).
T	F	7. After you use the cut or copy technique in Windows, you use the Replace command to place the cut or copied file or folder in a new location.
T	F	8. Long file names can include spaces and capital letters.
T	F	9. You can rename files, but not folders.
T	F	10. Deleting a file or folder always deletes it permanently.
T	F	11. The Windows Recycle Bin and Mac Trash are essentially the same feature.
T	F	12. You can find a file based on part of its name.

Circle the correct answer to each of the questions below:

1. The computer desktop is:
    A. The desk on which you've placed your computer.
    B. A program you use to keep your schedule.
    C. The starting point for your work with the computer, where you see icons for files and folders and menus for using programs.
    D. Both A and B.

2. An icon represents:
    A. A file.
    B. A folder.
    C. A program.
    D. Any of the above.

3. To display a shortcut menu (Windows) or contextual menu (Mac), you:
    A. Ctrl+click an icon (Windows and Mac).
    B. Right-click an icon (Windows) or Control+click an icon (Mac).
    C. Triple-click an icon (Windows and Mac).
    D. None of the above.

4. To permanently delete a file:
    A. Place it in the Recycle Bin or Trash, and then empty the Recycle Bin or Trash.
    B. Select it and press Delete.
    C. Select its file name and use the Delete key to remove the name.
    D. Select the file and press F10.

5. You use these features to find a file:
    A. File Snoop (Windows and Mac).
    B. Search Files (Windows) and Look for Files (Mac).
    C. Bob (Windows and Mac).
    D. Find (Windows and Mac).

Illustration 2

	A	B	C	D
1	**Go! Travel Consultants**			
2	**St. Louis Hotel Partners**			
3				
4	**Partner**	**Rate**	**Rate Code**	**Phone**
5	Hilton	$209	A445	314-555-0101
6	Hyatt	$199	C278	314-555-5600
7	Westin	$189	39393	314-888-4000
8	St. Regis	$179	40408	314-777-0303
9	Marlborough Inn	$159	IC4491	314-555-7600
10	Fleming House	$159	L22	314-111-0404
11				
12	St. Louis Arch			

Lessons 2–10
Exercises 1–65

6. Follow the new hyperlink. Connect to the Internet, if prompted. Your Web browser should launch and display the main Web page for the St. Louis site.

   ✓ *In recent Word versions, you have to Ctrl+click a hyperlink to follow it in any view.*

   ✓ *If your system doesn't prompt you to connect to the Internet since you were working offline in earlier exercises, you may need to connect manually. Consult your instructor if you need help.*

7. Close your Web browser and disconnect from the Internet.

8. Close the word processing program, saving the file.

   ✓ *If you insert a hyperlink in a presentation graphics file, you can click the hyperlink when you play the on-screen slide show to jump to the Web from the slide show.*

9. Start your spreadsheet program.

10. Open the **IC17-2** file.

11. Save the file as **STLHL2**.

12. Select cell A12 and enter **St. Louis Arch**.

    ✓ *Be sure to press Tab or Enter to finish your cell entry.*

13. Reselect cell A12.

14. Insert a hyperlink to the **STLHL** word processing file. The finished hyperlink should resemble the one shown in Illustration 2 on the following page.

    ✓ *You must enter the full path (including disk, folders, and file name) to the file. Generally, you can browse to find the file you need. If you're not sure where you've saved the file, get help from a lab partner or your instructor.*

15. Click the new hyperlink. Your word processing program launches and opens the **STLHL** file.

16. Close the word processing program. Save your changes and close the spreadsheet program.

Illustration 1

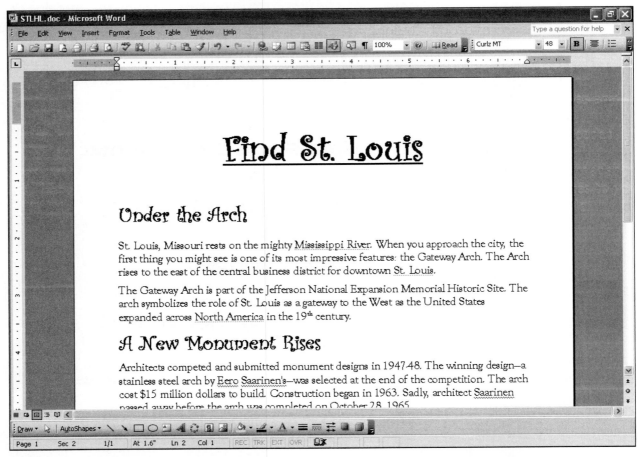

Directory of Files

Exercise	File Name	Page
1	None	—
2	None	—
3	None	—
4	None	—
5	None	—
6	WP06	50
7	WP07	52
8	WP08	54
9	WP09	56
10	WP10	58
11	WP11	60
12	WP12, WP12-2	62
13	WP13	65
14	WP14	67
15	WP15	69
16	WP16	71
17	WP17	73
18	WP18	75
19	WP19	78
20	WP20	80
21	WP21	82
22	WP22	85
23	WP23	88
24	WP24	90
25	WP25	93
26	WP26	95
27	WP27	97
28	None	—
29	WP29	102
30	WP30	104
31	WP31	106
32	WP32	108
33	WP33	110
34	WP34	112
35	WP35	114

Exercise	File Name	Page
36	WP36	118
37	WP37	120
38	WP38	125
39	WP39	129
40	WP40	133
41	WP41	136
42	WP42	140
43	WP43	143
44	WP44	146
45	WP45	151
46	WP46	154
47	None	—
48	WP48	158
49	WP49	161
50	WP50	163
51	WP51	165
52	WP52	168
53	None	—
54	None	—
55	WP55	176
56	WP56, WP56-2	179
57	WP57, WP57-2	181
58	WP58, WP58-2	185
59	None	—
60	WP60, WP60-2	192
61	WP61, WP61-2	195, 196
62	WP62	198
63	WP63	202
64	WP64, WP64-2, WP64-3	203
65	WP65	205

Exercise 17

❖ Insert Hyperlinks ❖ Use Hyperlinks

Notes

When you browse for information (either on the Web or in many online help systems), you click a **hyperlink** to display the next page of information that you want to review. The hyperlink can be a button or graphic, but more often a hyperlink is specially highlighted and underlined text. The leading applications (word processing, spreadsheet, database, and presentation graphics) all allow you to create hyperlinks right within your files. You can insert a hyperlink that opens your Web browser and displays a Web page, or you can insert a hyperlink that opens another file from a location on your hard drive.

You put together a document about the St. Louis arch some time ago for Go! Travel Consultants. You now want to insert a link to the City of St. Louis Web site, so that anyone using the document can jump online for more facts. Likewise, you have a spreadsheet of St. Louis Hotels that give Go! Travel Consultants clients special deals, and you want to add a hyperlink from that file to the St. Louis Arch document, for easy reference.

Vocabulary

hyperlink

Directions

1. Start your word processing program.
2. Open the **IC17** file.
3. Save the file as **STLHL**.
4. Select the document title, **Find St. Louis**.

   ✓ *Making a selection identifies what text will be formatted as a hyperlink.*

   ✓ *In many applications, you can merely type a Web page address in a file, and the application automatically recognizes the Web address and formats it as a hyperlink.*

5. Insert a hyperlink. Enter the City of St. Louis' Web site address, **http://stlouis.missouri.org/**, as the link address. The hyperlink appears in the document with the default hyperlink formatting. Illustration 1 on the following page shows what the hyperlink looks like at the top of the document.

   ✓ *The command for inserting a hyperlink may be found on the Insert or Create menu.*

   ✓ *In a word processing program, you can insert hyperlinks anywhere on a page. In a presentation graphics program, you have to insert a hyperlink in a text placeholder. In a spreadsheet program, you insert a hyperlink in a cell. In a database program, you have to first create a field that uses the hyperlink data type in the data table.*

Lesson 2
Create, Save, and Close a Document

Exercises 1–5

- ❖ **Create new documents**
- ❖ **Save new documents**
- ❖ **Close an open document**
- ❖ **Move the insertion point in the document**
- ❖ **Check spelling and grammar in a document**
- ❖ **Understand grammar and spell check options**

information from the database report looks when saved as a Web page and displayed in a Web browser.

10. Close the browser.

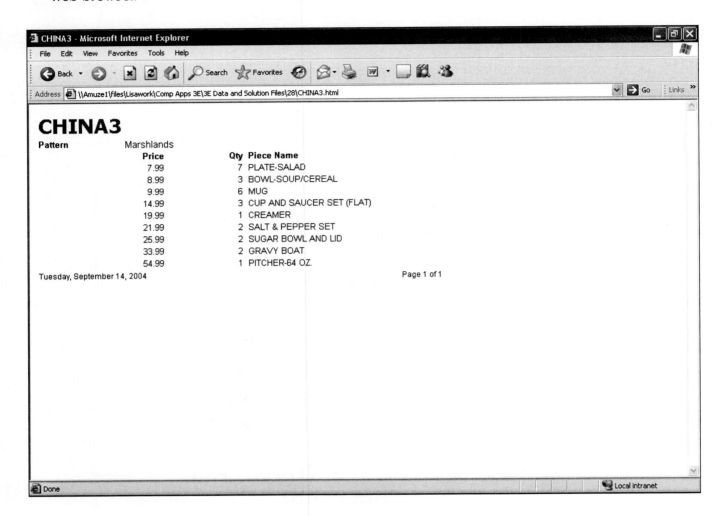

Exercise 1

❖ Create a Document ❖ Save a Document
❖ Close a Document

Notes

To create your message in a word processing **program**, you can create a blank **document** and then begin typing. Word processing programs offer a number of features that make it easy to create documents, as you'll find in this exercise. Note that you may also see a word processing program called a "word processor." A "word processor" used to be a separate machine capable of creating text-based documents only, as opposed to a fully-featured computer capable of running many different types of software. Today, however, you may see the term "word processor" used to mean "word processing program."

Imagine that you're preparing a paper about Thomas Jefferson for a history or political science class. In this exercise, type an introductory paragraph for the paper.

Vocabulary

program	insertion point	Backspace	save
document	word wrap	Delete	

Directions

1. Start the word processing program, if needed.
2. Create a new, blank document.
3. Leave the blinking **insertion point** at the top of the document.
4. Type the paragraph shown on the following page. When the insertion point reaches the end of each line, continue typing. The **word wrap** feature moves the insertion point to the beginning of the next line.
    - ✓ *If wavy lines appear under certain words you type, ignore them for now.*

5. If you make a mistake, press the **Backspace** key to delete the character to the left of the insertion point.
6. If needed, use the left and right arrow keys to move the insertion point within the text. Press the **Delete** key to delete the character to the right of the insertion point.
7. **Save** the document file; name it **JEFF**.
8. Close the document.

Exercise 16

❖ View Database Information in Web Format

Notes

Converting database information to Web format is more complicated. You probably won't want to publish the database data, but you might want to save a view or **object** such as a form, report, or query. Saving the object only (rather than data table list itself) results in a Web file with more attractive formatting and more useful information.

You want to start selling some of your replacement china on the Web, so you need to post a list of the available pieces that you've listed in a database. You want to start out by selling only one pattern so you made a query to place only that data in a report. Save that report as an HTML document now from your database program.

Vocabulary

object   export   convert

Directions

1. Start your database program.
2. Open the **IC16** database file.
3. Open the **CHINA3** report.
4. Choose the command for saving the file object in HTML or Web page format. (It usually appears on the File menu or a submenu of the File menu. Unlike the command used to save Web information from other applications, this command may be named **Export** or may have a longer name that starts with **Convert**.)

   ✓ *At least one of the top database programs (Access) lets you save database information as an interactive Web page called a data access page. You copy the data access page (which is in HTML format) and the database file on which it is based to a Web location so that users can use the data access page to view and work with selected data from the database.*

5. If your database program gives you the option of applying a Web template during the save operation, click OK to skip that step.

   ✓ *When you're working with other databases you can apply a template if you prefer.*

6. Name the file **CHINA3**, and finish saving the file. The database program will add a .htm or .html file name extension to the file for you.
7. Close the file and your database program. Do not save changes to the file if prompted to do so.
8. Launch your Web browser, but do not connect to the Internet.
9. Use the Web browser's command for opening files (or the address box) to open the **CHINA3** file. The illustration on the following page shows an example of how the

Despite his human flaws and foibles, Thomas Jefferson influenced the government of our country perhaps more than any other political figure. In writing the Declaration of Independence, Jefferson framed powerful political ideas in accessible, graceful language. Jefferson dedicated his life to applying those ideas to help build a lasting government for the United States of America.

8. Practice using the interactive tools (a list of slide names, buttons for navigating between various slides, and so on) to display the various slides in your Web browser. Notice that bulleted lists, tables, and other graphical elements translate well. The illustration below shows an example of how the information from the presentation graphics file looks when saved as a Web page and displayed in a Web browser.

9. Close the browser.

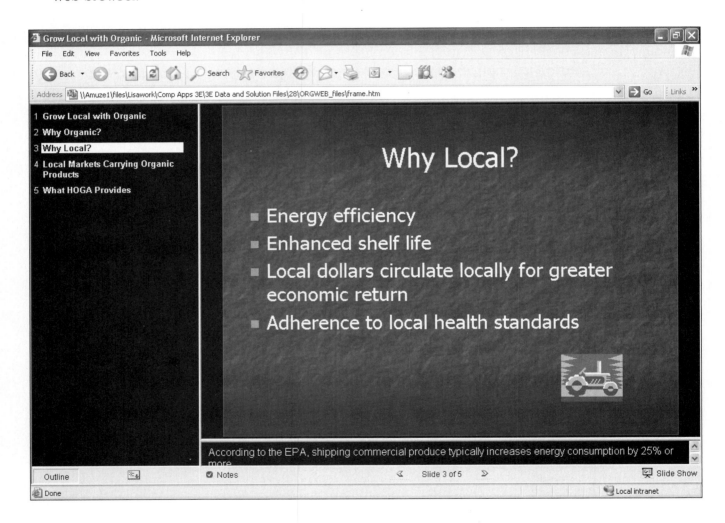

Exercise 2

❖ Create a Document ❖ Save a Document ❖ Close a Document ❖ Move Around the Document

Notes

Most word processing programs offer **templates**. When you use a template to create a new document, the template provides the design for the document and text. The template also might supply **placeholder text**—suggested text you replace with your own information. Try using a template to create a new document, and then practice moving around the document.

You work in the human resources department of a company called Crystal Communications. You need to send a memo to all employees to inform them of a benefits meeting. Create the memo in this exercise.

Vocabulary

template	placeholder text	drag	automatic completion

Directions

1. Create a new document using a memo template.

   ✓ *In recent versions of Word, you choose File | New and then click the On my computer link in the Templates section of the New Document task pane to find installed templates.*

2. Insert the company name as shown on page 42. If your memo template has Company Name Here placeholder text, use the Delete key to remove it, and then type the company name.

3. Enter the To:, From:, CC:, and Subject:/Re: information shown. (Insert the CC: line if your template doesn't include it. Also, the Date: line should automatically enter the current date; enter the date yourself if it doesn't appear.)

   ✓ *To replace the placeholder text for a line at the top of the memo, click the bold **here** to select the entire placeholder, then type the new text. If the bold **here** is absent, such as in a date, select the text and type the new text.*

4. If the body of the memo has a heading line, delete it.

5. **Drag** to select all the placeholder text in the body of the memo.

6. Type the new memo body text shown on page 42, pressing Enter once to start each paragraph, in this case.

Exercise 15

❖ Save a Presentation as a Web Page

Notes

You can also save a presentation graphics file as a Web page file. This allows you to take advantage of the design features in your presentation graphics program without forcing you to become an HTML expert. Generally, the presentation graphics program saves the entire presentation in HTML format and adds features to make it **interactive**. For example, you might see a list of titles for all the slides, and be able to click a title to display that "slide" on the Web.

You want to put your presentation for the Haywood Organic Growers Association on the Web. Open the presentation you created previously and save it for the Web.

Vocabulary

interactive   publish

Directions

1. Start your presentation graphics program.
2. Open the **IC15** presentation file. This presentation already has formatting applied with a presentation design template.
3. Choose the command for saving the file in HTML or Web page format. (It usually appears on the File menu.)

   ✓ *Some presentation graphics programs allow you to save a limited number of slides (or even one slide) and to include features like speaker notes in the Web version of the presentation. For example, you could save a slide that has a graph to create a Web page with that graph. If your presentation graphics program only enables you to save one slide at a time as a Web page, save slide 3 of this presentation as a Web page to complete this exercise.*

   ✓ *When you use the **Publish** button in the Save As dialog box when saving in Web format from PowerPoint 2003, you can further control the HTML output. For example, you can choose which slides to output and whether to include speaker notes.*

4. Name the file **ORGWEB**, and finish saving the file. The presentation graphics program will add a .htm or .html file name extension to the file for you.
5. Close the file and your presentation graphics program. Do not save changes to the file if prompted to do so.
6. Launch your Web browser, but do not connect to the Internet.
7. Use the Web browser's command for opening files (or the address box) to open the **ORGWEB** file.

✓ In many templates, the paragraph formatting adds extra white space between paragraphs, so that you need not press Enter twice.

✓ As you type certain words such as a day or month name, a small box or tip might pop up to display the full word. You can usually then press Enter or F3 to enter the rest of the word into the document. This **automatic completion** feature is called AutoComplete in Word; other word processing programs typically offer a similar feature.

7. Press Ctrl+Home to move the insertion point to the beginning of the document. Press Ctrl+End to move the insertion point to the end of the document.
8. Click anywhere in the second paragraph.
9. Press the up arrow key to move the insertion point up one line.
10. Use Ctrl+up arrow and Ctrl+down arrow to move to the beginning of different paragraphs in the document.
11. Save the document file; name it **INSURE**.
12. Close the document.

6. If available, select the option to save the selected range only.

7. Name the file **MM6MWEB**, and finish saving the file. The spreadsheet program will add a .htm or .html file name extension to the file for you.

8. Close the file and your spreadsheet program. Do not save changes to the file if prompted to do so.

9. Launch your Web browser, but do not connect to the Internet.

10. Use the Web browser's command for opening files (or the address box) to open the **MM6MWEB** file. The illustration below shows an example of how the information from the spreadsheet file looks when saved as a Web page and displayed in a Web browser.

11. Close the browser.

✓ *Generally, after you save information from an application as a Web (.htm or .html) file, you can open that file in any application that enables you to edit Web page files. Then, you can add any finishing touches to your newly-created Web information. In fact, most word processors now provide many features to enable you to improve basic Web pages.*

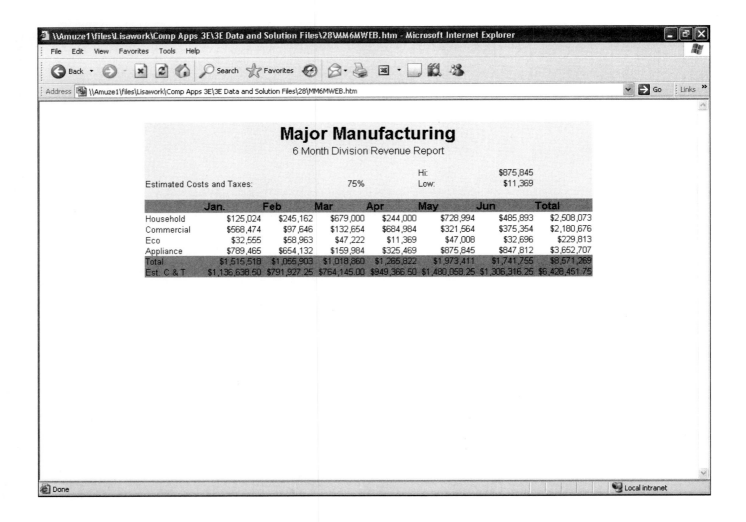

\\Amuze1\files\Lisawork\Comp Apps 3E\3E Data and Solution Files\28\MM6MWEB.htm - Microsoft Internet Explorer

File   Edit   View   Favorites   Tools   Help

Back   Search   Favorites

Address   \\Amuze1\files\Lisawork\Comp Apps 3E\3E Data and Solution Files\28\MM6MWEB.htm   Go   Links

Major Manufacturing
6 Month Division Revenue Report

| | | | Hi: | $875,845 |
| Estimated Costs and Taxes: | | 75% | Low: | $11,369 |

	Jan.	Feb	Mar	Apr	May	Jun	Total
Household	$125,024	$245,162	$679,000	$244,000	$728,994	$485,893	$2,508,073
Commercial	$568,474	$97,646	$132,654	$684,984	$321,564	$375,354	$2,180,676
Eco	$32,555	$58,963	$47,222	$11,369	$47,008	$32,696	$229,813
Appliance	$789,465	$654,132	$159,984	$325,469	$875,845	$847,812	$3,652,707
Total	$1,515,518	$1,055,903	$1,018,860	$1,265,822	$1,973,411	$1,741,755	$8,571,269
Est. C & T	$1,136,638.50	$791,927.25	$764,145.00	$949,366.50	$1,480,058.25	$1,306,316.25	$6,428,451.75

Done   Local intranet

Crystal Communications Memorandum

To: All Employees

CC: John Crystal, CEO

From: Human Resources

Date: 9/13/2005

Re: Benefits Meeting

As has been previously communicated, the cost of providing our premier employee benefits program has increased substantially due to factors beyond the company's control. Crystal Communications has explored a number of benefits alternatives.

Working with a number of local healthcare, insurance, and investment providers, Crystal Communications has developed a new benefits program. This new program will be available to all employees.

The new benefits program will be explained at an employee meeting next Thursday at 4 p.m. in the large conference room. Light refreshments will be provided.

If you cannot attend the meeting, please contact HR at extension 500.

1

Exercise 14

❖ Save a Spreadsheet as a Web Page

Notes

Spreadsheet information may be particularly vital to the operation of a company, so the company may want to make that information easily accessible to employees, customers, or stockholders. For example, the company may want to post sales results to its **intranet** (internal Internet) so the employees can monitor the company's performance. Or, the company might want to publish a list of products on a Web site to provide customers with more information, as demonstrated in this exercise. The leading spreadsheet programs now enable you to save spreadsheet information directly into a Web file.

Your boss in Finance at Major Manufacturing has asked you to save the spreadsheet of sales by division for the first six months of the year as a Web document, so it can be posted and distributed more easily. Handle that task from your spreadsheet program now.

Vocabulary

intranet

Directions

1. Start your spreadsheet program.
2. Open the **IC14** spreadsheet file.
3. Adjust formatting for this file if you wish before saving it as a Web page. (Although in this case, the example file already contains automatic formatting, so you may not need to make any formatting changes.)

   ✓ *While a spreadsheet program may not offer as many Web-specific formatting options as a word processing program, it's still worth applying the formatting to make your spreadsheet an attractive Web page. If you plan to link the Web page to other pages on your site, try to use formatting (colors and fonts) that's consistent with those other pages.*

4. Select the range **A1:H13**, the range that holds information on the first sheet.

   ✓ *Your spreadsheet program may enable you to save a selected range as the Web page. It also may allow you to save only the first worksheet (sheet or page) in the file, or all sheets in the file. If you can't save a selection only, as in this exercise, then save the first sheet in the file. If your spreadsheet program doesn't give you any choice of what to save, that likely means that you can only save the whole first sheet in the spreadsheet file as a Web page file.*

5. Choose the command for saving the file in HTML or Web page format. (It usually appears on the File menu.)

Exercise 3

❖ Create a Document ❖ Save a Document
❖ Close a Document
❖ Correct Spelling Errors

Notes

If you misspell words often, you can rely on your word processor for a little assistance. Leading word processing programs now offer automatic spelling help, correcting some typos for you automatically as you type. Take advantage of automatic spelling help in this exercise.

You own a hiking gear shop called Mountain Gear. In this exercise, you'll create an in-store flyer about some new equipment the store offers.

Vocabulary

No new vocabulary in this exercise.

Directions

1. Create a new, blank document.
2. Leave the blinking insertion point at the top of the document.
3. Type the paragraphs shown on the following page, allowing the word wrap feature to move the insertion point to the beginning of each new line. To start each new paragraph, press the Enter key twice.

   ✓ *Some versions of Word may automatically format the first line of the document as a headline the second time you press Enter without inserting a blank line. You can ignore that formatting for now.*

4. Make sure you type the circled words exactly as shown. The word processing program's spelling correction feature corrects these common typos and converts some special codes to typeset symbols.

   ✓ *If the automatic correction feature isn't working, consult online help or get help from your instructor to find out how to turn it on.*

   ✓ *Your word processing program might not correct all the circled words, because each word processing program contains its own list of spelling errors to correct. If you want more practice using this feature in your word processing program, create your own blank document and keep typing misspelled words to see which words your program corrects.*

5. Save the document file; name it **GEAR**.
6. Close the document.

   ✓ *In newer versions of Word, you can undo any automatic correction. Point to the corrected word, point to the blue underline that appears below the first letter, and then click the AutoCorrect Options button. Click on the Undo Automatic Corrections choice (the command name may change based on the type of correction made).*

Illustration 2

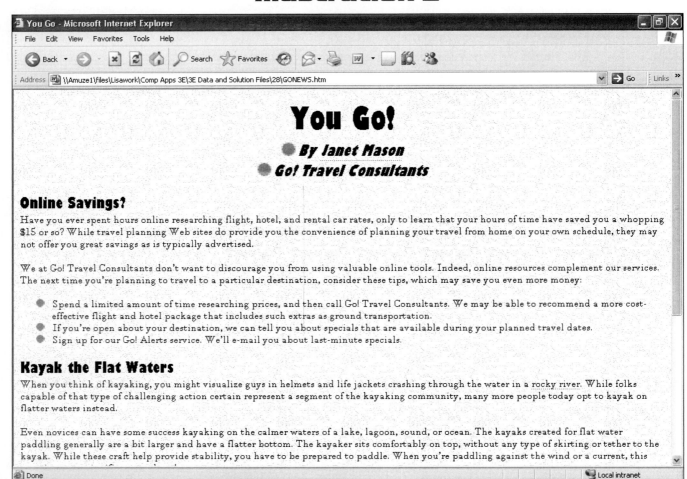

Address: \\Amuze1\files\Lisawork\Comp Apps 3E\3E Data and Solution Files\28\GONEWS.htm

You Go!

By Janet Mason
Go! Travel Consultants

Online Savings?

Have you ever spent hours online researching flight, hotel, and rental car rates, only to learn that your hours of time have saved you a whopping $15 or so? While travel planning Web sites do provide you the convenience of planning your travel from home on your own schedule, they may not offer you great savings as is typically advertised.

We at Go! Travel Consultants don't want to discourage you from using valuable online tools. Indeed, online resources complement our services. The next time you're planning to travel to a particular destination, consider these tips, which may save you even more money:

- Spend a limited amount of time researching prices, and then call Go! Travel Consultants. We may be able to recommend a more cost-effective flight and hotel package that includes such extras as ground transportation.
- If you're open about your destination, we can tell you about specials that are available during your planned travel dates.
- Sign up for our Go! Alerts service. We'll e-mail you about last-minute specials.

Kayak the Flat Waters

When you think of kayaking, you might visualize guys in helmets and life jackets crashing through the water in a rocky river. While folks capable of that type of challenging action certain represent a segment of the kayaking community, many more people today opt to kayak on flatter waters instead.

Even novices can have some success kayaking on the calmer waters of a lake, lagoon, sound, or ocean. The kayaks created for flat water paddling generally are a bit larger and have a flatter bottom. The kayaker sits comfortably on top, without any type of skirting or tether to the kayak. While these craft help provide stability, you have to be prepared to paddle. When you're paddling against the wind or a current, this

Exciting New Products from Mountain Gear

(teh) fall hiking season is (almots) here, so get ready! Mountain Gear has (terrfic) new products to ensure (yuor) safety and comfort on the trail.

If you need (nwe) boots, try the Rox (TM) line from Blazers. (when) you wear (thees), your feet will feel fine on even the toughest trails.

Also (chcek) out the new packs from Hammer. (Tehy) are 5% more spacious than prior models.

Don't (fogret) our Frequent Buyer Program, which offers (sepcial) deals and discounts!

13. Use the Web browser's command for opening files (or the address box) to open the **GONEWS** file. Illustration 2 on the following page shows an example of how the information from the word processing document file looks when saved as a Web page and displayed in a Web browser.

14. Close the browser.

✓ *To use a browser address box to open a file stored on your hard disk, enter the full path (including disk, folders, and file name) to the file, then press Enter.*

Illustration 1

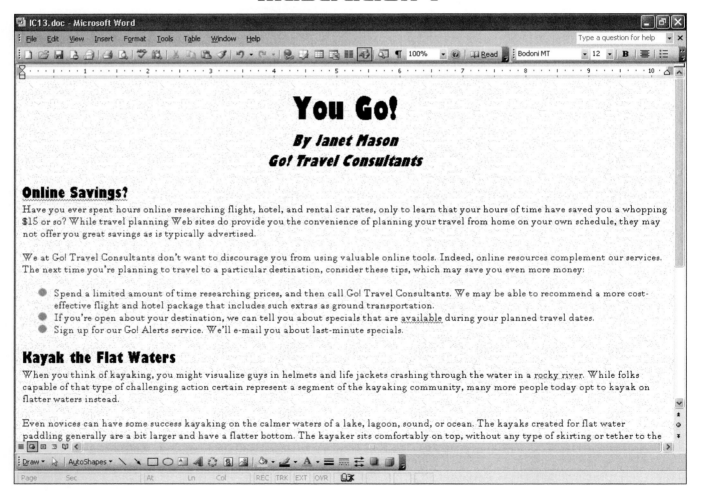

Exercise 4

❖ Create a Document ❖ Save a Document
❖ Close a Document ❖ Spell Check

Notes

In some cases, your word processing program identifies a word that may be misspelled, but leaves it up to you to make the correction. You can simply retype the word, or use the **spell check** feature to fix it.

Your American history instructor wants the class to commemorate the 100th anniversary of the Lewis and Clark expedition. Start your assignment now, typing the first few paragraphs of a report.

Vocabulary

spell check

Directions

1. Create a new, blank document.
2. Leave the blinking insertion point at the top of the document.
3. Type the paragraphs shown on the following page, allowing the word wrap feature to move the insertion point to the beginning of each new line. To start each new paragraph, press the Enter key twice.
4. Make sure you type the circled words exactly as shown. Notice that your word processing program displays wavy red underlining or uses some other technique to identify misspelled words.
5. Correct each misspelled word by editing it or by using the spell check feature in your word processing program.

✓ *Leading word processing programs also offer a shortcut for fixing flagged typos. For example, you can right-click (or Ctrl+click in Macintosh applications) the misspelled word with the wavy underline, then click a replacement word in the shortcut menu that appears. In other cases, you click a status bar button, then click the correct word.*

✓ *If you're using the Backspace key to make a correction in recent Word versions, you may see a narrow blue box appear under the word you're correcting. This tells you that Word may have an automatic correction for the word. (The blue box will only appear in such a case.) You can point to that box then click on the drop-down menu button that appears to display a menu of AutoCorrect options.*

6. Save the document file; name it **LC**.
7. Close the document.

Exercise 13

❖ Work with a Theme

Notes

Some word processing programs—notably recent versions of Word—include the **theme** feature. A theme includes a collection of styles, bullets, and background formatting that you can apply to a document. While the text and bullet formatting of a theme appears in a regular document file, some of the theme formatting only appears when you save the document as an HTML file.

✓ *Themes not only update the body text style but also the heading styles. So, you should apply heading styles as needed before "trying on" various themes in a file.*

The Go! Travel Consultants Web site also includes a page with a newsletter. Apply a theme to the document that holds the newsletter content, and then save the document as a Web page

Vocabulary

theme

Directions

1. Start your word processing program.
2. Open the **IC13** document file.
3. Scroll down until you see the bulleted list and review the initial appearance of the bullets.
4. Change to the Web (or Web layout) view.
5. Apply the theme of your choice. Illustration 1 on the following page shows an example of how the document looks with a theme applied.

   ✓ *Not all themes install by default. Either choose one of the installed themes, or consult your instructor to find out more about installing additional themes.*

6. Change to the Normal view to see what formatting does not apply to the document itself.
7. Change back to the Web (Web Layout) view.

8. Review the updated appearance of the bullets in the bulleted list. Notice that the theme applies a custom picture bullet.
9. Apply a bullet to the subtitle lines below the page title.

   ✓ *In this example document, adding the bullets provides a decorative element rather than setting off list items.*

10. Save the document as a Web page. Name the file **GONEWS**. The word processor will add a .htm or .html file name extension to the file for you.
11. Close the file and your word processing program.
12. Launch your Web browser, but do not connect to the Internet. (This may be called working offline on your system.)

Erly maps of North America prvide a telling look at how lttle of the geography had been expored. As on other contenants, exploration hear reqwired government leardership and funding.

President Thomas Jeffrson, hoping to find a watr route between the Atlantic and Picific Oceans, commissioned an expedition. Army ocifers Meriwether Lwewis and William Clark were to lead the xpedition

Illustration 2

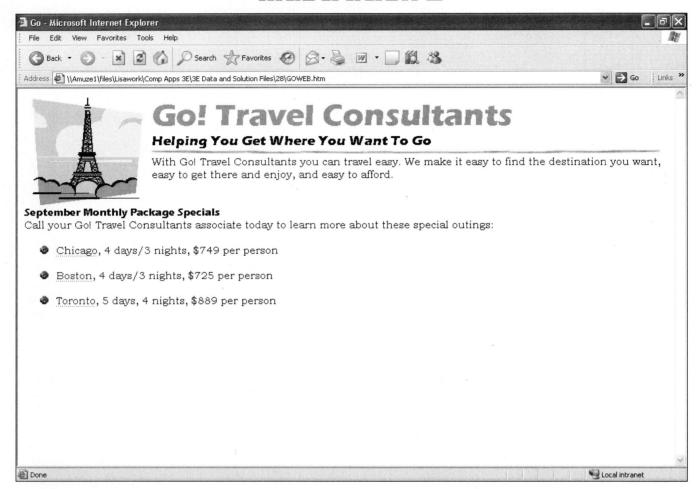

Exercise 5

❖ Create a Document ❖ Save a Document
❖ Close a Document ❖ Spell Check
❖ Grammar Check
❖ Spell Check and Grammar Check Options

Notes

In addition to checking your spelling, the most advanced word processing programs also include grammar checking. When the word processing program performs a **grammar check**, usually in conjunction with a spelling check, it compares the text in your document to a list of grammar rules, and identifies any phrase, sentence, or paragraph that may violate a grammar rule. See how this works in this exercise. Also explore the options for controlling how the spelling and grammar checker feature works in your word processing program. For example, if you don't want wavy underlines to appear below misspelled words, you can turn that feature off.

As the owner of the Mountain Gear shop, you want to thank your employees for a good year and announce a holiday party. Create a note to your employees in this exercise.

Vocabulary

grammar check

Directions

1. Create a new, blank document.
2. Leave the blinking insertion point at the top of the document.
3. Type the salutation and first paragraph shown on the following page, allowing the word wrap feature to move the insertion point to the beginning of each new line in the first paragraph.
4. Make sure you type the circled words and phrases exactly as shown. Notice that your word processing program displays wavy red or green underlining or uses some other

technique to identify misspelled words or grammar errors.

✓ *In most word processing programs, the grammar check feature works along with the spell check feature and is turned on (enabled) by default. If grammar checking isn't working for you, consult online help or your instructor to learn how to turn the grammar check feature on and use it.*

5. Display the options for controlling how the spelling and grammar checking works. Turn off the feature for checking spelling and grammar as you type.

7. Change the destination cities to **Chicago**, **Boston**, and **Toronto**. Don't change any other information in the bullet items.

   ✓ *If you have change tracking (revision marking) turned on when you make your edits, the tracking marks may appear in your final Web page. So, be sure to accept the changes you've made and turn off change tracking if you do not want to see those marks in a finished Web page.*

8. Insert an appropriate piece of clip art near the top of the page. Size and position the clip art as desired, adjusting wrapping settings as needed. Your Web page should now resemble Illustration 1.

   ✓ *You may discover as you position the clip art that certain positioning options aren't active. That's because your word processor prevents you from selecting formatting options that aren't supported by some Web browser programs.*

9. Use the command for saving the file as a Web page to save the file as **GOWEB**. (The word processor will add a .htm or .html file name extension to the file for you.)

10. Close the file and your word processing program.

11. Launch your Web browser, but do not connect to the Internet.

12. Use the Web browser's command for opening files (or the address box) to open the **GOWEB** file. Illustration 2 on the following page shows an example of how the information from the word processing document file looks when saved as a Web page and displayed in a Web browser.

    ✓ *To use a browser address box to open a file stored on your hard disk, enter the full path (including disk, folders, and file name) to the file, then press Enter.*

13. Close the browser.

Illustration 1

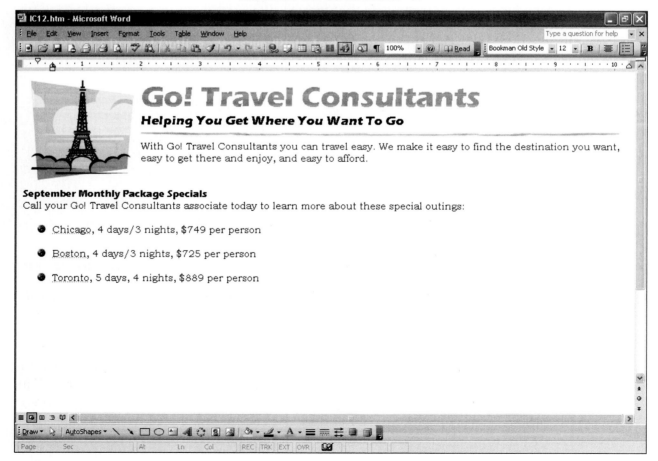

✓ *In some programs, you also can choose whether the word processing program should automatically correct misspellings as you type them.*

6. Type the rest of the text shown below. To start each new paragraph, press the Enter key twice. Notice that the word processing program no longer identifies spelling or grammar errors with wavy underlines.

7. Run your word processing program's spell check feature to correct the spelling and grammar errors in the document. Do not change the name in the last line, however.

✓ *Sometimes the grammar check feature flags word usage that is correct. If you think your version is correct, choose Ignore to remove the wavy underline.*

8. If the spell check and grammar check doesn't catch all the spelling and grammar errors, edit the text to correct them.

✓ *In some programs, you can make your own corrections (edits) right in the Spelling and Grammar dialog box, then click a button like the Change button to apply your change.*

9. Display the options for controlling how the spelling and grammar checking works. Turn the feature for checking spelling and grammar as you type back on.

10. Save the document file; name it **PARTY**.

11. Close the document.

Dear Colleagues:

Mountain Gear has has edperienced a tremendous year Thanks to all your efforts, sales and cutomer satisfaction are both grown.

Join me in celebrating our successs at a holiday party. The parrty at Juniper Brothers Restaurant at 7 p.m. on December 14. Please contact Rita to R.S.V.P for yourself and guste and to make a dinner selections.

Have a happyholiday season!

Janet Janitz

Exercise 12

❖ Edit a Web Page in Your Word Processor

Notes

If your word processor can only save documents in HTML format, you have to make sure that you've perfected a document before you save it in the HTML format. Now, though, you can typically use your word processing program to open and edit an existing HTML file. This gives you the opportunity to tweak the HTML file to improve its appearance and text. In this exercise, practice making some text and formatting changes to a really basic HTML file.

✓ *Your word processing program does not provide all the capabilities of an HTML editing program, however. You can use your word processing program to make modest formatting changes and edits to text. If you want to make more advanced changes like adding in scripts to automate Web page features, you'll need to use an HTML editing program.*

The Go! Travel Consultants Web site includes a page with monthly travel package specials. Edit the Web page in your word processing program to update the information about the specials and apply more attractive formatting to the Web content now.

Vocabulary

No new vocabulary in this exercise.

Directions

1. Start your word processing program.
2. Open the **IC12.HTM** Web page file in the word processing program.

   ✓ *Generally, you can choose File|Open and then select the type of file to open from the drop-down list named Files of Type (or something similar).*

   ✓ *The Web file should open in the Web view or Web layout view. If it doesn't, also switch to that view.*

3. Change the formatting of the first paragraph (headline) to 36-point Eras Bold ITC in the color of your choice.

   ✓ *You can experiment a bit more with text colors on a Web page because you don't have to worry about print quality. Just be sure that the text is dark enough (or light enough) in contrast to the page background.*

4. Change the formatting of the second paragraph (subhead) to 16-point Eras Bold ITC. Also add a colorful or decorative border (divider) below the paragraph. If you inserted a divider or line, left-align it.
5. Change the formatting of the text that reads **September Monthly Package Specials** to 12-point Eras Bold ITC.
6. Add the bullet of your choice to each of the paragraphs in the list of trips.

Word Processing

Lesson 3
Open and Edit Documents

Exercises 6–12

- ❖ Open an existing document
- ❖ Insert and delete text
- ❖ Work with proofreader's marks
- ❖ Print an open document
- ❖ Preview an open document
- ❖ Mark edits in a document
- ❖ Accept or reject edits
- ❖ Compare edited documents

Illustration 2

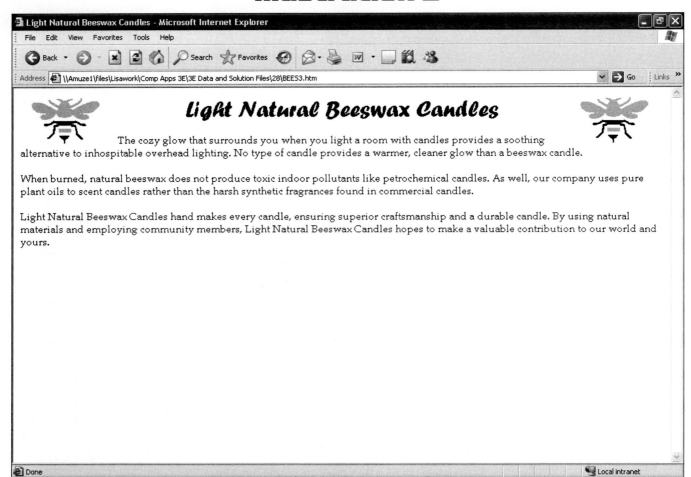

Exercise 6

❖ Open a Document ❖ Insert Text ❖ Print

Notes

You can revise a word processing document as you gather new information about your topic or audience. You can add text as needed, then save your new changes. Most word processing programs enable you to add text in either the default **Insert mode** or **Overtype mode**. Use Insert mode to insert new text at the insertion point, moving existing text to the right. Use Overtype mode to type over existing text. Typically, you can press the Insert key on the keyboard to switch between the two editing modes.

Imagine that your instructor for this class asked an essay question about the difference between Insert mode and Overtype mode. You previously drafted an answer to the question and saved it as a word processing file. Now, you're going to open that file and make changes to improve your answer.

Vocabulary

Insert mode
Overtype mode

open a file (document)
Save As

proofreading marks:
   insert text ∧
   change to lowercase /

Directions

1. Open the **WP06** document file.
2. Save the file as **INSOVR**.

    ✓ *When you save a file under a new name (using the **Save As** command), you really create a new copy of the file. The changes you make then appear only in the new file copy, not the original file.*

3. In the default Insert mode, make the changes for the first paragraph shown in the document on the next page.
4. Change to the Overtype mode.
5. Make the changes for the second paragraph shown. (You'll have to retype the existing text, as your changes will type over the existing text in Overtype mode.)

✓ *Check your work carefully after you use Overtype mode. You may accidentally type over text you need, or leave in unwanted text. Clean up any errors using the Backspace or Delete keys.*

6. Save the edited document file.
7. Print one copy of the document.

    ✓ *Your instructor may require you to submit a printout of the final document from each exercise you complete. If so, print the document and write your name and the exercise number on it for submission.*

8. Close the document.

4. Choose the command for saving the file in HTML or Web page format. (It usually appears on the File menu.)
5. Name the file **BEES3** and finish saving the file. The word processor will add a .htm or .html file name extension to the file for you.

   ✓ *If you see a message that text wrapping for graphics will be changed, simply continue the save.*

6. Close the file and your word processing program.
7. Launch your Web browser, but do not connect to the Internet. (This may be called **working offline** on your system.)

8. Use the Web browser's command for opening files (or the address box) to open the **BEES3** file. Illustration 2 on the following page shows an example of how the information from the word processing document file looks when saved as a Web page and displayed in a Web browser.

   ✓ *To use a browser address box to open a file stored on your hard disk, enter the full path (including disk, folders, and file name) to the file, then press Enter.*

9. Close the browser.

Illustration 1

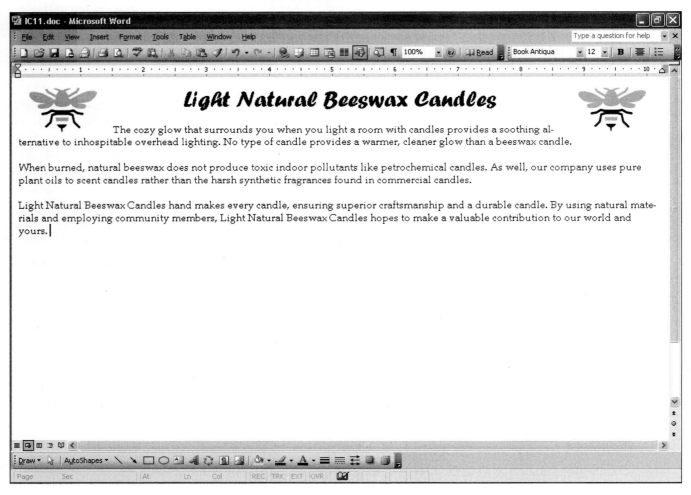

My word processing program offers two modes. I can use the mode I want to update a
document. Press the Insert key.

typing :Insert mode and Overtype mode

with new information — *to change between modes*

Adds text into a document, Overtype mode replaces text.

Insert mode *while* *to the right of the insertion point*

Exercise 11

❖ Save a Word Processing Document as a Web Page

Notes

Web browser programs read files stored in the **HTML** (Hypertext Markup Language) format. As recently as a few years ago, you had to know special HTML coding to develop Web pages. Then, software publishers began offering programs you could use to create Web pages without having to know all the coding. Now, you can save your word processing documents as Web pages directly— eliminating the need to copy or paste information from the document into the Web page creation program. In this exercise, you save an example Word processing document as a Web page.

You're starting to develop some Web site content for your business, Light Natural Beeswax Candles. Save a word document with basic information as a Web page now.

Vocabulary

HTML   background   working offline

Directions

1. Start your word processing program.
2. Open the **IC11** document file.

    ✓ It's best to convert only shorter documents into Web pages, because a long file would take a long time to load from a Web site.

3. If your word processing program offers a Web view (such as Web Layout view), switch to that view. It gives you an idea of how your document will look once you save it in HTML format. Illustration 1 on the following page shows you how the document might appear in a word processing program that offers a Web view.

    ✓ If your Web page contains graphics, bullets, and **backgrounds**, the word processing program may save a separate folder containing all the graphics files used to construct the Web page file. If you need to copy the Web page file to another location, be sure to copy that new folder holding the graphics, too. And never rename the folder. If the folder is in the wrong location or uses the wrong name, your page won't display with the correct formatting.

    ✓ If you're working in Word 2003, you may instead choose to save the file as a Single File Web Page (*.mht or *.mhtml), which does not require subfolders for supplemental items like graphics.

Exercise 7

❖ Open a Document ❖ Delete Text
❖ Preview ❖ Print

Notes

Good writers can communicate with a few precise words. You can delete text from a document to reduce wordiness or remove old information. In addition to inserting new words and phrases, you may need to insert other characters like **tabs** and **new paragraphs** to update a document you created previously. Proper punctuation and organization helps make information easier to understand. Before you print your edited document, you can use the **print preview** to see how it will look when printed. You can then print and close the document.

You're updating the seasonal work schedule for your employees at Mountain Gear. Make the changes to the schedule by editing a previous document in this exercise.

Vocabulary

tabs	proofreading marks:	insert tab character →	run in (delete
new paragraph	delete ℒ	insert space #	paragraph mark) ↶
print preview	new paragraph ¶	period ⊙	

Directions

1. Open the **WP07** document file.
2. Save the file as **WORK**.
3. Change to Insert mode, if needed.
4. Add the new tab characters, spaces, periods, and paragraphs shown on the following page.
5. Make the deletions and combine paragraphs as shown on the following page.

   ✓ When you add or combine paragraphs, don't forget to delete any extra leading space or insert a space to separate sentences, if needed. Some instructors may teach you to insert two spaces after each sentence. While you should follow your instructor's preference for the purpose of your class, it's no longer essential to type two spaces after each sentence. Modern word processing programs (and the fonts or lettering they use) automatically insert the correct amount of space if you press the spacebar once after a sentence.

   ✓ Usually, you can double-click a word to select it. You often can double-click in the margin to the left of a paragraph to select the paragraph.

   ✓ In your word processing program, you can drag with the mouse to select or highlight a block. Or, you can click at the beginning of the block, then press and hold the Shift key and press an arrow key as needed to extend the selection to the end of the block. Pressing the Delete key deletes an entire block of text that you've selected or highlighted.

Integration and Communications

Lesson 28
Work with Web Design Features

Exercises 11–19

- ❖ Save a word processing document as a Web page
- ❖ Work with Web page formatting in your word processing program
- ❖ Save a spreadsheet as a Web page
- ❖ Save a presentation as a Web page
- ❖ View database information in Web format
- ❖ Work with Word, Excel, and XML
- ❖ Insert and use hyperlinks

6. Save the edited document file.
7. View the document in print preview.
8. Close the print preview.

9. Print one copy of the document.
10. Close the document.

Mountain Gear¶Fall Schedule¶As the busy season approaches ~~quickly,~~ it's time to revise our staffing schedule. Please let me know as soon as possible if you cannot work the schedule ~~as noted~~ below:

~~Monday   1 5 pm   Gary~~
Tuesday⟶1-7 pm⟶ Gary, Shannon
Wednesday→1-7 pm⟶ Linda, Tom
Thursday⟶1-7 pm⟶ Linda, Drew
Friday→ ⟶1-9 pm⟶ Linda, Tom, Drew
Saturday ⟶1-9 pm⟶ Tom, Janet, Ted
Sunday ⟶1-5 pm⟶ Gary, Shannon
¶Remember that policies also change for the fall.

You may have a 15-minute break every two hours, but please make sure the register is covered.

Please give me 24-hour notice if you trade shifts.

~~You will be paid on Thursday by direct deposit.~~

22. Close the document and the word processing program.

23. Save the spreadsheet file and close the spreadsheet program.

CRYSTAL COMMUNITY COLLEGE
CLASS MEMORANDUM

TO: «FNAME» «LNAME» «STUDENTID»

FROM: JACK SCOTT, INSTRUCTOR, GERMAN I

SUBJECT: TEST 1 RESULTS

DATE: 10/6/2004

Congratulations! Everyone in the class performed well on this test.

«FName», here's your test score: **«Score»**

Here's a chart of the overall class results:

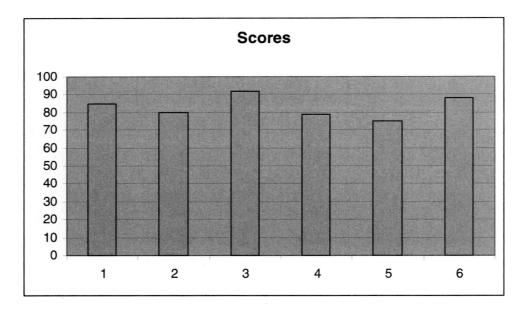

Exercise 8

❖ Open a Document
❖ Insert and Delete Text ❖ Print

Notes

Most often, you will need to both add and delete information to finalize the content of your documents. In this exercise, you practice making corrections and using features to insert text automatically. The exercise features a letter that's in the **full block style**.

You want to make a donation to a local food bank, Meals for All. You drafted a letter to accompany your donation earlier, but didn't have the proper contact information. Now you can finish the letter with the contact information, and more.

Vocabulary

full-block style letter
insert date feature
automatic text or glossary
  feature

salutation
closing
proofreading marks:
    make a correction
      two times x2

make a correction
  four times x4
change to uppercase ≡
close up/no space ◯
press Enter ↵

Directions

1. Open the **WP08** document file.
2. Save the file as **DONATE**.
3. Insert some spacing so that the top line of the document begins about 2.5 inches down from the top.

   ✓ *By default, most word processors have a margin (blank area) of about one inch at the top of the page, so you only need to insert another 1.5 inches.*

4. Use the **insert date feature**, if your word processing program has one, to add the date at the top of the document. (Otherwise, you can type the date.)

5. Make the rest of the changes shown in the example document on the following page.

   ✓ *You can work in Insert mode or Overtype mode as needed. You can even switch between the two modes as often as you want while editing your documents.*

   ✓ *Make sure you press Enter as needed to insert spacing between old and new paragraphs of text in the document.*

   ✓ *If your word processor asks whether you want help creating the letter, close the help feature.*

Exercise 10

❖ Critical Thinking

Notes

Test your integration skills by building a document using information from a word processor, spreadsheet, and database.

You're an instructor at Crystal Community College, and you need to create a memo to German I class members to report test skills. Integrate word processing, database, and spreadsheet information to create that memo now.

Vocabulary

No new vocabulary in this exercise.

Directions

1. Copy the **IC10** database file. Name the copy **GRADE**.
2. Start your word processing program.
3. Open the **IC10-2** document file and save the file as **GRADE2**.
4. Start the spreadsheet program.
5. Open the **IC10-3** file.

   ✓ *You don't have to save a copy of the exercise files when you just plan to copy information from them.*

6. Copy the chart in the spreadsheet.
7. Switch back to the word processing program.
8. Paste the chart at the end of the document.
9. Position and resize the pasted chart as you prefer.
10. Start the mail merge wizard or helper.
11. Create a form letter type merge document, using the open document (in the active window) as the main merge document.
12. Choose the command in the merge helper or wizard for opening an existing data source file.
13. Specify that you want to open a file from the database program. You may find the choice of file types on a drop down list named Files of type or something similar.
14. Open the **GRADE** database file.
15. If you're prompted to specify what table to use for the merge, select the **GRADE** table and continue the merge.
16. Choose to edit the main document next, so you can insert the merge field codes into the document.
17. Insert the merge field codes into the document, as shown in the illustration on the following page.
18. Format all the inserted fields in bold.
19. Merge the main document and database information to a new document.
20. Review the merged document (or print pages as directed by your instructor), then close the merged document without saving it.
21. Save your changes to the main merge document file.

6. Use your word processing program's **automatic text** or **glossary feature** (if available) to insert the **salutation** and **closing** text.

7. Save the edited document file.
8. Print one copy of the document.
9. Close the document.

X8

← Today's date

X4

←
Anna Bryce
Executive Director
Meals for All
1001 Deed Way
Indianapolis, Indiana 46250
X2
Dear Ms. Bryce:
X2

, Meals for All

Your organization has a terrific reputation for serving the community. Every time the
news reports about how many people you helped, I feel pride in having support you.
  media   've   ed

∧ I recently received a small donation, and I would like to continue my support.
   Meals for All must continue in its vital role.

        find
I enclosed my $100 donation. Please accept this gift in memory of John and Connie
Kosek and send a commemorative card to:
X2
Phyllis Kosek
54 Haley Lane
Fishers, IN 46038
X2
Sincerely,
X2
Your name

12. In the dialog box that appears, specify that you want to save the file in your spreadsheet format. (You may find this option on a drop-down list named Save as type.)
13. Change the file name to **SSENT3-2**, then finish exporting the query.
14. Switch to your spreadsheet program, and then open the **SSENT3-2** file.

15. Change column widths as needed, apply the Time number format to the **SightTime** entries, and add a quick sum formula totalling the **Count**.
16. Save the file and close it.
17. Close your spreadsheet program.
18. Switch to the database program, if needed, and close it and the **ENT3** file.

Exercise 9

❖ Open a Document ❖ Insert Text
❖ Delete Text ❖ Preview ❖ Print

Notes

In this exercise, you continue to practice making changes to a document, previewing the document, and printing.

You work at Mountain Gear, and you've been asked to reorder some men's hiking boots. Open and update a previous fax document for the new order.

Vocabulary

fax document

Directions

1. Open the **WP09** document file, an example **fax document**.
2. Save the file as **ORDER**.

   ✓ *Depending on the software version you're using, this document may contain background graphics. If you don't see them, you may be working in the Normal view rather than the Print Layout or Page Layout view. To change views, use the commands at the top of the View menu.*

3. Complete the recipient and sender information near the top of the document, as shown in the illustration on the following page.

   ✓ *When you edit or replace the information near the top of the document, make sure you make your changes to the right of the tab characters that are already in place, so that your entries align nicely.*

4. Replace the date entry with the current date.
5. Make the rest of the changes shown in the example document on the following page.

   ✓ *Some fax templates use increased spacing between lines. Exercise 21 will explain how to work more with line spacing.*

6. Save the edited document file.
7. View the document in print preview.
8. Close the print preview.
9. Print one copy of the document.
10. Close the document.

Exercise 9

❖ Export Database Data

Notes

Typically, database files hold some of the most mission-critical information tracked by a business. Once information has been entered into a database and verified, you need not retype the information to take advantage of it in another program. In fact, you can export data from any database table, and usually from any database query, as well. In this exercise, practice exporting database information.

Your Entomology professor has asked you to do some further work with the data in your moth and butterfly tracking database. Export the data now so that you can complete the required tasks.

Vocabulary

No new vocabulary in this exercise.

Directions

1. Make a copy of the **IC09** database file. Name the copy **ENT3**. (You don't need to start the database program, in most instances, to copy files.)
2. Start your database program and open the **ENT3** database file.
3. Use the command for exporting a table to start exporting the **ENT3** table.

   ✓ In Access 2003, you generally click the Tables choice at the left side of the database window, right-click on the table to export, and then click on Export.

4. In the dialog box that appears, specify that you want to save the file in your spreadsheet format. (You may find this option on a drop-down list named **Save as type**.)
5. Change the file name to **SSENT3**, then finish exporting the table.

6. Start your spreadsheet program, and then open the **SSENT3** file.
7. Change column widths as needed. Apply the Time number format to the data in the **SightTime** column, and add a quick sum formula to total the **Count** data.
8. Save and close the file.
9. Switch back to your database program and the **ENT3** file.
10. Display the queries in the file. (Generally you do this by clicking on a queries choice in the database window, or by choosing a similar command.)
11. Use the command for exporting a query to start exporting the **ENT3Q** query.

    ✓ In Access 2003, you generally right-click on the query to export, and then click on Export.

FACSIMILE TRANSMITTAL SHEET

TO: ~~Bob Timmons~~ ℓ Roger Carey	FROM: ~~Your name~~ ℓ Student's name
COMPANY: Blazers	DATE: 9/15/2005
FAX NUMBER: 555-4545	TOTAL NO. OF PAGES INCLUDING COVER: 1
RE: ~~New~~ ℓ Rox order	YOUR REFERENCE NUMBER: ~~0001~~ ℓ 2045

☐ URGENT   ☐ FOR REVIEW   ☐ PLEASE COMMENT   ☐ PLEASE REPLY   ☐ PLEASE RECYCLE

Mountain Gear would like to ~~ship~~ ℓ order the products listed below. Please call me at 555-2222 to provide your ~~payment~~ information.

↵ X2 Stock and shipping

Line →	Sex →	Color →	Size →	Quantity
Rox →	M →	Black →	9 →	2
Rox →	M →	Buff →	9 →	1
Rox →	M →	Black →	10 →	2
Rox →	M →	Buff →	10 →	2
Rox →	M →	Buff →	11 →	2

↵ X2

The above order will be considered active for ~~15~~ 30 days. If the order exceeds 300 lbs., delivery ~~will be free~~ ℓ must be made to our storage facility. Please call for more information about ~~our returns policy~~ ℓ that location.

5. Change the file name to **PL**, then finish saving the file.

   ✓ *In many cases, a program will warn you that saving to a particular format will remove special formatting like table formatting, font formatting, and graphics. In some cases, you may even see a preview of these changes, to decide whether or not to proceed with the Save As operation.*

6. Close the file in your word processing program, if needed, and then open it in Notepad. As you can see, the file won't necessarily look usable, due to the loss of the table formatting.

   ✓ *Often, you can make a copy of a word processing file that holds a table, convert the table to text, and then export the file to a generic format for a better result.*

7. Close the **PL** file and Notepad, returning to your word processing program.
8. Reopen the **IC08** file.
9. Use the command for saving a file in another format, usually an export command or the File|Save As command.
10. In the dialog box that appears, specify that you want to save the file in another format, such as WordPerfect 5.x for Windows format. (You may find this option on a drop-down list named Save as type.)

    ✓ *If you get a message that the WordPerfect converted is not installed, you can save in Rich Text Format or consult your instructor about installing the converter.*

11. Change the file name to **PL2**, then finish saving the file.
12. Close the file and your word processing program.
13. Start your spreadsheet program.
14. Open the **IC08-2** spreadsheet file.
15. Use the command for saving a file in another format, usually an export command or the File|Save As command.
16. In the dialog box that appears, specify that you want to save the file in .CSV (comma delimited) format. (You may find this option on a drop-down list named Save as type.)
17. Change the file name to **CSV**, then finish saving the file.
18. Close the file in your spreadsheet program, if needed, and then open it in Notepad.

    ✓ *When you close a file that you've exported, you generally want to close it without saving changes.*

19. Close the **CSV** file and Notepad, returning to your spreadsheet.
20. Reopen the **IC08-2** file.
21. Use the command for saving a file in another format, usually an export command or the File|Save As command.
22. In the dialog box that appears, specify that you want to save the file in another format, such as 1-2-3 format. (You may find this option on a drop-down list named Save as type.)
23. Change the file name to **CSV2**, then finish saving the file.
24. Close the file and your spreadsheet program.

Exercise 10

❖ Open a Document ❖ Insert Text
❖ Delete Text ❖ Preview ❖ Print

Notes

In this exercise, you work with a simple document to continue building your editing skills.

Your boss at Crystal Communications has asked you to prepare a project status report memo for your client, Major Manufacturing. Open the boss' first draft of the memo and finish it now.

Vocabulary

proofreading marks:
   transpose   ⁀

Directions

1. Open the **WP10** document file.
2. Save the file as **STATUS**.
3. Make the additions, deletions, and other changes shown in the example document on the following page.

   ✓ *Some word processing programs enable you to use a shortcut key combination (such as Shift+F3) to switch words between upper- and lowercase.*

   ✓ *You typically can double-click a word to select it. Then you can delete or replace the entire word.*

4. Spell check the document.
5. Save the edited document file.
6. View the document in print preview.
7. Close the print preview.
8. Print one copy of the document.
9. Close the document.

Exercise 8

❖ Save a Word Processing or Spreadsheet File in Another Format

Notes

There may be times when you need to share information with a colleague, but that colleague doesn't use the same software that you do. In such instances, most programs give you the ability to use the File|Save As command to save a file using another file type. Typically, you can save a file to use it in an earlier version of your software (such as Excel 5.0/95 rather than Excel 2003). You also often have the option to save a file for another application altogether, such as saving an Excel file for use in 1-2-3 or Quattro Pro. As a last resort, you typically also can save a file from many applications in a generic format such as plain text (.TXT), rich text (.RTF), or comma-separated values (.CSV). Most applications can read at least one of these generic formats. (And, you can even use one of those generic formats to move information between applications, if no direct import or export capability exists.) In this exercise, practice using File|Save As to change the format for a word processing document and a spreadsheet.

    ✓ *You also can use File|Save As to save application data in Web page (.HTML) format in most applications. Exercises 11, 14, 15, and 16 in Lesson 28 enable you to work with specific examples for converting application information to Web pages.*

Some of your colleagues at Meals for All would like some of the files you've prepared earlier, but in different file formats, because their computers use different software. Save the Progress Report word processing document you created earlier in the needed formats, as well as save a list of volunteers from a spreadsheet in an alternate format, so you can pass the information along.

Vocabulary

Save as type

Directions

1. Start the word processing program.
2. Open the **IC08** file.
3. Use the command for saving a file in another format, usually an export command or the File|Save As command.
4. In the dialog box that appears, specify that you want to save the file in the Plain Text format. (You may find this option on a drop-down list named **Save as type**.)

Memorandum

To ⟶ Tom Brandt, Major Manufacturing

From: ⟶ Your name, Crystal Communications

Date: ⟶ Today's date

Re: ⟶ Project Status Report

Crystal Communications continues to ~~strive to~~ provide superior service to major manufacturing. We have several projects in progress. We want to ensure that you are fully informed about ~~projects.~~ for Major Manufacturing, and
them

102 Product Label Design

This project was put on hold last month. We are still waiting for direction about resuming this project. ↵

103 Web Site

Your IT director has approved the Web site template. We have received the missing information from your engineering and sales departments. A pilot of the site will be available for review in two weeks. ↵

104 Product Catalog

The catalog template has been with your Sales department for two weeks. It is our understanding that a redesign may be required due to changes in the product mix.

Crystal Communications.
appreciates the opportunity to continue our service to Major Manufacturing

If you would like to schedule a meeting to review any of these projects in greater depth, please call me at 555-6464.

7. Confirm that you have finished the import operation, if needed, and open the new data table if it doesn't appear on its own.

✓ You can open the **IC07** spreadsheet file in the spreadsheet program to compare the original spreadsheet data to the copy of that data imported into the database table.

✓ Notice that when a spreadsheet includes cells that hold formulas, the database imports the calculated results, not the formulas themselves.

8. Delete the **Field3**, **Days of rain**, and **18** fields that were imported. These fields represented other columns of data from the spreadsheet, which aren't needed in the database.

9. Save your changes to the database, and close the database file and database program.

✓ You can sometimes export database information to a spreadsheet program, but that process is typically much more complicated.

Exercise 11

❖ Open a Document ❖ Mark Edits
❖ Accept or Reject Edits

Notes

Leading word processing programs can keep track of the changes that you and other users make in a document. This feature is called **document review** or **revision marking**. When this feature is on, the word processing program marks inserted text with underlining and deleted text with **strikethrough**, as in the example document on the following page. In addition, the word processing program usually assigns a different color to each user's corrections, so you can tell who made which changes. The word processing program also may place a mark in the margin beside each paragraph containing a change. To finish the document, you review the changes and decide which to **accept** (keep) and which to **reject** (undo).

> ✓ *In recent Word versions, you can choose File|Send To|Mail Recipient (For Review) to turn on revision marking and e-mail the file. The file recipient can make his or her changes, then click a special Reply with Change button on the Reviewing toolbar to e-mail the file back to you. Lesson 30 provides more information about e-mailing files.*

You need to revise the copy for a sales brochure about Crystal Communications. Make the changes as specified in this exercise.

Vocabulary

document review   strikethrough   reject
revision marking   accept

Directions

1. Open the **WP11** document file.
2. Save the file as **CC**.
3. Make the additions, deletions, and other changes shown in the example document on the following page.

> ✓ *The document review (revision marking) feature should be turned on in the **WP11** (**CC**) file. If the feature isn't on, consult online help or your instructor to learn how to turn it on. In recent Word versions, the Reviewing toolbar should appear automatically when revision marking is*

on. If it doesn't, right-click a toolbar and click Reviewing.

> ✓ *By default, Word now shows deleted material in balloons at the right side of the page in the Print Layout and Web Layout views, as well as in printouts. Click the Show button on the Reviewing toolbar, click Options, and then clear the Use Balloons in Print and Web Layout check box to return to using strikethrough to mark deletions.*

Exercise 7

❖ Spreadsheet and Database Integration

Notes

The data table in a database program looks quite similar to a spreadsheet, organizing information into rows and columns. In fact, you can often import information from a spreadsheet into a database. However, in the spreadsheet you import into the database program, you need to omit information like the spreadsheet title. You should place labels (which become field names) in the top row of the spreadsheet; the database program may call this row the **header row** (or the column heading row). Try moving information between the spreadsheet and database in this exercise.

You created a spreadsheet tracking rainfall for a science course. Now, your instructor wants your list of data in a database format. Prepare the data and import it into your database program now.

Vocabulary

header row

Directions

1. Start the database program and create a new, blank database. Name the database file **RAINDAT**.

2. Choose the command for importing information into the database.

   ✓ *This command might be something like File|Import or File|Get External Data|Import.*

3. In the dialog box that appears, specify that you want to import a file created in your spreadsheet program. (You may find this option on a drop-down list named Files of type.)

4. Open the **IC07** spreadsheet file.

5. At this point, your database may display a wizard or helper to assist you in this process. To complete the wizard, specify that the information to import is on the first sheet and that the first row in the spreadsheet includes column or field headings.

   ✓ *If you see a warning that some of the data in the first row cannot be used as a field name, just continue the wizard.*

6. Import the information into a new table, if your database uses separate tables, and name the new table **RAINDAT**. Use the **Day** field as the primary key field for the imported data.

4. Save the edited document file.
5. Review the changes.

   ✓ *In some word processing programs, you can rest the mouse pointer over a correction to display a pop-up note telling you who made the correction and when it was made.*

6. Accept the corrections that are numbered as follows in the illustration: 1, 2, 3, 4, 7, 11, 12, 13, 18, 19, 20, 21, 22, 23, 25, 26, and 27.
7. Reject the corrections that are numbered as follows in the illustration: 5, 6, 8, 9, 10, 14, 15, 16, 17, 24, and 28.

   ✓ *When you replace a word or phrase, your word processing program might treat the replacement as two separate corrections. If this happens, you need to accept or reject both the insertion in the text and the deletion in the balloon. If you're viewing revisions with strikethrough marks instead, select (highlight) both the cut and added text, then accept or reject both at the same time.*

8. Save the edited document.
9. Print one copy of the document.
10. Close the document.

About Crystal Communications

Who We Are
Founded in 1979, Crystal Communications dedicates itself to providing superior① communications services to local and regional companies. Clients throughout the③ Midwest have depended on Crystal Communications for timely dissemination of information through a variety of media.⑦   ⑤

| **Deleted:** excellent ② |
| **Deleted:** Illinois ④ |
| **Deleted:** accurate ⑥ |

Offerings   ⑩
⑧Our firm offers a full range of advertising and public relations services. We provide design, production, and printing. In addition, we offer communications planning, advertising, and media relations services.⑫

| **Deleted:** Crystal Communications ⑨ |
| **Deleted:** , as well as other services ⑪ |

Team   ⑬
Crystal Communications' team of more than 150 dedicated individuals continues to⑱ ⑭excite clients. The Word department serves up concise and creative text. The Creative department creates the concept for each publication. And the Account department offers innovative communication planning.   ㉑

| **Deleted:** amaze ⑮ |
| **Deleted:** Copy ⑰ |
| **Deleted:** Visual ⑲ |
| **Deleted:** Finally, the Print department composes and executes the finished document. ⑳ |

Fees   ㉒
Crystal Communications typically charges by the hour. However, we can accommodate a variety of relationships, including retainer, job, and multi-item contract plans.

| **Deleted:** job ㉓ |
| **Deleted:** terms ㉖ |

                    ㉔   ㉕

Founders
Catherine Baggett and Frederick Hanson combined more than 30 years of advertising and pubic relations experience to create Crystal Communications㉗

Promise
Your message will be Crystal clear if we bring it to the public's ear㉘

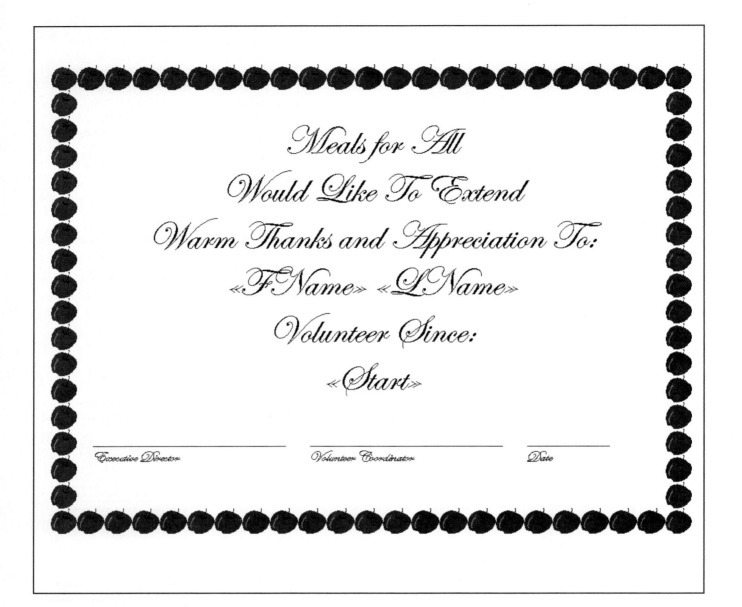

Meals for All

Would Like To Extend

Warm Thanks and Appreciation To:

«FName» «LName»

Volunteer Since:

«Start»

_____   _____   _____
Executive Director   Volunteer Coordinator   Date

Exercise 12

❖ Compare Edited Documents

Notes

You may encounter situations where you end up with multiple versions of the same document. You may have saved different versions of the document over time, making slight changes to each document. Or, you may have e-mailed a file to another person, who returned it with changes. In either case, you need a way to integrate changes from two versions of a document. You can use the document **compare** feature offered in leading word processor programs to do the job. The compare feature identifies changes between two versions of a document, and marks those changes in one of the document files. Then, you can review the revision marks and accept and reject changes as needed to finalize the document.

Before you leave Crystal Communications for the day, you have one more project. You need to merge different versions of the company rate schedule.

Vocabulary

compare

Directions

1. Open the **WP12** document file.
2. Save the file as **RATE.**
3. Open the **WP12-2** document file.
4. Save the file as **RATE2**.
5. Close the **RATE2** file. The **RATE** file should now appear on-screen, so that you can compare it with another document.
6. Start the compare feature.
   - ✓ In recent Word versions, choose Tools | Compare and Merge Documents.
7. Choose the **RATE2** file as the file you want to compare and merge, then perform the merge.
8. Review the changes in the **RATE2** file. Differences in the **RATE** file are marked as changes within the **RATE2** file.

- ✓ If you want, you can use the File | Save As command to save the merged document .

9. Accept the corrections that are numbered as follows in the illustration: 1, 2, 3, 4, 9, 10, 11, 12, 14, 15, 16, and 17.

   - ✓ Depending on your system setup and the software updates that have been installed, the compare feature might give you slightly different results. If your compared document looks different than the one shown in the illustration on the following page, alert your instructor about the differences so you can be evaluated fairly on your results.

   - ✓ If a balloon contains more than one revision, accepting or rejecting handles all the revisions in the balloon simultaneously.

Exercise 6

❖ Word Processing and Database Integration

Notes

Because merging database information into a word processing document is fast becoming one of the most vital business skills, you should practice this process again.

As volunteer coordinator for Meals for All, you're in charge of a banquet honoring volunteers. Create certificates now to honor the volunteers, and merge the volunteer information from a database.

Vocabulary

No new vocabulary in this exercise.

Directions

1. Make a copy of the **IC06** database file. Name the copy **MFAVOL**. (You don't need to start the database program, in most instances, to copy files.)
2. Start your word processing program.
3. Open the **IC06-2** file, and save it as **MFAVOL2**.
   - ✓ *In some database programs, you can start a merge from the database program, and create a new word processing document into which you can merge the information from a database file.*
4. Start the mail merge wizard or helper.
   - ✓ *Alternatively, you can display the merge toolbar in your word processing program and use its tools to set up the merge.*
5. Create a form letter type merge document, using the open document (in the active window) as the main merge document.
   - ✓ *You also can create an envelope or label document and merge your database information into them.*
6. Choose the command in the merge helper or wizard for opening an existing data source file.
7. Specify that you want to open a file from the database program. You may find the choice of file types on a drop-down list named Files of type or something similar.
8. Open the **MFAVOL** database file.
9. If a dialog box asking you what table to use for the merge appears, select the **MFAVOL** table and continue the merge.
10. Choose to edit the main document next, so you can insert the merge field codes into the document.
11. Insert the merge field codes into the document, as shown in the illustration on the following page.
12. Merge the main document and database information to a new document.
13. Review the pages of the merged document (or print it if required by your instructor), then close the merged document without saving it.
14. Save your changes to the main merge document file.
15. Close the document.

✓ *If you have trouble accepting or rejecting an insertion, click within the inserted text first.*

10. Reject the corrections that are numbered as follows in the illustration: 5, 6, 7, 8, 13, and18.

✓ *If you need to reinsert any spaces or hard returns as a result of the corrections, do so.*

11. Save the edited **RATE2** document.
12. Print one copy of the document.
13. Close both documents.

Crystal Communications
Rate Schedule*   — Deleted: Fee ②

Document Creation: — Deleted: creation ④
Writing: $40/hr.   — Deleted: 50 ⑥
Design: $45/hr.
Production: $25/hr.   — Deleted: 35 ⑧
Printing: As quoted

Communications:
Analysis: $50/hr.   — Deleted: Strategic ①
Writing: $50/hr. ②
Agency: $40/hr.
Agent: $40/hr. ③
Assistant: $25/hr.

Admin.: $15/hr.

Mileage and Expenses: ④   — Deleted: expenses ⑤
As allowable by law. ⑥   — Deleted: All are charged. ⑦

* As of 1/31/05 ⑧

Baker Remodeling
P.O. 4528
Fishers, IN 46038
317-555-6767

Today's Date

«FirstName» «LastName»
«Address1»
«Address2»
«City», «State» «ZIP»

Dear «FirstName»:

Thank you for your prior choice of Baker Remodeling to handle your remodeling needs. We are pleased to announce some exciting news and opportunities to you, our loyal customers.

Baker Remodeling recently moved to an expanded facility, and we have also added two additional project managers to our team. This means that Baker Remodeling is now equipped to handle more of your remodeling needs than any of the competition.

For a limited time, we are pleased to offer 10% off the cost of any project for our customers in «City». Please contact me at 317-555-6767 to learn more about this exciting offer.

Sincerely,

Allen H. Baker
President

Lesson 4
Text Alignments and Enhancements

Exercises 13–20

❖ **Align text in a document**
❖ **Center text in a document**
❖ **Apply text attributes**
❖ **Work with fonts and font sizes**
❖ **Use superscript, subscript, and symbols**
❖ **Insert bullets**
❖ **Insert numbers**
❖ **Correct errors with the Undo feature**

9. If you are prompted to specify what table to use for the merge, select the **ALLCLIENT** table and continue the merge.

   ✓ *You may also have the option of selecting a query you've previously created and merging only the records that match the query results.*

10. Filter the list of recipients so your letter will be merged only for clients with **Fishers** in the City field.

11. Choose to edit the main document next, so you can insert the merge field codes into the document.

12. Insert the merge field codes into the document, as shown in the illustration on the following page. You can merge information from some or all of the fields included in the **FISHM** database.

13. Merge the main document and database information to a new document.

   ✓ *Sometimes, the formatting or input mask you set for a field that holds a phone number or ZIP Code won't apply in the merged data. That is, your phone numbers will appear without parentheses or hyphens. In such cases, you may need to make a copy of the database or data table that holds the information to merge, reapply the input mask or formatting so that it saves needed parentheses and hyphens with the data, and then copy the information from and back into the affected field. In other cases, you can use more advanced formatting techniques (such as creating your own format for the affected fields in either the database or word processing program), but you'll need to consult the help feature and experiment on your own to come up with a format and method that works for your software.*

14. Print one copy of the merged document, then close the merged document without saving it.

15. Save your changes to the main merge document file.

16. Close the document.

Exercise 13

❖ Text Alignments ❖ Vertical Centering

Notes

Once you're satisfied with the words in your document, you can begin to work on the document's appearance. In this exercise, add spacing to the text in a party flyer to set off information. Also work with the text **alignment**—how the text in a paragraph lines up relative to the page margins (or indention settings, if any).

Your choral group will be having a benefit recital. Your director has asked you to finish the flyers inviting your fellow students to the event.

Vocabulary

alignment	right align	justify	vertically center
left align	center	distributed	

Directions

1. Open the **WP13** document file. Notice that all the text in the file aligns to the left margin, and that there are no extra spaces between paragraphs.
2. Save the file as **RECITAL**.
3. Insert extra lines between paragraphs as shown in the illustration on the following page.
   ✓ *When you increase the font size in a paragraph and then press Enter at the end of the paragraph, the blank line that's inserted is as tall as the new font size.*
4. Change the alignment for various paragraphs as shown in the illustration.
   ✓ *You must select a paragraph or place the insertion point within it to change the paragraph alignment.*
5. Vertically center all the text on the page.
   ✓ *If your word processor doesn't offer a feature for vertically centering page contents, use the Enter key to add blank lines at the top of the document and approximate the alignment you want.*
6. Save the edited document file.
7. View the document in print preview.
8. Close the print preview.
9. Print one copy of the document.
10. Close the document.

Exercise 5

❖ Word Processing and Database Integration

Notes

Your list of contacts may already be entered into your database program and you probably don't want to retype that information to create a word processing data document. In many instances, you can merge information you've already stored in a database data table into a word processing document. Generally, you use your word processing program's mail merge wizard or helper to accomplish the merge.

You have your own remodeling business, and you'd like to focus the marketing for your business within a particular town. Create a sales letter to mail to clients in that town, and merge the letter with client records from an existing database.

Vocabulary

No new vocabulary in this exercise.

Directions

1. Make a copy of the **IC05** database file. Name the copy **FISHM**. (You don't need to start the database program, in most instances, to copy files.)

   ✓ *Copy the file in a My Computer window or Windows Explorer.*

2. Start your word processing program.
3. Open the **IC05-2** file, and save it as **FISHM2**.
4. Start the mail merge wizard or helper.

   ✓ *Alternatively, you can display the merge toolbar in your word processing program and use its tools to set up the merge.*

5. Create a form letter type merge document, using the open document as the main merge document.

6. Choose the command in the merge helper or wizard for opening an existing data source file.
7. Specify that you want to open a file from the database program. You may find the choice of file types on a drop-down list named Files of type or something similar.

   ✓ *The mail merge helper or wizard in your word processing program might work differently. Follow the instructions on the screen to accomplish this operation.*

8. Open the **FISHM** database file.

   ✓ *Don't worry if it takes several moments for the merge helper to proceed. At this stage, it has to contact the database program and find the information in your database.*

Patriotic Hits from the 1940s

Center

X1

Presented by
The Songsters Choral Group

X2

November 12
7 p.m.
Quadrant Auditorium

X2

Right-align

Learn more about greats like
The Andrews Sisters and
The Glenn Miller Orchestra

X1

Justify

Your $1 admission donation will benefit the Meals for All food bank. Meals for All serves needy families in five counties.

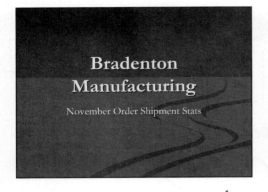

1

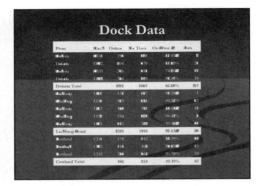

2

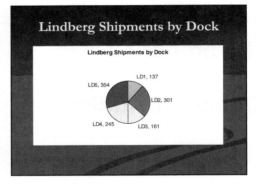

3

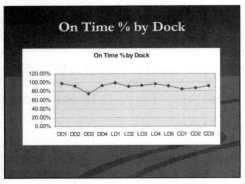

4

5

Exercise 14

❖ Text Alignments ❖ Text Enhancements
❖ Bold ❖ Italics ❖ Underline
❖ Double Underline

Notes

Changing the paragraph alignment helps set off and emphasize the whole paragraph. To emphasize a word or phrase within a paragraph, you can apply **attributes**. These formatting choices include **bold**, **italics**, **underline**, **words only underlining** (underlining with breaks between words), and **double underlines**. Try applying attributes and working with other formatting.

You want to make the project status report memo you created earlier for your client, Major Manufacturing, more attractive. Apply some formatting attributes now to highlight information in the memo.

Vocabulary

attributes	words only underlining	proofreading marks:
bold	double underlines	bold ～～～
italics		italics (ital)
underline		underline _____

Directions

1. Open the **WP14** document file.
2. Save the file as **STATUS2**.
3. Replace **"Your name"** with your name in the From: line.
4. Change the alignment for various paragraphs as shown in the illustration.
5. Apply bold, italics, underlining, words only underlining, and double underlines as shown in the illustration.

   ✓ *Most word processors offer icons or buttons you can click to apply basic formatting like bold and italics. However, you probably need to display a dialog box with text formatting choices to find*

   fancier attributes like words only underlining and double underlines.

   ✓ *Some word processors now offer decorative underlining styles using dots, dashes, and other symbols. Most word processors also enable you to change the text color, so you can create attractive color printouts. Be sure to choose a color that's dark enough to print clearly.*

6. Save the edited document file.
7. View the document in print preview.
8. Close the print preview.
9. Print one copy of the document.
10. Close the document.

12. Add three new slides using the title only layout, and enter **Orders Shipped by Plant**, **Lindberg Shipments by Dock**, and **On Time % by Dock**, respectively as the slide titles.

13. Switching back and forth between slides and programs as needed, copy each of the three charts from the spreadsheet and paste it onto each of the new slides. (The top chart goes on slide 3, the middle chart on slide 4, and the bottom chart on slide 5.)

   ✓ *When you paste a spreadsheet chart, it often pastes as an embedded (but not linked) object. You can then double-click it to display the spreadsheet's charting tools to make changes to the chart. Changing the pasted chart does not alter the original chart.*

14. Position and resize each chart as needed. The finished presentation slides should look similar to those in the illustration on the following page.

15. Save the presentation graphics file; name it **BRADEN**.

16. Print one copy of the presentation, with one slide per page.

17. Close the presentation graphics file, then close the presentation graphics program.

18. Switch back to the spreadsheet program and close the spreadsheet file.

19. Close the spreadsheet program.

<u>Memorandum</u>

Center, Underline

To: Tom Brandt, Major Manufacturing

From: Student name, Crystal Communications

Date: 7/14/04

Re: Project Status Report

Crystal Communications continues to provide superior service to *Major Manufacturing*. We have several projects in progress for *Major Manufacturing*, and we want to ensure that you are fully informed about them.

Justify

Center, Bold, Double underline

102 Product Label Design

This project was put on hold last month. We are still waiting for direction about resuming this project.

103 Web Site

Your IT director has approved the Web site template. We have received the missing information from your engineering and sales departments. A pilot of the site will be available for review in two weeks.

104 Product Catalog

The catalog template has been with your Sales department for two weeks. It is our understanding that a redesign may be required due to changes in the product mix.

Crystal Communications appreciates the opportunity to continue our service to *Major Manufacturing*. If you would like to schedule a meeting to review any of these projects in greater depth, please call me at 555-6464.

Words only underline

Exercise 4

❖ Presentation Graphics and Spreadsheet Integration

Notes

You can reuse your data and charts from a spreadsheet file in a presentation graphics file so you can take advantage of both the spreadsheet's calculating and charting capabilities and the presentation graphics program's tools for attractively presenting information. Practice using both applications in this exercise.

You work in logistics for Bradenton Manufacturing. You've been asked to make a presentation to the board about shipments for the prior month. Use information you've already created in your spreadsheet program to flesh out the presentation.

Vocabulary

No new vocabulary in this exercise.

Directions

1. Start your presentation graphics program, if needed.
2. Create a new presentation using the design template of your choice.
3. Choose the title slide layout for the first slide.
4. Enter **Bradenton Manufacturing** as the title and **November Order Shipment Stats** as the subtitle for the first slide.
5. Add a second slide that uses the title only layout, and enter **Dock Data** as the slide title. Make sure you're displaying the second slide in the normal view or the single slide view.
6. Start your spreadsheet program.
7. Open the **IC04** file.

8. Select the range **A4:F19** in the spreadsheet file.
9. Copy the range.
10. Switch to the presentation graphics file.
11. Paste the copied cells onto the second slide using the Paste command, then move, resize, and format it as needed.

   ✓ *If you have trouble adjusting the height of a row, be sure to check the font size applied to blank cells during the paste operation. Often, you'll have to click in a blank cell and reduce the font size applied in order to resize the row that holds the blank cell.*

   ✓ *When you resize a pasted or linked and embedded object, press and hold the Shift key while dragging a corner handle to keep the object sizing proportional.*

Exercise 15

❖ Change Font ❖ Change Font Size

Notes

The term **font** refers to the style of letters you use for text. The font you choose affects how your document looks. Some fonts have **serifs**, or cross-strokes at the ends of letters. Serifs look formal and make text easier to read. **Sans serif** fonts don't have serifs, making such fonts more casual and useful for **headings**. Some fonts look very fancy and ornate, while others look compressed, look extended, or look like handwriting (or **script**). Fancier fonts are typically called **decorative fonts** and are used primarily for personal or less formal documents, like flyers or party invitations. Always use script and decorative fonts sparingly, because they can be difficult to read. Word processors measure text size in **points**; each point equals $1/72^{nd}$ of an inch. Experiment with a few fonts and **font sizes** in this exercise.

Your choral director doesn't think the recital flyer you formatted earlier is quite jazzy enough. Apply some new fonts and make other changes to another version of the flyer file to help the document sell your performance.

Vocabulary

font	sans serif	script	points
serif	heading	decorative fonts	font size

Directions

1. Open the **WP15** document file.
2. Save the file as **RECITAL2**.
3. Change the alignment for various paragraphs as shown in the illustration on the following page.
4. Apply new fonts and font sizes as shown in the illustration.

   ✓ A font is really a set of characters (each letter, numeral, and special character such as an ampersand) in a particular style and particular point size. However, most word processors more generally use the term font to refer to the style of the letters only.

   ✓ If your system doesn't have one of the fonts shown in the illustration, just choose a similar font.

5. Apply different text attributes as shown in the illustration.
6. Save the edited document file.

   ✓ You can apply formatting as you type text, too. Simply choose the font, size, attributes, and alignment you want before typing. Then, you can change to other formatting settings as needed. For example, you can turn boldfacing on, type a few words that appear in bold, and then turn boldfacing off to resume typing regular text.

Memo

To: James Allen, First Community Bank

From: Janet Thomkins, Mountain Gear

Date: May 12, 2006

Re: 2005 Sales Data

Thank you for working with me on this financing request. As you can see from the information below, Mountain Gear experienced great success last year. We are well-positioned to expand our business and service the modest debt amount that you and I have discussed. If you need additional documentation of Mountain Gear's financial performance or would like to see any additional data, please call me and I will provide it promptly.

Product Line	Qtr 1	Qtr 2	Qtr 3	Qtr 4
Footwear	$12,504.65	$13,248.09	$17,382.93	$9,389.22
Outerwear	$2,258.99	$4,939.39	$19,393.99	$6,549.99
Sportswear	$2,390.90	$11,043.46	$9,397.21	$5,373.33
Gear	$15,888.23	$31,845.00	$27,301.10	$13,500.00
Accessories	$2,393.33	$2,920.55	$4,033.97	$3,783.77
Total	$35,436.10	$63,996.49	$77,509.20	$38,596.31
Annual Total:	$215,538.10			

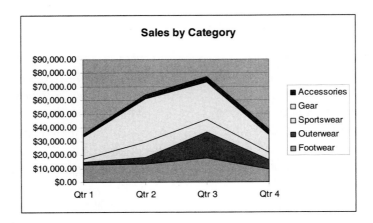

1

7. View the document in print preview.
8. Close the print preview.

9. Print one copy of the document.
10. Close the document.

Patriotic Hits

72-pt. Rage Italic, Bold

Decorative or double underline

from the 1940s

Right-align, 18-pt. Papyus

Presented by
The Songsters Choral Group

November 12

7 p.m.

Quadrant Auditorium

26-pt. Rage Italic, Bold

Learn more about greats like
The Andrews Sisters and
The Glenn Miller Orchestra

Center, 16-pt. Papyus

32-pt. Curlz MT, Bold

Center, 24-pt. Book Antiqua

Your $1 admission donation will benefit the Meals for All food bank. Meals for All serves needy families in five counties.

12. Adjust the size, position, and formatting of the pasted table as desired.
13. Position the insertion point after the table and add an extra blank line.
14. Switch back to the **MGMEMO2** spreadsheet file.
15. Select the top chart in the spreadsheet, and copy it.
16. Switch to the **MGMEMO** word processing file and paste the chart into the document as a linked object.

   ✓ *You also can insert an object like a chart that's **embedded**, but not linked. Use the Insert | Object command, then choose the type of object to insert, such as a chart from your spreadsheet program. Tools from the spreadsheet program appear in the word processing document, so you can create the chart. When you want to edit the chart object, double-click it to redisplay the spreadsheet program's charting tools. You can embed different types of objects in different types of programs.*

17. Make the chart smaller so it will fit on the first page, under the table. (Decrease the text size in the table to help it fit, if needed.) Position the chart as you want in the word processing document, then click outside the chart.
18. Save the word processing document.
19. Switch back to the **MGMEMO2** spreadsheet file, and click cell A1 to clear the blinking marquee around the chart, if needed.
20. Change the entry in cell C9 (which holds Qtr 2 sales for Accessories) to **2920.55**.

21. Change the entry in cell E8 (which holds Qtr 4 sales for Gear) to **13500**. Notice that the top chart updates to reflect your changes automatically.

   ✓ *You don't have to type the currency formatting when you change those cell entries.*

22. Save the spreadsheet file.
23. Switch back to the **MGMEMO** word processing file. The linked table and chart should also show the changes you made to the original information in the spreadsheet program, as shown in the illustration on the following page.

   ✓ *If the linked information doesn't update automatically, you can update it manually. Usually, you do so by choosing Edit | Links (or the applicable command in your application). In the list of links that appears, click the link to update, then click the button that updates the link. Update other links as needed, then close the dialog box.*

   ✓ *Note that if you e-mail a file with linked objects, the recipient might not be able to use the full file. However, you can break the links. Choose your program's command for editing links (Edit | Links). Click each link and click the button that breaks the link, then close the dialog box. Save and e-mail the file.*

24. Save the word processing file.
25. Print one copy of the document, then close the document.
26. Switch back to the spreadsheet program, and save and close the spreadsheet file.

Exercise 16

❖ Use Superscripts ❖ Use Subscripts

Notes

In some cases, you may need to position a character or word above or below the **baseline**—the invisible line on which normally-sized letters rest. **Superscript** characters appear far above the baseline, like the 2 in x^2. **Subscript** characters rest just below the baseline, like the 2 in H_2O. Use this exercise to practice formatting characters in superscript and subscript.

Your physics instructor has assigned a brief refresher project. You need to write a paper that gives a brief review of how to calculate the distance between celestial bodies based on the speed of light. Open the file that holds your paper now, and apply needed superscript and subscript formatting to finish the paper.

Vocabulary

baseline   superscript   subscript

Directions

1. Open the **WP16** document file.
2. Save the file as **LIGHTSP**.
3. Change the alignment for various paragraphs as shown in the illustration on the following page.
4. Apply new fonts and font sizes as shown in the illustration.
5. Apply different text attributes as shown in the illustration.
6. Format selected characters as superscript and subscript, as noted in the illustration.

   ✓ *Before you use superscript characters to create footnotes or endnotes, check to see whether your word processor has a feature that enables you to create footnotes or endnotes automatically. Exercises 40 through 43 in Lesson 7 give you practice with footnotes and endnotes.*

   ✓ *If your word processor enables you to copy formatting from one selection to another, you may find it faster to use that feature to copy subscript or superscript formatting than to reapply the formatting each time.*

7. Remove the extra tabs in the line where you applied superscript to make the top and bottom parts of each value better align.

   ✓ *Some word processing programs offer add-on components or programs that you can install and use to build equations.*

8. Save the edited document file.
9. View the document in print preview.
10. Close the print preview.
11. Print one copy of the document.
12. Close the document.

Exercise 3

❖ Word Processing and Spreadsheet Integration

Notes

Imagine you've created a related spreadsheet and word processing document, but you haven't finalized the information in either of them. Further, you want to use both a range of cells and a chart from the spreadsheet in the word processing document. You can use **linking and embedding** features to link the original information in the spreadsheet file to the pasted information (**linked objects**) in the word processing file. Then, whenever you make changes to the original information in the spreadsheet file, those changes will appear in the linked information in the word processing file, too. Work with this process in this exercise.

You own the Mountain Gear outfitter store, and you want to get a loan from your banker to expand the business. Create a memo to present the prior year's financial data to your banker.

Vocabulary

linking and embedding   linked object   Paste Special

Directions

1. Start your word processing program.
2. Open the **IC03** file.
3. Save the file as **MGMEMO**.
4. Start your spreadsheet program.
5. Open the **IC03-2** file.
6. Save the file as **MGMEMO2**.
7. Select the range **A4:E12** in the spreadsheet file.
8. Copy the range.
9. Switch to the **MGMEMO** word processing file.
10. Move the insertion point to the end of the document.
11. Paste the range of cells into the word processing document as a linked formatted text object. (If a Paste Options button appears in Word, choose Match Destination Formatting and link to Excel or Match Destination Table Style and Link to Excel.) The linked range of cells appears as a table in the word processing file.

   ✓ *You must use the **Paste Special** command on the Edit menu for this operation. In the dialog box that appears, specify that you want to paste the selection as a spreadsheet object, and that you want to link the pasted object to its original data. Then finish the paste operation.*

   ✓ *If the table's cell entries are indented within the table, causing odd wrapping, select the whole table and use the Format|Paragraph command to remove the indention.*

Center, 16-pt.
Arial Black

Calculating Distances with the Speed of Light

If you know the speed of light, you can use that value to calculate the distance between one celestial body and another.

The speed of light is widely held to be 186,000 miles per second.

So, let's say you're trying to find the distance, in miles, from the Earth to a body that's five light years away. The calculation is really a matter of multiplication.

To find the number of meters in a light year: *Subscript, underline*

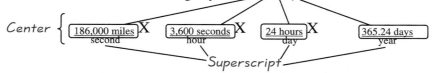

Center

You can then multiply the result, 5,869,552,896,000 miles per light year, by the number of light years to yield the total miles of distance. (For a less precise measure, use scientific notation to express the miles per light year as 5.8696×10^{12}.)

Superscript

So, for example, to find the total miles light would travel in the five light years between the Earth and the distant body, multiply the number of miles in a light year by five:

Center $\left\{ 5,869,552,896,000 \times 5 = 29,347,764,480,000 \text{ or } 2.9348 \times 10^{13} \text{ miles.} \right.$

Superscript

13. Adjust formatting for the pasted table as needed.

   ✓ When you perform a copy like this, you can edit the entries in the copied table without affecting the original entries in the spreadsheet file.

   ✓ If you end up with extra blank spaces at the bottom of the document, after the inserted table, be sure to delete spaces as needed to keep the document to a single page.

14. Click outside the finished table. The finished document should resemble the illustration shown below.
15. Save the word processing document file.
16. Print one copy of the document, then close the document.

Mike's Motors

2005 Sales by Model

Thank You for a Great Year!

The results below demonstrate the terrific performance by everyone on the sales team. Mike's Motors is now poised to become the state's leading dealership.

| Mike's Motors 2005 Sales by Model | | | | | | |
Model	Q1	Q2	Q3	Q4	Model Total	Model Average
LE	$35,000	$48,000	$27,000	$33,000	$143,000	$35,750
XL	$43,000	$66,000	$75,000	$61,000	$245,000	$61,250
RX300	$73,000	$53,000	$225,000	$57,000	$408,000	$102,000
F100	$27,000	$40,000	$53,000	$40,000	$160,000	$40,000
F250	$75,000	$56,000	$125,000	$200,000	$456,000	$114,000
Tundra	$22,000	$65,000	$45,000	$104,000	$236,000	$59,000
Tahoe	$75,000	$125,000	$253,000	$75,000	$528,000	$132,000
Total	$350,000	$453,000	$803,000	$570,000	$2,176,000	
Average	$50,000	$64,714	$114,714	$81,429	$310,857	

1

Exercise 17

❖ Change Font ❖ Change Font Size
❖ Use Symbols

Notes

Your computer keyboard offers a limited number of characters. With older word processing software, you could add **symbol characters** into a document by typing a special key combination, but you had to know which keys to press for a given character—and the key combination changed depending on the selected font. Within the last few years, most word processors have added a feature used to insert a symbol character into a document more easily. By making a few easy choices, you can insert a Greek character, accented letter, currency symbol, copyright symbol, or other decorative symbol into your document. As this exercise illustrates, it can be much easier to choose a symbol to insert than to remember and type a keyboard shortcut.

You volunteer for Meals for All, which will be holding a fundraiser run. You need to finish creating the signup form for the event. Do so in this exercise, by adding symbols where needed.

Vocabulary

symbol characters

Directions

1. Open the **WP17** document file.
2. Save the file as **SIGNUP**.
3. Change the alignment for various paragraphs as shown in the illustration on the following page.
4. Apply new fonts and font sizes as shown in the illustration.

   ✓ *When you need to specify a font size that's not one of the listed sizes, you can typically select the font size value, type a new value, and press Tab or Enter.*

5. Apply different text attributes as shown in the illustration.

6. Insert symbol characters from the Bookman Old Style and Wingdings fonts as shown in the illustration. If specified, press Tab before or after inserting a symbol.

   ✓ *Some paragraphs in this document feature tab stops already set for you. Be careful not to delete these tab stops. Exercise 26 in Lesson 5 gives you more practice with tab stops.*

   ✓ *While several "regular" fonts offer symbol characters in addition to the regular set of characters, some fonts consist of symbols only. These symbol fonts include Webdings and Wingdings, among others.*

Exercise 2

❖ Word Processing and Spreadsheet Integration

Notes

Software suites offer a number of features that enable them to work smoothly together. One key feature is that you can paste information between files in some applications. For example, if you create a range of data in a spreadsheet, you can **copy** that data into a word processing document. Usually, you select the range to copy, use the copy command, position the insertion point at the location where you want to **paste** the cells in the word processing document, then choose the paste command. The pasted cells usually appear as a table in the word processing document, and some of the formatting you applied in the spreadsheet program may even appear in the pasted table.

You're the sales manager for Mike's Motors, and you're creating a memo to inform the sales staff of the prior year's sales results. Finish the memo by pasting some spreadsheet information into the word processing document as a table now.

Vocabulary

copy   paste

Directions

1. Start your word processing program.
2. Open the **IC02** file.
3. Save the file as **CARMEM**.
4. Start your spreadsheet program.
5. Open the **IC02-2** file.
6. Select the range **A1:G13** in the spreadsheet file.
7. Copy the range.
   - ✓ You can use the copy button or icon, if one is available, or the Copy command on the Edit menu.

8. Close the spreadsheet file and program without saving any changes.
9. Switch to the **CARMEM** word processing document.
10. Move the insertion point to the end of the document.
11. Press Enter twice.
12. Paste the range of cells into the word processing document. The pasted range of cells appears as a table.
    - ✓ You can use the paste button or icon, or the Paste (or Paste Cells) command on the Edit menu.

7. Increase the text size of the inserted symbols as indicated in the illustration.

   ✓ *If the document increases to 2 pages after you format the specified symbols, you can decrease the size of other text to hold the example document to a single page.*

8. Save the edited document file.
9. View the document in print preview.
10. Close the print preview.
11. Print one copy of the document.
12. Close the document.

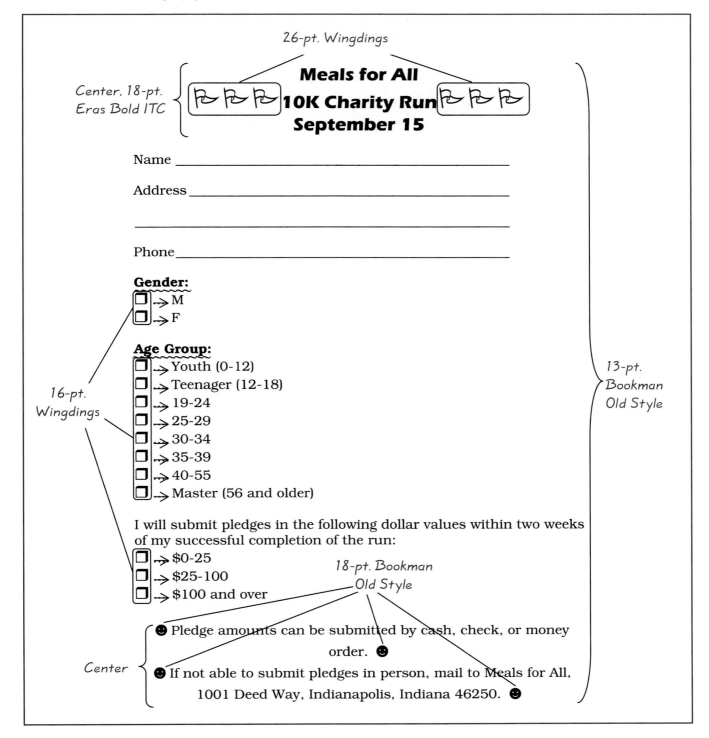

7. Save the presentation file; name it **FED**.
8. Print one copy of the presentation, with one slide per page.

9. Close the presentation file and the presentation graphics program.

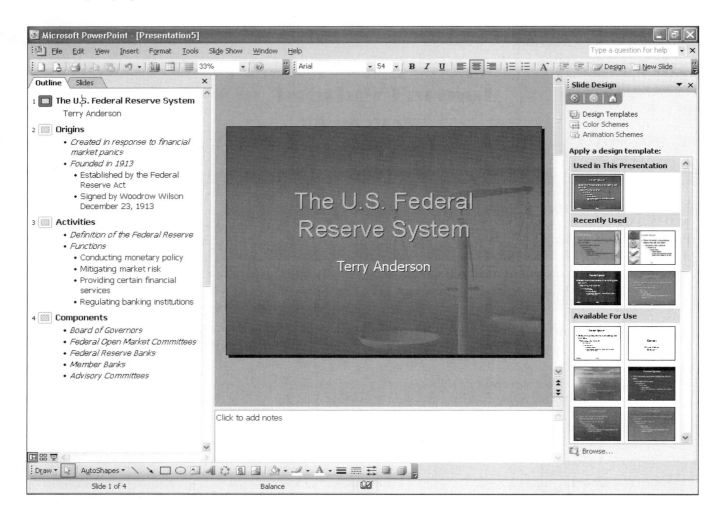

Exercise 18

❖ Change Font ❖ Change Font Size
❖ Use Symbols ❖ Use Bullets ❖ Undo

Notes

When you want to set off a list of items from the surrounding text and distinguish each item in the list, you can add **bullets** to the list. Most word processors offer a feature used to create a **bulleted list** automatically. When it applies bullets to the paragraphs (list items) you specify, the word processor also applies new indentation. When you make changes such as adding bullets to a list or deleting text, you can use the **undo** feature to reverse the changes.

Your boss at Mountain Gear has written a document about hiking safety for customers. Open the document now and apply new fonts, symbols, and bullets to make it more attractive and easier to read.

Vocabulary

bullets   bulleted list   undo

Directions

1. Open the **WP18** document file.
2. Save the file as **SAFE**.
3. Change the alignment for various paragraphs as shown in the illustration on page 77.
4. Apply new fonts and font sizes as shown in the illustration.
5. Insert symbol characters from the Webdings font as shown in the illustration, adding spacing where needed. (Use a similar font if the Webdings font is not available on your system.)
   - ✓ *In some word processors, you can use the automatic correct feature to enter some symbol characters. Type (c) to enter a ©, type (r) to enter a ®, or type (tm) to enter a ™. Or, you can insert those characters as symbols.*

- ✓ *After you've inserted a symbol, you can copy and paste it throughout the document.*

6. Increase the text size of the inserted symbols as indicated in the illustration.
7. Apply bullets in the appropriate style to specified paragraphs as shown in the illustration.
   - ✓ *In Exercise 17, you manually inserted symbols to create check boxes. Most word processors offer a check box bullet style, giving you a faster way to create a list of check box items. The top word processors also allow you to customize bullets or even use a graphic image as a bullet.*

Exercise 1

❖ Import a Word Processing Outline into a Presentation

Notes

If you've already created an outline for information in your word processing program using the proper heading styles, you can **import** or insert that outline directly into a presentation graphics file. This not only saves you the time of retyping all the outline information but also ensures that the presentation uses exactly the same information as the outline. Some presentation graphics programs will also examine the styles applied to the outline and create a new slide starting with every heading 1 (top level) heading in the outline.

Earlier you created an outline for a paper on the Federal Reserve System for the economics course. Now, your instructor wants you to present that information orally. Import your outline into your presentation graphics program so you can create your presentation.

Vocabulary

import

Directions

1. Start the presentation graphics program.
2. Create a new presentation using the design template of your choice.
3. Choose the command for importing or inserting a word processing outline into the presentation graphics program, and insert the **IC01** word processing file.

   ✓ *The command may appear on the File menu or Insert menu, and the command name might vary. For example, in PowerPoint 2003, the command is Insert|Slides from Outline. Also, if you get a message telling you the feature for inserting an outline hasn't been installed, ask your instructor to install it for you.*

   ✓ *You also can send an outline from Word 2003 directly to PowerPoint using the File|Send To|Microsoft Office PowerPoint command.*

4. If your presentation graphics program requires you to specify the beginning of each slide manually, use the presentation outline (switch to the outline view, if needed) to break the information into separate slides.

   ✓ *Hint: You use Shift+Tab and Tab to promote and demote text to different outline levels.*

5. Add a report title and your name to the blank slide that appears at the beginning of the presentation, if needed.
6. Change the titles on slides 2 through 4 to **Origins**, **Activities**, and **Components**, respectively. These shorter titles are more appropriate for a presentation. The presentation outline should now resemble the one shown in the illustration on the following page.

✓ *After you apply bullets to a list, you can insert a new item in the list. Move the insertion point to the end of one of the list paragraphs, press Enter, and type the new list item.*

8. Save the edited document file.
9. View the document in print preview.

✓ *When you use both bullets and symbols in a document, try to pick complementary designs.*

10. Close the print preview.
11. Delete the last bullet item near the bottom of the page.
12. Undo your deletion.

✓ *Some word processors let you undo several prior changes simultaneously.*

13. Print one copy of the document.
14. Close the document.

Integration and Communications

Lesson 27
Use Programs and Files Together

Exercises 1–10

- ❖ Integrate a word processing outline and a presentation
- ❖ Add a spreadsheet to a word processing document
- ❖ Add a spreadsheet to a presentation
- ❖ Use a database to create a merge document
- ❖ Import information from a spreadsheet to a database
- ❖ Save word processing or spreadsheet information in alternate formats
- ❖ Export a database's contents

Center {

Trail Safety Reminders From Mountain Gear

22-pt. Impact

26-pt. Webdings

You read the news articles every year. Hundreds of people encounter difficulty while enjoying natural beauty on the trail. Government agencies spend hundreds of thousands of dollars finding and evacuating lost and injured hikers—the hikers that survive such an ordeal, that is.

Many trail difficulties can be prevented using common sense preparation. For example, hundreds of hikers have difficulty with dehydration in the Grand Canyon each year because they fail to do a simple thing: take adequate water for everyone in the hiking party.

Mountain Gear would like to provide a few simple reminders about how you can have a more safe and enjoyable hiking experience. Take these basic steps before you leave on a hike:

Check bullets

- ✔ Research and plan your hiking route to assess the supplies you'll need. Always take water. For a short day hike, you may take additional snacks such as power bars or trail mix. Always have your trail map and a compass with you.
- ✔ Check the weather forecast and dress appropriately for weather conditions. Dress in layers, and bring gear for rain and other conditions you anticipate.
- ✔ Let someone know where you're going and when to expect you back. At a national park, you can register your plan with the ranger. By informing others of your plan, you ensure that others can begin searching for you as soon as possible should you not return in a timely fashion.

Once you're on the trail, follow these guidelines to stay safe:

Arrow bullets

- ➜ Stay on the marked trails and observe posted safety warnings. Many accidents and injuries occur when hikers leave the trail or venture into an unsafe area.
- ➜ Take breaks as frequently as needed, including drinking plenty of water. Drink water even when you're not yet thirsty, especially if you're hiking at higher altitudes.
- ➜ Do not touch or eat unfamiliar plants, or remove plant life from the wild. Also, do not approach wildlife.

Above all, respect your fellow hikers and remain ready to help when someone else has trouble.

_X2_

Center, 26-pt. Webdings {

12-pt. Garamond

Directory of Files

Exercise	File Name	Page
1	IC01	476
2	IC02, IC02-2	478
3	IC03, IC03-2	480
4	IC04	483
5	IC05, 1C05-2	486
6	IC06, IC06-2	489
7	IC07	491
8	IC08, IC08-2	493, 494
9	IC09	495
10	IC10, IC10-2, IC10-3	497
11	IC11	500
12	IC12	503
13	IC13	506
14	IC14	509
15	IC15	511
16	IC16	513
17	IC17, IC17-2	515, 516
18	IC18, IC18-2	518
19	IC19, IC19-2	519

Exercise	File Name	Page
20	None	—
21	None	—
22	None	—
23	None	—
24	None	—
25	None	—
26	IC26, IC26-2	535, 536
27	IC27, IC27-2	538
28	None	—
29	None	—
30	None	—
31	None	—
32	None	—
33	None	—
34	None	—

Exercise 19

❖ Change Font ❖ Change Font Size
❖ Use Symbols ❖ Use Numbers ❖ Undo

Notes

Most word processors now also offer a feature that automatically numbers a list of paragraphs, creating a **numbered list**. If you use this feature to number a list, you can add new items (paragraphs) within the list, and the word processor automatically renumbers all list items for you. In this exercise, you work with the numbering feature, as well as other formatting features and the undo feature.

You've been asked to create a document with basic computer troubleshooting steps for other students in your class. Apply formatting, including list numbering, to that document now.

Vocabulary

numbered list

Directions

1. Open the **WP19** document file.
2. Save the file as **TS**.
3. Change the alignment for various paragraphs as shown in the illustration on the following page.
4. Apply new fonts and font sizes as shown in the illustration.
5. Insert symbol characters (and any needed spacing) from the Wingdings font as shown in the illustration.
6. Increase the text size of the inserted symbols as indicated in the illustration.
   - ✓ *When you select a symbol to resize it, you may find that it appears to be formatted in a font other than the original font (like Wingdings) that you used to create it. If this creates a problem, simply reapply the proper font to the symbol.*

7. Apply numbering to specified paragraphs, as shown in the illustration.
   - ✓ *You also can apply numbering or bullets before you type a list. To do so, turn on the numbering or bullets feature. Type the list, pressing Enter to start each new list item. After you create the last item and press Enter, turn off the numbering or bullets.*

8. Save the edited document file.
9. View the document in print preview.
10. Close the print preview.
11. Delete the "Printer Troubleshooting" list.
12. Undo your deletion.
13. Print one copy of the document.
14. Close the document.

Intergration and Communications

Lessons 27-31
Exercises 1-34

Lesson 27
Use Programs and Files Together

Lesson 28
Work with Web Design Features

Lesson 29
Work on the Web

Lesson 30
Manage Your E-Mail

Lesson 31
Manage Your Time

24-pt. Wingdings

Center, 18-pt. Copperplate Gothic Bold

✪✪✪ ANDREWS HALL ꙮꙮꙮ
COMPUTER TROUBLESHOOTING TIPS

BASICS } *18-pt. Copperplate Gothic Bold*

12-pt. Century Schoolbook

Remember to practice these basic good habits when using your computer:

Numbered list

1. Use a surge suppressor.
2. Unplug the system and all peripherals during storms that include lightning.
3. Do not place the computer system unit on carpet or any other surface that will generate static electricity.
4. Be careful when eating or drinking around the computer. Spills kill!
5. If you don't perform regular backups of your full system, be sure to back up important files every few days or so. Save your documents every 10 minutes or so while working.

12-pt. Century Schoolbook

SYSTEM TROUBLESHOOTING } *18-pt. Copperplate Gothic Bold*

Numbered list

1. Press Ctrl+Alt+Delete (Windows) or Option+Command+power button (Mac) to restart the system.
2. If #1 fails, try pressing the system Reset button (if available).
3. If #2 fails, shut down the system. Wait until you hear the hard disk spin all the way to a stop. Check all cables and connections, then restart.
4. If all of the above fail, consult CCC (see below).

12-pt. Century Schoolbook

PRINTER TROUBLESHOOTING } *18-pt. Copperplate Gothic Bold*

Numbered list

1. Before powering up the printer, make sure that all cable connections are firm and that the printer has paper and ink or toner.
2. If the printer jams, follow the instructions for clearing the jam on the printer display.
3. If the print queue keeps stalling, delete and reinstall the printer. If you need help with this, consult CCC (see below).

Justify, 12-pt. Century Schoolbook

CAMPUS COMPUTER CENTER (CCC) } *18-pt. Copperplate Gothic Bold*

The Campus Computer Center provides 24-hour support services for students. For Web or chat help, go to **WWW.STATEU.EDU/CCC**. Otherwise, call **EXTENSION 599**.

26-pt. Wingdins

↓X2

Circle the correct answer to each of the questions below:

1. You can add new slides in this view:
   A. Single slide (normal).
   B. Outline.
   C. Small slides (slide sorter).
   D. Any of the above.

2. To work with bullet levels in the outline view, you:
   A. Use the arrow keys.
   B. Press Tab or Shift+Tab.
   C. Choose an outlining number.
   D. None of the above.

3. You can insert clip art:
   A. In a placeholder.
   B. Anywhere on a slide.
   C. On the slide master.
   D. Any of the above.

4. To change the font for text:
   A. Select the text and press F1 to display the Font dialog box.
   B. Use the font tool.
   C. Select its placeholder on the slide or master, and then use formatting toolbar choices or the Font dialog box.
   D. Type a font code.

5. You can make these transition choices:
   A. Transition type, sound, and automatic advance time.
   B. Transition type, flashing color, and overall presentation time.
   C. Transition type, slide order, and background music.
   D. Any of the above.

Exercise 20

❖ Critical Thinking

Notes

Applying formatting to a document helps make it more attractive and doesn't take much time. In this exercise, practice making your own formatting choices for an example document.

You work in the Eco Products division of Major Manufacturing. You've written a document about the company's environmentally-friendly flooring products, and you want to enhance it with various types of formatting now.

Vocabulary

No new vocabulary in this exercise.

Directions

1. Open the **WP20** document file.
2. Save the file as **FLOOR**.
3. Add extra spacing between paragraphs to better group and set off information.
4. Change the alignment for various paragraphs, as you prefer.
5. Apply new fonts and font sizes as needed.

   ✓ *When it comes to choosing fonts, a good rule of thumb is to use no more than three fonts per document, or even fewer if the document contains little text. Using too many fonts and attributes in a document results in the "ransom note effect," where the document looks as if it's pasted together from newspaper and magazine clippings.*

6. Apply bullets and numbering to lists as needed.
7. Apply attributes to text as needed.

   ✓ *You also can add attributes such as bold to the bullets and numbering you add. In more recent versions of Word, clicking on one bullet or number selects all the bullets or numbers in the list (showing a gray selection highlight), so that your formatting change will be applied to all the bullets or numbers in the list.*

8. Insert symbols to enhance the document.

   ✓ *If you want to center a row of decorative symbols, you will get a better result if you insert an odd number of symbols (five or seven works well) rather than an even number. Also, you can insert spaces between symbols to achieve a different effect.*

   ✓ *The Wingdings font includes circled number symbols that you can use to replace numbers in text for a unique look.*

9. Adjust the vertical alignment of the information in the document, if needed.
10. Save the edited document file.
11. View the document in print preview.
12. Close the print preview.
13. Print one copy of the document.
14. Close the document.

Quiz Break 7

Fill in your brief answers below:

1. A presentation is made up of separate pages called:
   _____

2. This controls how all the slides in the presentation look:
   _____

3. This controls what type of content an individual slide has:
   _____

4. The view where you can easily move slides around is called:
   _____

5. If you have more to say about a slide, you should enter your comments as:
   _____

6. When you print more than one slide on a page for your audience, you're printing a:
   _____

7. The default type of graph typically is a:
   _____

8. This type of chart diagrams how jobs or items relate:
   _____

9. You add this to a slide to control how it appears when you play the slide show on-screen:
   _____

10. When you set up a bulleted list to appear one item at a time, you've created a:
    _____

11. You can apply _____ to any slide element to add movement, and in some cases, set timings for automatic playback.
    _____

12. An inserted _____ (or movie) enables you to show actual footage of your product or service in use.
    _____

Word Processing

Lesson 5
Format and Edit Documents

Exercises 21–27

❖ **Set margins and indent text**
❖ **Adjust line spacing**
❖ **Set tabs**
❖ **Copy formatting in a document**
❖ **Copy and move text in a document**

Exercise 17

❖ Critical Thinking

Notes

This final presentation graphics exercise combines a number of the skills you've learned.

Keller Mortgage will have a booth in the local home show, and you want to set up a computer to play your presentation at the event. Set up the on-screen Keller Mortgage slide show by adding transitions and other effects.

Vocabulary

No new vocabulary in this exercise.

Directions

1. Open the **PG17** presentation file.
2. Save the file as **KELLER2**.
3. Change to the presentation design of your choice.
4. Add the transition of your choice to the first slide, setting the transition to advance to the next slide after five seconds.
5. Apply the transition to all slides in the presentation.
6. Apply a custom animation effect to one of the title slide elements, such as the title text or any background graphic. (You'll have to go to the title slide master to apply an animation effect to a background graphic.)
7. Apply a build effect to the bulleted lists on slides 2 and 5, reducing the size of the text on slide 5 if needed. Set up each build to automatically display the next bullet after two seconds.
8. Go to slide 1.
9. Spell check the presentation.
10. Run the on-screen slide show from slide 1.
11. Print the presentation with one slide per page.
12. Print the slides with the speaker notes.
13. Save and close the presentation file.

Exercise 21

❖ Indent Text ❖ Change Line Spacing

Notes

Indentation helps the reader identify new paragraphs or list items. You can apply a few different types of indents to a paragraph: **left** (indents all lines at the left), **right** (indents all lines at the right), **first line** (applies a left indent to the first line of the paragraph only), and **hanging** (applies a left indent to all lines but the first line). You also can apply different **line spacing** to a paragraph to adjust its appearance or follow formal document formatting guidelines. For example, you should use **double spacing** for most text in a report or in documents where you want to leave space for the reader to make notes. In other cases, you use single spacing for quotations (even in business letters, which normally require single spacing), and greater line spacing for other document text. Most business letters and brochures use single spacing, while school reports and legal documents often use double spacing. Practice adjusting indents and line spacing in this exercise.

You volunteered to create a progress report for the Meals for All food bank. You've already written the document, and now you're going to finish it by changing line spacing, indenting text, and applying other formatting.

Vocabulary

indentation	first line indent	double spacing	proofreading marks:
left indent	hanging indent	1.5 line spacing	left indent]
right indent	line spacing	single spacing	right indent [

Directions

1. Open the **WP21** document file.
2. Save the file as **MFA**.
3. Format the document heading and other text as shown in the illustration on page 84.
4. Apply double spacing to all text in the document.

   ✓ *Most word processors offer you a keyboard shortcut (such as Ctrl+A or Command+A) or a menu command (such as Edit|Select All) for selecting all the text in a document.*

5. Apply 1.5 line spacing to the paragraphs specified in the illustration.

6. Add hanging indents to the paragraphs shown in the illustration.

   ✓ *You must select a paragraph or place the insertion point within it to change the paragraph indent or paragraph line spacing.*

7. Add first line indents to the paragraphs shown in the illustration.

   ✓ *Using a tab to create a first line indent can create problems later if you combine paragraphs, because you have to remember to delete the tab. Use paragraph indent settings to add the first line indent instead.*

10. To preview the first part of the movie from the slide, right-click it and choose the command for playing it (Play Movie in PowerPoint).
11. Run the on-screen slide show from slide 1.

12. If the slide doesn't play automatically, click it or use the slide show controls to start it.
13. Print the presentation with one slide per page.
14. Save and close the presentation file.

8. Add left indents to the paragraphs shown in the illustration.

9. Indent the quotations from both sides, as shown in the illustration.

   ✓ *In most document styles, you should generally use **single spacing** and .5" left and right indentation for quotations greater than five lines or for numerous quotations. Some instructors may prefer that you also use a first line indent for the first paragraph after a heading; others don't. If in doubt about proper formatting, check with your instructor or consult the style guide recommended for the course.*

10. Insert extra blank lines as shown in the illustration.

11. Save the edited document file.

12. View the document in print preview.

13. Close the print preview.

14. Print one copy of the document.

   ✓ *Remember, if your instructor requires it, label and turn in a copy of the printed document.*

15. Close the document.

Exercise 16

❖ Add a Video Object
❖ Add an Animated GIF ❖ Play Back a Video Object During the Slide Show

Notes

With quality digital video cameras available for a thousand dollars or so, an organization can easily avoid employing professional videographers to create video of products, events, or services. And, you can easily include the video you create as a **video object (movie)** in your presentation for greater impact. You also may want to include animated GIFs—graphic files that include motion and are commonly seen on Web pages. Your movies and animations only playback when you run the slide show, the same as for other types of animations you apply.

Finish your Pet Country Club presentation by adding an animated graphic and video.

Vocabulary

video object (movie)

Directions

1. Open the **PG16** presentation file.
2. Save the file as **PETCC2**.
3. Add the transition of your choice to all slides in the presentation.
4. Display slide 5.
5. Insert the **PG16-2** animated GIF.

    ✓ *Presentation graphics programs now typically provide animated clip art or animated GIFs you can include in a slide show. In recent PowerPoint versions, click a slide layout with a content placeholder, then click the Insert Media Clip button on the placeholder.*

6. Display slide 6.

7. Insert the **PG16-3** video file.

    ✓ *In this instance, use the command for inserting the movie (Insert|Movies and Sounds|Movie from File in PowerPoint 2003), then navigate to the folder holding the book files. Choose All Files (*.*) from the Files of type drop-down list, and then insert either the .AVI or . WMV (Windows Media Video), depending on which movie format your system supports.*

8. If prompted, specify that the movie should playback automatically.
9. Resize the movie to **3"** high and proportionally wide, and position it in a central position on the slide.

Center, Bold, 18-pt. Antique Olive, Single line spacing {

Meals for All
Progress Report

↙ X1

Meals for All has completed yet another year of improvements in serving people in need. We worked hard to secure additional funds and food contributions, while reducing food delivery and client service expenses.

The following list summarizes our achievements for the year:

Hanging indent, 1.5 line spacing {

Dollar donations increased by 12 percent. The additional revenue enabled Meals for All to increase the number of households served by 13 percent.

Contributions from our food donor partners increased by seven percent. In particular, significant produce donations enabled Meals for All to deliver healthier food choices to clients.

Transportation costs decreased by two percent. We offset higher fuel costs by retiring our least efficient truck, replacing it with higher-mileage truck that was purchased through a special donor fund.

Staffing costs remained stable. While health benefit costs continue to grow, we were able to find alternate plans that kept costs in line.

First line indent {

Despite those accomplishments, more needs to be done as low income families continue to struggle. Meals for All will continue its regular programs. As you plan your charitable (and tax-deductible) donations for next year, we ask you to keep in mind that the following items are still on our wish list:

11-pt. Perpetua

1.5 line spacing { .5"

An updated computer system, so we can better communicate and share data with other county and regional agencies.

Another new delivery truck, as we anticipate that fuel costs will not decrease dramatically in the near future.

An upgraded refrigeration system, so that we can lower food storage costs while increasing the available storage space.

First line indent {

Meals for All would like to close this report by letting our clients speak to you. These are the people whom we serve through the generosity of donors like you.

Single line spacing { .5"

Even though a lot of companies in the area were closing, I never expected to be without a job for so long. Meals for All really came through for my family. I've got a new job, and once we're back on our feet, my family will be making a donation to Meals for All. (Jim D.)

↙ X1

Meals for All saved my family from having to choose between food and heat last winter. Thank you for keeping us both warm and fed. (Tanya L.)

.5"

Exercise 15

❖ Add Transitions ❖ Create Builds
❖ Animate Objects ❖ View the Slide Show

Notes

As you may have noticed when you displayed the finished presentation from the last exercise, adding multiple animation effects means you have to click or press the spacebar many times to run even a short presentation. To avoid this problem, you can add **advance timing** to slide transitions, which tells the presentation to advance to the next slide after the specified amount of time. In this exercise, you will practice creating timed transitions, as well as adding other slide show effects.

✓ *Some presentation templates (designs) may already apply animations to selected objects in a particular slide layout. If you see an unwanted animation, you can display the slide master, select the object, and remove the animation. You can also add animation to any object on the slide master. Use such animation sparingly, though, to avoid making presentation playback tedious.*

You want to leave your Meals for All presentation with the employers you visit, so employees can play it back on their own as they consider whether or not to volunteer. Set up the presentation for automatic playback, adding timed transitions and other effects.

Vocabulary

advance timing

Directions

1. Open the **PG15** presentation file.
2. Save the file as **VOL3**.
3. Add the transition of your choice to all slides in the presentation. Include the sound of your choice with the transition. Also set up the transition so that the slides advance automatically after five seconds.
4. Display slide 3.
5. Add the animation of your choice to the chart.

   ✓ *In some presentation graphics programs you can animate graphs or particular parts of graphs. If you have extra time, copy an exercise file and experiment on your own.*

6. Apply the same effect to the chart on slide 4
7. Apply a build effect to the bulleted lists on slides 2, 5, and 6. Use custom animation to specify that each bullet item should appear automatically after two seconds.
8. Display slide 5.
9. Increase the slide transition advance timing to eight seconds for this slide.
10. Run the on-screen slide show from slide 1.
11. Print the presentation with one slide per page.
12. Save and close the presentation file.

Exercise 22

❖ Copy Formatting

Notes

As you saw in the last exercise, it can be rather time consuming to apply the same formatting settings over and over in a document. Newer versions of the leading word processors offer a feature that enables you to copy formatting from one selection to another and from one paragraph to another. (This feature has the name **format painter** in Microsoft Office Word, for example.) In this exercise, practice with the **format copy** feature using a modified copy of the document you used in Exercise 18 of this section.

You want to make a few last changes to the Mountain Gear hiking safety document you worked on earlier. Open the document now and copy formatting from one location to another.

Vocabulary

format painter   format copy

Directions

1. Open the **WP22** document file.
2. Save the file as **SAFE2**.
3. Format the first line of the document as shown in the illustration on page 87.
4. Copy the formatting from the first line to the second line in the document.

   ✓ *The Format Painter button appears on Word's Standard toolbar. If you don't see the button at first, click the Toolbar Options button at the right end of the toolbar, then click the button in the drop-down palette that appears. If the button isn't in the initial palette, click Add or Remove Buttons at the bottom of the palette and then click Standard to see the full list of buttons available for the Standard toolbar.*

5. Adjust the paragraph formatting for the first item in the first bulleted list as shown in the illustration.

6. Copy that formatting to the rest of the items in the first bulleted list, as shown in the illustration.

   ✓ *You can drag over the paragraph to which you're copying the formatting. Or, if your word processor enables you to select a whole paragraph by double-clicking in the left margin, that technique may be faster.*

   ✓ *In Word, you can double-click the Format Painter button, copy the formatting to multiple locations, then click the button again to stop copying.*

   ✓ *If you are going to copy paragraph formatting, you should do the copying before you format selected words within those paragraphs. Otherwise, the previously formatted selections could change.*

Exercise 14

❖ Add Transitions ❖ Create Builds
❖ Animate Objects ❖ View the Slide Show

Notes

The text, clip art, and other objects on your slides don't have to just sit there on-screen. You can add an **animation effect** to a slide or a custom animation to any object. When the slide holding the object appears, the object appears after a brief pause. The animation effect you added to the object, like having it dissolve onto the screen, controls exactly how the object appears.

Jazz up your Mobile A Network presentation about mobile phones by adding transitions and animations in this exercise.

Vocabulary

animation effect

Directions

1. Open the **PG14** presentation file.
2. Save the file as **MPHONE2**.
3. Apply a dissolve or fade transition to all the slides in the presentation. Include a sound effect with the transition, such as a slide projector or laser sound effect.

   ✓ *If you're prompted to install sound effects, confirm whether or not you should do so with your instructor.*

4. Add the build effect of your choice to the bulleted list on slide 2.

   ✓ *When you add a build effect to a list or animate an object, the slide appears first, then the animated list or object. Also, some animation schemes and build effects include a sound effect by default. Others do not, so you can return to the pane or dialog box where you added the slide transition and re-specify the sound if desired.*

5. Display slide 5.

6. Add an animation effect to the chart.

   ✓ *In recent PowerPoint versions, you have to use the Slide Show | Custom Animation command (or right-click on an object and choose Custom Animation) to animate specific slide objects.*

7. Display slide 1.
8. Use custom animation settings to apply the animation effect of your choice to the slide title and subtitle. Set the animations so that the title animates first, followed by the subtitle.

   ✓ *If you have multiple subtitle lines, the lines display one at a time when animated. Also, you can use the custom animation feature to control the animation order of any slide on which you animate multiple objects, such as a slide that contains a bulleted list and clip art image.*

9. Run the on-screen slide show from slide 1.
10. Print the presentation with one slide per page.
11. Save and close the presentation file.

7. Change the text formatting for selected text in the item in the second bulleted list, as shown in the illustration.
8. Copy the text formatting to the other items in the bulleted list, as specified in the illustration.
9. Save the edited document file.
10. View the document in print preview.
11. Close the print preview.
12. Print one copy of the document.
13. Close the document.

Exercise 13

❖ Add Transitions ❖ Create Builds
❖ View the Slide Show

Notes

If you plan to display your slide show on your computer screen, you can add special effects that make it more interesting visually. A **slide transition** like a fade or shutter effect appears when you display the slide to which you applied the transition. A **build effect** displays each bulleted item on a slide in sequence, rather than displaying all the bullets simultaneously. (In some programs, you achieve this build effect by adding animation.)

Enhance your Haywood Organic Growers Association presentation with transitions to give it more impact when viewed on-screen.

Vocabulary

slide transition   build effect   running the slide show on-screen

Directions

1. Open the **PG13** presentation file.
2. Save the file as **ORGANIC3**.
3. Add a dissolve or wipe transition to all slides in the presentation.
4. Display slide 4.
5. Apply a checkerboard or blinds transition to slide 4 only.

   ✓ *A transition you apply to a single slide typically overrides any transition you earlier applied to all slides.*

6. Display slide 2.
7. Apply a wipe transition to slide 2 only.
8. Apply the build effect of your choice to each of the following slides: 2, 3, and 5

   ✓ *In some presentation graphics programs, you actually apply a custom animation effect to the bulleted list by clicking one bullet at a time and*

applying the desired animation. In other cases, such as in recent PowerPoint versions, you can apply an animation scheme to the slide itself, and the program automatically knows it should display the bullets one by one. However, not all animation schemes create the build effect when used with a bulleted list slide. And, take note of the fact that when you apply an animation scheme to a slide, the scheme may change any slide transition you applied earlier.

9. **Run the on-screen slide show** from slide 1.

   ✓ *Generally, you click the mouse or press a keyboard key to advance the presentation.*

10. Print the presentation with multiple small slides per page.
11. Save and close the presentation file.

24-pt. Bodoni MT Black

Trail Safety Reminders From Mountain Gear

Copy formatting

★ ★ ★ ★ ★

You read the news articles every year. Hundreds of people encounter difficulty while enjoying natural beauty on the trail. Government agencies spend hundreds of thousands of dollars finding and evacuating lost and injured hikers—the hikers that survive such an ordeal, that is.

Many trail difficulties can be prevented using common sense preparation. For example, hundreds of hikers have difficulty with dehydration in the Grand Canyon each year because they fail to do a simple thing: take adequate water for everyone in the hiking party.

Mountain Gear would like to provide a few simple reminders about how you can have a more safe and enjoyable hiking experience. Take these basic steps before you leave on a hike:

Copy format-ting

Center

✓ Research and plan your hiking route to assess the supplies you'll need. Always take water. For a short day hike, you may take additional snacks such as power bars or trail mix. Always have your trail map and a compass with you.

✓ Check the weather forecast and dress appropriately for weather conditions. Dress in layers, and bring gear for rain and other conditions you anticipate.

✓ Let someone know where you're going and when to expect you back. At a national park, you can register your plan with the ranger. By informing others of your plan, you ensure that others can begin searching for you as soon as possible should you not return in a timely fashion.

Once you're on the trail, follow these guidelines to stay safe:

Bold

➔ **Stay on the marked trails and observe posted safety warnings.** Many accidents and injuries occur when hikers leave the trail or venture into an unsafe area.

➔ **Take breaks as frequently as needed, including drinking plenty of water.** Drink water even when you're not yet thirsty, especially if you're hiking at higher altitudes.

➔ **Do not touch or eat unfamiliar plants, or remove plant life from the wild.** Also, do not approach wildlife.

Copy format-ting to the rest of the list

Above all, respect your fellow hikers and remain ready to help when someone else has trouble.

Lesson 26
Work with Slide Shows

Exercises 13–17

❖ **Work with transitions, builds, animation, and video**

❖ **Run a slide show**

Exercise 23

❖ Set Margins

Notes

The font size, paragraph alignment, indents, and line spacing settings you specify all affect how much text fits on each page in your document. In addition, you can change the size of the **margins**—the blank, unprinted area around the edge of each page—to fit more or less text on each page in a document. The margin settings are part of the **page setup**—settings that apply to each page in the document. (Lesson 7 in this section covers more of the page setup choices.) Most word processing programs set default margins of 1 inch for the top, bottom, left, and right sides of the document; Word documents have larger left and right margins of 1.25 inches by default.

You want to revisit the formatting of the Meals for All progress report you created earlier. You'd like to use larger, more readable text, but still limit the document to a single page. Try to do so by adjusting text and margin settings.

Vocabulary

margin	right margin	bottom margin	print view
left margin	top margin	page setup	page layout view

Directions

1. Open the **WP23** document file.
2. Save the file as **MFA2**.
3. Format all but the first two lines of the flyer in the 12.5-point font size.

   ✓ *You can usually apply a more specific font size by selecting the entry in the font size text box, typing the desired size, and pressing Enter or Tab.*

4. Move the insertion point to the end of the document. Notice that increasing the font size has caused the document to become two pages in length.
5. Move the insertion point back to the beginning of the document, at the left end of the first line.
6. Change the size of the top margin to **.5"**.

7. Change the size of the bottom, left. and right margins to **.75"**.
8. Move the insertion point to the end of the document. Decreasing the margin widths now enables all the text to fit on a single page, as shown in the illustration on the following page.

   ✓ *For a better look at the effects of margin or any other page setup changes, you can change the word processing program from its normal view to a **print** or **page layout view**. Choose a view using the commands on the View menu.*

9. Save the edited document file.
10. View the document in print preview.
11. Close the print preview.
12. Print one copy of the document.
13. Close the document.

Mobile Market Increasing   2

businesses or a joint venture with a foreign entity. The latter technique,

in particular, enabled the providers to tap into less expensive sources of

capital. Coupling that capital with explosive population growth in

markets like China enables rapid subscriber expansion.

By now, you may be wondering what the growth has looked like in

terms of sheer numbers. Here's a picture:

- U.S. subscribers: 123,000 (1990) to 45 million (2005)

- European subscribers: 75,000 (1990) to 35 million (2005)

- Asian subscribers: 45,000 (1990) to 215 million (2005)

- Other markets: 12,000 (1990) to 14 million (2005)[3]

The market factors that have generated such growth appear to be

in position to maintain the growth for at least two decades. Mobile A

Network predicts subscriber growth of 10% per year for the next five

years, with commensurate revenue growth.

---

[1] The Phone Group "Market Revisited" *Cell Phone World* 15.3 (March 2005): 67.
[2] Andrews, Phillip "Cost Efficiencies Examined" *Cell Phone World* 13.9 (September 2003): 55.
[3] The Phone Group, *15-Year Market Report* (Los Angeles: Phone Group Printworks, 2005) 22.

Meals for All
Progress Report

.5"

12.5 pt.

Meals for All has completed yet another year of improvements in serving people in need. We worked hard to secure additional funds and food contributions, while reducing food delivery and client service expenses. The following list summarizes our achievements for the year:

Dollar donations increased by 12 percent. The additional revenue enabled Meals for All to increase the number of households served by 13 percent.

Contributions from our food donor partners increased by seven percent. In particular, significant produce donations enabled Meals for All to deliver healthier food choices to clients.

Transportation costs decreased by two percent. We offset higher fuel costs by retiring our least efficient truck, replacing it with higher-mileage truck that was purchased through a special donor fund.

Staffing costs remained stable. While health benefit costs continue to grow, we were able to find alternate plans that kept costs in line.

Despite those accomplishments, more needs to be done as low income families continue to struggle.

.75"

Meals for All will continue its regular programs. As you plan your charitable (and tax-deductible) donations for next year, we ask you to keep in mind that the following items are still on our wish list:

An updated computer system, so we can better communicate and share data with other county and regional agencies.

Another new delivery truck, as we anticipate that fuel costs will not decrease dramatically in the near future.

An upgraded refrigeration system, so that we can lower food storage costs while increasing the available storage space.

Meals for All would like to close this report by letting our clients speak to you. These are the people whom we serve through the generosity of donors like you.

Even though a lot of companies in the area were closing, I never expected to be without a job for so long. Meals for All really came through for my family. I've got a new job, and once we're back on our feet, my family will be making a donation to Meals for All. *Jim D.*

Meals for All saved my family from having to choose between food and heat last winter. Thank you for keeping us both warm and fed. *Tanya L.*

.75"

.75"

.75"

Mobile Phone Market Continues to Grow
Mobile A Network

In the mobile phone marketplace's first 15 years, growth was limited by infrastructure costs. It was excessively expensive to erect even a single cell tower. Service providers had to rely on heavy investment by other communications companies, such as land-based phone companies, to enter any particular marketplace.

Today the picture looks dramatically different. Subscriber bases have grown substantially. In 2001, service revenues actually exceeded operating costs. Then in 2002, service revenues for the first time were able to cover up to 85% of infrastructure costs[1], as well.

Let's examine the factors contributing to this dramatic shift. First, by 2001, the mobile phone infrastructure achieved an average of 98% completion (in terms of cell phone towers) in the United States. This enabled the U.S. providers to shift capital investments to less costly network equipment that would multiply efficiency. The providers could sign on 15% more customers for each dollar invested in the infrastructure, as opposed to the earlier figure of being able to add 5% more customers for each infrastructure dollar[2]. That change alone spurred most of the providers over the profitability hurdle.

In addition, profitable providers became able to apply capital dollars to developing new markets in other countries. Providers chose one of two methods for doing so: a simple expansion of their own

Exercise 24

❖ Move Text ❖ Copy Text ❖ Set Margins

Notes

In addition to changing page margins, which you'll practice again in this exercise, you can **move** or **copy** text within a document to adjust how text reads and looks on the page. To move text, you **cut** it from its current location, and **paste** it into a new location. To copy text, you copy it and then paste it, leaving the original copy of the information in place. Practice copying and pasting, as well as resizing margins, in this exercise.

You are a realtor with Pro Realty. You're drafting a letter to clients to alert them about your latest listings. Improve your letter now by copying and moving text and adjusting the margins.

Vocabulary

move	cut	proofreading mark:
copy	paste	move text

Directions

1. Open the **WP24** document file.
2. Save the file as **PRO**.
3. Replace the **Today's date** and **Your name** placeholders with the date and your name.
4. Change the size of the top and bottom margins to **.75"**.
5. Change the size of the left and right margins to **1.5"**.

   ✓ *If you use a small font size (such as 10 points) for the body text in your document, increasing the left and right margin widths makes each line a bit shorter and more in proportion with the small text.*

   ✓ *Word 2003 offers an additional Gutter margin setting. Increase the value for this setting and specify a Gutter position to create a document with extra binding space along one edge.*

6. Move selections of text as specified in the illustration on page 92.

   ✓ *Look on the Edit menu in your word processing program to find the commands for cutting, copying, and pasting text. Most word processors also offer convenient buttons or icons for performing these commands.*

   ✓ *If you're working with recent Word versions, the Office Clipboard may appear when you begin using menu commands or toolbar buttons to cut, paste, and copy text. You can use the Office Clipboard to complete moving and copying text. After you finish, close the Office Clipboard by clicking the Close button in its upper-right corner.*

7. Copy selections of text as specified in the illustration.

Exercise 12

❖ Critical Thinking

Notes

This exercise applies all your presentation graphics skills.

You work for Mobile A Network, and much earlier you wrote a report about the mobile phone market. Develop a presentation based on that report now.

Vocabulary

No new vocabulary in this exercise.

Directions

1. Read through the report starting on the following page.
2. Create a new presentation, choosing an attractive presentation design.
3. Create a presentation that uses at least four slides.
4. Include at least one bulleted list slide, one slide with a graph, and one slide with a table.

   ✓ *Although you need not do so for this exercise, when you're entering data to graph in the datasheet in PowerPoint, you can drag over the cells that hold the values you've entered, then use the Format | Number command to format the values as currency. This change will show up on the value axis of the graph, if applicable. Alternatively, you can right-click the value axis, click on Format Axis, then use the Number tab to format the axis display only.*

5. Change the presentation design and the layout for one slide.
6. Add the date and page (slide) number in a footer for all slides except slide 1.
7. Change the title alignment on at least one slide.
8. Change the font and size for text on at least one slide.
9. Spell check the presentation.
10. Save the presentation as **MPHONE**.
11. Print and close the presentation.

8. If needed, correct spacing of the copied information, and correct punctuation and capitalization.
9. Save the edited document file.
10. View the document in print preview.
11. Close the print preview.
12. Print one copy of the document.
13. Close the document.

12. Display slide 5.
13. Enter the following bulleted list information:

- **Make your home more energy-efficient**
- **Reduce vapor infiltration**
- **Update your home's curb appeal**
- **Protect furniture and other possessions against fading**

14. Switch to the slide master view, then make these changes:

- Center the title text, if needed.
- Add slide (page) numbers. (Remember, in some programs, you have to choose the View|Header and Footer command to add page numbers.)
- Enter **Williams Windows** as the footer.
- Format the footer and slide (page) numbers with an 18-point script font.

15. Return to single slide view.
16. Add clip art to any slides you choose, or insert a shape that applies. The presentation should now look something like the illustration below.
17. Spell check the presentation.
18. Save the presentation as **WINDOW**.
19. Print and close the presentation.

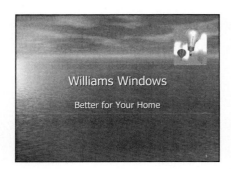

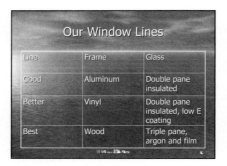
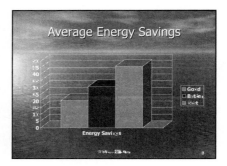
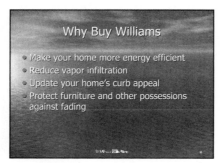

.75"

Pro Realty
222 Main Road
Weaverville, NC 28787

Today's Date

Dear Valued Client:

I am pleased to make the following new listings available for your inspection. *Move* Thank you for trusting me to serve your past real estate needs. Every Pro Realty agent strives to provide the highest level of service.

Even though you presently may not be in need of a new home, you may know of someone who is. Or, you may be considering a real estate investment.

.75"   .75"

Move

- **$299,900.** 4 bedroom, 2 bath home in exclusive Marion Farms. Seller has already relocated and is motivated!
- **$99,900.** Charming 2 bedroom, 1 bath cottage on 2 acres. Organic garden area and substantial shed.
- **$149,900.** 3 bedroom, 1 bath brick ranch. Desirable Marlowe school district.
- **$499,500.** Executive estate with architect-designed 5 bedroom, 4 bath home. Entertain in the gourmet kitchen.
- **$69,900.** Fixer-upper bungalow. Get a deal on the worst house in the best neighborhood.

Move

If you are interested in these properties or have any other real estate needs, please call me at **555-7676**.

Sincerely,

Your name

Copy

Buy the best from the best—Pro Realty.

.75"

Exercise 11

❖ Critical Thinking

Notes

In this exercise, you combine all the presentation graphics program skills you've practiced so far. Work on your own to create a presentation.

You are a proud sales associate for Williams Windows. Build a sales presentation for the company now.

Vocabulary

No new vocabulary in this exercise.

Directions

1. Create a new presentation, choosing a presentation design.
2. Make the first slide a title slide.
3. Switch to the outline view.
4. Enter the outline for the slides shown below.

---

1 ▣ **Williams Windows**
   Better for Your Home

2 ▣ **Who We Are**
   • Premier window manufacturer in the Southeast
   • Family-owned company
   • Employer of more than 200 dedicated associates

3 ▣ **Our Window Lines**

4 ▣ **Average Energy Savings**

5 ▣ **Why Buy Williams**

---

5. Display slide 3.
6. Switch to the single slide view.
7. Change the slide layout to one that includes a title and table (chart or graphic) placeholder.

8. Use the table placeholder to create a table with three columns and four rows, then enter the table information shown below.

Line	Frame	Glass
Good	Aluminum	Double pane insulated
Better	Vinyl	Double pane insulated, low E coating
Best	Wood	Triple pane, argon and film

9. Display slide 4.
10. Change the slide layout to one that includes a title and chart (or graphic) placeholders.
11. Create a column chart on the slide using the data below.
    ✓ It's easier to enter the data if you select the correct chart type first.

		A	B
		Energy Savings	
1 ⬛	Good	26.2	
2 ⬛	Better	31.8	
3 ⬛	Best	46	

Exercise 25

❖ Move Text ❖ Set Margins ❖ Change Case

Notes

In this exercise, you refresh three different skills: moving text, changing margins, and changing the case of text (that is, changing between **uppercase** and **lowercase**). This time, use **drag and drop** editing to move your text. With drag and drop editing, you use the mouse to drag a selection from one location in the document to another.

You are taking an economics class, and you've been assigned to write a paper about the U.S. Federal Reserve System. In this exercise, begin organizing your topics and research in an example document.

Vocabulary

uppercase
lowercase

drag and drop

proofreading mark:
    initial capitals ╱‾‾‾‾‾

Directions

1. Open the **WP25** document file.
2. Save the file as **RESERVE**.
3. Change the size of the left and right margins to **1.0"**.
4. Using drag and drop editing, move and copy selections of text as specified in the illustration on the following page, including moving list items to place them in the specified order.

   ✓ *Note that when you move items in a list that's been numbered automatically, the list renumbers itself.*

5. Make corrections to text formatting and the number of lines between paragraphs as needed. Also correct spacing between copied or moved sentences or list items.

6. Change the case of text as specified in the illustration.

   ✓ *You can use whatever technique you'd like to change case. You can make edits in your word processing program's Insert mode or type over characters in the Overtype mode. If your program offers a keyboard shortcut, such as pressing Shift+F3 to change the case of selected text or the word holding the insertion point, that may be an even faster way to change the case of letters and entire words.*

7. Save the edited document file.
8. View the document in print preview.
9. Close the print preview.
10. Print one copy of the document.
11. Close the document.

Illustration 2

Precision Software

Solutions for serious users

10/13/2004

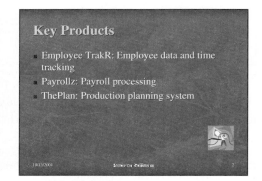

Key Products

- Employee TrakR: Employee data and time tracking
- Payrollz: Payroll processing
- ThePlan: Production planning system

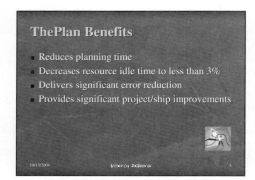

ThePlan Benefits

- Reduces planning time
- Decreases resource idle time to less than 3%
- Delivers significant error reduction
- Provides significant project/ship improvements

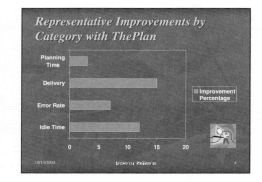

Representative Improvements by Category with ThePlan

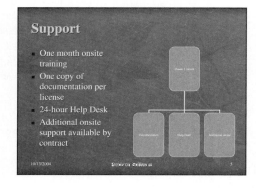

Support

- One month onsite training
- One copy of documentation per license
- 24-hour Help Desk
- Additional onsite support available by contract

Key Clients

- Associated Life & Health
- Major Manufacturing
- BigCo Environmental
- Amber Aluminum Products
- Macy & Clark Window

Copy

The United States Federal Reserve System

HISTORY

Move

Was founded in 1913 by Congress. Created by the federal reserve act, signed into law December 23, 1913 by woodrow wilson. Developed in response to periodic financial panics, especially a large one in 1907.

DEFINITION

Is the central bank for the United States.

PURPOSE

Move to arrange in the order given by number

3 1. Offers some financial services, such as maintaining the nation's payments system. Serves the U.S. government, the public, financial institutions, and foreign official institutions in this capacity.

4 2. Oversees and regulates banking institutions. Both monitors the safety and soundness of the banking and financial system and protects consumers.

1 3. Runs the U.S. monetary policy. Uses various tools to affect the economy's money and credit conditions. Full employment and stable prices are two monetary policy goals.

2 4. Stabilizes the financial system by using tools to combat risk in financial markets.

1"

SYSTEM COMPONENTS

1"

3 • member banks
5 • advisory committees
4 • federal reserve banks
1 • federal open market committees
2 • board of governors

Move to arrange in the order given by number

Illustration 1

Slide 1

Precision Software

Solutions for business users

1

Slide 2

Key Products

- Employee TrakR: Employee data and time tracking
- Payrollz: Payroll processing
- ThePlan: Production planning system

2

Slide 3

Purchase Decision

- What are your needs today?
- What will needs be tomorrow?
- Can your infrastructure handle tomorrow's needs?

3

Slide 4

ThePlan Benefits

- Reduces planning time
- Decreases resource idle time to less than 3%
- Delivers significant error reduction
- Provides significant project/ship improvements

4

Slide 5

Representative Improvements by Category with ThePlan

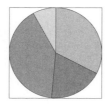

- Idle Time
- Error Rate
- Delivery
- Planning Time

5

Slide 6

Key Clients

- Associated Life & Health
- Major Manufacturing
- BigCo Environmental
- Amber Aluminum Products
- Macy & Clark Window

6

1

Exercise 26

❖ Create Tab Stops

Notes

When you press the Tab key, your word processor moves text so that it lines up with the next **tab stop** set for the paragraph. By default, most word processors have **left tab stops** set every .5" for every paragraph in the document. You can change the tab stop settings for a paragraph or set a different type of tab stop.

With a left tab stop, the left side of the text aligns to the tab stop. With a **right tab stop**, the right side of the text aligns to the tab stops. To align the center of a selection of text with the center of the tab stop, use a **center tab stop**. If you want to align dollar or decimal values in several lines, set a **decimal tab stop**, which aligns all the decimal points. In this exercise, you can work with setting each type of tab stop.

You are helping coach a track team for a local youth group called OnTrack. You've typed up the most recent workout times, and now you'd like to add some tab stops to improve the document's readability.

Vocabulary

tab stop
left tab stop

right tab stop
center tab stop

decimal tab stop
leader

Directions

1. Open the **WP26** document file.
2. Save the file as **TIMES**.
3. Select the two lines at the top of the document.
4. Set a right tab stop at **5"**.
   - ✓ *The tab settings you make apply to the paragraph that holds the insertion point or all selected paragraphs. That's why you have to select all the list items before you set tab stops.*
5. Click outside the selection to deselect it, then insert a tab (by pressing Tab) within each line to align the text as shown in the illustration on the following page.
6. Select the list of runner times.
7. Set a left tab stop at **1"**.
8. Set a center tab stop with a dotted leader at **2. 5"**.
9. Set a decimal tab stop with a dotted leader at **4"**.
   - ✓ A **leader** character repeats in the blank area leading up to the tab stop.
   - ✓ Recent versions of Word also offer a bar type tab stop. When you set this type of tab stop, Word draws a vertical line at the specified location in the document.

15. Make the following changes on the slide master:
    - Add a clip art image to a corner of the slide master.
    - Left align the title.
    - Enter **Precision Software** in the footer area.
    - Turn on display of the date and slide numbers.
    - Change the footer text to another font and increase its size to 16 points.

    ✓ *As with the slide (page) numbering, in some cases you have to turn on the date area and footer area display with a menu command.*

    ✓ *Sometimes, changes you make to the slide master apply to all slide layouts except title slides. In such a case, you have to display a different master to change the layout for title slides.*

16. Close the slide master view, and display slide 1.
17. Change **business** to **serious**.
18. Display the presentation in small slide view. The slides should now look like those in Illustration 2 on page 458.
19. Return to the single slide view.
20. Spell check the presentation.
21. Save your changes to the presentation.
22. Print and close the presentation.

10. Click outside the list to deselect it, then insert tabs (by pressing Tab) before the event, runner, and time on each line to align the text as shown in the illustration. Also insert tabs as shown between the labels in the first row of the list.

11. Delete the spaces that appear after the event and runner on each line of the list.

✓ *In Word, you can choose Tools|Options, click on the View tab, and then click Spaces under Formatting Marks to view the spaces as onscreen dots, making it easier to find and delete them.*

12. Save the edited document file.
13. View the document in print preview.
14. Close the print preview.
15. Print one copy of the document.
16. Close the document.

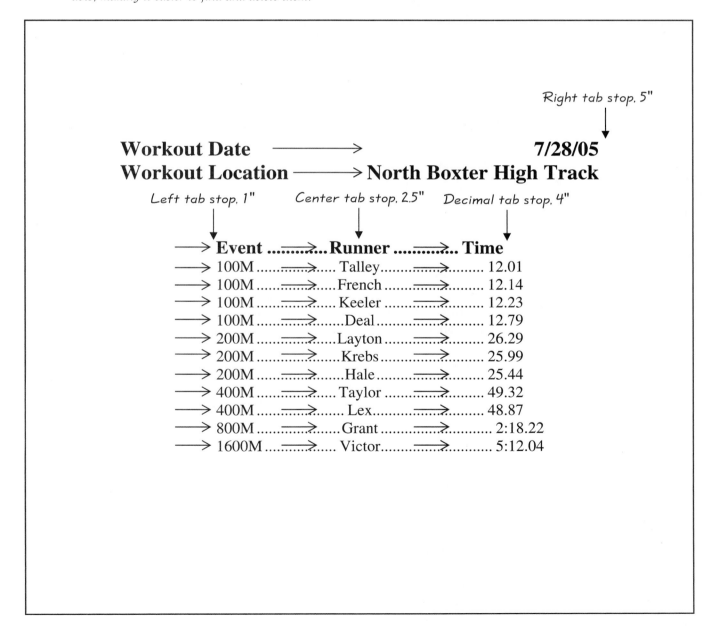

Exercise 10

❖ Align Text ❖ Change Fonts
❖ Change Slide Design (Template)
❖ Change Slide Layout ❖ Use Slide Master

Notes

This exercise reinforces your practice from the last exercise. Again, you will work with altering the appearance for individual slides and the presentation as a whole.

You are in sales for Precision Software. You're updating a sales presentation about your company's key products, including changing presentation information and applying more attractive formatting.

Vocabulary

date area

Directions

1. Open the **PG10** presentation file.
2. Save the file as **PROD**. The six presentation slides look like those in Illustration 1 on page 457.
3. Choose a new presentation template (design).
4. Delete slide 3.
5. Go to slide 4.
6. Add a new slide using the bulleted list layout, and enter **Support** as the slide title. (If the new slide doesn't become slide 5, move it to make it slide 5.)
7. Enter the following as the bulleted list:
   - **One month onsite training**
   - **One copy of documentation per license**
   - **24-hour Help Desk**
   - **Additional onsite support available by contract**
8. Change slide 5 to use the layout that includes a graph placeholder and bulleted list placeholder.

9. Undo the slide layout change.
   - ✓ *You can use the Undo button to undo a layout change that doesn't look right.*
10. Change slide 5 to use the layout that includes a graph beside the bulleted list.
11. Use the graph placeholder to create an org chart or diagram illustrating the bullet points you created in Step 7. (The first bullet point can be the top level of the chart.)
12. Go to slide 4. Change its chart from a pie chart to a bar chart.
   - ✓ *To reselect a chart and display the charting tools and commands, you typically must double-click the chart.*
13. Italicize the slide title.
14. Display the slide master view.

Exercise 27

❖ Critical Thinking

Notes

In this final exercise, you use several skills from this lesson to improve a document's appearance.

You have your own commercial and home cleaning business, Clean Partners. You're working on a basic newsletter to mail to customers.

Vocabulary

byline   initial caps

Directions

1. Open the **WP27** document file.
2. Save the file as **CLEAN**.
3. Format the top three lines of the document with any settings you choose.
4. Move the article titled **We Love to Serve You** to the end of the newsletter.

   ✓ *Don't forget to add or remove spaces or lines as needed when you move or copy text or change formatting. Also, empty blank lines at the end of your document can cause your word processing software to insert an extra blank page, so be sure to delete extra blank lines if this occurs.*

5. Apply 1.5 line spacing to the text of all the articles.
6. Change the titles for the first article, **New Cleaning Products Available Now**, from all uppercase to initial caps (the first letter of each word in uppercase and remaining letters in lowercase). Also change the article title and byline formatting as you choose.
7. Copy the formatting from the **New Cleaning Products Available Now** article title and

byline to the other two articles. (The third article will not have a byline.)

8. Format the quotations in the **We Love to Serve You** last article with the proper indent and line spacing settings for long quotations. Also fix the capitalization in the names of the persons quoted and format the names in italic.

   ✓ *Exercise 21 discussed proper settings for long quotations.*

9. Change the line spacing for the bulleted list in the **New Services to Love** article to single spacing.
10. Apply a first line indent for all article paragraphs except the quotation and bulleted list paragraphs.
11. Adjust the page margins so that all the articles fit on a single page.
12. Save the edited document file.
13. View the document in print preview.
14. Close the print preview.
15. Print one copy of the document.
16. Close the document.

Illustration 2

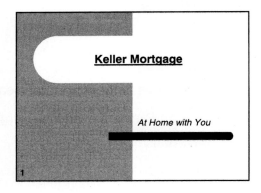

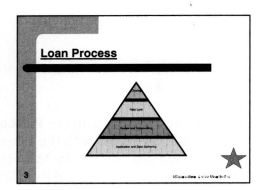

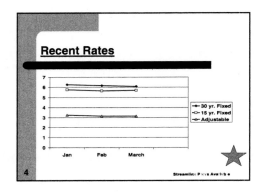

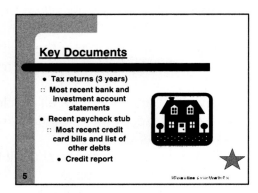

1

Word Processing

Lesson 6
Additional Formatting and Editing

Exercises 28–35

- ❖ Create and edit an outline
- ❖ Work with styles
- ❖ Use the thesaurus and hyphenation
- ❖ Find and replace text in a document
- ❖ Use comments
- ❖ Protect a document

Illustration 1

Slide 1

Keller Mortgage

At Home with You

Slide 2

Mortgages Offered

- Fixed rate, 15-30 year terms
- Adjustable rate, with a variety of adjustment and cap options
- Balloon
- Construction
- Interest only
- Home equity

Slide 3

Loan Process

Slide 4

Recent Rates

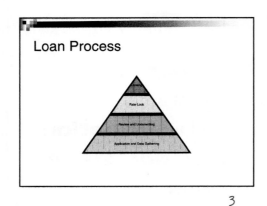

- 30 yr. Fixed
- 15 yr. Fixed
- Adjustable

Slide 5

Key Documents

Exercise 28

❖ Outline Text

Notes

Today's full-featured word processors offer an **outline view** that you can use to organize topics (**headings**) in a document. The outline view organizes the headings in your document by **outline level**. The major headings are called level 1, top-level, or Heading 1 headings. Subheadings are level 2 headings, subheadings under level 2 headings are level 3 headings, and so on. As you build your outline, you can **promote** a heading to a higher level or **demote** it to a lower level.

When you create a formal outline, such as an outline page for the beginning of a report, you need to adhere to formal outline style. Formal outline style calls for proper capitalization and includes at least two headings at every heading level. For example, if you add one level 2 heading under the first level 1 heading in your outline, you must add a second level 2 heading under that first level 1 heading. In addition, you must include proper **outline numbering**. While a number of outline numbering styles exist, the academic style you'll practice in this exercise uses Roman numerals for level 1 headings, capital letters for level 2 headings, and Arabic numerals for level 3 headings. Many word processors offer automatic outline numbering to help you apply the proper numbering style.

You are ready to begin writing your paper on the Federal Reserve System for the economics course. In this exercise, create an outline of the topics you plan to cover.

Vocabulary

outline view	outline level	promote	demote
headings			outline numbering

Directions

1. Create a new, blank document.
2. Switch to the outline view.
3. Enter the first five lines of the outline shown in the illustration on page 101. Do NOT type the outline numbers; you will apply those in a later step.
   - ✓ Use Tab and Shift+Tab to choose the heading level for each new line in your outline.
   - ✓ If you're creating an outline for a more casual or personal document, you don't have to follow the formal outline style of having at least two headings at each level.

4. Turn on automatic outline numbering, if available, and choose the numbering style shown in the illustration.
   - ✓ In Word, choose Format | Bullets and Numbering, click the Outline Numbered tab, click the outline numbering style to use, then click OK. If your word processor doesn't offer automatic numbering, enter the numbering manually.

14. Make the following changes on the slide master:

    - Underline the title.

    - Enter **Streamline Plans Available** in the **footer** area. Center the text if it doesn't center automatically. Change the text to Arial Black font (or another font without serifs) in 12-point size.

    - Draw a star or starburst shape in the lower-right corner. Fill it with the color and pattern of your choice.

    - Add a page number.

    ✓ *You may have to turn on the slide (page) numbering feature using a menu command. Otherwise, even though the slide or page number appears on the master, it won't print. The menu command also may give you the option of turning on features like page numbering for the title slide. In recent PowerPoint versions, this menu command is View | Header and Footer.*

15. Display the presentation in small slide view. The slides should now look like Illustration 2 on page 454.
16. Return to the single slide view.
17. Spell check and then print the presentation.
18. Save your changes to the presentation.
19. Close the presentation.

5. Continue entering the outline shown in the illustration on the following page.

   ✓ *Because you use the Tab key to control outline levels in the outline view, how do you enter a Tab when you need one, such as after an outline number? Most word processors offer an alternate key combination, such as Ctrl+Tab, for entering Tabs in the outline view. Alternately, you can type your outline information in the normal view, then switch to the outline view and apply outline levels.*

6. Save the file as **RESERVE2**.

7. Switch back to the normal view or page (print) layout view to see how your outline looks.

   ✓ *Notice that the word processing program applies different formatting for each heading level, so you can identify heading levels in views other than outline view. If the formatting does not appear, make sure you turn on that capability. To do so in Word, choose Tools | AutoCorrect Options. Click the AutoFormat As You Type tab, and check the Built-in Heading styles check box.*

8. Switch back to the outline view.

9. Print one copy of the outline.

10. Turn off the outline numbering.

    ✓ *In Word, choose Format | Bullets and Numbering, click the Outline Numbered tab, click None, then click OK. If your word processor doesn't offer automatic numbering, delete the numbering manually.*

11. Print another copy of the outline.

    ✓ *Remember, if your instructor requires it, label and turn in a copy of the printed documents.*

12. Close the document.

Exercise 9

❖ Align Text ❖ Change Fonts
❖ Change Slide Design (Template)
❖ Change Slide Layout ❖ Use Slide Master

Notes

You can adjust the appearance of your presentation slides at any time. In this exercise, you practice changing text in a single location, changing the design for the entire presentation, and changing the layout for a slide.

You're the president of Keller Mortgage, a small hometown lender. Update the company's sales presentation now.

Vocabulary

presentation template (design)   slide master   footer

Directions

1. Open the **PG09** presentation file.
2. Save the file as **KELLER**.
3. Insert a new title slide.
4. Enter **Keller Mortgage** as the title and **At Home with You** as the subtitle.
5. Make sure the title slide is the first slide in the presentation. The presentation should now resemble Illustration 1 on page 453.
6. Choose a new **presentation template (design)**.
7. Center the title on slide 1, if needed.
8. Italicize the subtitle text.
9. Display slide 5.
10. Change the slide to the layout that includes placeholders for both a bulleted list and clip art graphic.

   ✓ In recent PowerPoint versions, click the drop-down arrow near the top right of the task pane and then click on Slide Layout to redisplay the layout choices.

   ✓ If you choose a slide layout that removes the placeholder for text, a chart, or clip art image you've added to a slide, the presentation graphics program may delete that material altogether or move it to an unexpected location.

11. Enter the following list, then select an appropriate clip art image:

   • **Tax returns (3 years)**
   • **Most recent bank and investment account statements**
   • **Recent paycheck stub**
   • **Most recent credit card bills and list of other debts**
   • **Credit report**

12. Center and bold the text in the bulleted list.
13. Display the **slide master** view.

✛ I. **The Origins of the U.S. Federal Reserve System**
    ▭ *A. Created in response to financial market panics*
    ✛ *B. Founded in 1913*
        ▭ 1. **Established by the Federal Reserve Act**
        ▭ 2. **Signed by Woodrow Wilson December 23, 1913**
✛ II. **The Activities of the Federal Reserve System**
    ▭ *A. Definition of the Federal Reserve*
    ✛ *B. Functions*
        ▭ 1. **Conducting monetary policy**
        ▭ 2. **Mitigating market risk**
        ▭ 3. **Providing certain financial services**
        ▭ 4. **Regulating banking institutions**
✛ III. **The Components of the Federal Reserve System**
    ▭ *A. Board of Governors*
    ▭ *B. Federal Open Market Committees*
    ▭ *C. Federal Reserve Banks*
    ▭ *D. Member Banks*
    ▭ *E. Advisory Committees*

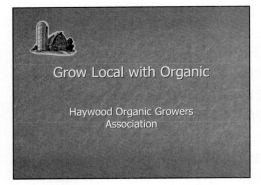

Grow Local with Organic

Haywood Organic Growers
Association

1

Why Organic?

- Food without chemicals or genetic engineering is healthier food
- Organic food has better flavor
- Organic food has superior shelf life
- Consumers prefer organic produce in blind taste tests

2

Why Local?

- Energy efficiency
- Enhanced shelf life
- Local dollars circulate locally for greater economic return
- Adherence to local health standards

3

Local Markets Carrying Organic Products

Earth Good	Grove Market
Haywood Food Co-op	Marshall Tailgate Market
Taylor Food Co-op	Canton Tailgate Market
Fine Foods	Clyde Tailgate Market

4

What HOGA Provides

- Seed capital for new organic farmers and producers
- Mentoring for completion of organic certifications
- Resources and information regarding best practices, pricing, and labor concerns

5

HOGA Officers

Steve Simon
Executive Director

Gail Johnson
Outreach Director

Mark Rogers
Program Director

Al Paulson
Resource Director

6

1

Exercise 29

❖ Edit an Outline

Notes

You may not create the perfect outline right away. You can edit your outline text using the same techniques you use to edit normal text—moving, copying, deleting, inserting new text, and so on. In addition, you can promote or demote selections to another heading level (or **outline level**, if you prefer that term). To check your work, you can **collapse**, or hide, subheadings and text below a particular heading or outline level. **Expand** a heading to redisplay the subheadings and text it holds. In this exercise, you make changes to an outline and learn how to work with outline text.

You are a member of your county council. In preparation for an upcoming council meeting, you've prepared an outline of remarks you'd like to make to attendees. Update that outline with a few changes now.

Vocabulary

outline level   collapse   expand

Directions

1. Open the **WP29** document file.
2. Save the file as **COUNTY**.
3. Change to the normal or page (print) layout view, if needed.
4. Enter the following normal body text after the **Identifying needs** level 1 heading:
   The county has previously failed to perform adequate research before approving budget allocations and planning.
   - ✓ *If you use the outline view to create an outline, the word processing program applies special formatting to the heading levels. When working in another view, you can click at the end of a heading line and press Enter to create a new paragraph that automatically becomes a normal body text paragraph. This makes it easy to flesh out your outline. It's more difficult to add text in*

   outline view, where you often need to choose a button or command to create a body text paragraph.

5. Enter the following normal body text after the **Meeting needs** level 1 heading:
   We can meet needs while better managing costs.
6. Return the insertion point to the beginning of the document.
7. Switch to the outline view.
8. Make the outline changes shown in the illustration on the following page.
   - ✓ *To change a heading's level, place the insertion point within the heading. Press Tab to demote the heading or Shift+Tab to promote it. To promote or demote multiple headings at the same level, select the headings first.*

10. Enter **Local Markets Carrying Organic Products** as the slide title.
11. Select the table placeholder (button), and create a table that's two columns by four rows.
12. Enter the following table information:

Earth Good	Grove Market
Haywood Food Co-op	Marshall Tailgate Market
Taylor Food Co-op	Canton Tailgate Market
Fine Foods	Clyde Tailgate Market

13. Left-align the slide title.
14. Display the small slide view.
15. Rearrange the slides into the order shown on the following page.
16. Return to the single slide view, go to the last slide, and delete it.
17. Save your changes to the presentation.
18. Close the presentation.

9. Select the **Meeting needs** heading, and collapse it to hide both the text and level 2 headings under it.
10. Expand the **Meeting needs** heading to redisplay the text and level 2 headings under it.
11. Collapse the outline so that it shows only level 1 and level 2 headings.
12. Print the outline.
13. Expand the outline so it shows all text and headings.
14. Save the edited document file.
15. Close the document.

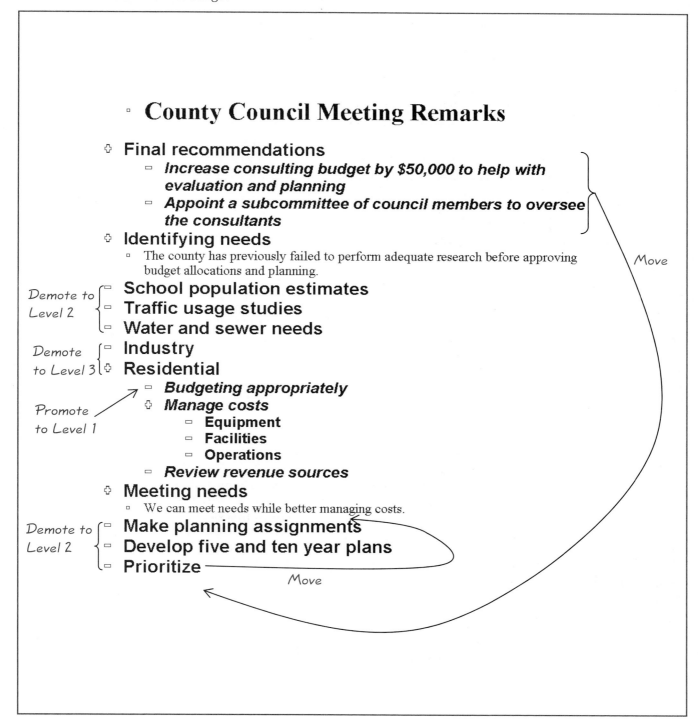

Exercise 8

❖ Add New Slides ❖ Insert a Table on Slides ❖ Insert an Organization Chart on Slides ❖ Move Slides ❖ Delete Slides ❖ Align Text

Notes

You can use additional slide layouts to present information. **Tables** align rows and columns of data, while an **organization chart** shows the arrangement of jobs in a group or organization. In addition to adding more information, you may want to change how text lines up (its **alignment**) to alter the appearance of certain slides.

You need to add some additional information to the presentation you created for the Haywood Organic Growers Association (Exercise 4), such as a chart of the organization leadership and a list of local markets. Make those changes and more now.

Vocabulary

table   organization chart   alignment

Directions

1. Open the **PG08** presentation file.
2. Save the file as **ORGANIC2**.
3. Insert the clip art image of your choice anywhere on slide 1. Insert clip art images on at least two other slides.

   ✓ *Some presentation graphics programs treat decorative graphics and icons as clip art, too.*

4. Insert a slide with placeholders for a title and a single large graph or organization chart.
5. Enter **HOGA Officers** as the slide title.
6. Select the diagram or organization chart placeholder (button) to start making the chart, and choose the organization chart diagram type, if required.

7. Enter the following titles and names, with the first one on the top level of the organization chart:

   • **Steve Simon**
     Executive Director
   • **Gail Johnson**
     Outreach Director
   • **Mark Rogers**
     Program Director
   • **Al Paulson**
     Resource Director

8. Left align the title text on the HOGA Officers slide.
9. Insert a slide with placeholders for a title and a single large graph or table.

Exercise 30

❖ Hyphenate Text
❖ Change a Word Choice (Thesaurus)

Notes

Using a **hyphen** to split a word and move part of it to the next line can increase the length of each line (in left-aligned text), so the right side of the paragraph looks more even. **Hyphenating** justified text also can eliminate a loose appearance in some lines of text. Top-notch word processing programs can hyphenate your text automatically or make it easier for you to specify where a hyphen should fall.

In addition, such programs offer a **thesaurus** feature, which enables you to select a word, find a synonym, then insert the synonym in place of the original word. Work with hyphens and the thesaurus in this exercise.

You have your own business, Light Natural Beeswax Candles. You drafted a description of the product, and now you want to work with hyphenation and word choice in the document.

Vocabulary

hyphen   hyphenate   thesaurus

Directions

1. Open the **WP30** document file.
2. Save the file as **BEES**.
3. Turn on automatic hyphenation. Your word processing program inserts hyphens in the document where needed.

   ✓ *Some word processing programs don't offer the hyphenation and thesaurus features by default. If you try to use either feature and receive a message telling you it's not installed, ask your instructor to install it for you.*

   ✓ *In Word 2003, use the Tools|Language| Hyphenation command to work with hyphenation settings.*

4. Use the thesaurus to find a synonym for the circled words in the illustration on the following page. Replace the words with synonyms.

   ✓ *Notice that as you make changes to the text, the word processing program adds and removes hyphens as needed. If you add hyphens manually (by typing hyphen, pressing Spacebar, and typing the rest of the word until it wraps to the next line), you have to remove them manually—which can lead to stray hyphens in your document.*

   ✓ *In Word 2003, the Research task pane shows you the thesaurus search results. Click the arrow beside a suggested word in the pane and then click Insert to replace the word you selected in the*

Illustration 3

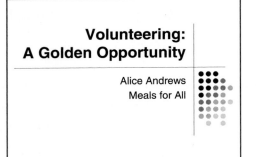

**Volunteering:
A Golden Opportunity**

Alice Andrews
Meals for All

1

Why Volunteer?

- Do something direct for those in need
- Give back to your community
- Show needy people that they deserve human dignity
- Help put your daily wants and needs in their proper perspective

2

Clients Served

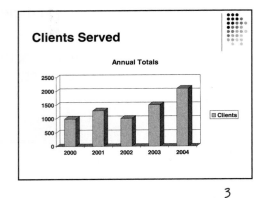

3

Types of People Served

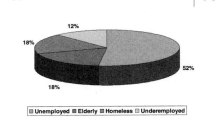

4

Volunteer Jobs

- Publicity assistant
- Fund drive assistant
- Client greeter/assessment
- Food pickup driver
- Food stocker
- Client shopping counselor

5

Let's Make It Work

- Flexible schedule times available
- Tax-deductible expenses verified
- Fun and camaraderie expected
- Fulfillment guaranteed

6

1

document. Then right-click on the next word to look up in the document, point to Synonyms to display a list of similar words, and then click on Thesaurus if you need to look the word up.

5. Save the edited document file.

6. View the document in print preview.
7. Close the print preview.
8. Print one copy of the document.
9. Close the document.

Light Natural Beeswax Candles

The warm glow that surrounds you when you light a room with candles provides a soothing alternative to harsh overhead lighting. No type of candle provides a warmer, cleaner glow than a beeswax candle.

When burned, natural beeswax does not generate toxic indoor pollutants like petrochemical candles. As well, our company uses pure plant oils to scent candles rather than the harsh artificial fragrances found in commercial candles.

Light Natural Beeswax Candles hand makes every candle, ensuring superior craftsmanship and a durable candle. By using natural materials and employing community members, Light Natural Beeswax Candles hopes to make a positive contribution to our world and yours.

Illustration 1

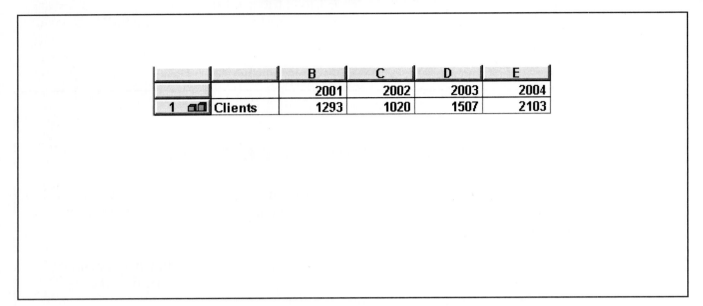

		B	C	D	E
		2001	2002	2003	2004
1	Clients	1293	1020	1507	2103

Illustration 2

		A	B	C	D
		Unemployed	Elderly	Homeless	Underemployed
1	Client segment	52	18	18	12

Exercise 31

❖ Apply a Style

Notes

In Exercise 28, you saw how your word processing software automatically assigns special formatting to help you tell the difference between headings of different heading levels. Each heading level uses a few different formatting settings—font, size, and attributes, for example. Collectively, these attributes form a **style**.

If you create a new, blank document in your word processor, a few styles will be available to you: one for normal text and a few for headings. If you use a template to create your document, it will offer even more styles. This exercise lets you try applying a style to text, to save you the trouble of applying several separate formatting settings and to see how styles can improve formatting consistency.

You work for a small construction firm and are preparing a project estimate for a client. You've typed the estimate information into the document, and now you want to apply some styles that already exist in the file to the document text.

Vocabulary

style   paragraph style

Directions

1. Open the **WP31** document file.
2. Save the file as **PROJEST**.
3. Apply styles to the text as shown in the illustration on the following page.

   ✓ Most styles are **paragraph styles** that apply both text and paragraph formatting settings. Click in a paragraph to place the insertion point, then choose a style for that paragraph. Or, you can select multiple paragraphs before applying the style. In recent Word versions, choose Format, Styles and Formatting to display the available styles in the task pane window at the right.

   ✓ If you don't want to use a menu command to apply styles, most word processing programs also offer a style list on either a toolbar or the status bar.

4. Insert tabs where shown in the illustration on the following page.
5. Save the formatted document file.
6. View the document in print preview.
7. Close the print preview.
8. Print one copy of the document.
9. Close the document.

Exercise 7

❖ Open a Presentation ❖ Add New Slides
❖ Insert a Graph on Slides ❖ Move Slides

Notes

You can insert a graph on a slide to compare data or show trends. Practice with this exercise.

✓ *Some presentation graphics programs use the term* **chart** *rather than* **graph**.

You want to enhance the presentation you created in Exercise 3 to recruit volunteers for the Meals for All food bank. Add some chart slides to the presentation to demonstrate the need for your organization's services.

Vocabulary

chart	datasheet	bar or column chart	plot area
graph	pie chart	legend	

Directions

1. Open the **PG07** presentation file.
2. Save the file as **VOL2**.
3. Insert a slide with placeholders for a title and a single large chart.
4. Enter **Clients Served** as the title for the new slide.
5. Select the chart placeholder (button), and enter the chart data shown in Illustration 1 on the following page.

   ✓ *Sometimes, you have to delete example data cells (cells that you haven't edited already) in the* **datasheet** *to ensure your graph is correct.*

6. Add **Annual Totals** as the chart title.
7. Display slide 5.
8. Insert a slide with placeholders for a title and a single large chart.
9. Enter **Types of People Served** as the title for the new slide.

10. Select the chart placeholder (button), and enter the graph data in Illustration 2. (These numbers represent percentages.)
11. Change the graph to the **pie chart** type in 3D. (The default chart type is usually a **bar** or **column chart**.)
12. Move the **legend** to the bottom of the graph and add percentage value labels.

    ✓ *If a border appears around the* **plot area** *(the area that holds the actual chart series like the pie in this case), you should also remove it. Click the plot area to select it, right-click on the plot area, and then choose Format Plot Area.*

13. Spell check the presentation.
14. Display the small slide view.
15. Rearrange the slides into the order shown in Illustration 3 on page 447.
16. Save your changes to the presentation.
17. Close the presentation.

Project Estimate } *Estimate Title*

Client: Dena White
⟶ 223 Whitmire Drive
⟶ Indianapolis, IN 46225   } *Client*
⟶ 317-555-5555

Project Description: Build 16 ft. x 10 ft. deck with three steps and railing } *Description*

Material   Quantity   Cost
4 x 4 posts   10 $150.00
2 x 12, 10 ft. each   15 $225.28
Ipe decking, 10 ft. each   50 $750.00   } *Items*
Fasteners   n/a $25.35
Footing materials   n/a $85.67
Stain   2 gal. $47.95
Labor   40 hrs. $800.00

Estimate Total: $2,084.25 } *Estimate Total*

11. Display the small slide (slide sorter in PowerPoint) view.
12. Rearrange the slides into the order shown below.

    ✓ *You can drag a slide thumbnail to the desired position in the small slide view. In recent PowerPoint versions, you can drag the slide thumbnail on the **Slides tab** at the left side of the Normal view.*

13. Save your changes to the presentation.
14. Close the presentation.

Crystal Community College and You

1

Get a Degree in...

- Nursing
- Radiology
- Computer technology
- Communications technology
- Business administration
- And more!

2

The CCC Difference

- Expert instructors with full professional credentials
- More accreditations than any other community college
- Small class sizes guaranteed for an enhanced learning experience
- Superior career counseling and job placement track record

3

Come Grow with Us

- Program enrollment begins June 15
- Financial aid and other assistance available
- Evening programs accommodate your working schedule
- Online courses enable flexible scheduling

4

More About CCC

- Centrally-located campus
- Four multimedia labs
- On-campus health care
- Affordable cafeteria
- Accessible by public transportation

5

Exercise 32

❖ Find and Replace Text

Notes

You can use a word processor's **find and replace** feature to find a word and then replace it with another word. In this exercise, you practice replacing multiple occurrences of a company name and car model name in a sales letter. Using find and replace in a case like this ensures that you find all instances of the name or word you want to replace.

Previously, the Clean Partners, Inc. cleaning company operated under a different name. You want to update a document with old brochure information to reflect the new name, as well as make some other changes. Use the find and replace feature to update the document.

Vocabulary

find and replace

Directions

1. Open the **WP32** document file.
2. Save the file as **CLEANBR**.
3. Make sure you start the find and replace operation from the top of the document.
4. Find each occurrence of **Sparkle Cleaning** and replace it with **Clean Partners**.

   ✓ *You also can specify that the replacement text use different formatting than the original text.*

5. Replace each occurrence of **555-3434** with **444-3434**.
6. Find the first and third occurrences only of **business** and replace them with **commercial**. At this point, you should have replaced all the circled words in the illustration on the next page.

   ✓ *You can choose to replace all occurrences of the word simultaneously or to review each found word and determine whether or not to replace it.*

7. Return the insertion point to the top of the document.
8. Refer to the illustration on the following page, and replace the words (and phrases) marked for deletion as indicated by the marked insertions using find and replace.

   ✓ *Make sure you replace only the words indicated in the illustration, not other matching words, too.*

   ✓ *After you replace one instance of a word, you can cancel the find and replace operation or enter new words to find and replace.*

9. Save the edited document file.
10. View the document in print preview.
11. Close the print preview.
12. Print one copy of the document.
13. Close the document.

Exercise 6

❖ Open a Presentation ❖ Add New Slides
❖ Insert Clip Art on Slides ❖ Move Slides

Notes

Rarely will you create a perfect presentation the first time through. You may need to add more slides or rearrange slide order. You may also want to include slides with illustrations that emphasize your point.

You work for Crystal Community College, presenting information about your school to high school seniors in your state. Update your presentation now with a new slide and clip art.

Vocabulary

open a presentation file   placeholder   Slides tab
clip art   resize

Directions

1. **Open** the **PG06** presentation file.
2. Save the file as **CCC**.
3. Insert a new slide with the title layout.

   ✓ *Generally, inserting a new slide places it after the current slide in the presentation.*

4. Enter **Crystal Community College and You** as the slide title.
5. Add a **clip art** picture with some type of academic subject matter to the title slide.

   ✓ *When a slide doesn't hold a **placeholder** for clip art, use the Insert|Picture|Clip Art command or its equivalent to view clip art choices. (In PowerPoint 2003, you must next click on the Organize clips link in the task pane.) Then insert or copy and paste the clip art. In some cases, you can drag the clip art from the gallery dialog box and drop it onto the slide.*

6. **Resize** the clip art to an appropriate size and move it to a central position on the slide.

7. Insert a new slide using a layout with both a bullet list and a clip art placeholder.
8. Enter the following slide title and bullet list:

   More About CCC
   - **Centrally-located campus**
   - **Four multimedia labs**
   - **On-campus health care**
   - **Affordable cafeteria**
   - **Accessible by public transportation**

9. Insert an appropriate piece of clip art using the clip art placeholder on the slide.

   ✓ *In recent PowerPoint versions, placeholders include buttons for inserting six types of content: tables, charts, clip art, pictures, diagrams or organization charts, and media clips. In this case, be sure to click on the button for inserting clip art.*

10. Spell check the presentation.

Sparkle Cleaning, Inc.

Who We Are

Sparkle Cleaning, Inc. provides the finest residential and business cleaning services. When you trust Sparkle Cleaning to handle your cleaning needs, you release yourself from cleaning work, freeing up your time for more important ~~pursuits~~ engagements. Our large staff of dedicated workers will ensure that your home or business environment ~~emits~~ shines with the sparkle of health and ~~cleanliness.~~ tidiness.

What We Provide

Sparkle Cleaning offers the full array of residential and business cleaning services. Our regular service provides:

- Cleaning bathroom vanity, toilet, and tub. Mopping bathroom floor.
- Cleaning kitchen sink and countertops. Mopping kitchen floor.
- Vacuuming all rooms.
- Light dusting of desks and other items.

Sparkle Cleaning also can provide these and other services ~~by special arrangement.~~ as requested.

- Window cleaning
- Plant watering
- Making beds with fresh sheets.
- Thorough cleaning of stove and microwave.
- Unload dishwasher.

How You Can Become a Client

All the pros here at Sparkle Cleaning would love to serve you, your family members, and your business colleagues. Call 555-3434 to make an appointment for ~~a personalized~~ customized service quotation.

Sparkle Cleaning, Inc. 555-3434

Lesson 25
Edit and Enhance Slides

Exercises 6–12

- ❖ **Add slides to a presentation**
- ❖ **Enhance a presentation with clip art and design templates**
- ❖ **Format slide text with decorative fonts and text alignments**
- ❖ **Work with charts and tables on slides**
- ❖ **Design a slide master**

Exercise 33

❖ Use Comments

Notes

Comments provide another useful document editing feature in some word processing programs. Unlike tracked changes, comments typically appear in a special balloon, box, or pane in the word processing program. The original author of the document or others can respond to the comment right in that balloon, box, or pane. Each writer's name or initials identify his or her comments and responses. While you cannot incorporate a comment directly into a document like a tracked change, you can copy and paste text from a comment into the document, before deleting the comment.

The Clean Partners, Inc. brochure text has been forwarded to you for your review. Use the comments feature now to communicate your thoughts about the information in the brochure text.

Vocabulary

comments

Directions

1. Open the **WP33** document file.
2. Save the file as **CLEANBR2**.
3. Add the comments shown in the illustration on the following page.

   ✓ Your word processing program marks the comments with the initials specified in the program's user information. If your instructor indicates, you should update the user information with your name and initials before adding your comments. In Word, you can change user information by choosing Tools|Options and then clicking the User Information tab.

   ✓ You can select a word or phrase to which you want to apply the comment. The word processor will then typically highlight the selection along with adding the comment.

4. Hide the comments.

   ✓ In Word 2003, the Reviewing toolbar appears when you insert the first comment. You can use the Reviewing toolbar to work with your comments. For example, use the Show button and its menu to hide and redisplay comments.

5. Delete the last comment.
6. Save the edited document file.
7. View the document in print preview.
8. Close the print preview.
9. Print one copy of the document, with the comments displayed.

   ✓ Typically, the comments will print when displayed on screen and will not print when they're hidden.

10. Close the document.

1 □ **Major Manufacturing Sales Results**
Six months ending June 30

2 □ **Sales by Division**
- Household: $2,508,073
- Commercial: $2,180,676
- Eco: $229,813
- Appliance: $3,652,707

3 □ **Overall Total**
- $8,571,269
- 12% revenue increase
- 7.5% operating income increase
- 14% unit sales increase

4 □ **Focus Areas**
- Improve shipping performance
- Reduce unit rejections to 10 per 1,000
- Replace aging data systems
- Outsource payroll functions
- Enhance employee training

5 □ **Key Opportunities**
- Eco division could begin growing by 40% per year. See acquisitions in this space.
- Small competitors have nabbed 5% of market share. Acquire key small competitors.
- Resource efficiencies. Implement conservation policies and new methods before competitors.

1

Clean Partners, Inc.

Comment: Shouldn't we have a title with more punch?

Who We Are
Clean Partners, Inc. provides the finest residential and commercial cleaning services. When you trust Clean Partners to handle your cleaning needs, you release yourself from cleaning work, freeing up your time for more important engagements. Our large staff of dedicated workers will ensure that your home or business environment shines with the sparkle of health and tidiness.

What We Provide
Clean Partners offers the full array of residential and commercial cleaning services. Our regular service provides:

Comment: Let's indicate how often we clean with our regular service.

- Cleaning bathroom vanity, toilet, and tub. Mopping bathroom floor.
- Cleaning kitchen sink and countertops. Mopping kitchen floor.
- Vacuuming all rooms.
- Light dusting of desks and other items

Comment: We should probably clarify what we mean by "items."

Clean Partners also can provide these and other services as requested:
- Window cleaning
- Plant watering
- Making beds with fresh sheets.
- Thorough cleaning of stove and microwave.
- Unload dishwasher.

Comment: We should also note that we can offer the regular service with a special schedule.

How You Can Become a Client
All the pros here at Clean Partners would love to serve you, your family members, and your business colleagues. Call 444-3434 to make an appointment for a customized service quotation.

Clean Partners, Inc. 444-3434

Comment: What about a slogan to make our name more memorable?

Exercise 5

❖ Critical Thinking

Notes

The more presentations you create, the more comfortable you'll be. This exercise gives you additional practice in entering and working with a presentation.

You work in Finance at Major Manufacturing and need to create a presentation to share sales data with employees. Create slides to communicate that information now.

Vocabulary

No new vocabulary in this exercise.

Directions

1. Create a new presentation, choosing a presentation design.
2. Make the first slide a title slide.
3. Switch to the outline view.
4. Enter the outline for the five slides shown below.
5. Return to the single slide view.
6. Display slide 1.
7. Spell check the presentation.
8. View the presentation in small slide view.
9. Save the presentation file as **MM6M**.
10. Print the slides with multiple small slides per page.
11. Close the presentation file.

Exercise 34

❖ Protect a Document ❖ Specify Exceptions
❖ Add a Password

Notes

E-mail viruses, identity and information theft, and other privacy concerns have become increasingly common problems for both individual and corporate computer users. Virus protection and other types of programs provide the right protection in some circumstances. However, when you *want* to share a document that includes sensitive information, you need other tools, instead. Leading word processing programs give you one or more ways to apply **protection** to a document. For example, in Word 2003, you can prevent recipients of your document from applying disallowed styles; prevent all document changes; allow readers to add only tracked changes, comments, or form fill-in information; or apply a password for opening or editing the document.

You are the director of Manufacturing Group 2 for Major Manufacturing. You want to send a memo confirming an employee's promotion and raise. Apply a password to that memo now, as well as making the document read-only, except for the memo header information.

Vocabulary

protection   exceptions

Directions

1. Open the **WP34** document file.
2. Save the file as **PROMOTE**.
3. Use the protection settings to start the process for making the document read-only.

   ✓ *In Word 2003, choose Tools|Protect Document and then work in the Protect Document task pane to set protections.*

   ✓ *If your word processing program doesn't enable you to control who can edit a document and how it can be edited, skip to Step 12.*

4. Select the first six lines of the document.

5. Make an **exception** so that all users (Everyone) can edit those lines in the document.
6. Start the protection.
7. Apply **student1** as the protection password.

   ✓ *In Word 2003, a yellow highlighted area will appear to indicate the area of the document that can be edited. (Other word processing programs may use a different method to identify protected text.)*

8. Save the document file.
9. Attempt to change the salary rate increase to **6%**. You will not be able to make the change.

Illustration 3

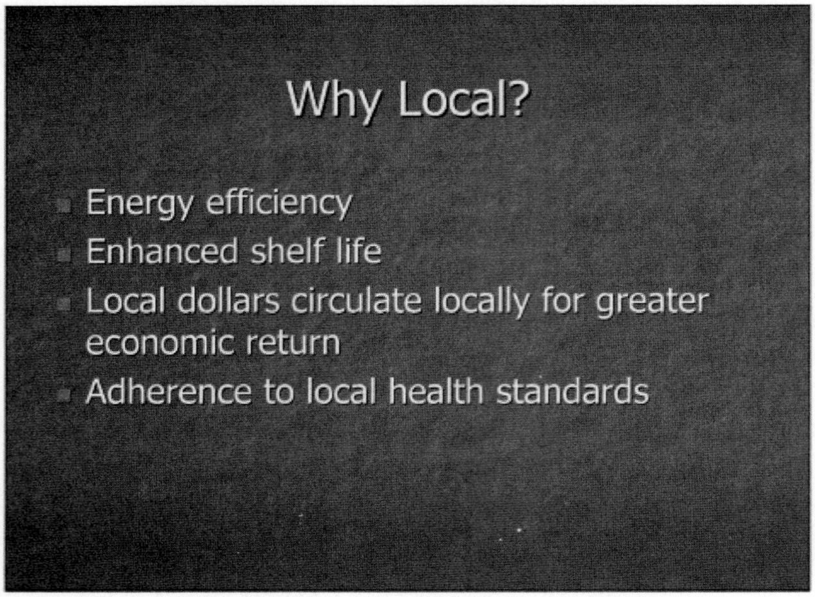

Why Local?

- Energy efficiency
- Enhanced shelf life
- Local dollars circulate locally for greater economic return
- Adherence to local health standards

According to the EPA, shipping commercial produce typically increases energy consumption by 25% or more.

This area has experienced Hepatitis outbreaks caused by improperly handled foods imported from other countries.

3

10. Close the document.
11. Reopen it. You were not prompted for a password (the earlier password only enables you to control the editing protection).
12. Apply **student2** as the password for opening the document.

    ✓ *In Word 2003, choose Tools | Options, and then click on the Security tab to find document password settings.*

13. View the document in print preview.
14. Close the print preview.
15. Save and close the document.
16. Reopen the document, entering the **student2** password.
17. Close the document.

Illustration 2

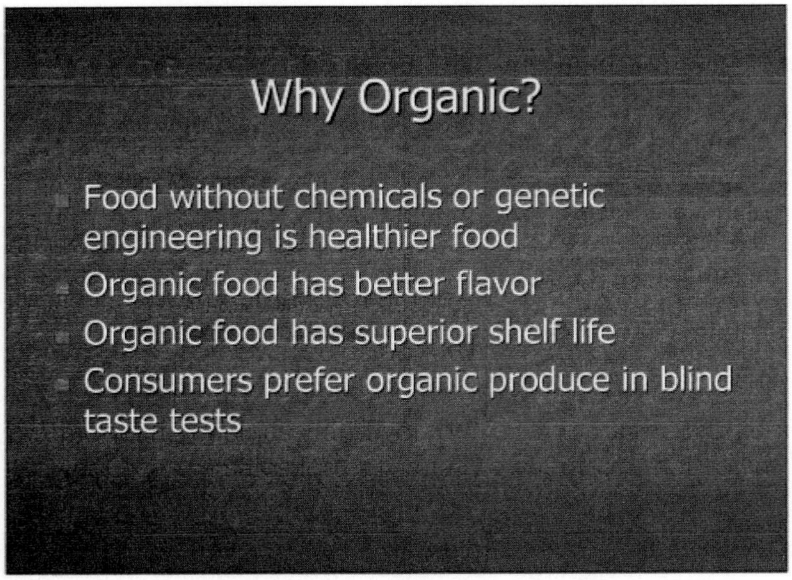

Why Organic?

- Food without chemicals or genetic engineering is healthier food
- Organic food has better flavor
- Organic food has superior shelf life
- Consumers prefer organic produce in blind taste tests

The average commercially-grown produce item tested by the EPA and FDA in 2000 was contaminated by three or more chemicals.

Taste testing conducted in 2002 by Best Product Reports.

2

Exercise 35

❖ Critical Thinking

Notes

You covered a lot of ground in the preceding exercises in this lesson. Refresh a few of your skills here.

You are a dentist, and you're writing an informational newsletter telling clients how to prevent tooth stains. Make some changes to the document now, add a comment because a colleague will review the document for you, and then assign a password.

Vocabulary

No new vocabulary in this exercise.

Directions

1. Open the **WP35** document file.
2. Save the file as **TOOTH**.
3. Add some new text on the blank line immediately after the **Stain Causes** heading.
4. Change to the outline view, and apply outlining levels to the document headings.
   - ✓ Hint: *You should end up with at least three level 1 headings and two level 2 headings.*
   - ✓ Hint: *If you use Shift+Tab to promote the headings in Word, Word also applies the heading style formatting. If you use the Promote and Demote buttons instead, you'll have to select the text and then apply the heading level styles.*
5. Change back to normal or print layout view.
6. Turn on automatic hyphenation.
7. Delete any blank lines that are no longer needed due to the outline style formatting.
8. Use Find and Replace to replace **tetracycline** with **certain antibiotics**.
9. Use the Thesaurus to replace the word **proven** in the second sentence of the document.
10. Select the second paragraph under the **At Home** heading, and add the following comment:
    Perhaps mention a price range for kits?
11. Specify **6tooth6** as the password for opening the document.
12. Save the edited document file.
13. View the document in print preview.
14. Close the print preview.
15. Print one copy of the document, with the comment displayed.
16. Close the document.

Illustration 1

1 ▣ **Grow Local with Organic**
    Haywood Organic Growers Association

2 ▣ **Why Organic?**
- Food without chemicals or genetic engineering is healthier food
- Organic food has better flavor
- Organic food has superior shelf life
- Consumers prefer organic produce in blind taste tests

3 ▣ **Why Local?**
- Energy efficiency
- Enhanced shelf life
- Local dollars circulate locally for greater economic return
- Adherence to local health standards

4 ▣ **What HOGA Provides**
- Seed capital for new organic farmers and producers
- Mentoring for completion of organic certifications
- Resources and information regarding best practices, pricing, and labor concerns

1

Quiz Break 2

Circle the correct answer to each of the questions below:

T	F	1. You have to press Enter at the end of every line when you type text.
T	F	2. Word processor file names can only have eight characters.
T	F	3. Most word processing programs today can check both spelling and grammar.
T	F	4. You can have the spelling checker ignore all instances of a word.
T	F	5. You can see how a printout will look before you send it to the printer.
T	F	6. You can center text two ways: vertically and horizontally between the margins.
T	F	7. You generally click a toolbar button to insert a symbol.
T	F	8. You generally click a toolbar button to apply or remove automatic bullets and numbering.
T	F	9. If you move text within a list created using automatic numbering, it will renumber itself.
T	F	10. You use the Margins dialog box to change margins.
T	F	11. Most word processing programs offer at least four types of tab stops.
T	F	12. Word processing programs hyphenate text automatically by default.

Fill in your brief answers below:

1. When you insert text within existing text, you are using this mode: _____

2. When you add text by typing new text over old text, you are using this mode: _____

3. Superscript text appears: _____

4. Subscript text appears: _____

5. If you make a mistake, you can use this feature to back up and remove it: _____

6. With this feature, you use the mouse to copy and move text: _____

7. Use this type of tab stop to align numbers and dollar values: _____

8. Use this feature to replace a word you've selected with a more appropriate or descriptive word: _____

9. Assign heading levels in this view: _____

10. A collection of formats saved under a name so you can apply the formatting quickly is called a: _____

Exercise 4

❖ Create a Presentation
❖ Create Speaker Notes
❖ Save a Presentation ❖ Print a Presentation

Notes

You need to keep slides concise, but you may need to provide additional information when you give your presentation. Presentation graphics programs enable you to enter and print notes for each slide to use while you're speaking.

You lead the Haywood Organic Growers Association, and you want to create a presentation to for a meeting of the local Chamber of Commerce. Create the presentation, with speaker notes, now.

Vocabulary

speaker notes

Directions

1. Create a new presentation, choosing a presentation design.
2. Make the first slide a title slide.
3. Switch to the outline view.
4. Enter the outline for the four slides shown in Illustration 1 on the following page.
5. Switch to the **speaker notes** view or click in the pane where you enter speaker notes.
6. Display slide 2 and enter the notes shown in Illustration 2 on page 438.
7. Display slide 3 and enter the notes shown in Illustration 3 on page 439.
8. Spell check the presentation.
9. Save the presentation file as **ORGANIC**.
10. Print the slides with the speaker notes.
11. Close the presentation file.

Circle the correct answer to each of the questions below:

1. You move around in a document by:
    A. Clicking with the mouse to position the insertion point.
    B. Pressing an arrow key.
    C. Scrolling with the scroll bar and then clicking with the mouse.
    D. All of the above.

2. Using the document review or revision marking features does the following:
    A. Marks additions and identifies who made them.
    B. Generates a new edited copy of the document.
    C. Marks deletions and identifies who made them.
    D. A and C only.

3. To set off a long quotation in a document, you generally:
    A. Triple space it.
    B. Single space it and indent by .5 inch from the left and right margin.
    C. Double space it and format it all in bold.
    D. None of the above.

4. To reuse formatting in a document, you can:
    A. Copy text with the formatting you want, then replace the copied text so the new text uses the formatting you want.
    B. Copy or paint the formatting from one selection to another.
    C. Apply a style that has the formatting you want.
    D. B and C only.

5. This feature can help you make edits throughout the document:
    A. Find and Replace.
    B. AutoEdit.
    C. Word Highlight.
    D. Fast Edit.

6. This feature enables you to communicate your thoughts about a document without editing the document text:
    A. Document Marker.
    B. Whisper.
    C. Comments.
    D. Sidelines.

7. Most word processors enable you to control who can open a document by:
    A. Assigning a password.
    B. Creating a user list.
    C. Checking users.
    D. Asking for bounceback.

1 ▦ Volunteering:
A Golden Opportunity
Student's Name
Meals for All

2 ▦ Why Volunteer?
- Do something direct for those in need
- Give back to your community
- Show needy people that they deserve human dignity
- Help put your daily wants and needs in their proper perspective

3 ▦ Volunteer Jobs
- Publicity assistant
- Fund drive assistant
- Client greeter/assessment
- Food pickup driver
- Food stocker
- Client shopping counselor

4 ▦ Let's Make It Work
- Flexible schedule times available
- Tax-deductible expenses verified
- Fun and camaraderie expected
- Fulfillment guaranteed

1

Word Processing

Lesson 7
Working with Multiple-Page Documents

Exercises 36–44

- ❖ Use special views for multi-page documents
- ❖ Create page and section breaks in a document
- ❖ Work with multiple-page letters and reports
- ❖ Enhance a document with headers, footers, and page numbers
- ❖ Add headers and footers to multiple-page documents
- ❖ Use endnotes
- ❖ Practice moving and copying text in multiple-page documents

Exercise 3

❖ Create a Presentation ❖ Choose Views
❖ Save a Presentation ❖ Print a Presentation

Notes

When you create a presentation, you need to both arrange information on each slide and organize the slides in a logical order. Use the **single slide (normal) view** to perfect slides one at a time. Use the **outline view** to enter information. Use the **small slide (slide sorter) view** to rearrange slides in the presentation.

You are the volunteer manager for the Meals for All food bank. A number of large local businesses have agreed to allow you to make a presentation to employees so you can recruit more volunteers. Write and print a handout for your presentation now.

Vocabulary

single slide (normal) view   outline view   small slide (slide sorter) view   handouts

Directions

1. Create a new presentation, choosing a presentation design.
2. Make the first slide a title slide.
3. Switch to the outline view in your presentation graphics program.
4. Enter the text for the four slides shown on the following page. (Enter your name on the title slide.)

   ✓ *Don't put too much information on a slide. Six bulleted items fit nicely on a slide using the single-column bulleted list layout. When in doubt, use fewer bullet points per slide.*

5. Switch to the single slide view.

6. Use the method of your choice to display slide 1.
7. Switch to the small slide view.
8. Redisplay slide 3 in the single slide view.
9. Save the presentation file as **VOL**.
10. Print the presentation outline.
11. Print the presentation with four small slides per page.

    ✓ *Some presentation graphics programs call printouts with multiple slides per page **handouts**.*

12. Close the presentation file.

Exercise 36

❖ Use Reading Layout View
❖ Use Document Map View
❖ Use Thumbnails View

Notes

When you're working in one of the usual views in a word processing program, you can only see a part of a particular document page on-screen at any given time. This makes it slower to read or move around in the document, because you have to scroll frequently or quickly.

Many word processing programs now offer additional views to help you more quickly read and scroll through a document. For example, Word 2003 offers **reading layout view**, which hides unneeded toolbars and divides the document into multiple enlarged screens of information, for more comfortable reading. Word also offers the **document map** and **thumbnails views**, which enable you to jump to a particular point in a document by clicking a document heading or page thumbnail, respectively, in a pane that appears at the left side of the screen. Other word processing programs offer their own views to help you read and navigate a document.

You are reviewing a multi-page document for your dental practice. Use various views to make it easier to read through and navigate the document.

Vocabulary

reading layout view   document map view   thumbnails view

Directions

1. Open the **WP36** document file.
2. Display the document in reading layout view or the equivalent in your word processing program.
3. Scroll down so that screens 2 and 3 appear.

   ✓ *You can display a navigation pane of headings or thumbnails in document map view by clicking the Document Map or Thumbnails buttons on the Reading Layout toolbar.*

   ✓ *You also can press PgDn and PgUp to scroll by two screens at a time.*

4. Scroll down again so that screens 3 and 4 appear.
5. Return to the first page of the document.
6. Switch back to print (page) layout or normal view.
7. Display the document map or the equivalent in your word processing program.
8. Click the **Stain Cures** heading in the map to display that section of text on-screen.
9. Click the **At the Dentist** heading in the map to display that section of text on-screen.

Mike's Motors

Sales Procedures
12/4/06

1

Meet and Greet

- Do not let a customer remain unattended for more than three minutes
- Make eye contact, introduce yourself, and always shake hands with both spouses
- Ask about their current needs
- Suggest one or more models or cars in stock

2

If Not Interested...

- Provide one of your business cards
- Point out the Web site address on the business card and encourage the customer to check for upcoming deals
- Shake hands and bid a polite good-bye

3

If Interested...

- Escort customer indoors
- Offer refreshments
- Provide model brochure (new models)
- Provide datasheet (old and new models)
- Encourage a test drive and accompany customer

4

If Pricing Requested...

- Give our "dealer best pricing" value
- Negotiate price and parameters
- Have price approved by sales manager
- Input loan application information and forward to finance manager
- On all approvals and agreements, finalize payment and delivery details

5

After the Sale...

- Meet customer for actual payment and delivery
- Send a dealer greeting card with handwritten "Thank You" message

6

10. Press Ctrl+Home to return to the top of the document.
11. Display the thumbnails or the equivalent in your word processing program.

   ✓ In Word 2003, *displaying the thumbnails automatically hides the document map.*

12. Click on the thumbnail for page 2 to display that page.

13. Click on the thumbnail for page 1 to display that page.
14. Turn off the thumbnails view to return to the print layout or normal view.
15. Close the document.

Kayak the Flat Waters

When you think of kayaking, you might visualize guys in helmets and life jackets crashing through the water in a rocky river. While folks capable of that type of challenging action certain represent a segment of the kayaking community, many more people today opt to kayak on flatter waters instead.

Even novices can have some success kayaking on the calmer waters of a lake, lagoon, sound, or ocean. The kayaks created for flat water paddling generally are a bit larger and have a flatter bottom. The kayaker sits comfortably on top, without any type of skirting or tether to the kayak. While these craft help provide stability, you have to be prepared to paddle. When you're paddling against the wind or a current, this can give you a significant workout!

You can still mix it up a bit with this type of kayak. It's fun to take one out at the ocean shoreline and catch a wave to surf back in. Just be sure to wear a helmet and lifejacket for that type of action. You're sure to get flipped under the water and some of the spills can be rough.

If you've never tried a kayak and aren't prepared for the whitewater, try the flat water. For less than $100 a day, you can rent all the equipment you need to have a blast. If you're renting a beach house, set aside a day or so for kayaking fun.

Do the New Cruising

If prior cruise ship vacation experiences have left you with a "been there, done that" feeling that makes you write off cruises today, you might want to think again. Today's cruise vacation companies have some great options that will appeal to even jaded cruise veterans.

For example, many cruise ships now work in conjunction with clubs and groups to provide special interest cruise packages. You can learn about investing or cooking while taking a cruise, for example. Or, you can sign up for a cruise that includes intensive yoga or fitness instruction.

If you don't want to think or sweat that much but still want an interesting cruise experience, consider a luxury cruise. Some adults-only ships feature a smaller number of passengers, specialty cuisine, and more. Or, try a cruise destination that you wouldn't otherwise visit, such as Alaska or Costa Rica.

Directory of Files

Exercise	File Name	Page
1	None	—
2	None	—
3	None	—
4	None	—
5	None	—
6	PG06	443
7	PG07	445
8	PG08	448
9	PG09	451
10	PG10	455
11	None	—
12	None	—
13	PG13	465
14	PG14	466
15	PG15	467
16	PG16, PG16-2, PG16-3	468
17	PG17	470

Online Savings?

Have you ever spent hours online researching flight, hotel, and rental car rates, only to learn that your hours of time have saved you a whopping $15 or so? While travel planning Web sites do provide you the convenience of planning your travel from home on your own schedule, they may not offer you great savings as is typically advertised.

We at Go! Travel Consultants don't want to discourage you from using valuable online tools. Indeed, online resources complement our services. The next time you're planning to travel to a particular destination, consider these tips, which may save you even more money:

❖ Spend a limited amount of time researching prices, and then call Go! Travel Consultants. We may be able to recommend a more cost-effective flight and hotel package that includes such extras as ground transportation.
❖ If you're open about your destination, we can tell you about specials that are available during your planned travel dates.
❖ Sign up for our Go! Alerts service. We'll e-mail you about last-minute specials.

Presentation Graphics

Lessons 24-26
Exercises 1-17

Lesson 24
Create, Save, and Print a Presentation

Lesson 25
Edit and Enhance Slides

Lesson 26
Work with Slide Shows

Exercise 38

❖ Format a Multiple-Page Letter
❖ Use Headers/Footers

Notes

When a document contains multiple pages, it is helpful to add information to each page to identify the document. You can set up a **header** to appear at the top of each page, or a **footer** to appear at the bottom of each page. A header or footer can contain any information you want: the document's title, subject, author, date printed, and so on.

You also can set up automatic **page numbering** within a header or footer, so the word processing program prints the proper page number on each page of a printout. In this exercise, work with the formatting of a two-page letter, and set up header/footer information for the second page of the letter.

You're president of Go! Travel Consultants. You've written a letter to a key corporate client about discounts that you've negotiated. Format that letter with footer and page numbering to improve its appearance.

Vocabulary

header   footer   page numbering

Directions

1. Open the **WP38** document file.
2. Save the file as **GOLET**.
3. Replace the **Today's Date** placeholder at the top of the letter with the actual date.
4. Set the left, right, top, and bottom margins to **1.5"**.
5. Move down the document. Replace the name **Scott King** with your own name. Notice that there's an automatic page break after the closing, **Sincerely**.
6. Move the insertion point to the beginning of the paragraph that begins with **It has certainly been a pleasure...,** before the closing.
7. Insert a page break.
8. Leave the insertion point at the new beginning of the second page.
9. Create a footer that includes the name of the company (**Go! Travel Consultants**), the date, and page numbering.

Circle the correct answer to each of the questions below:

1. You can enter database information in:
   A. The database list or table, also called the datasheet.
   B. The entry window.
   C. A form that you create.
   D. Both A and C.

2. You control these settings when you print a database object:
   A. Rotation.
   B. Whether or not headings print.
   C. Orientation.
   D. B and C.

3. When you want a query criterion to compare data to a test or want to create a calculated query field, you:
   A. Enter an expression using operators in the query design view or grid.
   B. Create a formula in a spreadsheet and paste it in the query design view or grid.
   C. Create a special table for the query.
   D. None of the above.

4. The fastest way to sort a database is typically to:
   A. Use the Ascending and Descending commands.
   B. Triple-click the field name.
   C. Click in a field and use a sorting button.
   D. Create a sort object.

5. When creating a report, you control:
   A. The table or query used.
   B. Grouping.
   C. Sorting.
   D. All of the above.

✓ While you can add both a header and footer to a document, in most cases it's sufficient to add one or the other. If you use both a header and footer, make sure you don't place duplicate information in the header and footer. Also, in most letters and reports, you don't want to include a header or footer on the first page or a title page.

✓ In most word processing applications, the header or footer area has a center tab stop set up in the center of the area and a right tab stop set up at the far right. You can use these tab stops to align various parts of the headers and footers.

10. Adjust the center and right tab stops, if needed, to more appropriate locations. You may need to do this because you changed the document margins, and footer (and header) elements look best when they conform to the document margins.

✓ You may need to select dates and page numbers inserted as fields to be able to move the tab stops using the tab stop markers on the ruler.

11. Format the footer to use 11-point Times New Roman font. Also apply boldface to the footer.
12. Turn off the footer display for the first page.
13. Use the print preview or page (print) layout view to examine both pages of the letter. Only the second page should have a footer, as shown in the example that begins on the next page.
14. Save your changes to the document file.
15. Print one copy of the document.
16. Close the document.

Quiz Break 6

Circle the correct answer to each of the questions below:

T	F	1. Some database programs divide information into tables.
T	F	2. Database programs require you to specify a format for each field.
T	F	3. Database programs require you to specify special capitalization for each field.
T	F	4. Entering data in a database resembles entering information in a spreadsheet.
T	F	5. You can drag or double-click on the right side of a field name (column heading) to resize the on-screen or printed field width.
T	F	6. Resizing a field on-screen also changes the field size in the database (table) design.
T	F	7. Changing the font, size, and so on of the database (table or datasheet) on-screen changes its printed appearance, as well.
T	F	8. You cannot change the field type after you've created the database.
T	F	9. You can find a matching record quickly with the find feature.
T	F	10. Finding and querying are the same.
T	F	11. You can save a query and use it again.
T	F	12. You can save a report and use it again.

Fill in your brief answers below:

1. A column of similar information about each item in the database is called a: _____

2. A row of all the information about a single entry in a database is called a: _____

3. To view a database element before printing it, use the _____ feature.   _____

4. Use the _____ feature to create a quick list of records matching criteria you specify.   _____

5. _____ a field to temporarily remove it from view.   _____

6. _____ a field to permanently remove it from the database.   _____

Today's Date

Janet Cahill
Purchasing Department
Major Manufacturing
100 Commerce Loop
Indianapolis, IN 46201

Dear Ms. Cahill:

Thank you for placing your confidence in Go! Travel Consultants. As you know, we worked hard to win Major Manufacturing's business. We want to ensure we do everything we can to keep that business, providing your company with the most cost effective travel services available.

I am pleased to report to you the results of our recent negotiations with key travel partners for Major Manufacturing. We were able to work with those partners to achieve the cost guidelines that you specified at our last meeting. Specifically:

- Excel Air agreed to a **five percent fare reduction** for seven states in the Midwest. Additionally, every tenth business class upgrade will be complimentary.

- Upper Hotel Group agreed to a **three percent rate reduction** for lodging nationwide. Further, it will provide a **10 percent rate reduction** for rental of facilities such as seminar rooms and equipment.

- Rapid Rentals agreed to a **seven percent rate reduction** for car rentals nationwide (reservation 24 hours in advance required).

Each of these vendors has already signed the applicable agreement. Go! Travel Consultants will deliver the necessary discount program cards for your employees to Major Manufacturing within the next two weeks.

Exercise 25

❖ Critical Thinking

Notes

You've now learned a number of powerful skills for viewing and using the data in your databases. Practice with skills such as finding records, querying, sorting, and reporting now.

Your Entomology professor has asked you to report some information from your database of butterfly and moth sightings. Use your new database skills to respond to those requests in this exercise.

Vocabulary

No new vocabulary in this exercise.

Directions

1. Create a copy of the **DB25** database file. Save the copy as **ENT2**.
2. Open the **ENT2** database file (and table, if your database program uses separate tables).
3. Find each record with **Indian Blanket** in the **Species** field.
4. Return to the first record in the database (data table).
5. Close the data table, if needed.
6. Create a query that lists records with **SightDate** entries later than **6/20/05** and with **Moth** in the **Type** field. Name the query **ENT2Q**. (This query finds the number of moths observed during the second week of the assignment.)
7. Open (run) the query, then save and close it.

   ✓ *If your instructor wants you to print and submit a copy of the query, the sorted table, or either of the reports you create, do so.*

8. Open the **ENT2** table.
9. Sort the database in ascending order by the **Count** field.
10. Close the table, saving the table design.
11. Create a report using the data in the **ENT2** table, using all fields except the ID field. Do not group or sort the table, and choose the layout and design of your choice. Name the report **ENT2R1**. Finish and preview the report, then close the report.

    ✓ *Saving the table design saved the table in sorted order. That means you don't have to apply the sort in the report.*

12. Create another report using the data in the **ENT2Q** query, using all fields except the ID field. Apply the settings of your choice. Name the Report **ENT2R2**. Finish and preview the report.
13. Close the report.
14. Close the database file.

It has certainly been a pleasure providing travel services to Major Manufacturing. Our firm looks forward to a long and beneficial relationship with your company. If you have any additional needs or issues to discuss, please contact me at my office.

Sincerely,

Scott King
President
Go! Travel Consultants

Illustration 2

Overstock Sale Pricing

Company	SalePrice	Line	Gend	Color	NoInStock	FullPrice
Blazers	$49.49	Adventure	F	Black	18	$65.99
Blazers	$49.49	Adventure	M	Black	15	$65.99
Blazers	$52.50	Kix	F	Brown	19	$70.00
Blazers	$54.00	Kix	M	Brown	20	$72.00
Blazers	$90.59	Cascade	F	Brown	13	$120.79
Lindross	$68.24	Winger	M	Burgundy	18	$90.99
Screech	$67.49	LightWing	F	Gray	27	$89.99
Screech	$74.99	Fleming	M	Gray	23	$99.99
Trail Boss	$54.74	Linda	F	Black	18	$72.99
Western	$52.49	Cali	F	Burgundy	18	$69.99

Wednesday, October 13, 2004

Exercise 39

❖ Format a Multiple-Page Report or Document
❖ Use Headers/Footers

Notes

The longer your document becomes, the more valuable a header or footer can be. For example, if a reader photocopies a single page of the document to give to others, he or she will know exactly where that photocopy came from.

You're still working on the Go! Travel Consultants newsletter document from Exercise 37. In this exercise, add a header and footer to a copy of that document file.

Vocabulary

No new vocabulary in this exercise.

Directions

1. Open the **WP39** document file.
2. Save the file as **GO2**. This document includes a section break inserted to create a title page and a page break to align a heading at the top of the third page.
3. Set the left, right, top, and bottom margins for the whole document to **1.25"**.
4. Move the insertion point to the second page of the document.
5. Create a header that reads **You Go! Newsletter**.

   ✓ *To set up a header or footer for any section in a document, the insertion point must be in that section. If your document has no sections, a header or footer applies to the entire document. In that case, you set up a first page header or a first page footer.*

6. Center the header text and format it in 12-point Gill Sans Ultra Bold Condensed font (or a similar font).

7. Create a footer that includes the date, page number, and company name.
8. Format the footer in 12-point Gill Sans Ultra Bold Condensed font (or a similar font).
9. Move the insertion point to the first page (section) of the document.
10. Turn off the header and footer display for the first page (section) of the document.

    ✓ *To turn off the header and footer in some word processing programs, you specify that the first page should display a different header and footer, and then you leave the header and footer areas blank.*

11. Use the print preview or page (print) layout view to examine all pages of the report. The illustration that begins on the following page shows how the document should look.
12. Save your changes to the document file.
13. Print one copy of the document.
14. Close the document.

Illustration 1 (Page 2 of 2)

| | | M | Fender | Black | 12 | $99.99 |

Company   _Trail Boss_

Gender	Line	Color	NoInStock	FullPrice
F	Linda	Brown	4	$72.99
F	Linda	Black	18	$72.99
M	Keller	Brown	8	$75.99

Company   _Western_

Gender	Line	Color	NoInStock	FullPrice
F	Cisco	Black	4	$82.50
F	El Paso	Black	10	$102.00
F	Cali	Burgundy	18	$69.99
M	El Paso	Black	12	$102.99
M	Cali	Burgundy	12	$73.99
M	Cisco	Black	12	$85.50

Wednesday, October 13, 2004

You Go!

By Janet Mason
Go! Travel Consultants

Illustration 1 (Page 1 of 2)

Sale Items by Company

Company   *Blazers*

Gender	Line	Color	NoInStock	FullPrice
F	Kix	Brown	19	$70.00
F	Adventure	Black	18	$65.99
F	Rox	Black	12	$75.99
F	Cascade	Brown	13	$120.79
M	Rox	Black	8	$79.99
M	Adventure	Black	15	$65.99
M	Kix	Brown	20	$72.00
M	Spectrum	Umber	9	$55.75
M	Cascade	Brown	11	$120.79
M	Spectrum	Umber	9	$55.75

Company   *Lindross*

Gender	Line	Color	NoInStock	FullPrice
F	Winger	Burgundy	12	$85.99
M	Winger	Burgundy	18	$90.99

Company   *Screech*

Gender	Line	Color	NoInStock	FullPrice
F	LightWing	Gray	27	$89.99
F	Owl	Gray	10	$77.95
F	LightWing	Brown	8	$89.99
M	Fleming	Gray	23	$99.99
M	Owl	Gray	12	$79.95

Company   *TopLine*

Gender	Line	Color	NoInStock	FullPrice
F	Fender	Black	7	$95.99
F	LowRide	Gray	7	$65.99
M	LowRide	Gray	12	$69.99

Wednesday, October 13, 2004

Page 1 of 2

You Go! Newsletter

Kayak the Flat Waters

When you think of kayaking, you might visualize guys in helmets and life jackets crashing through the water in a rocky river. While folks capable of that type of challenging action certain represent a segment of the kayaking community, many more people today opt to kayak on flatter waters instead.

Even novices can have some success kayaking on the calmer waters of a lake, lagoon, sound, or ocean. The kayaks created for flat water paddling generally are a bit larger and have a flatter bottom. The kayaker sits comfortably on top, without any type of skirting or tether to the kayak. While these craft help provide stability, you have to be prepared to paddle. When you're paddling against the wind or a current, this can give you a significant workout!

You can still mix it up a bit with this type of kayak. It's fun to take one out at the ocean shoreline and catch a wave to surf back in. Just be sure to wear a helmet and lifejacket for that type of action. You're sure to get flipped under the water and some of the spills can be rough.

If you've never tried a kayak and aren't prepared for the whitewater, try the flat water. For less than $100 a day, you can rent all the equipment you need to have a blast. If you're renting a beach house, set aside a day or so for kayaking fun.

Do the New Cruising

If prior cruise ship vacation experiences have left you with a "been there, done that" feeling that makes you write off cruises today, you might want to think again. Today's cruise vacation companies have some great options that will appeal to even jaded cruise veterans.

For example, many cruise ships now work in conjunction with clubs and groups to provide special interest cruise packages. You can learn about investing or cooking while taking a cruise, for example. Or, you can sign up for a cruise that includes intensive yoga or fitness instruction.

If you don't want to think or sweat that much but still want an interesting cruise experience, consider a luxury cruise. Some adults-only ships feature a smaller number of passengers, specialty cuisine, and more. Or, try a cruise destination that you wouldn't otherwise visit, such as Alaska or Costa Rica.

Today's Date   2   Go! Travel Consultants

6. Create a grouping level using the **Company** field.

   ✓ *When you specify a field as a **grouping level**, the report groups information by the entries in that field. You can set up grouping levels within grouping levels to create a more complicated report.*

7. Sort the report information in ascending order by the **Gender** field.

   ✓ *This choice sorts the records within each **Company** group, according to the entries in the **Gender** field.*

8. Choose an align left layout and portrait orientation for the report.

9. Choose a report style that's corporate or formal.

10. Name the report **Sale Items by Company**, and finish the report creation process.

11. If the finished report doesn't appear on-screen, display it.

12. Print one copy of the report. Illustration 1 starting on the following page shows how this printed report should look.

    ✓ *It's not unusual for some of the text in a report to appear cut off or for a page break to be awkward, as in the examples here. You can handle that by changing to the view for designing a report and adjusting the report formatting—after you've created and previewed the report.*

13. Close the report.

14. Start the report creation process.

15. Verify that the report will use the data from the **BSALE4Q** query.

16. Add all fields but the **ItemNo** field to the report.

17. Do not add any grouping level.

18. Sort the report information in ascending order by the **Company** field.

19. Specify a second sort to sort information in ascending order by the **SalePrice** field.

    ✓ *This choice sorts the records according to **Company**, then by **SalePrice**.*

20. Choose a tabular layout and portrait orientation for the report.

21. Choose a report style that's casual.

22. Name the report **Overstock Sale Pricing**, and finish the report creation process.

23. If the finished report doesn't appear on-screen, display it.

24. Print one copy of the report. Illustration 2 shows how this printed report should look.

25. Close the report.

26. Close the database file.

You Go! Newsletter

Online Savings?

Have you ever spent hours online researching flight, hotel, and rental car rates, only to learn that your hours of time have saved you a whopping $15 or so? While travel planning Web sites do provide you the convenience of planning your travel from home on your own schedule, they may not offer you great savings as is typically advertised.

We at Go! Travel Consultants don't want to discourage you from using valuable online tools. Indeed, online resources complement our services. The next time you're planning to travel to a particular destination, consider these tips, which may save you even more money:

❖ Spend a limited amount of time researching prices, and then call Go! Travel Consultants. We may be able to recommend a more cost-effective flight and hotel package that includes such extras as ground transportation.
❖ If you're open about your destination, we can tell you about specials that are available during your planned travel dates.
❖ Sign up for our Go! Alerts service. We'll e-mail you about last-minute specials.

Exercise 24

❖ Create, Format, and Print a Report
❖ Group Data

Notes

A data table (datasheet) presents information in a boring format. Printing forms may not yield the right results, because you have less control over which records print when you print forms. You can get the best of both worlds by printing a **report**. Because reports are designed to summarize database information for formal purposes, they use more attractive formatting. And, you can base a report on a query (rather than the entire database) to limit the information stored in the report.

You can further improve upon the formatting in your reports by **grouping** the information in them. Like sorting, grouping places all the records with a particular entry together in the report, so you can see all the related records. Unlike with sorted information, however, the report applies special formatting to the grouped information, so each group is easy to identify.

You want to apply more attractive formatting to your Mountain Gear boot sale database, so you can generate information about the sale pricing to your employees. Try generating reports from the database now.

Vocabulary

report   grouping   grouping level

Directions

1. Create a copy of the **DB24** database file. Save the copy as **BSALE4**.
2. Open the **BSALE4** database file.
3. Start the report creation process.

   ✓ *Some database programs offer a wizard or helper to lead you through the report creation process. In Access, it's much easier to use a wizard to create a report.*

4. Verify that the report will use the data from the **BSALE4** table (assuming your database program uses a separate name for each table; otherwise just use the data table view of your database program).
5. Add all fields but the **ItemNo** field to the report.

Exercise 40

❖ Footnotes ❖ Page Numbers

Notes

Many word processing programs now include features to help you set up **footnotes** with a minimum of effort. You don't have to worry about formatting the numbers as superscript or estimating how much space the footnote requires at the bottom of the page. Just position the insertion point after the text that requires a **citation**, use the command for inserting a footnote, and type the footnote text. Your word processing program takes care of the numbering and most of the formatting for you.

In addition, if your document requires page numbers but not a full header or footer, you can turn on **automatic page numbering** to supply numbers for your pages.

In Exercise 16, you wrote a brief explanation of how to use the speed of light to calculate the distance between celestial bodies. Complete the assignment now by adding footnotes and page numbering.

Vocabulary

footnotes   citation   automatic page numbering

Directions

1. Open the **WP40** document file.
2. Save the file as **LIGHTSP2**.
3. Set the left, right, top, and bottom margins for the whole document to **1.5"**.
4. Add a page break after the document title.
5. Add your name to the title page. Format the page and text as you want.
6. Turn on automatic page numbering.
7. Set up the page numbers to display at the bottom-right corner of the page, and turn off the page number display for the first page.
8. Create the two footnotes shown in the illustration on page 135.

   ✓ *In the most recent versions of Word, you use a new command (Insert|Reference|Footnote) to add each footnote.*

   ✓ *You do have to enter and format the footnote text by hand, even though your word processing program will add and format the numbers, allow the proper spacing for the footnotes, and add a divider line. Be sure to follow the footnote style, such as MLA style, required by your school and course instructors. The desired style may vary from course to course.*

9. Use the print preview or page (print) layout view to examine all pages of the document.
10. Save your changes to the document file.
11. Print one copy of the document.
12. Close the document.

Illustration

Pattern	Qty	Code	Piece Name	Diameter	Capacity	Price
Abundance	8	FRR	BOWL-FRUIT/DESSERT (SAUCE)-RIM	5.5		9.99
Abundance	2	SP	PLATE-SALAD	8.25		11.99
Abundance	9	CERR	BOWL-CEREAL/RIM	6.5		12.99
Abundance	1	SAL	SALT SHAKER			13.99
Abundance	1	CUPFL	CUP ONLY-(FLAT)	2.625		14.99
Abundance	14	CSFL	CUP AND SAUCER SET (FLAT)	2.625		17.99
Abundance	2	CR	CREAMER			19.99
Abundance	2	SU	SUGAR BOWL AND LID			25.99
Abundance	1	SAP	SALT & PEPPER SET			27.99
Abundance	1	PIT24	PITCHER-24 OZ.	4.125		45.99
Abundance	1	TPCP	TEA/COFFEE POT	5.125	6 CUP	79.95
Adrienne	4	SAU	SAUCER ONLY			6.99
Adrienne	16	BB	PLATE-BREAD AND BUTTER	6.5		7.99
Adrienne	13	SP	PLATE-SALAD	8.25		11.99
Adrienne	3	FR	BOWL-FRUIT/DESSERT (SAUCE)	5.75		19.99
Adrienne	14	CSFT	CUP AND SAUCER SET (FOOTED)	3		19.99
Adrienne	9	DP	PLATE-DINNER	10.5		23.99
Adrienne	2	CR	CREAMER			26.99
Adrienne	1	NILIR	NIGHT LIGHT HC			29.99
Adrienne	16	SOC	BOWL-SOUP/COUPE	7.625		33.99
Adrienne	1	CHPFDR	CHEESE PLATE-FOOTED W/DOME HC			34.99
Adrienne	2	SU	SUGAR BOWL AND LID			34.99
Adrienne	2	SERPR	PLATE-SERVING-W/CTR HDL (DP)HC			39.99
Adrienne	1	CAFMR	CAKE STAND/METAL PEDESTAL HC			49.99
Adrienne	2	ST2R	TRAY-SERVING/2 TIER-DP/SP HC			55.99
Adrienne	2	ST3R	TRAY-SRV/3TIER-DP/SP/BB HC			64.95
Adrienne	2	OV10	VEGETABLE-OVAL	10.125		69.95
Adrienne	1	GR2	GRAVY BOAT AND UNDERPLATE			69.95
Adrienne	2	RCV	VEGETABLE-ROUND COVERED		42 OZ	149.95
Marshlands	7	SP	PLATE-SALAD	8.375		7.99
Marshlands	3	SOCE	BOWL-SOUP/CEREAL	7.25		8.99
Marshlands	6	MUG	MUG	3.875		9.99
Marshlands	3	CSFL	CUP AND SAUCER SET (FLAT)	3		14.99
Marshlands	1	CR	CREAMER	4.375	8 OZ	19.99
Marshlands	2	SAP	SALT & PEPPER SET			21.99
Marshlands	2	SU	SUGAR BOWL AND LID	3.375		25.99
Marshlands	2	GRA	GRAVY BOAT			33.99
Marshlands	1	PIT64	PITCHER-64 OZ.	8.5		54.99
Shalimar	6	BB	PLATE-BREAD AND BUTTER	6.375		8.99
Shalimar	10	FR	BOWL-FRUIT/DESSERT (SAUCE)	5.375		12.99
Shalimar	7	SP	PLATE-SALAD	7.625		12.99
Shalimar	11	CERC	BOWL-CEREAL/COUPE	5.875		14.99
Shalimar	6	SOC	BOWL-SOUP/COUPE	7.375		17.99
Shalimar	2	DP	PLATE-DINNER	10		21.99
Shalimar	10	CSFT	CUP AND SAUCER SET (FOOTED)	2.125		25.99
Shalimar	1	CR	CREAMER			29.99
Shalimar	1	SU	SUGAR BOWL AND LID			37.99
Shalimar	2	CRN	BOWL-CRANBERRY	5		39.99
Shalimar	1	OV10	VEGETABLE-OVAL	10.5		47.99
Shalimar	1	GR	GRAVY BOAT/ATTACHED UNDERPLAT			57.99
Shalimar	1	RDV	VEGETABLE-ROUND DIVIDED	10.125		65.95
Shalimar	1	PL16	PLATTER-OVAL SERVING	16.25		79.95
Shalimar	1	RCV	VEGETABLE-ROUND COVERED			99.95

Calculating Distances
with the Speed of Light

Your Name

7. Click in the Code column, and resort the database in ascending order to return the database records to their original order.

   ✓ *Some database programs may provide the capability to undo a sort (as long as you haven't saved your changes). Look for a command like Remove Filter/Sort or Undo Sort.*

8. Choose the command in your program that enables you to set up a more complicated sort based on multiple fields.

   ✓ *In Access, this command has an odd name: Records|Filter|Advanced Filter/Sort. In Approach, you may find the command on the Browse|Sort submenu.*

9. If the **Code** field appears as part of the sort by default, specify (not sorted) as its sort order using the Sort drop-down list or equivalent option in your program.

10. Add the **Pattern** field to the sort.

11. Set it up to sort in ascending order.

12. Add the **Price** field to the sort next, to specify it as the secondary sort.

13. Set it up to sort in ascending order.

14. Click the button or choose the command that applies the sort. (This might actually be the Apply Filter/Sort button or command.)

   ✓ *Access 2003 includes a Save as Query button so you can save a sort like this to reapply it later.*

15. Look again at the records that have **Abundance** in the **Pattern** field. Now look at the Price column for those records. The records are now in order by price, as are all other sets of records for other china patterns.

16. Format the data table (datasheet) in a 9-point size and resize the columns as needed to eliminate unneeded space and show the full field names (as for the **Piece Name** field).

17. Save your changes to the data table or database.

   ✓ *The next time you open the table, it appears in the sorted order. So, if you need your original data intact, you may want to copy the database file or table, and make your sorting changes to that copy.*

   ✓ *On the other hand, if your database includes an AutoNumber field and you haven't deleted any records, you can sort the database by the AutoNumber field (whatever its name is) to return the database to its original order.*

18. Print one copy of the sorted data using portrait orientation, **.25"** top and bottom margins, and no print headings. An example of the resulting printout appears on the following page.

19. Close the open data table, if needed, then close the database file.

If you know the speed of light, you can use that value to calculate the distance between one celestial body and another.

The speed of light is widely held to be *186,000 miles per second*[1].

So, let's say you're trying to find the distance, in miles, from the Earth to a body that's five light years away. The calculation is really a matter of multiplication.

To find the number of meters in a light year[2]:

$$\frac{186{,}000 \text{ miles}}{\text{second}} \times \frac{3{,}600 \text{ seconds}}{\text{hour}} \times \frac{24 \text{ hours}}{\text{day}} \times \frac{365.24 \text{ days}}{\text{year}}$$

You can then multiply the result, 5,869,552,896,000 miles per light year, by the number of light years to yield the total miles of distance. (For a less precise measure, use scientific notation to express the miles per light year as 5.8696×10^{12}.)

So, for example, to find the total miles light would travel in the five light years between the Earth and the distant body, multiply the number of miles in a light year by five:

$$5{,}869{,}552{,}896{,}000 \times 5 = 29{,}347{,}764{,}480{,}000 \text{ or } 2.9348 \times 10^{13} \text{ miles.}$$

---

[1] Calvin Combs, *Basic Physics Facts* (Minneapolis: PPress, 2004) 12.
[2] Bloom, Jane "Working with Distances" *Celestial Bodies* 17.2 (December 2003): 78.

2

Exercise 23

❖ Sort a Database

Notes

When you **sort** a database, you place the records in a particular order based on the entries in a field. For example, you can sort the database according to the entries in a date field, sort based on names, sort by state, and so on. You can sort in **ascending** order: from A to Z, from smallest to largest, or from the earliest date to the latest. Sorting in the reverse order is a **descending** sort. In most database programs, you can sort by a single field or by multiple fields. When you sort using multiple fields, the field the database uses to sort first by is the **primary sort** field, and the field the database resorts by is the **secondary sort** field. Specify both sorts at the same time, rather than performing them separately, however. Say you have a contact database. You set it up to sort by state (the primary sort), then to sort the already sorted data by last name (the secondary sort) without disturbing the primary sort results. So, for example, such a sort would group the Indiana records, then order them by last name: Appleton (IN), Jones (IN), Smith (IN), and so on. The records for all other states would remain grouped, too, but would be resorted by last name.

You've decided your database of china items will be more useful to you if you've sorted it. Tackle that task now.

Vocabulary

sort	descending	secondary sort
ascending	primary sort	

Directions

1. Create a copy of the **DB23** database file. Save the copy as **CHINA3**.
2. Open the **CHINA3** database file.
3. Open the **CHINA3** table (assuming your database program uses a separate name for each table; otherwise just use the data table or datasheet view of your database program).
4. Click in the **Pattern** field, if needed.

5. Sort it in ascending order.
   - ✓ *For a simple sort, you click in the field to sort by to specify that field as the sort field, then click a button or icon or choose a command to perform the sort.*
6. Look at the records that have **Abundance** in the **Pattern** field. Now look at the Price column for those records. Notice that the records for the Abundance china pattern are not in order by price.

Exercise 41

❖ Footnotes ❖ Headers ❖ Page Numbers
❖ Widow/Orphan Lines

Notes

A **widow** occurs when the last line of a paragraph follows a page or column break, so that the line appears by itself at the top of the new page or column. When the first line of a paragraph appears at the bottom of a page or column, with the rest of the paragraph appearing on the following page or column it is called an **orphan**. Removing widows and orphans to keep more text together makes the paragraph easier to read.

You've now written a more extensive report about Thomas Jefferson for your American History course. Finish the document now by adding footnotes, headers, and page numbers.

Vocabulary

widows   orphans   keep together

Directions

1. Open the **WP41** document file.
2. Save the file as **JEFF2**.
3. Turn on automatic page numbering.
4. Set the page numbers to display at the bottom center of each page, and turn off the page number display for the first page.
5. Fix the paragraph on the bottom of page 1 to eliminate the orphan there.

   ✓ *Leading word processing programs offer a feature that automatically eliminates widows and orphans. You typically find this feature among the paragraph formatting choices. More than likely, though, the feature for controlling widows and orphans will be turned on by default for all paragraphs in your word processing program.*

   ✓ *In the case of Step 5, the feature that eliminates widows and orphans actually moves the paragraph to page 2, so the orphan isn't standing alone.*

6. Step 5 generally creates a widow at the top of page 3. Fix the paragraph at the bottom of page 2 to eliminate the widow at the top of page 3.

   ✓ *In the case of Step 6, the feature that eliminates widows and orphans actually may not work. Your word processing program may also offer a **keep together** feature. You can use the keep together feature, instead, in Step 6. The keep together feature generally keeps a heading paragraph with the first text of paragraph that follows it, so that the heading paragraph never becomes an orphan.*

7. Create the two footnotes shown in the illustration that begins on the following page. (One is on page 1; the second is on page 2.)
8. Use the print preview or page (print) layout view to examine all pages of the report.
9. Save your changes to the document file.
10. Print one copy of the document.
11. Close the document.

10. Use the query design grid to create a new **calculated field** that multiples the **FullPrice** field entry by **.75** for each record (this finds 75% of the original value, or 25% off). Name the new field **SalePrice**.

   ✓ *Creating a calculated field tells the query to perform mathematical or other operations using the contents of other fields. To create this calculated field in the Access 2003 query design grid, you would click in the Field cell for the next blank column, and type* **SalePrice:[FullPrice]*.75**. *In that expression, the new field's name precedes the colon, and the name of the field holding the data to be calculated is enclosed in square brackets.*

11. Set up the calculated field to display in currency format.

   ✓ *To do so, right-click on the field in the query design grid, click Properties, and use the Format setting on the General tab of the Properties dialog box.*

12. Save your changes to the query.
13. Open (run) the query.
14. Save and close the query.

15. Create another new query with the same criteria you specified for the **BSALE3Q** query. Name the new query **BSALE3Q2**.

   ✓ *Hint: You can copy the* **BSALE3Q** *query in some database programs.*

16. If needed, display the view where you design or enter criteria for the query.
17. For the **Company** field, enter **Blazers** to add another criterion. Now, when you run the query, records must match both criteria, and the query will perform the calculation specified by the calculated field.
18. Save your changes to the query.
19. Open (run) the query.
20. Print one copy of the query results (landscape orientation, no print headings). The illustration below shows the results of this second query.

   ✓ *You change the page setup for the query results in the same way that you change the page setup for the data table (datasheet) itself.*

21. Save and close the query.
22. Close the database file.

ItemNo	Line	Company	Gender	Color	NoInStock	FullPrice	SalePrice
0007 Adventure		Blazers	M	Black	15	$65.99	$49.49
0008 Adventure		Blazers	F	Black	18	$65.99	$49.49
0017 Kix		Blazers	M	Brown	20	$72.00	$54.00
0018 Kix		Blazers	F	Brown	19	$70.00	$52.50
0030 Cascade		Blazers	F	Brown	13	$120.79	$90.59

Thomas Jefferson: Author of Our Independence

Despite his human flaws and foibles, Thomas Jefferson influenced the government of our country perhaps more than any other political figure. In writing the Declaration of Independence, Jefferson framed powerful political ideas in accessible, graceful language. Jefferson dedicated his life to applying those ideas to build a lasting government for the United States of America.

After a brief stint with a tutor at his family home, Jefferson was sent to live with other instructors who provide a classical education of studies in Greek, Latin, history, literature, geography, and natural science. Moving on to William and Mary College in Williamsburg, Virginia, Jefferson developed an interest in the law. He studied law for five years. In 1767, he began practicing law in Virginia while maintaining his primary source of income from his family's plantation.

Jefferson's focus on political matters developed soon after. He served in the Virginia Burgess, applying his leadership to the following matters[1]:

- The Townshend Acts
- Committee of Correspondence
- The Richmond Convention

---

[1] Linda Franklin, *Early Jefferson* (Williamsburg: W&M Press, 1976) 144.

Exercise 22

❖ Query a Database Using Operators and Multiple Criteria

Notes

A query also can compare records to a mathematical test. For example, you could find all the records with a value greater than a particular value or all the records with a date entry before a particular date in a field holding date entries. You create such comparisons by entering **operators** along with the other criteria information. In addition, you can perform calculations in a query to produce a **calculated field**.

In Exercise 17, you made some changes to your boot sale database. Since then, you've added some additional records, so you want to use a query to find particular items on the sale list. Also, you need to apply a standard discount percentage to come up with the sale price for each boot listed, which you'll handle in a query as well.

Vocabulary

operators   calculated field

Directions

1. Create a copy of the **DB22** database file. Save the copy as **BSALE3**.
2. Open the **BSALE3** database file.
3. Start the query creation process.
4. Verify that the query will use the data from the **BSALE3** table (assuming your database program uses a separate name for each table; otherwise just use the data table view of your database program).
5. Add all fields to the query.
6. If you're given the choice of showing detail or summary information in the query, show detail information.
7. Name the query **BSALE3Q**.

8. After you've set up the basic query, display the view where you design or enter criteria for the query.
9. For the **NoInStock** field, enter **>12** as the test or comparison that the query should apply.
   - ✓ This tells the query to display all records with an entry greater than 12 in the NoInStock field.
   - ✓ You also can use the > < >= and <= operators with dates. Your database program may require you to insert number signs around the date in the entry, as in >#1/1/00#, or the program may enter the number signs for you.

Jefferson's experience with the Burgess made him a key figure as the Continental Congress formed to fight the British Government's oppression of the colonies. In 1775, Jefferson was among the drafters of a document explaining why the colonies were making a stand against Britain.

In 1776, after Jefferson had become a fully-elected delegate to the Congress, he joined a committee of five congressman whose mission it was to draft a declaration that explained a resolution that the colonies should be free and independent. The committee members asked Jefferson to create the first draft of the declaration, which he later corrected along with John Adams and Benjamin Franklin.

The document incorporated ideas of European philosophers like John Locke, including notions such as government by consent and the natural rights of the individual. The original draft even denounced slavery and the slave trade[2], although that language was removed as a result of debate.

On July 2, 1776, Congress passed the resolution declaring the colonies independent. After debate and correction by the full body, the Declaration of Independence was formally adopted by Congress on July 4, 1776. The document was distributed throughout the colonies, so that inhabitants would know that America was a free nation.

---

[2] Maxim, Lea "Ideas in the Declaration" *Great Political Documents* 19.3 (Fall 1993): 45.

2

✓ Your database application may offer a cell or text box (perhaps named **Or**) for entering a second criteria for a particular field. For example, you could enter **Shalimar** as the second criterion to find records with either Marshlands or Shalimar in the **Pattern** field.

✓ Or, you can enter criteria in more than one query field, so when you run the query you'll see only records that match both criteria.

10. Save your changes to the query.
11. Open (run) the query.

✓ In some database applications, you run the query by switching from the query design view to a query datasheet (data table) view.

✓ Displaying (running) the query doesn't affect the original data table.

12. Print one copy of the query results (portrait format, no titles), which appear as in the illustration below. (Don't worry if your query results include an empty record at the bottom. That's normal in some programs, and the empty record does not print.)
13. Save and close the query.
14. Close the database file.

Pattern	Qty	Piece Name	Price
Marshlands	3	CUP AND SAUC	14.99
Marshlands	7	PLATE-SALAD	7.99
Marshlands	3	BOWL-SOUP/C	8.99
Marshlands	6	MUG	9.99
Marshlands	1	CREAMER	19.99
Marshlands	2	SUGAR BOWL	25.99
Marshlands	2	GRAVY BOAT	33.99
Marshlands	2	SALT & PEPPER	21.99
Marshlands	1	PITCHER-64 0Z	54.99

While Jefferson went on to make many other contributions to the United States of American, including serving as its third president, he will be perhaps remembered most and most fondly for writing the Declaration of Independence.

3

Exercise 21

❖ Query a Database Using a Single Criterion

Notes

A **query** works much more like filtering. You use a query to limit the list of records that appears on-screen, so that you can print or use only those records. As with a filter, you tell the database to find records that match a **criterion**—matching information or a statement you specify for a particular field. The extra benefit from a query is that you can save the query within the database. Then you can open the query at any time without having to re-enter your criteria.

You want to be able to find all the pieces from the Marshlands pattern in your CHINA database. Build a query to do so now.

Vocabulary

query   criterion

Directions

1. Create a copy of the **DB21** database file. Save the copy as **CHINA2**.
2. Open the **CHINA2** database file.
3. Start the query creation process.

   ✓ *Many database programs offer a wizard or helper you can use to create queries. Use that method, if available, for the exercises in this lesson. Also, different database programs handle the query creation process very differently, so if you have problems building a query, consult online help in your application to learn more.*

4. Verify that the query will use the data from the **CHINA2** table (assuming your database program uses a separate name for each table; otherwise just use the data table view of your database program).
5. Add only the **Pattern**, **Qty**, **Piece Name**, and **Price** fields to the query.

   ✓ *Leaving a field out of the query means that it doesn't display in the query results. Then you don't need to hide the field before you print the query results.*

6. If you're given the choice of showing detail or summary information in the query, show detail information.
7. Save the query and name it **CHINA2Q**. (Even though a table and form can use the same name, a table and query may not.)
8. After you've set up the basic query, display the view where you design or enter criteria for the query.
9. In the **Pattern** criteria field, enter **Marshlands** as the criteria that the query should match. When you run or open the query, the database program will display only records with Marshlands in the Pattern field.

Exercise 42

❖ Edit Headers and Footnotes ❖ Endnotes

Notes

You may want to make changes to the headers and footnotes that you've included in a document. You practice those techniques in this exercise. In addition, you learn to work with **endnotes**. An endnote contains the same information as a footnote, but appears in a list collected at the end of the document. In contrast, each footnote appears on the page that holds the citation the footnote identifies. In top word processing programs, you can convert existing footnotes to endnotes, or add an endnote automatically.

You work for Mobile A Network, a mobile phone service provider. You've written a report about the state of the industry. Improve the report now by adjusting the header and completing the endnotes.

Vocabulary

endnote

Directions

1. Open the **WP42** document file.
2. Save the file as **MOBILE**.
3. Edit the page 2 header so the title information reads **Mobile Market Increasing**. Leave the header page numbering in place.

   ✓ You use the same technique to edit either a header or footer. Display the header or footer to edit, make the changes you want, and close the header or footer.

4. In the second footnote, change the page number to **55**.

   ✓ If you're working in a view that displays footnotes or endnotes, like the page layout or print layout view, you can click right in the footnote or endnote and make the changes you want. In the normal view, you usually have to display the footnote or endnote contents in order to edit them.

5. Convert both the footnotes to endnotes.

   ✓ Hint: If you right-click a footnote in recent Word versions, the shortcut menu offers a command for the conversion.

6. Begin the process for inserting a third endnote (the one shown on page 2 of the illustration that begins on the following page).
7. If your word processing program uses a different numbering scheme for endnotes (as in **i**, **ii**, **iii**, for example), change the endnote options to number the endnotes with Arabic numerals, like footnotes (as in **1**, **2**, **3**).
8. Finish creating the third endnote, shown at the bottom of page 2 in the illustration.
9. Use the print preview or page (print) layout view to examine all pages of the report.
10. Save your changes to the document file.
11. Print one copy of the document.
12. Close the document.

9. Close the **CHINA** data table, then open the **CHINA** form (or switch to the form view in your database program).
10. Find all the records with **8.99** in the **Price** field. Count and record the total.

11. Close the database file, closing any open forms and data tables first, if required.

Student Name:

Today's Date:

No. of Matching Records with Marshlands in the Pattern Field:

No. of Matching Records with PLATE-DINNER in the Piece Name Field:

No. of Matching Records with 8.99 in the Price Field:

Mobile Phone Market Continues to Grow
By Will Terrell
Mobile A Network

In the mobile phone marketplace's first 15 years, growth was limited by infrastructure costs. It was excessively expensive to erect even a single cell tower. Service providers had to rely on heavy investment by other communications companies, such as land-based phone companies, to enter any particular marketplace.

Today the picture looks dramatically different. Subscriber bases have grown substantially. In 2001, service revenues actually exceeded operating costs. Then in 2002, service revenues for the first time were able to cover up to 85% of infrastructure costs[1], as well.

Let's examine the factors contributing to this dramatic shift. First, by 2001, the mobile phone infrastructure achieved an average of 98% completion (in terms of cell phone towers) in the United States. This enabled the U.S. providers to shift capital investments to less costly network equipment that would multiply efficiency. The providers could sign on 15% more customers for each dollar invested in the infrastructure, as opposed to the earlier figure of being able to add 5% more customers for each infrastructure dollar[2]. That change alone spurred most of the providers over the profitability hurdle.

In addition, profitable providers became able to apply capital dollars to developing new markets in other countries. Providers chose one of two methods for doing so: a simple expansion of their own

Exercise 20

❖ Find a Record

Notes

Finding a record is different from filtering records. The **find** generally just scrolls down the data table and displays the matching record. (You also can perform a find when you're using a form to display the matching record in the form.) If more than one record matches the information you specify for the find, you can typically click a button named something like **Find Next** to display each subsequent matching record. A find differs from filtering in another way. You can only find records based on entries in a single field, rather than being able to use multiple fields. However, if you've got a really long list of data in the database, the find feature can help you to more quickly display a record if you need to edit it or otherwise use its information.

You run a company called China Finds, which finds and sells replacement china pieces. Use the find feature now to look for items in your CHINA database.

Vocabulary

find   Find Next

Directions

1. If your instructor requires it, be prepared to write down and submit your exercise results (a count of the items as instructed, in a format like the illustration on the next page).
2. Create a copy of the **DB20** database file. Save the copy as **CHINA**.
3. Open the **CHINA** database file.
4. Open the **CHINA** table (assuming your database program uses a separate name for each table; otherwise just use the data table view of your database program).
5. Find all the records with **Marshlands** in the **Pattern** field. Count and record the total.

    ✓ *To start a find, you have to click in the field that holds the information you want to match. Then you choose the Edit|Find command (or the equivalent in your program), enter the*

information to match in the appropriate text box of the dialog box that appears, and click the Find Next button (or its equivalent) to find the first match. You then can use the Find Next button to find subsequent matching records, until you see a message that there are no more matching records.

    ✓ *You can click the button for canceling or closing the find dialog box when you find the record with which you want to work.*

6. Go back to the first record by pressing Ctrl+Home.
7. Find all the records with **PLATE-DINNER** in the **Piece Name** field. Count and record the total.
8. Go back to the first record.

Mobile Market Increasing 2

businesses or a joint venture with a foreign entity. The latter technique,

in particular, enabled the providers to tap into less expensive sources of

capital. Coupling that capital with explosive population growth in

markets like China enables rapid subscriber expansion.

By now, you may be wondering what the growth has looked like in

terms of sheer numbers. Here's a picture:

- U.S. subscribers: 123,000 (1990) to 45 million (2005)

- European subscribers: 75,000 (1990) to 35 million (2005)

- Asian subscribers: 45,000 (1990) to 215 million (2005)

- Other markets: 12,000 (1990) to 14 million (2005)[3]

The market factors that have generated such growth appear to be

in position to maintain the growth for at least two decades. Mobile A

Network predicts subscriber growth of 10% per year for the next five

years, with commensurate revenue growth.

---

[1] The Phone Group "Market Revisited" *Cell Phone World* 15.3 (March 2005): 67.
[2] Andrews, Phillip "Cost Efficiencies Examined" *Cell Phone World* 13.9 (September 2003): 55.
[3] The Phone Group, *15-Year Market Report* (Los Angeles: Phone Group Printworks, 2005) 22.

Lesson 23
Find Records and Query a Database

Exercises 20-25

❖ **Find matching records one at a time**

❖ **Create a simple query**

❖ **Use operators to create a more powerful query**

❖ **Sort the database**

❖ **Use a report**

Exercise 43

❖ Move and Copy Text from One Page to Another

Notes

You practiced moving and copying information within a document in Lesson 5. In those instances, you moved and copied information within a single page.

You want to do more to promote your company, Light Natural Beeswax Candles. You're going to improve a company description document by moving and copying text from one page to another.

Vocabulary

No new vocabulary in this exercise.

Directions

1. Open the **WP43** document file.
2. Save the file as **BEES2**.
3. Refer to the illustration that starts on the following page. Select the text marked as Selection A on page 1.
4. Move Selection A to the specified location on page 2 of the document.

   ✓ *While you can use the drag and drop feature to move and copy text between pages of a document, it's much more difficult because the document may scroll too slowly or quickly.*

   ✓ *In recent Word versions, a Paste Options button appears when you paste copied or cut text in a document. Click this button to see options for pasting the selection with or without its formatting. After a second paste, the Clipboard may open in the Task Pane. You can use the pane or click its Close (X) button to close it.*

5. Select the text marked Selection B.
6. Move Selection B to the specified location on page 1 of the document.

   ✓ *If you move text containing a footnote, the footnote itself moves to the page that contains the moved text.*

7. Select the text marked as Selection C.
8. Copy Selection C to the specified location on page 1 of the document.

   ✓ *As you move and copy text between pages, don't forget to check the spacing between lines and paragraphs. Use Enter and the spacebar to adjust the spacing where required. Delete extra spacing.*

9. Save your changes to the document file.
10. Print one copy of the document.
11. Close the document.

11. Hide the **SSN** field.
12. Filter the data table to display only records with **checks** in the **Sold** field.
13. Print a copy of the data table in portrait orientation, without headings.
    - ✓ *The printout contains only information shown in the filter.*
14. Remove the filter.
15. Redisplay the **SSN** field.
16. Increase the font size to 11 points, and adjust the column widths as needed.
17. Filter the data table to display only records with **Charles** in the **LName** column.
18. Change the top margin of the page to **2"** and choose the landscape orientation.
19. Print one copy of the data table.
20. Remove the filter or turn off filtering to redisplay all the records.
21. Save the database.
22. Close the database file, closing any open data tables first, if required.

PN	FName	LName	SSN	Work	Price	Sold	SDate
011	Taylor	Long	506-21-3099	La Playa	650	no	
012	Janey	Flick	780-45-6700	Catch Me	1050	yes (check)	7/9/05
013	Cris	Charles	211-83-0385	16 Tons	1600	yes (check)	7/10/05
014	Opal	Lynn	410-57-8887	Coming Home for Now	375	no	

Copy
section C ⟶
here.

Section A

Light Natural Beeswax Candles

Light Natural Beeswax Candles has been serving candle customers for more than 12 years. We appreciate our customers, so we provide purchasing convenience. Purchase candles on our Web site, by phone, or by faxing an order from our catalog.

Light Natural Beeswax Candles
888-555-8181 for More Information

Creating a Comfortable Home

The cozy glow that surrounds you when you light a room with candles provides a soothing alternative to inhospitable overhead lighting. No type of candle provides a warmer, cleaner glow than a beeswax candle.

Move
section B ⟶
here.

Benefits of Beeswax

When burned, natural beeswax does not produce toxic indoor pollutants like petrochemical candles. As well, our company uses pure plant oils to scent candles rather than the harsh synthetic fragrances found in commercial candles.

Finally, beeswax is a natural product. Bees produce the wax while producing honey. Rather than discarding the wax during the honey extraction process, beekeepers rescue it and make it available for sensible applications like candles and cosmetics. If it's safe enough to use as makeup, it's certainly safe enough to burn!

Exercise 19

❖ Critical Thinking

Notes

Conclude this lesson by repeating a number of skills to reinforce your ability to alter and print a database.

You've realized you need to track artist Social Security Numbers in your art gallery database, because you have to report the amounts you pay the artists for their sales to the IRS. Add that new field now, as well as making additional changes and printing the database.

Vocabulary

No new vocabulary in this exercise.

Directions

1. Create a copy of the **DB19** database file. Save the copy as **ART3**.
2. Open the **ART3** database file.
3. Open the **ART3** table (assuming your database program uses a separate name for each table; otherwise use the data table view of your database program).
4. Delete the **FSALE** field. You've adopted a new policy only to show pieces that are for sale.
5. Enter **250** in the Price field for record 4, and **650** in the Price field for record 6.
6. Format the PN field to display with three digits (000).
7. Insert a new field named **SSN** after (to the right of) the **LName** field. Set it up as a text field with a width of 12, using the Social Security Number input mask and storing the values with the mask symbols.

   ✓ *Save your changes to the table as needed throughout this exercise.*

8. In the new **SSN** field, enter the new social security numbers for the artists in the appropriate records (repeat an SSN as needed for an artist with multiple works in the database):

Jean Flynt	**010-55-9283**
Cris Charles	**211-83-0385**
Randall Plemmons	**785-41-3022**
Taylor Long	**506-21-3099**
Keller Mahoney	**305-87-6690**
Miranda Miles	**034-62-7575**
Opal Lynn	**410-57-8887**
Lisa Charles	**317-91-0404**

9. Enter the new records shown in the illustration on the following page. (You can press Tab to move past the **PN** AutoNumber field in each record.)
10. Change the font size to 9 points, then adjust the field sizes to eliminate blank space and display all fields correctly.

Why Our Candles Are Superior

Light Natural Beeswax Candles hand makes every candle, ensuring superior craftsmanship and a durable candle. By using natural materials and employing community members, Light Natural Beeswax Candles hopes to make a valuable contribution to our world and yours.

Section B

Move
section A →
here.

Beeswax Candles—Naturally!

Section C

Illustration 2

ID	SighDate	SightTime	Species	Type	Location	Count
3	6/14/2005	4:00 AM	Luna	Moth	Front Porch	1
6	6/16/2005	5:30 AM	Polyphemus	Moth	Front Porch	1
8	6/17/2005	6:00 AM	Eastern Tent Caterpillar Moth	Moth	High Point Trail	12
13	6/18/2005	10:00 PM	Willow Tentmaker	Moth	Front Porch	2
15	6/20/2005	5:45 AM	Polyphemus	Moth	Garage	1
16	6/20/2005	6:15 AM	Indian Blanket	Moth	Front Porch	3
18	6/21/2005	7:00 AM	Willow Tentmaker	Moth	Tree in Yard	1
22	6/22/2005	9:00 PM	Darling Underwing	Moth	Tarry Lane	2
23	6/23/2005	6:15 AM	Luna	Moth	Back Deck	1
25	6/25/2005	800 AM	Indian Blanket	Moth	Front Porch	1
28	6/26/2005	7:15 AM	Easter Tent Caterpillar Moth	Moth	Beacon Hill	5

Exercise 44

❖ Critical Thinking

Notes

In this exercise, work on your own to create page or section breaks, footers, page numbers, and footnotes.

You work for Go! Travel Consultants, and you're preparing a brief document about the St. Louis Arch. Finish the document with some formatting and footnotes now.

Vocabulary

No new vocabulary in this exercise.

Directions

1. Open the **WP44** document file.
2. Save the file as **ARCH**.
3. Refer to the illustration that starts on the following page to complete the steps.
4. Insert a section break of the type that also inserts a page break to create the first page.
5. Set up a footer for the first page (section) that includes the date, centered in the footer area.
6. Format the footer in 14-point Goudy Old Style (or a similar font), bold.
7. Insert a page break where needed to create the third page.
8. Set up a footer for pages 2 and 3 that includes the date at the left and page numbering at the right.
9. Format the footer in 14-point Goudy Old Style (or a similar font), bold.
10. Create the footnotes shown for pages 2 and 3.
11. Save your changes to the document file.
12. Print one copy of the document.
13. Close the document.

Illustration 1

ENT   10/13/2004

ID	SightDate	SightTime	Species	Type	Location	Count
1	6/13/2005	2:00 PM	Spicebrush Swallowtail	Butterfly	Kerry Quad	2
2	6/13/2005	3:15 PM	Monarch	Butterfly	Kerry Quad	1
3	6/14/2005	4:00 AM	Luna	Moth	Front Porch	1
4	6/14/2005	12:00 PM	Northern Pearly Eye	Butterfly	North Library Lawn	2
5	6/15/2005	11:00 AM	American Painted Lady	Butterfly	North Library Lawn	4
6	6/16/2005	5:30 AM	Polyphemus	Moth	Front Porch	1
7	6/16/2005	11:30 AM	Spring Azure	Butterfly	Beacon Hill	18
8	6/17/2005	6:00 AM	Eastern Tent Caterpillar Moth	Moth	High Point Trail	12
9	6/17/2005	1:30 PM	Eastern Pine Elfin	Butterfly	Anderson Corner	3
10	6/17/2005	3:30 PM	Spicebrush Swallowtail	Butterfly	Loma Library	2
11	6/18/2005	12:30 PM	Alfalfa Sulphur	Butterfly	Back Yard	10
12	6/18/2005	1:30 PM	Viceroy	Butterfly	Back Yard	2
13	6/18/2005	10:00 PM	Willow Tentmaker	Moth	Front Porch	2
14	6/19/2005	3:00 PM	Yellow Eastern Tiger Swallowtail	Butterfly	Wayles Meadow	20
15	6/20/2005	5:45 AM	Polyphemus	Moth	Garage	1
16	6/20/2005	6:15 AM	Indian Blanket	Moth	Front Porch	3
17	6/20/2005	2:15 PM	Monarch	Butterfly	Wayles Meadow	4
18	6/21/2005	7:00 AM	Willow Tentmaker	Moth	Tree in Yard	1
19	6/21/2005	4:05 PM	Spring Azure	Butterfly	Keller Quad	10
20	6/22/2005	12:00 PM	Yellow Eastern Tiger Swallowtail	Butterfly	Arboretum	18
21	6/22/2005	12:15 PM	Monarch	Butterfly	Arboretum	1
22	6/22/2005	9:00 PM	Darling Underwing	Moth	Tarry Lane	2
23	6/23/2005	6:15 AM	Luna	Moth	Back Deck	1
24	6/24/2005	11:45 AM	Alfalfa Sulphur	Butterfly	Miller Quad	3
25	6/25/2005	8:00 AM	Indian Blanket	Moth	Front Porch	1
26	6/25/2005	1:05 PM	Northern Pearly Eye	Butterfly	Miller Quad	3
27	6/25/2005	3:25 PM	Northern Checkerspot	Butterfly	Loma Library	2
28	6/26/2005	7:15 AM	Eastern Tent Caterpillar Mothe	Moth	Beacon Hill	5
29	6/26/2005	10:00 AM	Spicebrush Swallowtail	Butterfly	Wayles Meadow	11
30	6/26/2005	2:15 PM	Viceroy	Butterfly	Back Yard	1

Page 1

Find St. Louis
Under the Arch

St. Louis, Missouri rests on the mighty Mississippi River. When you approach the city, the first thing you might see is one of its most impressive features: the Gateway Arch. The Arch rises to the east of the central business district for downtown St. Louis.

The Gateway Arch is part of the Jefferson National Expansion Memorial Historic Site. The arch symbolizes the role of St. Louis as a gateway to the West as the United States expanded across North America in the 19th century.

Today's Date

8. Use your database program's filter feature to display only the records with **Moth** as the **Type** field entry.

✓ *The filter feature works quite differently in different database applications. Often, you can display a "form"—a dialog box or list of the fields in the database. You open a drop-down list for the field to select what entry to match. After selecting entries, apply the filter by clicking a button on the dialog box or in the toolbar.*

✓ *If the form appears with an entry in any field by default, clear that choice, or the filter won't work.*

✓ *You can filter the records by more than one field. For example, you could use two fields in the filter form to display only records with **Moth** in the **Type** field and a **SightDate** later than 6/20/05. You specify that second filter test by entering a test like **>6/20/05** in the **SightDate** field of the filter form before applying the filter. (The method for entering a test or criterion like this may vary quite a bit from program to program.) Or, you could enter a formula like **=6/20/05** to filter for records with that **SightDate** only.*

9. Change the left and right margins to **.5"**, turn off print headings, and choose portrait orientation. Print a copy of the filtered data table. (The printout should look like Illustration 2 on page 406.)

✓ *Again, the printout includes only the information visible on screen, not records hidden due to the filter.*

10. Remove the filter or turn off filtering to redisplay all the records.
11. Save the data table.
12. Close the database file, closing any open data tables first, if required.

A New Monument Rises

Architects competed and submitted monument designs in 1947-48. The winning design—a stainless steel arch by Eero Saarinen's—was selected at the end of the competition. The arch cost $15 million dollars [1] to build. Construction began in 1963. Sadly, architect Saarinen passed away before the arch was completed on October 28, 1965.

Since its completion, the arch has won numerous awards and competitions and has been considered a wonder of the modern world.

---

[1] Kevin Angelo, *Local St. Louis* (St. Louis: Very Press, 1984) 95.

Today's Date   2

Exercise 18

❖ Hide Fields ❖ Filter Records
❖ Turn Off Printed Headings

Notes

If you want to view only certain information for each record on the screen, you can **hide fields** to remove them temporarily from your view. Hiding a field doesn't delete its contents, so you can redisplay the field at any time. Similarly, you can **filter** the records in the database to show only records that have something in common—an identical or similar entry in one or more fields.

You're taking an Entomology class during the summer session. Your instructor has asked you to track butterfly and moth sightings for a two-week timeframe. Work with that database in this exercise, then print the data requested by your instructor.

Vocabulary

hide fields   filter

Directions

1. Create a copy of the **DB18** database file. Save the copy as **ENT**.
2. Open the **ENT** database file.
3. Open the **ENT** table (assuming your database program uses a separate name for each table; otherwise use the data table view of your database program).
4. Because the **ID** field is an AutoNumber field, you don't necessarily need to see it all the time. Hide that field.

   ✓ *To hide a column (field), select the column, if required in your database program. Then use the command for hiding columns (it may be found on the View or Format menu). Alternatively, you can right-click the field name and click the command for hiding a column or field. Note that the command for redisplaying (unhiding) columns is found on the same menu as the command for*

   hiding columns. If the database program presents a list of hidden columns, you click a check box to check any column that you want to appear on screen.

5. Resize all columns so their entries display correctly, and so that they will all fit on a single page on a portrait orientation printout. (Use print preview as needed.)
6. Print a copy of the data table in portrait orientation. (The printout should look like Illustration 1 on page 405.)

   ✓ *Notice that the hidden field doesn't print. You also can hide columns to customize a printout.*

7. Redisplay the **ID** column (field) and adjust its column width to eliminate unneeded space.

Fun Arch Facts[2]

- Height: 630 ft. or 192 meters
- Width: 630 ft. or 192 meters
- Completed: 1965
- Foundation: Sinks 60 ft. into the ground
- Skin: ¼" thick
- Total Weight, Steel: 5,199 tons (4,644 metric tons)
- Total Weight, Concrete: 38,107 Tons (34,570 metric tons)
- Sways: Up to an inch in 20 mph winds
- Operated by: The National Park Service
- Getting to the top: Take the unique internal tram system

---

[2] The National Parks Service, *Monumental History* (Alexandria: Government Press, 1975) 225.

Today's Date   3

Illustration 2

ItemNo	Line	Company	Gender	Color	NoInStock	FullPrice
0001	Rox	Blazers	M	Black	8	$79.99
0002	Rox	Blazers	F	Black	12	$75.99
0003	Fleming	Screech	M	Gray	23	$99.99
0004	LightWing	Screech	F	Gray	27	$89.99
0005	Linda	Trail Boss	F	Brown	4	$72.99
0006	Keller	Trail Boss	M	Brown	8	$75.99
0007	Adventure	Blazers	M	Black	15	$65.99
0008	Adventure	Blazers	F	Black	18	$65.99
0009	LightWing	Screech	F	Brown	8	$89.99
0010	Linda	Trail Boss	F	Black	18	$72.99
0011	LowRide	TopLine	M	Gray	12	$69.99
0012	LowRide	TopLine	F	Gray	7	$65.99

Word Processing

Lesson 8
Formatting Columns and Tables

Exercises 45–53

❖ **Work with newspaper-style columns**
❖ **Set custom widths in columns**
❖ **Table basics**
❖ **Format and edit a table**
❖ **Sort information in a table**

8. Add the new entries for the **Color** and **NoInStock** fields, as shown in Illustration 1 below.

9. Add the new (shaded) records shown at the bottom of the illustration.

10. Reinsert an **ItemNo** field as the first field. Set it up as an AutoNumber field and the primary key. Also format it to display four places (**0000**).

11. Change the font size for the data table to 12 points, and adjust column widths, if needed, so each table cell entry and field name appears completely.

12. If your database program enables you to adjust the datasheet (both on screen and in printouts), display horizontal gridlines only and change the color of the gridlines to a dark color.

13. Confirm that the table is in the portrait orientation, set the top margin to **2"**, and set the left and right margins to **.5"**.

✓ *In most database programs, you use a Page Setup command to change the margin settings.*

14. Turn off printing of the headings (the file title, date, and page number). This setting is generally part of the Page Setup command.

✓ *If you want to look at your layout before you print the data table, use the print preview feature.*

✓ *If your printout doesn't fit on a single page, you can reduce the font size to help it fit.*

15. Save your changes to the data table again.

16. Print one copy of the table. Illustration 2 on the following page shows how the printed table looks.

17. Close the database file, closing any open data tables first, if required.

Illustration 1

Line	Company	Gender	Color	NoInStock	FullPrice	PercentOff
Rox	Blazers	M	Black	8	$79.99	35%
Rox	Blazers	F	Black	12	$75.99	35%
Hard Hike	TopLine	M			$129.99	35%
Hard Hike	TopLine	F			$119.99	35%
Fleming	Screech	M	Gray	23	$99.99	25%
LightWing	Screech	F	Gray	27	$89.99	25%
Linda	Trail Boss	F	Brown	4	$72.99	20%
Keller	Trail Boss	M	Brown	8	$75.99	20%
Adventure	Blazers	M	Black	15	$65.99	20%
Adventure	Blazers	F	Black	18	$65.99	20%
LightWing	Screech	F	Brown	8	$89.99	
Linda	Trail Boss	F	Black	18	$72.99	
LowRide	TopLine	M	Gray	12	$69.99	
LowRide	TopLine	F	Gray	7	$65.99	

Exercise 45

❖ Create Newspaper-Style Columns

Notes

If you format document text in newspaper-style columns (or **newspaper columns**), the word processing program fills the first column all the way to the bottom, then wraps text to the next column to the right. Formatting text in columns can enable you to use a small font size and therefore fit more information on each page. You can use as many columns as you need, but two or three columns usually works best for a letter-sized page in the portrait orientation (with the short edge of the page at the top). If the columns are too narrow, the text can be difficult to read.

As an employee of Go! Travel Consultants, you are continuing your work on a brochure you're developing about the Gateway Arch in St. Louis. Format the document text into columns to make it look a bit neater.

Vocabulary

newspaper columns

gutter

landscape orientation

three-panel brochure

balance

column break

Directions

1. Open the **WP45** document file.
2. Save the file as **ARCH2**.
3. Change the page margins to **.75"** on all sides.
4. Click to position the insertion point to the left of the heading, **Under the Arch**.
5. Format the following text (not the entire document) into two columns. When you create the columns, specify that a line should appear between the columns. When you create the columns, change the spacing between columns to **.4"**. Your word processing program should adjust the default column width to accommodate the smaller width.

   ✓ Traditionally, the spacing between columns is called the **gutter**. However, in recent versions of Word, the term gutter refers to extra white space left along the edges of a document for binding.

   ✓ Generally, when you format only part of the document into columns, the word processing program inserts a section break. (Remember, you can use sections to apply different types of page formatting within the same document.) In this case, the section is a continuous section, because the section break doesn't create a new page.

   ✓ If your word processing program doesn't use section breaks, it may or may not enable you to format part of a document in multiple columns. You can also create a text box to hold information that you want to format in one wide column. The Desktop Publishing section of this book reviews how to create objects like text boxes.

Exercise 17

❖ Add Records ❖ Delete Records
❖ Modify the Data Table ❖ Change Margins
❖ Turn Off Printed Headings

Notes

Adding and removing fields affects the width of your database printouts. In addition, you can adjust the printout **margins** and eliminate printed headings to have more control over the appearance of any printout. Add and remove fields, add and remove records, and work more with print settings in this exercise.

You've reviewed the boot sales database for the Mountain Gear store, and you've discovered you need to make some changes. Make the needed changes and print the database now.

Vocabulary

margins

Directions

1. Create a copy of the **DB17** database file. Save the copy as **BSALE2**.
2. Open the **BSALE2** database file.
3. Open the **BSALE2** table (assuming your database program uses a separate name for each table; otherwise use the data table view of your database program).
4. Using the view that enables you to make design changes to the table, first delete the **ItemNo** field.

   ✓ *Because you're going to delete records from the database, you want to remove the numbers. Then, after you delete records, you'll add a new ItemNo (AutoNumber) field to renumber them, so all the numbers will be sequential. You also can add an AutoNumber field after you create the database (and do any desired sorting) to number the records.*

5. Add the lightly shaded fields (**Color** and **NoInStock**) shown in Illustration 1 on the following page. Set up the **Color** field to use the text data type, with a size of **10**. Set up the **NoInStock** field to use the number data type. Be sure to insert the fields in the position shown in the illustration on the following page.
6. Using the data table, delete the records that appear with darker shading in the illustration on the following page. Assume it's because you've decided not to put those items on sale.
7. Delete the **PercentOff** field. It appears with darker shading in the illustration on the following page. Because you'll apply the same discount percentage for all the on-sale boots, you no longer need this field.

6. If your word processor prompts you to change views when you apply the column changes, do so.

7. Center the **Find St. Louis** heading and increase the font size to 48 points.

8. Click to position the insertion point at the beginning of the **Fun Arch Facts** heading. You want this information to span the whole page width.

   ✓ *When you format a letter-sized page in **landscape orientation** (wide rather than tall) with three columns, you actually can fold the page into a **three-panel brochure** by folding along the gutter lines. You typically fold the far right panel over the center panel, then the far left panel over the other two.*

   ✓ *If you print on two sides of the page, the information on the "outside" of the brochure needs to appear out of order on the page. The brochure "cover" information should appear in the far right column on that side. To print on both sides of the paper with a laser printer, print the first side first. Turn the printout over (you may need to rotate it, as well), and feed it back through the printer to print the second page.*

   ✓ *You may need to experiment a bit to know how to feed the paper to print the second side, so practice with some scrap paper first.*

9. Format the text from that point forward in one column.

   ✓ *After you complete Step 9, your word processing program should **balance** the information that's formatted in two columns. That is, the word processor should move some text from the first column into the second column, so that both columns are about equal in length. You can manually shift information from one column to the next by inserting a **column break**. Usually, you can insert a break by pressing Ctrl+Shift+Enter or by using the command for creating a column break in your word processing program.*

10. Press Enter to add a blank line between the two-column text and the section beginning with the **Fun Arch Facts** heading. The finished document should look like the illustration on the following page.

11. Save your changes to the document file.

12. Print one copy of the document.

13. Close the document.

Illustration 2

ID	Pet	Type	In	LName	HPhone	TPhone	Days	Vac	Other
2	Kipper	Dog	10/6/2006	Kimble	(212)555-0303	(595)333-9993	2	☑	Playtime
3	Baby	Cat	10/6/2006	Stevens	(212)666-9333	(904)333-3333	1	☑	Medicine
5	Blip	Bird	10/7/2006	Lion	(212)666-4444		7	☐	Medicine
6	Bo	Dog	10/7/2006	Poland	(212)888-0099	(292)333-6565	2	☑	Playtime
7	Rika	Dog	10/7/2006	Poland	(212)888-0099	(292)333-6565	2	☑	Playtime
8	Flyntt	Other	10/7/2006	Keller	(212)444-6464	(704)222-2244	4	☐	
9	Pepper	Cat	10/7/2006	Sullivan	(212)555-7878		1	☑	
10	Johnny	Dog	10/8/2006	Little	(212)555-8888	(204)777-4444	3	☑	Bath
11	Liza	Bird	10/8/2006	Dantz	(212)666-2121	(845)010-2204	3	☐	
12	Smiley	Dog	10/8/2006	Simpson	(212)555-3303		2	☑	Medicine

Page 1

Find St. Louis

Under the Arch

St. Louis, Missouri rests on the mighty Mississippi River. When you approach the city, the first thing you might see is one of its most impressive features: the Gateway Arch. The Arch rises to the east of the central business district for downtown St. Louis.

The Gateway Arch is part of the Jefferson National Expansion Memorial Historic Site. The arch symbolizes the role of St. Louis as a gateway to the West as the United States expanded across North America in the 19th century.

A New Monument Rises

Architects competed and submitted monument designs in 1947-48. The winning design—a stainless steel arch by Eero Saarinen's—was selected at the end of the competition. The arch cost $15 million dollars to build. Construction began in 1963. Sadly, architect Saarinen passed away before the arch was completed on October 28, 1965.

Since its completion, the arch has won numerous awards and competitions and has been considered a wonder of the modern world.

Fun Arch Facts

- Height: 630 ft. or 192 meters
- Width: 630 ft. or 192 meters
- Completed: 1965
- Foundation: Sinks 60 ft. into the ground
- Skin: ¼" thick
- Total Weight, Steel: 5,199 tons (4,644 metric tons)
- Total Weight, Concrete: 38,107 Tons (34,570 metric tons)
- Sways: Up to an inch in 20 mph winds
- Operated by: The National Park Service
- Getting to the top: Take the unique internal tram system

Illustration 1

ID	Pet	Type	In	FName	LName	HPhone	TPhone	Days	Vac	Other
1	Shandy	Dog	10/6/2006	Myra	Wood	(212)666-9899	(393)444-9992	3	Yes (check)	Bath
2	Kipper	Dog	10/6/2006	Kenneth	Kimble	(212)555-0303	(595)333-9993	2	Yes (check)	Playtime
3	Baby	Cat	10/6/2006	Linda	Stevens	(212)666-9333	(904)333-3333	1	Yes (check)	Medicine
4	Fritz	Cat	10/7/2006	Mark	Walls	(212)555-5555	(222)777-9999	2	No	
5	Blip	Bird	10/7/2006	Candy	Lion	(212)666-4444		7	No	Medicine
6	Bo	Dog	10/7/2006	Lisa	Poland	(212)888-0099	(292)333-6565	2	Yes (check)	Playtime
7	Rika	Dog	10/7/2006	Lisa	Poland	(212)888-0099	(292)333-6565	2	Yes (check)	Playtime
8	Flyntt	Other	10/7/2006	Keith	Keller	(212)444-6464	(704)222-2244	4	No	
9	Pepper	Cat	10/7/2006	Dana	Sullivan	(212)555-7878		1	Yes (check)	
10	Johnny	Dog	10/8/2006		Little	(212)555-8888	(204)777-4444	3	Yes (check)	Bath
11	Liza	Bird	10/8/2006		Dantz	(212)666-2121	(845)010-2204	3		
12	Smiley	Dog	10/8/2006		Simpson	(212)555-3303		2	Yes (check)	Medicine

Exercise 46

❖ Use Columns with Custom Widths

Notes

Equally-sized columns work well when a document has a lot of paragraph text to fill the columns. If, on the other hand, you want to set off a brief list or information that's less important, you can place that information in a slightly narrower column. This formatting not only makes the most of the available space but also creates an interesting appearance for the document.

You're working on another version of the newsletter for Go! Travel Consultants. In this instance, set up the document text to use two columns of different widths.

Vocabulary

No new vocabulary in this exercise.

Directions

1. Open the **WP46** document file.
2. Save the file as **GO3**.
3. Change the left and right page margins to **1"**.
4. Click to position the insertion point to the left of the first heading, **Online Savings?**.
5. Format the text from that point forward in two columns. Size the left column to **2.5"** and the right column to **3.6"**, with **.4"** spacing between columns. Also, add a line between columns.

   ✓ *In some word processing programs, you may need to clear a checkbox that sizes columns equally before you can specify unequal widths for the columns.*

6. Scroll down the document to see how it looks.
7. Click to position the insertion point to the left of the heading **Kayak the Flat Waters**.
8. Insert a column break to shift that heading and the information that follows it to the next column. The finished document should resemble the illustration on the following page.
9. Save your changes to the document file.
10. Print one copy of the document.
11. Close the document.

5. Delete the field that uses darker shading (**FName**) in the illustration on the following page. All you need is the pet's name and the owner last name for your list.

  ✓ *If you try to delete a field that already holds some data, the database program displays a warning message that deleting the field deletes any contents (entries) in that field, as well. You can choose to proceed with or cancel the deletion.*

  ✓ *You can delete a field in the data table. You can right-click the field name, click the Delete Column command, then confirm the deletion.*

6. Using the data table, delete the records shown in darker shading in the illustration on the following page. These owners came to the kennel, but decided not to drop their pets off after all.

  ✓ *Likewise, when you delete a record, your database program should prompt you to confirm the deletion, because you cannot undo a record deletion.*

  ✓ *You can delete a record, right-click the gray border box at the left end of the record, click the Delete or Delete Record command, then confirm the deletion.*

  ✓ *Note that when you delete an autonumbered record, the remaining records are not renumbered.*

7. Add the new (lightly shaded) records shown at the bottom of the illustration. Note that the **Type** field offers a value list, from which you can choose the proper entry.

  ✓ *In most database programs, the new records you add are appended to the end of the database list, even if the list doesn't contain an AutoNumber field. You can later sort the data to change its order. The AutoNumber feature also does not renumber entries in that field to account for deleted records. It simply eliminates the deleted numbers, leaving gaps (skipped numbers) in the AutoNumber field entries.*

  ✓ *Remember that you can enter the date in another format and skip entering punctuation with the phone numbers. The field formatting applies the displayed formats for you.*

8. Save your changes to the data table.
9. Change the font size for the data table to 12 points and apply the bold attribute.
10. Adjust column widths, if needed, so each table cell entry and field name appears completely.
11. Save your changes to the data table again.
12. Print one copy of the table in landscape orientation. Illustration 2 on page 399 shows how the printed table looks.
13. Close the database file, closing any open forms and data tables first, if required.

You Go!
By Janet Mason
Go! Travel Consultants

Online Savings?

Have you ever spent hours online researching flight, hotel, and rental car rates, only to learn that your hours of time have saved you a whopping $15 or so? We at Go! Travel Consultants don't want to discourage you from using valuable online tools. Indeed, online resources complement our services. The next time you're planning to travel to a particular destination, consider these tips, which may save you even more money:

- ❖ Spend a limited amount of time researching prices, and then call Go! Travel Consultants. We may be able to recommend a more cost-effective flight and hotel package that includes such extras as ground transportation.
- ❖ If you're open about your destination, we can tell you about specials that are available during your planned travel dates.
- ❖ Sign up for our Go! Alerts service. We'll e-mail you about last-minute specials.

Kayak the Flat Waters

When you think of kayaking, you might visualize guys in helmets and life jackets crashing through the water in a rocky river. While folks capable of that type of challenging action certain represent a segment of the kayaking community, many more people today opt to kayak on flatter waters instead.

Even novices can have some success kayaking on the calmer waters of a lake, lagoon, sound, or ocean. The kayaks created for flat water paddling generally are a bit larger and have a flatter bottom. The kayaker sits comfortably on top, without any type of skirting or tether to the kayak. While these craft help provide stability, you have to be prepared to paddle. When you're paddling against the wind or a current, this can give you a significant workout!

You can still mix it up a bit with this type of kayak. It's fun to take one out at the ocean shoreline and catch a wave to surf back in. Just be sure to wear a helmet and lifejacket for that type of action. You're sure to get flipped under the water and some of the spills can be rough.

If you've never tried a kayak and aren't prepared for the whitewater, try the flat water. For less than $100 a day, you can rent all the equipment you need to have a blast. If you're renting a beach house, set aside a day or so for kayaking fun.

Exercise 16

❖ Add Records ❖ Delete Records
❖ Modify the Data Table

Notes

As information accumulates, your database must grow and change. You may need to **add records** to the database, such as entering records for new product orders. You may need to **delete records**, such as removing information about a vendor you no longer use. In addition to adding and removing records, you can modify the data table itself by **inserting and deleting fields** of information.

✓ *The example database table for this exercise uses a special text field formatted to offer a drop-down list (also called a **value list**) of entries that you can choose from. To create such a list, you can use the **Lookup Wizard** or similar tool offered in your database program. (Or, hint, look at these table fields in the example file in the table design view to see the settings used to create them.) When a text field is formatted in this way, you can press Tab to move to the field, click on the drop-down list arrow that appears, and then click a choice in the list. Or, you can type the first part of the entry (until the full entry appears in the cell), and then press Tab.*

You've been using a modified version of the database shown in Exercise 7 to check pets into the Pet Country Club kennel. Modify the database now, adding and deleting fields and records.

Vocabulary

add records	insert and delete fields	Lookup Wizard
delete records	value list	

Directions

1. Create a copy of the **DB16** database file. Save the copy as **CHECKIN2**.
2. Open the **CHECKIN2** database file.
3. Open the **CHECKIN2** table (assuming your database program uses a separate name for each table; otherwise use the data table view of your database program).
4. Use the view that enables you to make design changes to the table, and add the lightly shaded field (**ID**) shown in Illustration 1 on page 398. Use the AutoNumber data type for the field and set up the field as the primary key.

✓ *While you can add (and delete) fields (columns) in the data table view, that method doesn't give you the option of choosing a data type and format. When using the design view for the table, be sure to insert the field in the location (order) in which you want it to appear.*

✓ *In the view for changing the table design, you can generally insert a new row for the new field to shift the field into the location you want relative to other fields (as opposed to at the bottom of the list of fields). Right-click the field above which you want to insert the new field, then click the Insert Rows or Insert Field command.*

Exercise 47

❖ Create a Table ❖ Change Table Column Width

Notes

Formatting text into columns is the best choice to help you align longer blocks of text. When your document needs to include many columns of short entries, you can create a table in the document instead. A table in a word processing document resembles a spreadsheet. The table arranges information into **rows** and **columns**, with each row/column intersection forming a **cell** into which you enter information. When you create the table, you indicate how many rows and columns it should have, based on the information you plan to enter. A dashed or dotted gray **column grid** identifies the cells for you. (Some word processing programs may include border lines along with the column grid, so that the table prints with borders by default.)

You're gathering some cell phone growth statistics for your boss at Mobile A Network. Present those statistics in a basic table to make the data easier for your boss to review.

Vocabulary

rows   columns   cells   column grid

Directions

1. Create a new, blank document.
2. Save the file as **MOBSTAT**.
3. Type the title lines shown in the illustration on the following page.
4. Press Enter three times after the third title line to insert blank lines.

   ✓ *If you insert a table at the first line of the document, some word processing programs won't let you move it or insert text above it later. So, it's a good practice to insert at least one blank line above a table in a new document.*

5. Insert a table that has five columns and five rows.

   ✓ *You can work with tables in the normal view or the page (print) layout view.*

6. Enter the table information as shown in the illustration.

   ✓ *As in a spreadsheet program, use the Tab key to move from cell to cell in a table or Shift+Tab to move the other direction.*

   ✓ *If the text you enter doesn't fit on a single line in a cell, the word processing program automatically wraps the text within the cell. You also can press Enter within a cell to create multiple lines (paragraphs) of text.*

7. Center the table column headings (the entries in the top row of the table) and format them in 14-point Times New Roman font. Also apply boldface to them.

Illustration 2 (Page 2 of 2)

Festival	Arts and Crafts Festival
Start	9/4/2006
End	9/5/2006
City	Ft. Lauderdale
State	FL
WebSite	www.artfestival.com

Festival	North Georgia State Fair
Start	9/23/2006
End	10/3/2006
City	Marietta
State	GA
WebSite	www.northgeorgiastatefair.c

Festival	Arts and Crafts Fair
Start	9/9/2006
End	9/10/2006
City	Bethany Beach
State	DE
WebSite	www.bethanybeachartsfesti

Festival	Smallwood Festival
Start	9/11/2006
End	9/12/2006
City	Westminster
State	MD
WebSite	

8. Resize the first column to make it wider.

   ✓ *When you point to the right border or gridline of a column, the mouse pointer changes to a resizing pointer; you can then drag to resize the column. Alternatively, you can use a command (usually found on the Table menu) to enter a precise width measurement for a column.*

9. Resize the second through fifth columns to make them a bit more narrow. The document should now resemble the illustration below.

   ✓ *You can select multiple columns to resize them simultaneously. To select a column, point to its top border or gridline until the pointer changes to a selection pointer. Click to select a single column. Drag right to select multiple columns.*

10. Save your changes to the document file.
11. Print one copy of the document.
12. Close the document.

U.S. Mobile Phone User Growth
By Quarter
March 31, 2006

Region	Q1	Q2	Q3	Q4
Northeast	150,000	252,000	139,000	179,000
Southeast	176,000	202,000	87,000	42,000
Northwest	56,000	49,000	123,000	28,000
Southwest	175,000	209,000	310,000	164,000

Illustration 2 (Page 1 of 2)

Festival	American Music Festival
Start	9/1/2006
End	9/4/2006
City	Virginia Beach
State	VA
WebSite	www.beacheventsfun.com

Festival	Mule Days
Start	9/23/2006
End	9/26/2006
City	Benson
State	NC
WebSite	www.bensonmuledays.com

Festival	Poppy Mtn. Bluegrass Festival
Start	9/14/2006
End	9/18/2006
City	Morehead
State	KY
WebSite	www.poppymountainbluegra

Festival	Peanut Festival
Start	9/25/2006
End	9/26/2006
City	Plains
State	GA
WebSite	www.plainsgeorgia.com

Festival	Outdoor FoodFest
Start	9/18/2006
End	9/18/2006
City	Hilton Head
State	SC
WebSite	www.hiltonheadisland.com/

Festival	Seafood Sampler
Start	9/16/2006
End	9/17/2006
City	Norfolk
State	VA
WebSite	www.festeventsva.org

Festival	OctoberFest
Start	9/16/2006
End	9/19/2006
City	Huntsville
State	AL
WebSite	www.huntsville.gov/fest

Festival	Bull Durham Blues Festival
Start	9/9/2006
End	9/11/2006
City	Durham
State	NC
WebSite	www.hayti.org

Festival	Horseshoe Riverbend Festival
Start	9/10/2006
End	9/11/2006
City	Clifton
State	TN
WebSite	www.cityofclifton.com

Festival	Home Garden Tour
Start	9/1/2006
End	9/12/2006
City	Cary
State	SC
WebSite	www.scfmca.org/gardentour

Exercise 48

❖ Create a Table ❖ Change Table Column Width
❖ Format Table Data

Notes

You can change the default font and alignment for the information you enter in table cells. You also can set up tab stops for a table column, or format a cell's contents as a bulleted list.

You're updating the seasonal work schedule you created earlier for employees at Mountain Gear. In this exercise, present the schedule as a table in the document, and apply some formatting choices to the table contents.

Vocabulary

No new vocabulary in this exercise.

Directions

1. Open the **WP48** document file.
2. Save the file as **WORK2**.
3. Click to place the insertion point on the second blank line following the paragraph that ends with **...schedule below:**.

   ✓ *When you insert a table, it usually looks more attractive when there's blank space above and below it.*

4. Insert a table that has five columns and seven rows.
5. Enter the table information as shown in the illustration on the following page.
6. Select all the table cells.

   ✓ *You can drag to select table cells. In addition, your word processing program may offer a Table menu command or button that pops up near the table for selecting the entire table.*

   ✓ *If you want to format only part of the text in a table cell, such as applying bold to only one word in the cell, drag within the cell to select that text.*

7. Decrease the font size for all the text to 10 points.

   ✓ *In most cases, row height adjusts automatically when you change the font size or add more text to a cell in the row.*

8. Format the text in the first row in bold.

   ✓ *Point to the left border or gridline of the row until the pointer changes to a selection pointer, then click to select the whole row.*

9. Resize the first, second, and third columns to make them narrower, so they don't have as much wasted space. This should automatically help the entries in the fourth column each fit on a single line.

   ✓ *If you accidentally select some of the cells in the column before you try to resize the column width,*

10. Redisplay the **FESTIVAL2** form. Notice that the font changes you made in the table do not appear in the form.

   ✓ *To change the font, use the design view (or the view your database program offers for entering forms), select all the fields and field labels, then change the font. Save your changes to the form, then redisplay the form data.*

11. Print one copy of the form in portrait orientation, with two columns and the column layout that prints records down and then across, and **.15"** row spacing. Illustration 2 starting on the following page shows how the printed form looks.

   ✓ *The printout will use two pages, as shown in this book.*

   ✓ *The row spacing setting refers to the setting that inserts blank space between each record, making the form printout easier to read. When you print a form view, the pages may break in odd locations, so that part of a record's shaded form background may be cut off at the bottom or top of the page. You can adjust the row spacing setting as needed to minimize this problem in your printouts.*

12. Close the database file, closing any open forms and data tables first, if required.

Illustration 1

Festival	Start	End	City	State	WebSite
American Music Festival	9/1/2006	9/4/2006	Virginia Beach	VA	www.beacheventsfun.com
Mule Days	9/23/2006	9/26/2006	Benson	NC	www.bensonmuledays.com
Poppy Mtn. Bluegrass Festival	9/14/2006	9/18/2006	Morehead	KY	www.poppymountainbluegrass.com
Peanut Festival	9/25/2006	9/26/2006	Plains	GA	www.plainsgeorgia.com
Outdoor FoodFest	9/18/2006	9/18/2006	Hilton Head	SC	www.hiltonheadisland.com/hospitalityassociation/
Seafood Sampler	9/16/2006	9/17/2006	Norfolk	VA	www.festeventsva.org
OctoberFest	9/16/2006	9/19/2006	Huntsville	AL	www.huntsville.gov/fest
Bull Durham Blues Festival	9/9/2006	9/11/2006	Durham	NC	www.hayti.org
Horseshoe Riverbend Festival	9/10/2006	9/11/2006	Clifton	TN	www.cityofclifton.com
Home Garden Tour	9/1/2006	9/12/2006	Cary	SC	www.scfmca.org/gardentour.html
Arts and Crafts Festival	9/4/2006	9/5/2006	Ft. Lauderdale	FL	www.artfestival.com
North Georgia State Fair	9/23/2006	10/3/2006	Marietta	GA	www.northgeorgiastatefair.com
Arts and Crafts Fair	9/9/2006	9/10/2006	Bethany Beach	DE	www.bethanybeachartsfestival.com
Smallwood Festival	9/11/2006	9/12/2006	Westminster	MD	

your word processing program will resize the selected cells only, not the entire column. To avoid this problem, select the whole column to resize, or click in a cell in another column before resizing.

10. Select the cells in the first and second columns.
11. Center the text in those columns.
12. Select the text in the top cell in the fifth column.
13. Center the text in the top cell in the fifth column.
14. Select all the cells but the top cell in the fifth column.
15. Create a decimal tab stop at about the midpoint of the column.

   ✓ *It's sometimes easiest to use rulers to set tab stops when you're working within table cells.*

16. If needed, insert a tab to the left of the entry in all of the cells but the top cell in the fifth column, to align the text to the new decimal tab.

   ✓ *In most word processing applications, remember that you have to press Ctrl+Tab to insert a tab within a table cell.*

17. Click outside the table so you can see the results of your changes. The finished document should look like the illustration on the following page.
18. Save your changes to the document file.
19. Print one copy of the document.
20. Close the document.

Illustration 1

Day	Hours	Employees	Tasks	Sales Goal
Tuesday	1-7 p.m.	Gary, Shannon	Clean restroom, clean counters	$575.00
Wednesday	1-7 p.m.	Linda, Tom	Vacuum floors	$625.50
Thursday	1-7 p.m.	Linda, Drew	Stock merchandise, mark sale items	$715.25
Friday	1-9 p.m.	Linda, Tom, Drew	Place sale signage, clean restroom	$1,500.00
Saturday	1-9 p.m.	Tom, Janet, Ted	Vacuum floors	$1,950.75
Sunday	1-5 p.m.	Gary, Shannon	Organize stock	$875.25

Exercise 15

❖ Edit Records ❖ Change Fonts
❖ Change Attributes

Notes

If you prefer working with a database form, you also can make changes to your records using a form. This method may slow you down somewhat, but since the form isolates information from one record at a time, you can more easily double-check the information for a single record.

You asked an editorial assistant to make some changes to the database holding the list of festivals that you created earlier (Exercise 10). You've discovered that the assistant made some errors, and you've received updates from some festival organizers. So, update the database now using a data form, work with both the data table and form, and then print the form.

Vocabulary

No new vocabulary in this exercise.

Directions

1. Create a copy of the **DB15** database file. Save the copy as **FESTIVAL2**.
2. Open the **FESTIVAL2** database file.
3. Open the **FESTIVAL2** form (assuming your database program uses a separate name for each form; otherwise use the form view of your database program). This form includes all of the fields in the database.
4. Using the form, make changes to each record as indicated in the shaded cells of Illustration 1 on the following page. (Each shaded cell holds a corrected entry you should make in the applicable field of the specified record.)
   ✓ As you update your database, you'll most likely make changes to a field or two in a few records at a time.

   ✓ If you leave the insertion point in a particular field and click the button for displaying the next record, that next record appears with the insertion point in the same field.

5. Save your changes, if needed, and close the form.
6. Open the **FESTIVAL2** data table (assuming your database program uses a separate name for each table; otherwise use the data table view of your database program).
7. Change the font size for the data table to 12 points and apply the bold attribute.
8. Adjust column widths so that each table cell entry and field name appears completely.
9. Save your changes to the database data table, and close the table.

Illustration 2

Mountain Gear
Fall Schedule

As the busy season approaches, it's time to revise our staffing schedule. Please let me know as soon as possible if you cannot work the schedule below:

Day	Hours	Employees	Tasks	Sales Goal
Tuesday	1-7 p.m.	Gary, Shannon	Clean restroom, clean counters	$575.00
Wednesday	1-7 p.m.	Linda, Tom	Vacuum floors	$625.50
Thursday	1-7 p.m.	Linda, Drew	Stock merchandise, mark sale items	$715.25
Friday	1-9 p.m.	Linda, Tom, Drew	Place sale signage, clean restroom	$1,500.00
Saturday	1-9 p.m.	Tom, Janet, Ted	Vacuum floors	$1,950.75
Sunday	1-5 p.m.	Gary, Shannon	Organize stock	$875.25

Remember that policies also change for the fall. You may have a 15-minute break every two hours, but please make sure the register is covered. Please give me 24-hour notice if you trade shifts.

Illustration 2

CLIENT3   10/12/2004

ID	FirstName	LastName	Address1	Address2	City	State	ZIP	HomePh	WorkPh
001	Linda	Williams	124 Avery Lane	Apt. 200	Indianapolis	IN	46208	(317)555-2727	
002	Joe	Scott	10995 College Ave.		Fishers	IN	46038	(317)888-0202	(317)888-7389
003	Fred	Lindstrom	8802 Charleston Way	C	Fishers	IN	46038	(317)555-0101	(317)555-9999
004	Vivian	Crowder	245 Broad Ave.		Indianapolis	IN	46201	(317)555-7878	(317)555-7777
005	Tom	Cantrell	455 Murdock Circle	Apt. B4	Greenwood	IN	46119	(317)777-4545	(317)777-9000
006	Petra	Gott	103 Maxwell Rd.		Indianapolis	IN	46254	(317)555-3838	(317)555-0001
007	Ruby	Pope	248 Whitaker Rd.		Greenwood	IN	46119	(317)777-2904	
008	Vicky	Wayne	1148 Black Oak Rd.		Fishers	IN	46038	(317)888-3827	(317)888-1221
009	Gene	Taylor	12 Priscilla Ln.		Indianapolis	IN	46268	(317)555-6701	
010	Carolynnne	Rose	60 Hilltop Dr.	#3	Greenwood	IN	46119	(317)777-4849	(317)777-4040

Page 1

Exercise 49

❖ Create a Table ❖ Change Table Column Width
❖ Format Table Data ❖ Add Borders/Shading

Notes

Not only can you format the text within the table cells, but you can also format the cells themselves. You can apply shading within any cell or choose a different border color and weight for the cell. Combine different shading and border choices within the table to create an interesting effect or to highlight the most important information in the table.

You own Light Natural Beeswax Candles, and you're putting together your 2006 wholesale price list. Add a table of prices in this exercise, and then apply some attractive formatting to the table cells.

Vocabulary

No new vocabulary in this exercise.

Directions

1. Open the **WP49** document file.
2. Save the file as **BEEPRI**.
3. Set all the page margins to **1.5"**.
4. Format the first two lines (paragraphs) of text in 16-point Forte (or a similar font) and center them.
5. Click to place the insertion point on the second blank line following the paragraph that ends with **...and other wholesale customers**.
6. Insert a table that has four columns and six rows.
7. Enter the table information as shown in Illustration 1 on the following page.
8. Select the top row of the table.

    ✓ *Point to the left border or gridline of the row until the pointer changes to a selection pointer, then click to select the whole row.*

9. Format the text in 12-point Forte (or a similar font).
10. Add rose shading to the selected cells.

    ✓ *In your word processing program, you probably use the same command for adjusting cell borders and shading that you used for working with paragraph borders and shading.*

    ✓ *Keep contrast in mind when you choose cell shading. If the shading is too dark, the cell text may become difficult to read, unless you format the text in a lighter color.*

11. Resize the first column so that it's approximately **2"** wide.
12. Select all rows but the first row in the table.
13. Add light green shading to the selected cells.

    ✓ *The contrasting shading calls attention to the first row.*

14. Select all the table cells.

✓ *You can't edit the entry in an AutoNumber field, like the **ID** field.*

✓ *When you change a cell entry in the data table, you can use the Tab key or an arrow key to move to the next cell.*

6. Change the font and font size for the data table to 11-point Century Schoolbook and apply italics.

   ✓ *In many database programs, any font change you make applies to all the table contents, even if you select only a particular column or record.*

7. Readjust column widths again so that each table cell entry can display on a single line, but don't include unnecessary blank space.

8. Save your changes to the database data table.

9. Print one copy of the data table in landscape orientation. Illustration 2 on the following page shows approximately how the printed table should look.

   ✓ *Most database programs offer a Page Setup command which you use to change the printout orientation setting.*

   ✓ *If your printout doesn't fit on a single page, you can change the margins to help it fit. You'll review how to change margins in Exercise 17.*

10. Close the database file, closing any open forms and data tables first, if required.

Illustration 1

ID	FirstName	LastName	Address1	Address2	City	State	ZIP	HomePh	WorkPh
001	Linda	Williams	124 Avery Lane	Apt. 200	Indianapolis	IN	46208	317-555-2727	
002	Joe	Scott	10995 College Ave.		Fishers	IN	46038	317-888-0202	317-888-7389
003	Fred	Lindstrom	8802 Charleston Way	C	Fishers	IN	46038	317-555-0101	317-555-9999
004	Vivian	Crowder	245 Broad Ave.		Indianapolis	IN	46201	317-555-7878	317-555-7777
005	Tom	Cantrell	455 Murdock Circle	Apt. B4	Greenwood	IN	46119	317-777-4545	317-777-9000
006	Petra	Gott	103 Maxwell Rd.		Indianapolis	IN	46254	317-555-3838	317-555-0001
007	Ruby	Pope	248 Whitaker Rd.		Greenwood	IN	46119	317-777-2904	
008	Vicky	Wayne	1148 Black Oak Rd.		Fishers	IN	46038	317-888-3827	317-888-1221
009	Gene	Taylor	12 Priscilla Ln.		Indianapolis	IN	46268	317-555-6701	
010	Carolynne	Rose	60 Hilltop Dr.	#3	Greenwood	IN	46119	317-777-4849	317-777-4040

15. Format all cells to have 1½-point sea green borders along the bottom and top of each cell only.

   ✓ *To achieve this effect, it's easier to apply the all or grid border style, then remove only the vertical borders.*

16. Click outside the table so you can see the results of your changes. The finished document should look like Illustration 2.
17. Save your changes to the document file.
18. Print one copy of the document.
19. Close the document.

Illustration 1

Item	Color	Case Quantity	Unit Price
3" round pillar, geranium	White	36	$2.99
3" round pillar, orange	Orange	36	$2.99
6" square pillar, cinnamon	Red	24	$10.99
6" square pillar, ginger	Green	24	$10.99
Votive assortment	Assorted	144	$.49

Illustration 2

Light Natural Beeswax Candles
2006 Wholesale Prices

Light Natural Beeswax Candles has been serving candle customers for more than 12 years. We appreciate our customers, so we provide purchasing convenience. Call 888-555-8181 to place an order. The prices below reflect our favored rates for resellers, event planners, and other wholesale customers.

Item	*Color*	*Case Quantity*	*Unit Price*
3" round pillar, geranium	White	36	$2.99
3" round pillar, orange	Orange	36	$2.99
6" square pillar, cinnamon	Red	24	$10.99
6" square pillar, ginger	Green	24	$10.99
Votive assortment	Assorted	144	$.49

Note: Sales tax not included. Prices subject to change.

Exercise 14

❖ Edit Records ❖ Change Fonts
❖ Change Attributes

Notes

You can make changes to the records in your database data table to update information as it changes. Also, you can change the formatting of the cell contents in the data table, to control how the data looks on-screen and when printed.

You've discovered some errors in your client database, and you need to make corrections. Also, you want to format the data table so that you can print a list of client information. Tackle both of these tasks now.

Vocabulary

No new vocabulary in this exercise.

Directions

1. Create a copy of the **DB14** database file. Save the copy as **CLIENT3**. This is a version of a database file you've worked with in a previous exercise.

   ✓ Some database programs do not offer a Save As command, so you have to use My Computer or a Windows Explorer window to copy the file and rename the copy. However, if your database program offers a Save As command, use it because it'll be faster.

2. Open the **CLIENT3** database file.
3. Open the **CLIENT3** table (assuming your database program uses a separate name for each table; otherwise use the data table view of your database program).
4. Resize columns as needed to show the contents of each field. You also can make some columns, such as the **ID** field column, smaller to allow room for the other, wider field columns.

   ✓ You can drag the right border of the column heading to change the column width. In some applications, you can double-click the right border in the column heading, which resizes the column to fit the longest entry in the column. Those same applications allow you to resize multiple columns at once, by selecting the columns and double-clicking the right border in any one of the column headings.

5. Make changes in the data table to each record as indicated in the shaded cells of Illustration 1 on the following page (Each shaded cell holds a corrected entry for the applicable field of the specified record.) Assume you need to make these changes to correct a few errors in the database.

Exercise 50

❖ Insert and Delete Table Columns and Rows

Notes

Just as you may need to edit regular paragraph text, you may need to make changes to the information in your table at a later time. To edit the contents of a table cell, click in the table cell and use regular editing techniques (Delete, Backspace, and so on) to make your changes. You may find, however, that you need to add a column or row, or delete a column or row.

You've realized the mobile phone growth statistics document that you created in Exercise 47 is incomplete. Update the document now with the latest information about the Mobile A Network. This will require you to work more with rows and columns.

Vocabulary

automatic table formatting

Directions

1. Open the **WP50** document file.
2. Save the file as **MOBSTAT2**.
3. Delete the **Northwest** row from the table.
   - ✓ When you delete a row, any rows below it slide up to fill the gap. When you delete a column, all columns to the right slide left to fill the gap.
4. Insert two new rows below the Northeast row.
   - ✓ To insert more than one row, you would select as many rows as you need to insert first. (That is, select two rows to insert two new rows.) New rows appear above the selected row(s). Similarly, columns you insert appear to the left of the selected column(s).
5. Make these entries in the first two columns of the two new rows:

Northwest/Alaska	**136,000**
Puerto Rico	**45,000**

6. Make these entries in the next three columns of the two new rows:

99,000	**105,000**	**62,500**
32,000	**37,000**	**19,000**

7. Insert a new column to the right of the **Q4** column.
   - ✓ You can use a command to insert a new column to the right of an existing table column in recent Word versions. Click a cell in the column beside which you want to insert a new column. Then choose Table|Insert|Columns to the Right.

10. Enter the following information in the new column:

Losses
33,000
9.000
4,000
21,000
20,000

Lesson 22
Edit and Enhance a Database

Exercises 14–19

- ❖ **Work with fonts and font attributes**
- ❖ **Edit records**
- ❖ **Adjust margins in a data table**
- ❖ **Practice inserting and deleting records**
- ❖ **Apply filters**

11. Select the entire table.

12. Use automatic table formatting to apply new formatting to the table. Do not apply the last row or last column formatting.

✓ **Automatic table formatting** (also called Table AutoFormat in Word) applies text formatting, column width and alignment settings, and borders and shading to the table. This erases any formatting you applied previously. However, you can change formatting settings after applying the automatic format to override the automatic formatting choices.

13. Click outside the table to see the results of your changes. The finished document should look like the illustration below, but will have the automatic formatted that you applied. (Compare it with the finished document from the last exercise to see the effect of your changes.)

14. Save your changes to the document file.

15. Print one copy of the document.

16. Close the document.

U.S. Mobile Phone User Growth
By Quarter
March 31, 2006

Region	Q1	Q2	Q3	Q4	Losses
Northeast	150,000	252,000	139,000	179,000	33,000
Northwest/Alaska	136,000	99,000	105,000	62,500	9,000
Puerto Rico	45,000	32,000	37,000	19,000	4,000
Southeast	176,000	202,000	87,000	42,000	21,000
Southwest	175,000	209,000	310,000	164,000	20,000

ItemNo	Line	Company	Gender	FullPrice	PercentOff
1	Rox	Blazers	M	$79.99	35%
2	Rox	Blazers	F	$75.99	35%
3	Hard Hike	TopLine	M	$129.99	35%
4	Hard Hike	TopLine	F	$119.99	35%
5	Fleming	Screech	M	$99.99	25%
6	LightWing	Screech	F	$89.99	25%
7	Linda	Trail Boss	F	$72.99	20%
8	Keller	Trail Boss	M	$75.99	20%
9	Adventure	Blazers	M	$65.99	20%
10	Adventure	Blazers	F	$65.99	20%

Exercise 51

❖ Insert and Delete Table Columns and Rows
❖ Calculate

Notes

Because tables in word processing documents can contain **values**, you may want to create formulas that perform calculations using the values in the table. You can enter a **table formula** into any cell in the table to calculate values. As in a spreadsheet program, you identify a cell by its **column letter** and **row number**, which form the **cell address**. (Unlike a spreadsheet you can't see the column letters and row numbers; starting from the upper-left cell of the table, which is A1, row numbers increase going down and column letters increase going right.) In some applications, you also can use the term **LEFT** in a formula to perform a calculation on the cell entries to the left and **ABOVE** to perform a calculation on the cell entries above. Each formula starts with a symbol like an equals sign. Formulas can include **functions**, which offer a shortcut method for performing a calculation. Try creating formulas in a word processing table in this exercise. (If you want a more clear understanding of formulas and functions, consult the help feature or the Spreadsheet section of this book.)

You need to make some changes to the table you created for the 2006 wholesale price list for Light Natural Beeswax Candles (Exercise 49). Adjust the table in this exercise, including adding formulas to perform some calculations.

Vocabulary

values	column letter	cell address
table formula	row number	function

Directions

1. Open the **WP51** document file.
2. Save the file as **BEEPRI2**.
3. Delete the **Color** column.
4. Insert two new rows above the row that has **Votive assortment** in the left cell.

5. Make the following entries in the new rows:

6" round pillar, geranium	26	$9.99
6" round pillar, orange	26	$9.99

6. Select the cells in the **Unit Price** column.

Exercise 13

❖ Critical Thinking

Notes

In this exercise, you will practice many of the database skills you've developed so far. In the steps below, you create a database, adjust the field formats, enter several records into the data table, and work with the data table appearance. Database and spreadsheet programs can hold similar lists of information, as you'll see here, although it's best to use the spreadsheet program if you're planning to perform a lot of calculations. (You can also share information between your spreadsheet and database programs.)

You own the Mountain Gear shop, and you've decided to track some of the information for your boot sale in a database. Create the database and enter that data now.

Vocabulary

No new vocabulary in this exercise.

Directions

1. Create a new database file, naming the database **BSALE**.
2. Refer to the illustration on the following page to see the information to include in the database. Add the appropriate fields, specifying the field name, data type, and size, if applicable.
3. Save your changes to the database. (Save the table and name it **BSALE**, if needed.)
4. Create a primary key.

5. Double-check the field formats, and apply any special formatting as needed.
   - ✓ Hint: Set up the **FullPrice** field as currency, and the **PercentOff** field as text with a special format—@@%. Redisplay the data table (or datasheet).
6. Enter the records shown in the illustration.
7. Save your changes to the database.
8. Change the widths for any columns in the data table as needed.
9. Preview and print one copy of the data table.
10. Close the database file.

7. Add a decimal tab at about the 4" mark so that the unit prices align.
8. Add a new column to the right of the **Unit Price** column.
9. Enter **Case Price** in the top cell of the new column.
10. Enter formulas in the **Case Price** column to multiply the entries in the **Case Quantity** and **Unit Price** columns on the same row.

   ✓ *You cannot type a formula directly into a table cell. Instead, use the command for creating formulas in the word processing program. A dialog box will assist you in building the formula, list available functions, and give you formatting choices for the calculated values.*

   ✓ *In formulas, * is the symbol for multiplying and / is the symbol for dividing.*

11. As you create the formulas, format the formulas to display results with a dollar sign, thousands separator, and two decimal places.
12. Click in the **Case Quantity** cell for the **Votive assortment** row.
13. Change the cell entry to **125**.
14. Recalculate the value in the **Case Price** cell for the **Votive assortment** row.

   ✓ *If your word processing program doesn't recalculate values automatically, you probably need to click in the cell to recalculate, then press a shortcut key such as F9. This is faster than recalculating information yourself and changing cell entries.*

15. Select the entire table.
16. Use automatic table formatting to apply new formatting to the table. Do not apply the last row or last column formatting.
17. Click outside the table so you can see the results of your changes.
18. Adjust the width of the **Item** column so that each of its entries appears on a single line. The finished document should resemble the illustration on the following page, but with the automatic formatting that you selected.
19. Save your changes to the document file.
20. Print one copy of the document.
21. Close the document.

ID	OutDate	Title	Item	Paid	Days	CID	CPhone
1	1/20/06	Prince of Tides	2938444	6	3	177	317-849-9999
2	1/20/06	Seven Year Itch	1029939	4	2	388	317-848-2222
3	1/21/06	Funny Face	1399399	4	2	222	317-298-5757
4	1/21/06	Kill Bill Vol. 1	3882828	6	3	225	317-298-5687
5	1/21/06	Kill Bill Vol. 2	3897739	6	3	225	317-298-5687
6	1/21/06	Rushmore	3777939	4	2	272	317-252-0909
7	1/22/06	Memento	3689393	4	2	304	317-221-9843
8	1/22/06	El Mariachi	3563838	4	2	199	317-299-4141

Light Natural Beeswax Candles
2006 Wholesale Prices

Light Natural Beeswax Candles has been serving candle customers for more than 12 years. We appreciate our customers, so we provide purchasing convenience. Call 888-555-8181 to place an order. The prices below reflect our favored rates for resellers, event planners, and other wholesale customers.

Item	Case Quantity	Unit Price	Case Price
3" round pillar, geranium	36	$2.99	$ 107.64
3" round pillar, orange	36	$2.99	$ 107.64
6" square pillar, cinnamon	24	$10.99	$ 263.76
6" square pillar, ginger	24	$10.99	$ 263.76
6" round pillar, geranium	26	$9.99	$ 259.74
6" round pillar, orange	26	$9.99	$ 259.74
Votive assortment	125	$.49	$ 61.25

Note: Sales tax not included. Prices subject to change.

Exercise 12

❖ Open a Form ❖ Enter Records
❖ Preview a Database Form
❖ Print a Database Form

Notes

In this exercise, you review how to use a form to create the records in a database. In addition, you print the database while viewing the form, so you can compare a form printout with the data table printout you made in the last exercise.

Use the database form to enter some records in the movie rental database you created to track your business' movie rentals, and then preview and print the form.

Vocabulary

No new vocabulary in this exercise.

Directions

1. Create a copy of the **DB12** database file. Save the copy as **MOVIE3**.
2. Open the **MOVIE3** database file.
3. Open the **MOVIE3** form or switch to the form view in your database program.
4. Enter the records listed in the illustration on the following page.

   ✓ *When you create a form that you intend to use for data entry, you may need to set up the field formatting or input mask for the form, too, and adjust width of the input text box for the field. In this case, the MOVIE3 form in the exercise file has the proper formatting set up for the field where you enter the phone number, so you don't need to enter parentheses or hyphens. Use the view for designing forms in your database program to specify field formatting, when necessary. Try to match the field formatting you*

   set up in the data table to reduce the possibility of errors.

   ✓ *If the **CPhone** field text box in the form isn't wide enough, switch to the view you use to edit the form design in your database program, and make the field wide enough to display the full phone number entry.*

5. Save your database entries.
6. Use the database program's print preview feature to see how a printout of the database would look. In this case, the database program formats the printout in the form layout.
7. Use the buttons in the preview window to see how many pages the printout will be.
8. Print one copy of the database.
9. Save the database.
10. Close the database file, closing any open forms or preview windows first, if required.

Exercise 52

❖ Sort Information

Notes

While you can insert and remove rows and move text between rows to alphabetize or reorder information in a table, that process could get time consuming. The task would be even more complicated if you had to reorder the table information based on the contents of more than one column. Most word processing programs offer a **sort** feature that orders the contents of the rows in a table according to sorting choices you specify. Perform a few separate sorts in this exercise.

As the owner of Mountain Gear, you need to do a little financial work. In this exercise, take a look at the current payables for the company, and sort that information in various ways so that you can better schedule your payments.

Vocabulary

sort   descending   criteria
header row   ascending

Directions

1. Open the **WP52** document file.
2. Save the file as **PAYA**.

   ✓ If your table contains a row of labels at the top (a **header row**), like the table in the document for this exercise, make sure you indicate its presence by choosing the correct option when you perform the sort. Otherwise, the sort may move the header row.

3. Sort the table in the document in descending number (numerical) order by the **P.O. Number** column.

   ✓ **Descending** order is Z-A order or from the largest to the smallest number. **Ascending** order sorts information from A-Z order or from the smallest to the largest number.

   ✓ You must click in the table before performing the sort. It isn't important where you click. The sort operation moves all the information in each row together. That is, you can't select a column and then sort or reorder the data in that column only without disturbing the information in other columns.

4. Sort the table in ascending text (alphabetical) order by the **Vendor** column.
5. Sort the table in the document in ascending date order by the **Due Date** column.

   ✓ Most word processors also enable you to sort consecutive paragraphs or items in a bulleted or numbered list. Select the paragraphs to sort, then perform the sort, which will be based on the first word or number (depending on whether you choose to sort alphabetically or by number) in each selected paragraph or list item.

Item	PurchasePrice	PurchaseYear	InHome	PaidOff
46" plasma TV	6500	2004	yes (check)	no
HP notebook computer	2500	2003	yes (check)	yes (check)
2004 Ford F150	13755	2004	no	no
1850 antique step cupboard	3500	2003	yes (check)	yes (check)
Oversized Kilim rug	2500	2000	yes (check)	yes (check)
KitchenMaster side-by-side fridge	1200	2002	yes (check)	no
KitchenMaster range	775	2002	yes (check)	no
36" TV	455	1999	yes (check)	yes (check)
Art print	250	1998	yes (check)	yes (check)
Digital camera	375	2003	yes (check)	yes (check)

6. Perform a single sort based on two sorting choices (**criteria**). First, specify to sort in ascending text order by the **Vendor** column. Then specify to sort in ascending date order by the **Due Date** column. Perform the sort.

7. Click outside the table to see the sort results. The finished document should look like the illustration below.
8. Save your changes to the document file.
9. Print one copy of the document.
10. Close the document.

Mountain Gear
Current Payables

P.O. Number	Due Date	Amount	Vendor
1001	1/1/2006	50.63	Denver
1098	1/10/2006	883.59	Denver
1076	1/8/2006	1,389.90	Footworks
1070	1/8/2006	2,662.57	Footworks
1084	1/9/2006	5,347.95	Footworks
1049	1/5/2006	1,531.62	High Vista
1047	1/5/2006	3,071.47	High Vista
1004	1/1/2006	200.61	Outdoor Action
1035	1/4/2006	1,537.59	Outdoor Action
1038	1/4/2006	209.98	Sport Shades
1019	1/2/2006	993.60	Spryster

10. Now experiment with the **PurchaseYear** field. Its entries are shorter than the field width, so you want to change the field width. Change to the view that enables you to create and design fields.

11. Change the width (size) of the **PurchaseYear** field to **3** and then save the database design. Your database program should display a warning that "data will be lost." This means that the longest entry in the field is longer than three characters, and resetting the field width to three characters would cause the database program to discard all but the first three characters of each entry in the field. You don't want to do this, so cancel the save.

   ✓ *Why do you want to set your fields to a width approximating the longest entry? Because if a database contains thousands of entries, the "empty space" in fields can add up and cause the database file to perform slowly, especially on slower computer systems with less memory.*

   ✓ *When in doubt, count the number of characters in the longest entry in a field before you reduce the field size.*

12. Change the width of the **PurchaseYear** field to **8** characters and save the database design. Because you're making the field larger than the four characters in a year entry, you can continue the save if you see any warnings.

13. Change the formatting of the **PurchasePrice** field, a Currency field, to have **0** (zero) decimal places. This will make the entries in those fields display in a more compact format. Save the database design.

14. Redisplay the database in the view you use to enter records in the data table. Notice that the **PurchaseYear** column display hasn't really changed, despite the fact that you've altered the field width.

15. Notice that the **InHome** and **PaidOff** field columns have unnecessary blank space when displayed on-screen. Change the column width (not the field width) so that these columns take up less space when you view the data table.

16. Increase the column width of the **Item** field so you can see all of the longest entries.

17. Use the database program's print preview feature to see how a printout of the database would look.

   ✓ *Generally, the database program will print whatever view of the data currently appears on-screen. Display the data table to print your database in a tabular format. Display a form to print your database using the formatting supplied by the form. Display a report to print it, and so on. However, you can't print the views you use to design your data table, forms, and reports.*

18. Print one copy of the database.
19. Save the database.
20. Close the database file, closing any open data tables or preview windows first, if required.

Exercise 53

❖ Critical Thinking

Notes

In this exercise, revisit the table building and formatting skills you developed throughout this lesson.

You are the instructor of an Advanced Algebra class. Create, edit, and format a table with student test score results. The table will include a column that totals the scores from three tests.

Vocabulary

No new vocabulary in this exercise.

Directions

1. Create a new, blank document.
2. Save the file as **PROD**.
3. Enter and format the document title lines as shown in the illustration on the followng page.
4. Create and enter the table text shown in the illustration.
5. Enter formulas in cells as indicated in the illustration. Format the formula results in the **Class Average** row to display with 0 decimal places. Add a new row below the row that has **L2044** in the far left column.
6. Make the following entries in the first four cells of the new row:

L2L2099	68	79	81

7. Enter a formula to calculate the Total for the new row.
8. Recalculate the values in the Class Average row.
9. Format the table with automatic table formatting. This time, do apply the last row and last column formatting.
   - ✓ *Not all automatic formats apply specific formatting to the far-right column, even if you choose to apply it. The formatting for the far-right and bottom columns will vary depending on the AutoFormat applied.*
10. Center the entries for all columns except the first one.
11. Save your changes to the document file.
12. Print one copy of the document.
13. Close the document.

Exercise 11

❖ Open a Data Table ❖ Enter Records ❖ Change Field Width ❖ Preview a Data Table ❖ Print a Data Table

Notes

Changing the column width in a data table, a skill you practiced in the last exercise, only changes how information displays. To change how much information a field can contain, in characters, you have to change the **field width**, or the size of the field in characters. (As noted in an earlier exercise, you only can change the size of fields with Text and Memo data types.)

Your financial planner has advised you to put together an inventory of your home's contents for insurance purposes. Add the first several records to your home inventory database now, adjust field lengths, and then preview and print the data table.

Vocabulary

field width

Directions

1. Create a copy of the **DB11** database file. Save the copy as **HOMEINV**.
2. Open the **HOMEINV** database file.
3. Open the **HOMEINV** table, if needed.
4. Start entering the records listed in the illustration on page 383. When you reach the **Item** entry for the fourth record, you should encounter a problem. You can't type the full item name into the field.
5. Change to the view that enables you to create and design fields. (Some database programs call this the design view.)
6. Notice that the field size for the **Item** field is set to **20** (it can hold 20 characters), making the field too small to accept your entry.

7. Change the field size so it can hold entries up to **45** characters.
8. Return to the view where you enter records, and enter the rest of the records listed in the illustration.

   ✓ *Save your changes to the database design whenever required by your program or whenever the program prompts you to do so. Generally, every time you make a change to a field or column, you need to save your changes to the database design.*

   ✓ *You may need to correct the **Item** field entry for the fourth record to continue. Click in the field to make the needed corrections.*

9. Save your database entries.

Advanced Algebra Test Scores

18-pt. Franklin Gothic Heavy

Student ID	Test 1	Test 2	Test 3	Total
L2076	99	89	95	
L2088	87	85	81	
L2102	99	98	99	
L2065	75	95	80	
L2044	78	82	87	
L2133	55	75	85	
Class Average				

Average the values above for individual tests and the Total.

Sum the three test values.

Festival	Start	End	City	State	WebSite
American Music Festival	9/3/06	9/6/06	Virginia Beach	VA	www.beacheventsfun.com
Mule Days	9/23/06	9/26/06	Benson	NC	www.bensonmuledays.com
Bluegrass Festival	9/14/06	9/18/06	Morehead	KY	www.poppymountainbluegrass.com
Peanut Festival	9/25/06	9/26/06	Plains	GA	www.plainsgeorgia.com
Outdoor FoodFest	9/18/06	9/18/06	Hilton Head	SC	www.hiltonheadisland.com/food
Seafood Sampler	9/18/06	9/19/06	Norfolk	VA	www.festeventsva.org

Lesson 9
Merge Documents

Exercises 54–59

- ❖ **Merge basics**
- ❖ **Work with main and data documents**
- ❖ **Use conditions when merging**
- ❖ **Create envelopes and labels**

Exercise 10

❖ Open a Data Table ❖ Enter Records
❖ Change Column Width

Notes

When you create a database, its table uses a default column width, so that each column in the table uses the same width. This is appropriate for fields that hold about 15 characters of information. However, if you set up a field for longer entries, those entries may appear cut off when you display the table. Or, if a field holds a currency amount or yes/no response, the field may contain unnecessary blank space. You can change the **column width** for various columns in a data table to ensure the columns better display the field entries.

You're a magazine editor compiling a list of upcoming festivals in surrounding states for publications. Enter the first several records now, and then adjust the datasheet column widths.

Vocabulary

column width

Directions

1. Create a copy of the **DB10** database file. Save the copy as **FESTIVAL**.
2. Open the **FESTIVAL** database file.
3. Open the **FESTIVAL** table, if needed.
4. Enter the records listed in the illustration on the following page.

   ✓ *If your database program offers a hyperlink field type, you can create a field for Web URLs in your database tables. A hyperlink field recognizes your Web URL entries as hyperlinks. You can click one of the hyperlinks to launch your Web browser and display the indicated Web site.*

5. Save your database entries. Notice that the **Festival** and **WebSite** columns are too narrow to display their full entries.

6. Resize the **Start**, **End**, and **State** columns to make them slightly smaller, about as wide as the field names.

   ✓ *In most database programs, you can use a command to specify a precise width, in characters, for columns in the data table. To specify an approximate column width for a field column, drag the right border of the field name to resize. To size the field to fit its widest entry, you can double-click on the border to the right of the field name.*

7. Resize the **Festival** and **WebSite** columns so that each column can show its widest entry. This causes the data table to be much wider. Save your changes to the database.
8. Close the database file, closing any open data tables first, if required.

Exercise 54

❖ Create Main and Data Document s ❖ Merge

Notes

You've probably seen a form letter: a company prepares numerous copies of the same letter, inserting a different recipient name in each copy of the letter. This approach creates a personalized copy of the letter for each recipient. You can use your word processing program's **mail merge** feature to accomplish the same process.

When you mail merge, you create a **main document** (or merge document), which holds the text common to all copies of the document. You also create the **data document** (data source), the document that holds the unique information that will be combined with the main document to create personalized copies. The data document divides information into **records** and **fields**. Each record is the set of data that pertains to one recipient or one copy of the document. All records use the same fields, or specific pieces of information like a first name, last name, address, and so on. The top row of the data document table lists the field names.

> ✓ *The Mail Merge Wizard in Word 2002 and Word 2003 saves the data document (or address list) as an Access database (.mdb) file by default. However, you also can enter data in a Word document in a table, as in previous Word versions. The first row of the table should hold the field names.*

To tell the word processing program where to merge the fields for each record, you insert **merge field codes** into the main document. Your word processing program may offer a wizard or other helper program to help you with the process.

You are the Executive Director of the Meals for All food bank. You want to send a letter to key donors who have not made a contribution recently. Create the data document and main document (your letter) from scratch, and then merge them.

Vocabulary

mail merge	data document	fields
main document	records	merge field codes

ID	FirstName	LastName	Address1	Address2	City	State	ZIP	HomePh	WorkPh
001	Linda	Williams	124 Avery Ct.	Apt. 2	Indianapolis	IN	46208	317-555-2727	317-555-0393
002	Joe	Scott	10995 College Ave.		Fishers	IN	46038	317-888-0202	317-888-7389
003	Fred	Lindstrom	8802 Charleston Way	C	Indianapolis	IN	46254	317-555-0101	317-555-9999
004	Vivian	Crowder	245 Broad Ave.		Indianapolis	IN	46201	317-555-7878	317-555-7777
005	Tim	Cantrell	455 Murdock Circle	Apt. B4	Greenwood	IN	46119	317-777-4545	317-777-9000
006	Petra	Gott	103 Maxwell Rd.		Indianapolis	IN	46254	317-555-3838	317-555-0001
007	Ruby	Pope	248 Whitaker Rd.		Greenwood	IN	46119	317-777-2937	
008	Vicky	Wayne	48 Black Oak Rd.		Fishers	IN	46038	317-888-3827	317-888-1221
009	Gene	Taylor	12 Priscilla Ln.		Indianapolis	IN	46268	317-555-6701	
010	Carolyn	Rose	60 Hilltop Dr.		Greenwood	IN	46119	317-777-4849	317-777-4040

Directions

1. Create a new, blank document.
2. Start the merge wizard or helper in your word processing application.
   - ✓ *Different word processing programs handle merging very differently. If your word processing program requires you to create the main or data document before starting its merge helper, or uses an order that's different from the order presented here, then follow the required process for the exercises in this lesson.*
3. Select the letter or form letter type for the main document and use the current (blank) document as the main document.
4. Create a new data file (data source). It will include **Title**, **First Name**, **Last Name**, **Address Line 1**, **City**, **State**, and **ZIP Code** fields in the new data document.
   - ✓ *The merge wizard may present most of these fields for you by default. You can add any missing fields by creating a custom field or customizing the list. You also can delete unneeded fields by customizing the list.*
   - ✓ *The examples in this Lesson use only one field, Address Line 1, for street addresses. In real life, though, you want to use two address fields to provide space for an apartment or suite number.*
5. Enter records in the data file as shown in Illustration 1.
   - ✓ *Avoid accidentally adding additional spaces at the end of an entry in a field. This could create spacing problems in the finished document or other problems if you try to merge selected records.*
6. Save the data document; name it **REMD**.
7. Make sure that all the entries are selected. Do not sort the list. Continue with the merge.
8. Create the text of the main document, including the merge field codes, as shown in Illustration 2.
   - ✓ *Different word processing programs may use slightly different characters to set off the field codes. Some use pairs of single angle brackets (<>), some use pairs of double angle brackets (<<>>), and some use other characters.*
   - ✓ *Don't forget to insert spacing and punctuation where needed between merge field codes. For example, if you don't insert a space between the First Name and Last Name field codes, the word processing program will run those two fields together in the merged copies of the document. Press Enter after a merge field code to start a new paragraph.*
   - ✓ *In Word 2002 and 2003, you also can use the Insert Address Block button on the Merge toolbar to insert a code that represents all the address-related fields at the top of a letter. However, this approach doesn't give you flexibility over such items as including a job title for the addressee.*
9. Save the main document; name it **REM**.
10. Merge the main and data documents to a new document.
11. Page through the merged documents to inspect them.
12. Print one copy of the merged letters, then close the merged document without saving it.
13. Save the main document and close it.
14. Save the data document and close it.

Illustration 1

Title	First Name	Last Name	Address Line 1	City	State	ZIP Code
Mr.	Donald	Hawkins	32 Pleasant Circle	Indianapolis	IN	46256
Mrs.	Amanda	Faber	6483 Crest Blvd.	Indianapolis	IN	46210
Mr.	Thomas	Wayne	110 Allen Ct., Apt. C	Indianapolis	IN	46268
Ms.	Selena	Draper	12034 Meridian St.	Indianapolis	IN	46250

Exercise 9

❖ Open a Data Table
❖ Enter Records

Notes

Using the database itself (data table) to enter records resembles working in a spreadsheet. Each column in the table holds a field, and each row holds a record. Enter information in a field, then press Tab to move to the next field. Press Tab after entering the last field of information for a record to move to the first field for the next record.

Now that you've created the client database for your home remodeling business (in Exercise 3), add some client records. In this case, use the datasheet to make your entries.

Vocabulary

No new vocabulary in this exercise.

Directions

1. Create a copy of the **DB09** database file. Save the copy as **CLIENT2**.
2. Open the **CLIENT2** database file.
3. Open the **CLIENT2** table (assuming your database program uses separate data tables; otherwise, use the data table view in your program).
4. Enter the records listed in the illustration on the following page.
   - ✓ If you can't see all the fields on-screen at once, just keep pressing Tab as needed. As you use Tab to move to fields further to the right, the database information scrolls so you can see the field holding the insertion point.

   - ✓ In this case, the ID field has been specially formatted to display three digits. In recent Access versions, you apply this format by entering **000** in the Format text box in the table design view, with the ID field selected. Formatting has also been applied to the phone number fields, so you don't have to type in hyphens or other characters.

5. Save your changes to the database.
6. Close the database file, closing any open data tables first, if required.

Illustration 2

Meals for All
1001 Deed Way
Indianapolis, Indiana 46250

Today's Date

«Title» «First_Name» «Last_Name»
«Address_Line_1»
«City», «State» «ZIP_Code»

Dear «Title» «Last_Name»:

Thank you for your continued support of Meals for All.

If you received our recent Progress Report, then you know that Meals for All has been judicious in using the dollars provided by donors like you. Meals for All must ensure that as many clients as possible benefit through your donations.

While we achieved many goals last year, more work in the serving the community always awaits. We have the following items on our wish list for next year:

❖ An updated computer system, so we can better communicate and share data with other county and regional agencies.
❖ Another new delivery truck, as we anticipate that fuel costs will not decrease dramatically in the near future.
❖ An upgraded refrigeration system, so that we can lower food storage costs while increasing the available storage space.

If you haven't already allocated your donation dollars for this year, «Title» «Last_Name», please consider helping your fellow community members through another contribution to Meals for All. If you have any questions about our programs, please feel free to contact me at 888-555-9090.

Sincerely,

Anna Bryce
Executive Director
Meals for All

✓ A Yes/No field may contain only a check box. *Click the check box to specify "yes," and click it again to clear the check box and change your answer to "no." You often can press the spacebar to toggle the check mark on and off.*

5. Save your additions to the database.
6. Close the form.
7. Open the data table. (The table uses the name **ART2** if your database program can save multiple tables of information per database.)

   ✓ *The data table now contains the records you entered using the form.*

8. Redisplay the form. (Its name is **ART2** if your database program uses separate form names.)
9. Use the Page Down key or next record button to display record 5.
10. Display record 10.
11. Use the Page Up key or previous record button to display record 7.
12. Use the first record button to go back to the first record.
13. Save your changes to the database.
14. Close the database file, closing any open forms and data tables first, if required.

PN	FName	LName	Work	FSale	Price	Sold	SDate
1	Jean	Flynt	Blazing	yes (check)	250	no	
2	Cris	Charles	Walking Lightly	yes (check)	750	no	
3	Randall	Plemmons	Whirled	yes (check)	550	yes (check)	6/17/05
4	Taylor	Long	Maya	no		no	
5	Jean	Flynt	Remembrance	yes (check)	275	yes (check)	6/24/05
6	Keller	Mahoney	Tripped	no		no	
7	Miranda	Miles	On a Clear Day You Can See Clearly	yes (check)	1250	yes (check)	6/24/05
8	Opal	Lynn	Where I've Been	yes (check)	125	no	
9	Miranda	Miles	Been a Long Day	yes (check)	1000	no	
10	Lisa	Charles	Football	yes (check)	625	yes (check)	7/7/05

Exercise 55

❖ Open and Edit Main and Data Documents
❖ Merge

Notes

You don't have to create a document from scratch to perform a merge. You can use an existing document, specify a data document, insert merge fields, and perform the merge. In this exercise, you set up a letter as a merge letter, create the data document, and complete the merge.

You chose to take a biology course to fill your undergraduate science requirement. Use a merge to create flash cards to help you remember key bones in the human body.

Vocabulary

No new vocabulary in this exercise.

Directions

1. Open the **WP55** document file.
2. Save the file as **BONES**. This document includes a table and labels, but no information within the table.
3. Start the merge wizard or helper in your word processing application.
4. Choose a letter type main document and use the open **BONES** document as the main document.

   ✓ *You can use the letter main document type even if your document isn't a letter, as in the example in this exercise. In other words, choose the letter type for any document that's not an e-mail message, envelope, label, or directory.*

5. Create a new data file (data source) with only two fields: Create **Scientific Name** and **Common Name**.

6. Enter records in the data document as shown in Illustration 1.
7. Save the data document; name it **BONESD**.
8. Make sure that all the entries are selected. Do not sort the list. Continue with the merge.
9. Edit the main document to insert the merge field codes in the table, as shown in Illustration 2. Also select each merge field code, increase its font size to 22 points, and apply bold.

   ✓ *Formatting the merge field code applies the same formatting to the merged text in each copy of the merged document.*

   ✓ *Some table cells will likely appear to resize after you insert and format the merge field codes. For example, the entries in the top row of the table may snap to a single line, because formatting the field codes causes the far left and right columns to increase in width. However, when you preview the merged information, the top row entries may again use two lines.*

Exercise 8

❖ Open a Form ❖ Enter Records
❖ Display Different Records

Notes

Many beginning computer users may prefer to use a form to enter and view database information. Because the form displays a single record at a time (like a single page), you can focus on the record you're working with. Also, if your database contains many fields, they may not all fit on the screen when you're working with a **data table**, so you can create a form that displays all the fields for each record, instead. After you enter records, you can click buttons (**next record**, **previous record**, **first record**, and **last record**) to move through the records.

You want to start entering the data for your art gallery database that you created in Exercise 2. Open a version of the file that has a data entry form and enter and view records.

Vocabulary

data table   previous record button   last record button
next record button   first record button

Directions

1. Create a copy of the **DB08** database file. Save the copy as **ART2**.

   ✓ *Some database programs do not offer a Save As command, so you have to use My Computer or a Windows Explorer window to copy the file and rename the copy. However, if your database program offers a Save As command, use it because it'll be faster.*

2. Open the **ART2** database file.
3. Open the **ART2** form (assuming your database program uses a separate name for each form; otherwise use the form view of your database program).

4. Enter the records listed in the illustration on the following page. You'll leave some fields blank due to unsold pieces or pieces that are not for sale.

   ✓ *Use the Tab key to move between fields and to create each new record. Notice that you don't have to enter the dollar signs for currency values, and that the date fields apply formatting to dates you enter. Remember, the field data type and field format you specify when you create the database (or table or data table) determine how the information you enter displays in the database, even in a form based on the data table.*

   ✓ *You can't make an entry in an AutoNumber field like the **PN** field; press Tab to move past such a field. The database program fills in the appropriate information for you.*

10. Merge the main and data documents to a new document.
11. Page through the merged documents to inspect them.
12. Print one copy of the merged flash cards, then close the merged document without saving it.
13. Save the main document and close it.
14. Save the data document and close it.

Illustration 1

Scientific name	Common name
Clavicle	Collar bone
Femur	Thigh bone
Fibula	Thin lower leg bone
Humerus	Upper arm
Patella	Kneecap
Radius	Shorter lower arm bone
Scapula	Shoulder blade
Sternum	Breastbone
Tibia	Thick lower leg bone
Ulna	Longer lower arm bone

Illustration 2

Key Bones in the Human Body
Biology 104—Prof. Cameron

Scientific Name		Common Name
«Scientific_Name»	=	«Common_Name»

Lesson 21
Add Records and Print a Database

Exercises 8–13

❖ **Work with forms and tables**
❖ **Add records**
❖ **Adjust column and field width**
❖ **Preview and print a database**

Exercise 56

❖ Edit the Data Document
❖ Merge with Conditions

Notes

The data document for a merge is essentially a database—a list of records—stored in a word processing table. (For more information on the databases you create in a database program, see the Database section of the book.) You may need to add to your list of records (data document) over time.

✓ *In Word 2002 and 2003, you can use a database file you created in Access as the data source. However, you cannot use the Mail Merge Wizard to add records to the database from within Word. Word's Mail Merge Wizard can only edit data source tables stored in a Word document or those created directly in the Mail Merge Wizard (as a database table). So, the remaining exercises in this lesson use merge information stored in a Word document table.*

For example, if your merge document confirms customer orders, you'll need to add a record for each new order to the data document. Similarly, you may not need to merge all the records listed in your data source document. For example, if you need to generate shipping records for orders received on a range of dates only, you need to **merge with conditions** (**query** the list of data) to select only those records for the current day on the merge.

You are the residential manager of Best Arms, an apartment complex owned by Best Property Management. You need to send a letter to residents whose leases will be up soon, reminding them to renew. Add records for new tenants to the data document and use conditions to merge only letters for tenants who need to renew leases.

Vocabulary

merge with conditions   query

Pet Country Club

Check In

Pet Name:		Check in date:	
Owner Name:		Length of stay:	
Home Phone:		Vaccinations verified?	
Travel Phone:		Other services:	

Directions

1. Open the **WP56** document file.
2. Save the file as **RENEWD**. This is an example data document.
3. Open the **WP56-2** document file.
4. Save the file as **RENEW**. This document is a standard lease renewal reminder used by your company.
5. With the **RENEW** document active, start the merge wizard or helper in your word processing application.
6. Choose a letter type main document and use the open **RENEW** document as the main document.
7. Choose to use the **RENEWD** file as the data document (data source) rather than creating a new data document.
8. Add the records shown in Illustration 1 to the data document.

   ✓ *If the Edit button in the Mail Merge Recipients dialog box in Word doesn't work, close the dialog box, click the Edit Recipient List choice in the task pane, and then click the Edit button again.*

   ✓ *While you can manually add new records into the data document file, it's not always easy to place new records at the end of an existing table. If the order of the records in the table doesn't matter to you, then feel free to edit the data document manually. Otherwise, you can use the feature provided by the mail merge wizard or helper to edit the data document.*

9. Specify merge conditions (query options) to merge only the new orders (orders with a **Lease Date** of 11/1/05 or later).

   ✓ *You typically can use the mail merge wizard or helper to sort the records in the data document, if needed. For example, you could sort by Customer to place the customer records in alphabetical order. If you're creating a bulk mailing, postal regulations require that you sort the pieces to be mailed by ZIP Code.*

10. Edit the main document to add your name and merge field codes, as shown in Illustration 2. (Add and remove blank lines and adjust other document formatting as needed.)
11. Merge the main and data documents to a new document.
12. Page through the merged documents to inspect them.
13. Print one copy of the merged document, then close the merged document without saving it.
14. Save the main document and close it.
15. Save the data document and close it.

Illustration 1

Lease Date	First Name	Last Name	Address Line 1	Apt.	City	State	ZIP Code
11/4/05	Jen	James	1019 Wander Way	D	Indianapolis	IN	46268
11/12/05	Steve	Carroll	1204 Anderson	C	Indianapolis	IN	46268
11/13/05	Ken	Glass	1000 Phillips Ct.	B	Indianapolis	IN	46268

Exercise 7

❖ Critical Thinking

Notes

In this exercise, you practice creating a database and form on your own.

You run Pet Country Club, a boarding and grooming facility for pets. Previously, clients had filled out the form (shown on page 373) to give you information when checking in a pet. Now, plan and create a database file to use to gather the check in information.

Vocabulary

No new vocabulary in this exercise.

Directions

1. Get a copy of the database planning worksheet from Appendix B.
2. Refer to the example pet check-in form on the following page, and fill out the database planning worksheet to plan the database fields. (Use **CHECKIN** as the file name.)

   ✓ *Your fields should not be identical to those on the example card. Remember, you'll want to break some types of information into multiple fields for more sorting options. Don't forget field types like yes/no fields.*

3. Create the database file, naming the database **CHECKIN**.
4. Add the appropriate fields, including the name, data type, description, and size, if applicable.
5. Save your changes to the database (saving and naming the table **CHECKIN**, if needed).
6. Do not create a primary key if your database program prompts you to do so.
7. Format the phone fields to display in (800)555-1234 format.
8. Create a form that displays all the fields in the database.
9. Finish and save the form (and database).
10. If you have to name the form, use the name **CHECKIN** again.
11. If the finished form doesn't appear on-screen automatically, view it.
12. Redisplay the database grid (table or datasheet).
13. Redisplay the database form.
14. Save your changes to the database.
15. Close the database file.

Illustration 2

Best Arms ★ 8902 Zionsville Road ★ Indianapolis, IN 46268 ★ 888-555-2323

October 1, 2005

«First_Name» «Last_Name»
«Address_Line_1» «Apt»
«City», «State» «ZIP_Code»

Dear «First_Name»:

It has been a pleasure having you as a tenant at Best Arms. Residents like you make Best Arms one of the premier apartment complexes in the Indianapolis metropolitan area.

Our records show that your lease was signed last year on the following date: **«Lease_Date»**. As such, it will soon be up for renewal.

Please drop by the rental office soon or call me at 555-2323 to begin the renewal process or to provide notice of your intention to depart.

Best regards,

Student's name
Residential Manager
Best Arms

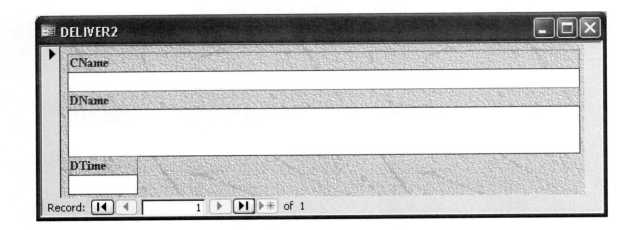

Exercise 57

❖ Edit the Data Document
❖ Merge with Conditions ❖ Prepare Envelopes

Notes

Because you can add records into your merge data document, you can reuse your main document and merge setup as many times as needed. This saves you the trouble of starting over with each mailing. You also can **merge envelopes** using the same data document you used to merge the main document. Try adjusting a data document and merging a letter and envelopes in this exercise.

You run an independent company, Testmasters, that grades law enforcement entrance exams. Prepare letters now to mail to applicants who have passed the latest exam.

Vocabulary

merge envelopes

Directions

1. Open the **WP57** document file.
2. Save the file as **EXAMD**. This is an example data document.
3. Open the **WP57-2** document file.
4. Save the file as **EXAM**.
5. With the **EXAM** document active, start the merge wizard or helper in your word processing application.
6. Choose a letter type main document and use the open **EXAM** document as the main document.
7. Choose to use the **EXAMD** document file as the data document (data source) rather than creating a new data document.
8. Add the records shown in Illustration 1 into the data document.
   - ✓ *If the Edit button in the Mail Merge Recipients dialog box in Word doesn't work, close the dialog box, click the Edit Recipient List choice in the Task Pane, and then click the Edit button again.*

9. Specify merge conditions (query options) to merge only the records for applicants that have passed the exam (records with a **Passing** entry in the **P_or_F** field).
10. Edit the main document to add your name and the merge field codes, as shown in Illustration 2. Apply bold to the merge field codes where shown. Save the document.
    - ✓ *After you save the main document with field codes in place and the data document specified, the field codes and links to the data document remain in place the next time you open the main document. You can reuse that same data document for the next merge, or use another data document.*
    - ✓ *You don't have to insert all the fields from the data document into the main merge document. Even if you don't insert a field, you can use it to specify a merge condition.*

Exercise 6

❖ Create a Form

Notes

In the last exercise, you created a form that displayed all the fields for each record, one record at a time. Create another form in this exercise. This time, set up the form to display only selected fields. You might use such a form when you only need to work with a few pertinent fields in the database.

When you're making your courier deliveries, you don't need to fill in all the fields immediately, so a form with a limited number of fields seems like an ideal solution. (Your plan is that you will enter the data for the rest of the database fields in advance, when you schedule your deliveries for the day.) Use a copy of the delivery database file you planned in Exercise 1 to create a quick form.

Vocabulary

No new vocabulary in this exercise.

Directions

1. Create a copy of the **DB06** database file. Save the copy as **DELIVER2**.
2. Open the new **DELIVER2** database file.
3. Create a form for the database (or the **DELIVER2** table in the database, in database files that can hold multiple tables).
4. Add only the following fields to the form:
   - CName
   - DName
   - DTime
5. Choose a layout for the form. The layout determines how the form arranges the fields. For example, the justified layout arranges the fields to fill a rectangular area where possible.
6. Choose form style, if prompted.
7. Finish and save the form (and database).
8. If you have to name the form, use the name **DELIVER2** again.
9. If the finished form doesn't appear on-screen automatically, view it. It should resemble the illustration on the following page, but may use a different layout or style.
10. Redisplay the database grid (table or datasheet).
11. Redisplay the database form.
12. Close the database file.

✓ If you want the merged information to use formatting other than the formatting specified when you insert the merge field code, you can select the merge field code and change its formatting. This changes the appearance of the merged information without affecting the merge itself.

11. Merge the main and data documents to a new document.

12. Page through the merged documents to inspect them.

13. Print one copy of the merged letters, then close the merged document without saving it.

14. Close the **EXAM** and **EXAMD** document and data files, saving them when prompted, then create a new, blank document.

15. Use the merge wizard or helper in your word processing program to change the blank file to a new main document of the envelope type.

16. Choose settings as needed to set the envelope with the standard business envelope (#10) size.

17. Choose the **EXAMD** document file as the data document (data source) for the envelope merge, too.

18. Specify merge conditions (query options) to merge only the records for applicants that passed (records with a **Passing** entry in the **P_or_F** field).

19. Insert the merge fields to address the envelope, as shown in Illustration 3. Delete any return address inserted by the merge wizard.

✓ Your word processing program's merge wizard or helper may display a dialog box that you can use to insert the fields. The envelope document also may have a placeholder area (basically a text box that displays a gray hatched outline when you click in it) to designate the approximate area where you should insert the merge fields. Click in this placeholder area before you start inserting merge fields.

✓ In Word, you also can include a postal bar code field above the address field. This field uses the ZIP Code field entry for this record to generate a bar code used by the U.S. Postal Service to facilitate mailing.

20. Merge the main (envelope) and data documents to a new document.

21. Page through the merged documents to inspect them.

22. Print one copy of the merged envelopes, then close the merged document without saving it.

✓ For the purposes of this exercise, you can print each envelope on plain paper. You only can print envelopes, labels, and special paper sizes if your printer provides that capability. If your printer can print special items, be sure to place the envelopes, labels, or special paper in the appropriate feed location or paper tray before printing.

✓ If you want to include a return address for envelopes that you create, edit the main envelope document before merging it. Simply enter and format the return address information in the upper-left corner of the main envelope document.

✓ Further, if you have a large mailing and want to qualify for bulk mailing rates, you would need to sort the records by ZIP Code before merging them. (It's best to do this before merging either the main document or the envelopes, so you don't spend your time hand-sorting the printed copies of the main document to match up each copy with its envelope.) The postal service requires that bulk-mailed items be sorted by ZIP Code. Then you would select all the text in the document with the merged envelopes and convert it to all uppercase (so the postal service's equipment can scan the recipient information). As bulk mailing rules change relatively frequently, check with your postmaster to learn how to prepare your bulk mailing.

23. Save the main envelope document file; name it **EXAME**.

24. Close the main envelope document.

10. Redisplay the database grid (table or datasheet).

11. Redisplay the database form.
12. Close the database file.

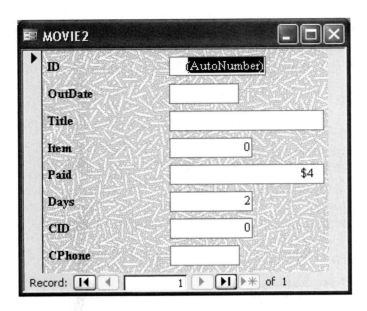

Illustration 1

First Name	Last Name	Address Line 1	City	State	ZIP Code	Score	P or F
Skip	Smith	8905 West End	Charlotte	NC	28277	87	Passing
Philip	Brown	2204 Beech Grove Lane	Charlotte	NC	28278	69	Failing

Illustration 2

TESTMASTERS, INC.
CHARLOTTE ST. LOUIS SEATTLE

January 20, 2006

«First_Name» «Last_Name»
«Address_Line_1»
«City», «State» «ZIP_Code»

Dear «First_Name»:

You recently took a law enforcement exam administered by Testmasters, Inc.

We have now scored the exams, and here is your result:

«Score»
«P_or_F»

Congratulations on your passing grade. Your local law enforcement agency will be contacting you soon to discuss the next step in the law enforcement application process.

Best regards,

YOUR NAME
TESTMASTERS, INC.

Exercise 5

❖ Create a Form

Notes

After you arrange the fields in the database, your database program may by default display fields in a grid that resembles a spreadsheet. (Your program may call this grid the database table or **datasheet**.) If you want a better way to enter and view records in your database program, you can create a **form**. A form provides an attractive layout for the fields in your database. In most database programs, the form displays one record on-screen at a time. Depending on how you format it, the form can display all the fields for each record or can display only the fields you really need to use.

Practice creating a form for the **MOVIE** database you created in the last exercise.

Vocabulary

datasheet   form

Directions

1. Create a copy of the **DB05** database file. Save the copy as **MOVIE2**.

   ✓ Some database programs do not offer a Save As command, so you have to use My Computer or a Windows Explorer window to copy the file and rename the copy. However, if your database program offers a Save As command, use it because it'll be faster.

2. Open the new **MOVIE2** database file.

   ✓ If you see a security warning when you open a database file for this book, click on Open to continue opening the file.

3. Create a form for the database (or the **MOVIE2** table in the database, in database files that can hold multiple tables).

   ✓ If your database program offers a wizard or other method to help you automatically create a form, you can use that method.

4. Add all the fields in the database to the form.

5. Choose a layout for the form. The layout determines how the form displays the fields. For example, the columnar layout displays the fields in a column, as in the illustration on the following page.

6. Choose form style, if prompted.

7. Finish and save the form (and database).

8. If you have to give a name to the form, use the name **MOVIE2** again.

9. If the finished form doesn't appear on-screen automatically, view it. It should resemble the illustration on the following page, though it may use a different layout or style.

   ✓ Depending on the database program you're using, you may need to change to a form view to view the form if it doesn't display automatically. If your database program will save several forms, you display the list of forms and then double-click the form you want to see; the form opens in its own window.

Illustration 3

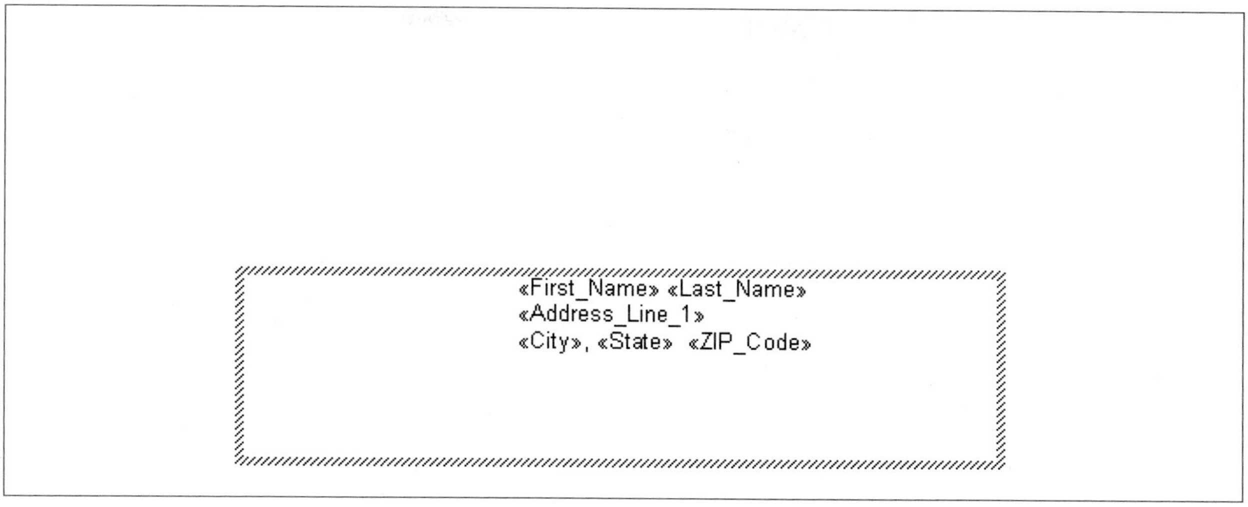

«First_Name» «Last_Name»
«Address_Line_1»
«City», «State» «ZIP_Code»

Input Mask, which both alters the display format of the data and saves added characters like hyphens along with the data. The method you use—Format or Input Mask—depends on whether you want to include formatting characters if you export the database data.

✓ Your database program may prompt you to save your work each time you start to make a change (or finish making a change) to the field format.

5. Format the **CPhone** field to display in the (800)555-1234 format.

✓ Hint: In Access 2003, you can enter (@@@)@@@-@@@@ into the Format text box for the field when in Design view. When you use this method, the formatting does not appear until you press Enter to finish making an entry in the field.

✓ The format choice for a Yes/No field controls how the database treats the user's choice behind the scenes rather than how the field entries appear on-screen. The database can treat the field selection as a Yes/No, True/False, or On/Off entry.

6. Set up the **Paid** field to display with zero decimal places.
7. Create a default value of **4** for the **Paid** field and **2** for the **Days** field.
8. Save your changes to the database.
9. Close the database file.

Database Planning Worksheet

Database Information

Student Name: Jan Taylor

Date: 10/4/06

Database Purpose: To track movie check outs

File Name: MOVIE

Field Information

Description	Name	Data Type	Size (Width)
Rental number	ID	AutoNumber	N/A
Check out date	OutDate	Date/Time	N/A
Name of movie	Title	Text	30
Movie item number	Item	Number	N/A
Amount paid for rental	Paid	Currency	N/A
Days rented	Days	Number	N/A
Client ID number	CID	Number	N/A
Client phone number	CPhone	Text	13

Exercise 58

❖ Edit the Main Document ❖ Prepare Labels

Notes

You may want to make changes to the main document you've created to provide new information, make the document more attractive, or add or remove field codes. You can use this exercise to practice making changes to a main document. Also review here how to **merge labels** using the same data source, so you can see how to create a mailing label for each letter or document you need to send.

You want to do some additional marketing for your Clean Partners cleaning service. You've created a postcard to offer a discount to residential and commercial cleaning customers. Merge the postcards and create mailing labels for them now.

Vocabulary

merge labels

Directions

1. Open the **WP58** document file.
2. Save the file as **OFFERD**. This is an example data document.
3. Open the **WP58-2** document file.
4. Save the file as **OFFER**.
5. With the **OFFER** document active, start the merge wizard or helper in your word processing application.
6. Choose a letter type main document and use the open **OFFER** document as the main document.

    ✓ Even though this document uses a postcard size, it's still considered a "form letter" in the mail merge feature.

7. Choose to use the **OFFERD** document file as the data document (data source) rather than creating a new data document.

8. Edit the main document to add the merge field codes, as shown in Illustration 1. Save the document.
9. Merge the main and data documents to a new document. (Merge all the records.)
10. Page through the merged documents to inspect them.

    ✓ Because the main document uses an irregular paper size, you may end up with a blank page at the end of the merged document. This can sometimes result from a merge due to paper and font sizes.

11. Print one copy of the merged cards (use plain paper for the purposes of this exercise and don't print any final blank page that results from the merge), then close the merged document without saving it.

Exercise 4

❖ Create the Database ❖ Save the Database
❖ Work with Field Formats

Notes

Databases provide an ideal method of keeping a list of products or items in a collection. When a database contains the applicable fields, you can easily **find** a single product among thousands or create informative **reports**.

You can change the **field format** for database fields. A database field format works somewhat like a number format in a spreadsheet program, controlling how entries in the field display. For example, you can adjust a currency field to display with 0 or 2 decimal places. You can have a text field for Social Security Numbers display in 111-22-3333 format so you don't have to type the hyphens in each entry. (You can similarly format phone number and ZIP Code fields.) For many types of fields, you can create a **default value**, so you don't have to make any entry at all in that field unless you need to enter a value other than the default value.

You have a movie rental business. Create a database to track when customers check out movies from your store.

Vocabulary

find   reports   field format   default value

Directions

1. Create a new database file (and table, if needed). Name the file **MOVIE**. (Use the same name later when you save the table.)
2. Create a primary key. (If your database program uses tables, this step may come later.)
3. Create the fields shown in the database planning worksheet on the following page, using the correct field name, description, data type, and size.
4. Format the **OutDate** field to display with the dd-mmm-yy format , or something similar.

✓ You must be working in the view that allows you to manually build fields (called the design view in some database programs). Using a wizard to create a table doesn't let you customize fields extensively.

✓ Field format choices change depending on the selected field type. Your database program may give you a few different options for formatting a field. You may be able to specify the formatting using a Format text box or choice; in this case, the format appears during display only. Format characters are not stored with the data. Or, as in Access 2003, you may be able to specify an

12. Close the **OFFER** and **OFFERD** document and data files, saving the files when prompted, then create a new, blank document.

13. Use the merge wizard or helper in your word processing program to change the blank document to the labels (mailing label) type.

14. Set up the mailing label main document to use a common mailing label size, such as the Avery 2160 Mini-Address label size, or something comparable.

15. Choose to use the **OFFERD** document file as the data document (data source) for the label merge.

16. Insert the merge fields to create address labels. (Position them as you would on an envelope.)

   ✓ Your word processing program's merge wizard or helper may display a dialog box that you can use to insert the fields. Otherwise, you probably only need to set up the merge fields on the first label and then click on an Update All Labels button, as for Word 2003 label merges.

17. Merge the main (mailing label) and data documents to a new document. (Merge all the records.) The merged labels should resemble Illustration 2.

18. Print one copy of the merged mailing labels (on plain paper for the purpose of this exercise), then close the merged document without saving it.

   ✓ Again, if you were preparing labels for a bulk mailing, the records would have to be sorted by ZIP Code and the recipient's address information would need to be printed in all uppercase characters.

19. Save the main mailing label document file; name it **OFFERL**.

20. Close the main document.

Illustration 1

<<First_Name>> <<Last_Name>>
Let Clean Partners, Inc. help you
with Spring Clearning!

We'll give you
<<Discount>>
off your next extra <<Type>>
clearning service.*

*Applicable only to services in addition to your
regularly-scheduled services.

Database Planning Worksheet

Database Information

Student Name: Steve Price

Date: 9/14/06

Database Purpose: To track client names and phone numbers

File Name: CLIENT

Field Information

Description	Name	Data Type	Size (Width)
Client I.D. number	ID	AutoNumber	N/A
Client's first name	FirstName	Text	15
Client's last name	LastName	Text	25
First line of street address	Address1	Text	30
Second line of street address	Address2	Text	30
City	City	Text	15
State	State	Text	2
ZIP code	ZIP	Text	10
Client's home phone	HomePh	Text	13
Clients's work phone	WorkPh	Text	13

Illustration 2

Lana Kerr
1856 Hendersonville Road
Charlotte, NC 28277

Harmony Lord
849 Sand Hill Road
Charlotte, NC 28278

Jim Davidson
200 Riverside Avenue
Charlotte, NC 28278

Ann Griffin
75 Ivy Lane
Charlotte, NC 28278

Sandra Fairview
25 Broadway St.
Charlotte, NC 28277

Garren Owen
56 Central Ave.
Charlotte, NC 28278

Ray Adams
7 West Professional Park
Charlotte, NC 28278

Exercise 3

❖ Create the Database   ❖ Save the Database

Notes

Although you can keep a list of names and phone numbers in any of a few different software programs, your database program is best suited to keeping this type of information for you.

You've started a small remodeling business, and you need to create a database to hold your client contact information. Create the basic database now.

Vocabulary

No new vocabulary in this exercise.

Directions

1. Create a new database file (and table, if needed). Name the file **CLIENT**. (Use the same name later when you save the table.)
2. Create the fields shown in the database planning worksheet on the following page, using the correct field name, description, data type, and size.

   ✓ *Notice that this database uses a lot of fields. This is helpful because breaking records down into more fields enables you to sort the data in more ways later. For example, you can't sort a database by last name if a single field contains the first and last name. And you can't sort by ZIP Code if a single field contains all of the address information. Use a copy of the database planning worksheet from Appendix B to help you decide how to break information into fields.*

   ✓ *The size of the ZIP field, 10, allows enough room for a ZIP+4 ZIP Code: five characters, a hyphen, and four more characters. The sizes for the phone number fields accommodate entries using parentheses and a hyphen, as in (800)555-1234.*

3. Set up the **ID** field as the primary key.
4. Save your changes to the database.
5. Close the database file.

Exercise 59

❖ Critical Thinking

Notes

Complete your work with merging by creating a merge document and data document from scratch, merging selected records, and creating and merging matching envelopes.

You operate your own dental practice. You've recently started accepting increased insurance coverage from a particular insurance plan, and want to inform patients using that plan of their enhanced benefits.

Vocabulary

No new vocabulary in this exercise.

Directions

1. Using the mail merge helper or wizard in your word processing application, create the main merge letter document and data documents shown in Illustrations 1 and 2. Name the main document **COVER** and the data document **COVERD**.

   ✓ *In this case, you can use the merge wizard or helper's automated feature to create the list as a database file (adding and deleting fields as needed), or create the list as a table in a word processing document.*

2. Specify merge conditions (query options) to merge only the records that have **BlueCo** in the **Insurer** field.

3. After typing letter text and inserting field codes, apply appropriate formatting to the main document. (The first illustration uses 24-point Rage Italic font for the letterhead information and 20-point Rage Italic to emphasize other text in the letter.)

4. Merge the main and data documents to a new document.

5. Print a copy of each letter and close the merged document without saving it.

6. Create an envelope document and merge envelopes to match the letters you merged.

7. Print a copy of each envelope (on plain paper) and close the merged envelope document without saving it.

8. Save the main envelope document as **COVERE**.

9. Save the main letter document and close it.

10. Save the data document and close it.

6. Make a copy of your finished planning worksheet to turn in to your instructor, if required.
7. Start your database program, if needed.
8. Create a new database file (and table, if needed). Name the file **ART**. (Use the same name later when you save the table.)

   ✓ *Do not create a **primary key** if the database program prompts you to do so. The primary key field a database program adds usually is an AutoNumber field that numbers the records you enter, although it can be another type of field that has a unique entry for every record. You can tell the database program to create the primary key for you in other instances, but do not do so in this instance because you're adding your own AutoNumber field.*

9. Create the fields shown in the database planning worksheet below, using the correct field name, description, data type, and size.

   ✓ *If your database program offers a **wizard** to help you through the process of creating a table or database fields, you can try using it. However, you have the most control if you use the database **view** that's designed for creating fields, sometimes called a design view. The steps in this section assume you'll use whichever method you prefer.*

10. Save your changes to the database.

    ✓ *In a database program that uses tables of data within each database file, you will have to save and close the table before closing the database file. The rest of this book's database coverage assumes you'll use the correct saving and closing method for your database program.*

11. Close the database file.

Database Planning Worksheet

Database Information

Student Name: Your name

Date: Today's date

Database Purpose: To track artwork

File Name: ART

Field Information

Description	Name	Data Type	Size (Width)
Piece number	PN	AutoNumber	N/A
Artist first name	FName	Text	15
Artist last name	LName	Text	25
Work name	Work	Text	50
For sale?	FSale	Yes/No	N/A
Sale price	Price	Currency	N/A
Sold?	Sold	Yes/No	N/A
Date sold	SDate	Date/Time	N/A

Illustration 1

Mark Myers, DDS
802 Ellipse Parkway
Fishers, IN 45038
800-555-6262

Today's Date

«First_Name» «Last_Name»
«Address_Line_1»
«City», «State» «ZIP_Code»

Dear «*First_Name*»:

Everyone here at the dental practice has appreciated having you as a patient. Your loyalty enables us to continue providing the best and latest in dental treatment techniques.

We are excited to announce an added benefit to you. We recently started accepting an enhanced plan from your insurer:

«*Insurer*»

We hope that this change enables you to enjoy lower pricing for the services we provide.

We look forward to seeing you for your next appointment.

Sincerely,

Exercise 2

❖ Plan the Database ❖ Create the Database
❖ Save the Database

Notes

Databases may also include any of three other data types. **Currency** fields hold dollar and cent entries, like prices. An **AutoNumber** field sequentially numbers each new record you add to your database, so you could later return the records to the original order after you sorted it in another order. A **Yes/No** field prompts the database user to choose yes or no or click a check box to fill in the field. After you plan your database, it takes only minutes to create the database itself and define the fields.

You just started a small art gallery, and want to use database software to track the pieces you've represented. Plan and create that database now.

Vocabulary

Currency	Yes/No	wizard
AutoNumber	primary key	view

Directions

1. Copy the database planning worksheet from Appendix B.
2. Fill out the **Database Information** section of the database planning worksheet. (Use **ART** as the file name.)
3. Cover up all columns except the **Description** column in the **Field Information** section of the database planning worksheet on the following page. You're going to practice planning the database first to see how well you do. The **Description** column lists the descriptions for several fields that you'll need. Copy these entries to your blank database planning worksheet.

✓ *You might want to limit a field's size to keep entries short or to help you see more fields at a time. For example, you don't need a long field size if you know a field will contain a phone number or ZIP Code.*

4. Fill out the database planning worksheet with field information that you think is appropriate. (Enter **N/A** as the **Size** for any field that the database sizes automatically based on the data type.)
5. Uncover the database planning worksheet on the following page to see how you did. Correct your copy of the database planning worksheet, if needed.

Illustration 2

First Name	Last Name	Address Line 1	City	State	ZIP Code	Insurer
Jennifer	White	9801 Whitley Way	Fishers	IN	46038	BlueCo
Kimberly	Terrell	11061 N. Meridian St.	Fishers	IN	46038	Winders
Terence	Kendall	8706 Sunblest St.	Fishers	IN	46038	Owen Insurers
Ken	Kimball	9208 Allen Lane	Fishers	IN	46038	BlueCo
Linda	Frank	6970 Level Loop	Fishers	IN	46038	Winders

3. Look at the example database planning worksheet below. The **Field Information** section lists the descriptions for several fields that you'll need and gives an example of how to fill in the information for the fields. Copy these entries to your blank database planning worksheet.

   ✓ *The data type (field type) controls what type of information you can enter in a field and how that information looks and acts in the database. For example, you can't enter text into a number field. Or, if you enter dates in a text field, the database program might not be able to sort the dates correctly.*

4. Finish filling out your copy of the database planning worksheet with field information that you think is appropriate. (Enter **N/A** as the **Size** for any field in which the database size is automatically based on the data type.)

✓ *Different database programs have different rules about field names. Some programs let you use long names and include spaces. Others require you to stick with short, one-word names. Consult your instructor or the Help feature in your database program to verify the field name rules in your database program.*

✓ *You use the Text data type for entries that combine text and numbers, like a street address. Also use the Text data type for numbers without calculations, like phone numbers, part numbers, and ZIP Codes. Eventually, you'll be able to set up the database to automatically format an entry like a phone number with hyphens or parentheses in the right locations.*

5. Make a copy of your finished planning worksheet to turn in to your instructor, if required.

Database Planning Worksheet

Database Information

Student Name: *Your name*

Date: *Today's date*

Database Purpose: *Enter a purpose*

File Name: *Enter a suggested file name*

Field Information

Description	Name	Data Type	Size (Width)
Customer name	*CName*	*Text*	35
Customer account no.			
Delivery date			
Drop location phone			
Drop street address			
City			
State			
ZIP code			
Received by and notes			
Delivery time			

Lesson 10
Work with Multiple Documents and Repetitive Text

Exercises 60–65

❖ **Copy and move text between documents**

❖ **Work with automatic text entries**

❖ **Use text shortcuts**

❖ **Create and run macros**

❖ **Insert a file into a document**

Exercise 1

❖ Plan the Database

Notes

Use a **database** program to organize lists of information, such as a list of customers or a list of products. All the information for one entry—like one product or customer—forms a **record**. Each individual piece of information in a record—the product name, item number, price, and so on—is a **field**. Before you enter your list of records in the database (or **data table**, as the list is sometimes called), you should plan and define the fields.

In this exercise, you plan a database that will use a few different **data types**. **Text** fields hold alphanumeric information; **Date/Time** fields hold dates and times; **Number** fields hold numeric entries; and **Memo** fields hold alphanumeric information but can be larger than text fields. In addition to the data type, you give each field a name. You can also change the **field size** (its width in characters) for some fields depending on the data type. (Typically, you only need to give the size for Text fields, and perhaps one or two other field types in your database program.)

✓ *Some database programs—notably Microsoft Office Access—enable you to add more than one list of information in a single database file; in these programs, you create each list as a separate **table** in the database. For the purposes of this book, the word "database" will refer to a list of records, whether you create it in a database file or in a table within a database file. If you're working with a program that requires you to create a table within a database file, you'll need to create both a new database file and a new table whenever this book instructs you to create a new database. In such cases, save your table with the same name as the database file itself.*

You make deliveries for a local courier service. Rather than logging your deliveries on paper, you've decided to carry a small notebook computer and enter the deliveries into a database. Plan the database fields now.

Vocabulary

database	data table	Date/Time	field size
record	data type (field type)	Number	table
field	Text	Memo	

Directions

1. Copy the database planning worksheet from Appendix B.

   ✓ *While you're at it, make four copies. You'll need copies for other exercises in this lesson.*

2. Fill out the **Database Information** section of the database planning worksheet. Suggest your own name for the database file.

Exercise 60

❖ Use Multiple Documents
❖ Copy Text from One Document to Another

Notes

When you can avoid retyping information, you enjoy two benefits. First, you save typing time. Second, you reduce errors (assuming the text you copy was error-free). So, if you have a document that contains information you want to reuse, you can copy that information from its original document to another document. To accomplish this kind of copy operation, you have to open both windows and **switch between document windows**, as in this exercise. (Alternatively, you can use the Arrange All command on the Window menu to show both document windows simultaneously.) When you have multiple windows open, the window holding the insertion point is called the **active window**.

You own Fine Knits yarn shop. You want to copy some information from a brochure you've created to a flyer about an upcoming knitting class.

Vocabulary

switch between document windows   active window   boilerplate text

Directions

1. Open the **WP60** document file.
2. Save the file as **KNIT**.
3. Open the **WP60-2** document file.
4. Save the file as **KNIT2**.
5. Refer to Illustrations 1 and 2. Copy the selections marked in the first illustration to the locations identified in the second illustration.

   ✓ For each copy operation, you select and copy text from the brochure document, switch to the other document, click to position the insertion point, then paste the copied information into place. Most word processing applications enable you to use the Window menu to switch between open documents.

   ✓ In recent Word versions, a Paste Options button appears by default when you paste a selection. Exercise 63 in this lesson demonstrates how to work with this button and others like it.

6. In the **KNIT2** document file, adjust the number of blank lines between paragraphs and the number of spaces between words and sentences as needed to accommodate the pasted text. Also, if Selection C pastes with a bullet, turn off the bullet.

   ✓ You can save yourself some work by selecting text to copy very carefully. Try not to select paragraph markers (which appear as a selected blank space at the end of a selected paragraph), or if needed, press Shift plus an arrow key to select or deselect spaces between words and punctuation marks as needed.

Lesson 20
Plan, Create, and Save a Database Table and Form

Exercises 1–7

- ❖ **Plan a database**
- ❖ **Create a database**
- ❖ **Save a database**
- ❖ **Work with forms**

7. Change the font formatting of the inserted Selection F text to 12-point Century Schoolbook to match other document text.

8. Save your changes to the **KNIT2** document file.

9. Print one copy of the **KNIT2** document.

10. Close both documents; do not save changes to the **KNIT** file if prompted.

✓ *General text that you develop to reuse in documents is often called* **boilerplate text**.

Illustration 1

Fine Knits
...a nice little yarn shop
222-A Atherton St.
Asheville, NC 28801
828-555-0404

Selection F

Why Knitting?
Because knitting provides:
* A relaxing outlet for stress
* A sense of productivity and accomplishment
* A way to be creative
* A way to meet other knitters

Selection E

Fine Knits has provided the Asheville community with fantastic yarns, knitting and crocheting supplies, patterns, and classes for more than 20 years. We serve everyone—from beginning knitters to experienced textile artists.

Yarns
Our buyers at Fine Knits travel all over the country to major knitting shows to learn about the best of the new yarns as they become available. Here are just a few examples of the terrific yarns we carry:
* Tarryton Knubby Wool   *Selection C*
* Ika Silk/Wool Blend Light
* Fun Zone Curly
* KnitIt Ribbon Pastels

Classes
Staff members and guest instructors work with Fine Knits to provide a variety of great classes. Here are just a few:
* Beginners: Sassy Striped Scarf
* Intermediate Boxy Fall Sweater   *Selection A*
* Advanced: A Cardigan to Die For

Selection B

How to Find Us
Fine Knits is located in Atherton Plaza. From Main Avenue, turn east (right if you're coming from the south, left if you're coming from the north) onto Creston Blvd. Go ½ mile, and then turn left onto Atherton St. Fine knits is in the middle of the second block, on the left.

Selection D

Directory of Files

Exercise	File Name	Page
1	None	—
2	None	—
3	None	—
4	None	—
5	DB05	368
6	DB06	370
7	None	—
8	DB08	375
9	DB09	377
10	DB10	379
11	DB11	381
12	DB12	384
13	None	—
14	DB14	389
15	DB15	392
16	DB16	396
17	DB17	400
18	DB18	403
19	DB19	407
20	DB20	410
21	DB21	412
22	DB22	414
23	DB23	416
24	DB24	419
25	DB25	424

Illustration 2

Come and Knit with Us at Fine Knits!

Class Name:	∧ *Insert selection A.*
Class Level:	∧ *Insert selection B.*
Yarn:	∧ *Insert selection C.*
Date:	Saturday, October 12
Time:	10 a.m.-2 p.m.
Location:	∧ *Insert selection D.*

If you've never knitted before, here's what you'll experience when you try:

∧ *Insert selection E.*

Contact Information:

∧ *Insert selection F.*

Database

Lessons 20-23
Exercises 1-25

Lesson 20
Plan, Create, and Save a Database Table and Form

Lesson 21
Add Records and Print a Database

Lesson 22
Edit and Enhance a Database

Lesson 23
Find Records and Query a Database

Exercise 61

❖ Save and Insert Repetitive Text

Notes

When you work for a particular organization, you may find yourself typing the organization's name or other key information time and time again. To save time and effort, you can save phrases and paragraphs you use repeatedly as **repetitive text** or **automatic text** entries. (Saved text may also be called a **glossary entry**.) You give each saved repetitive text entry a unique name so you can use that name to **insert** the repetitive text entry later.

  ✓ *If your word processing program doesn't offer a repetitive text (automatic text or glossary) feature, you can create a macro to insert text that you type and format. Exercise 65 covers macros.*

You need to put together a list of the inventory from a particular yarn maker for Fine Knits yarn shop. Use the repetitive text feature to save time with this task.

Vocabulary

repetitive text   automatic text   glossary entry   insert

Directions

1. Open the **WP61** document file.
2. Refer to Illustration 1. Save each selection of text as repetitive text or automatic text, using the name specified in the illustration.

  ✓ *The formatting may make it more complicated to save the repetitive text entry. If you want to save all the formatting, apply the formatting to the whole paragraph, select the whole paragraph, and save it as the repetitive text entry. Also, be careful not to select any extra spaces or punctuation that appear at the end of the text for your repetitive text entry. If you do, those spaces or punctuation will be included each time you insert the entry.*

  ✓ *Note that each of the repetitive text entry names in Illustration 1 has at least four characters. Word requires a repetitive text entry name to have at least four characters in order to display a ScreenTip of the repetitive text entry. (Word's Help system indicates that the names must have five characters, but that appears to be a typo in the Help system.)*

  ✓ *If your word processing program gives you a choice of where to save the repetitive text entries, make sure you save them to the default document template or any other location that makes them available to all documents.*

3. Close the **WP61** file without saving changes, if prompted to do so.

Circle the correct answer to each of the questions below:

1. You move around in a spreadsheet by:
   A. Clicking with the mouse to position the cell selector.
   B. Pressing an arrow key.
   C. Scrolling with the scroll bar and then clicking with the mouse.
   D. All of the above.

2. If you want to have a cell entry line up across several cells, you have to:
   A. Move the entry to a cell that is approximately in the location you want.
   B. Change column widths until the entry looks right.
   C. Select the cells over which to align information, and then choose the Span Cells command.
   D. Select the cells over which to align the information, and then choose the Center Across Selection alignment.

3. To select an entire row or column, you:
   A. Click the row number or column letter.
   B. Use the Select|Row command and enter a row or column letter.
   C. Select a cell in the row or column, then press Shift or Ctrl.
   D. None of the above.

4. These are example functions:
   A. AVERAGE.
   B. SUBTRACT.
   C. SUM.
   D. A and C only.

5. This function can display different messages based on a logical test:
   A. COUNT.
   B. CHOOSE.
   C. THEN.
   D. IF.

4. Open the **WP61-2** document file.
5. Save the file as **YARNS**.
6. Refer to Illustration 2. Insert (and expand) the repetitive text entries where indicated by the repetitive text entry names in the illustration.

   ✓ *Some word processing programs give you the option of using a shortcut key or combination to insert the repetitive text entry. In such a case, you type the name of the repetitive text entry into the document, then press the shortcut keys to expand the name to the full entry. In Word, you can simply press Enter once the ScreenTip for the repetitive text entry appears.*

   ✓ *Often, repetitive text entry names are not case sensitive. So even if you create a repetitive text entry with capital letters in its name, you can type the repetitive text entry name in all lowercase letters and your word processor should still prompt you to enter the repetitive text entry.*

7. Save the document, and print one copy.
8. Close the document file.

Illustration 1

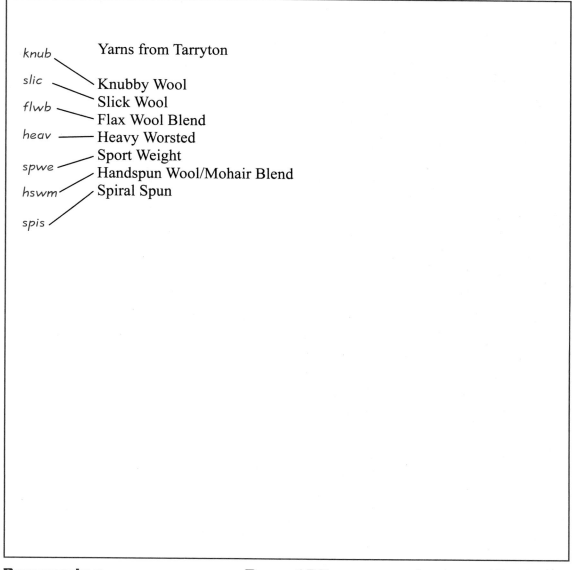

knub
slic
flwb
heav
spwe
hswm
spis

Yarns from Tarryton

Knubby Wool
Slick Wool
Flax Wool Blend
Heavy Worsted
Sport Weight
Handspun Wool/Mohair Blend
Spiral Spun

Quiz Break 5

Fill in your brief answers below:

1. A program that organizes labels, values, and calculations is called a: _____
2. The intersection of a row and column on a spreadsheet holds a: _____
3. When a spreadsheet file holds multiple "pages," each page is identified as a: _____
4. Each location on a spreadsheet is identified by its: _____
5. When you select an area that spans multiple rows and/or columns on a spreadsheet, you have selected a: _____
6. A calculation expression you enter is called a: _____
7. Entries can include a pre-programmed calculation called a: _____
8. Calculation expressions can work with values from: _____
9. A reference to a cell in a calculation expression can be either _____ or _____, which controls how the spreadsheet treats that reference if you copy the calculation expression. _____
10. You use a _____ or _____ to create a chart. _____

Circle the correct answer to each of the questions below:

T	F	1. You have to start every label with a special character.
T	F	2. You have to start every formula with a special character.
T	F	3. To change a cell entry, you have to delete the existing entry first.
T	F	4. You can use a template to create a preplanned spreadsheet.
T	F	5. You can use a fill alignment to repeat a cell entry within and across selected cells.
T	F	6. If you enter a formula wrong, it will simply display the wrong result.
T	F	7. You can change the way dates display in cells.
T	F	8. In most spreadsheets, you can click a toolbar button to start a formula that sums cell entries.
T	F	9. You use the drag and drop feature to copy a cell entry or formula to cells across the row or down the column.
T	F	10. You can use the shrink to fit feature to help a spreadsheet printout fit on a single page.
T	F	11. You can only print a spreadsheet with gridlines.
T	F	12. In most spreadsheet programs, you have to export data to chart it.

Illustration 2

Tarryton Yarn Inventory
Fine Knits Yarn
April 1, 2006

Yarn	Color	Skeins
spis	Gray	6
spis	Black	4
hswm	Green	12
hswm	Heather	16
hswm	Heather Gray	20
spwe	Buff	12
spwe	White	23
flwb	Baby Blue	7
flwb	Taupe	9
flwb	Pearl	12
knub	Gray/Green	4
knub	Gray/Blue	3
slic	Orange	4
slic	Yellow	9

13. Add a chart title.
14. Finish creating the chart, position it on the spreadsheet under the data, and resize it if needed.
15. Specify a print range.

16. Add a footer with the page number to the spreadsheet, and set up the printout to center information both horizontally and vertically on the printed page.
17. Print one copy in portrait orientation.
18. Save your changes to the spreadsheet file.
19. Close the spreadsheet file.

Exercise 62

❖ Save and Insert Repetitive Text
❖ Delete Repetitive Text Entries

Notes

Work with repetitive text entries again in this exercise. Saved repetitive text entries reduce the amount of time you spend typing document text, but you may encounter instances where you no longer need a repetitive text entry. In such instances, you can delete a saved repetitive text entry. Just display the list of repetitive text entries, choose the one you want, and delete it.

A particular instructor has agreed to teach a class at the Fine Knits yarn shop, and you need to send a confirmation letter. Use the repetitive text feature to save time with this task, by saving information from the brochure document you saw in Exercise 60 and reusing the text now.

Vocabulary

No new vocabulary in this exercise.

Directions

1. Open the **WP62** document file.
2. Refer to Illustration 1. Save each selection of text as repetitive text or automatic text, using the name specified in the illustration.

   ✓ To save the formatting for selected words only (not the paragraph) apply the formatting to those words and select those words only (not the paragraph mark) to save as the repetitive text entry.

   ✓ You must save each repetitive text entry under a unique name. You want the names to be long enough to be easy to remember, but short enough to type quickly before pressing the shortcut key entry that inserts the repetitive text entry.

3. Close the **WP62** file without saving changes, if prompted to do so.
4. Create a new document.

5. Refer to Illustration 2. Enter the text for the document as shown. Also insert repetitive text entries where indicated in the document.

   ✓ Insert all the repetitive text entries as new paragraphs.

   ✓ In recent Word versions, you can display the new AutoText toolbar to give you quick access to repetitive text entries. To find your custom entries, click the All Entries button on the toolbar and then point to the Normal (for the Normal template) category.

6. Adjust the number of lines between paragraphs and the number of spaces between words and sentences as needed.
7. Format all inserted text except for the **Addy** repetitive text entry as 12-point Times New Roman.

Exercise 29

❖ Critical Thinking

Notes

Work with functions, charting, and printing to review your skills in this exercise. Here, you'll also work with page orientation, gridlines, and printing.

You run a small convenience store chain, and have created a spreadsheet to track sales for each store over a five-week period. Finish creating the spreadsheet formulas and chart, and print now.

Vocabulary

No new vocabulary in this exercise.

Directions

1. Open the **SS29** spreadsheet file.
2. Save the file as **SALES**.
3. Enter **Week 1** in cell B3.
4. Fill the entry from cell B3 through F3 to enter headings through the fifth week.
5. Assign the **S_** plus the store number (as in S_101) as the range name for the range holding its sales data. Name each of the three store sales ranges.

   ✓ *You can't assign a range name like "S101," because the spreadsheet will interpret it as a cell address. Adding an underscore solves this problem.*

6. In each cell in the range G4:G6, enter a formula that sums the values to the left, using the range name as the argument.
7. In cell B7, add a formula that sums the values above. Fill the formula right through cell G7.

8. Apply the formatting of your choice to the spreadsheet. (You can use automatic formatting, if you wish.) Increase columns widths as needed.
9. In cells B9 and B10, respectively, enter formulas that find the maximum and minimum values in the range of weekly sales values.
10. Select the noncontiguous ranges A3:F4 and A6:F6.

    ✓ *To select non-contiguous ranges, remember to select the first range, press and hold the Ctrl key, then select the second range.*

11. Use the chart wizard or helper to create a 3-D area chart of the data.
12. Specify that cells A4 and A6 holds the names for series 1 and series 3, respectively.

    ✓ *In the second wizard dialog box, click the Series tab. Click the series to name in the Series list, then use the Name control to specify the cell that holds the series name.*

8. Add bullets (whatever style you wish) to the inserted **ACard** and **IkaL** repetitive text entries.
9. Save the new letter document as **CLASS**.
10. Print one copy of the document.

11. Delete the repetitive text entries you saved for this exercise.
   ✓ *In Word 2003, choose Insert | AutoText | AutoText to display the list of AutoText entries so that you can work with them.*
12. Close the document file.

Illustration 1

Fine Knits
...a nice little yarn shop
222-A Atherton St.
Asheville, NC 28801
828-555-0404

Addy

Why Knitting?
Because knitting provides:
   * A relaxing outlet for stress
   * A sense of productivity and accomplishment
   * A way to be creative
   * A way to meet other knitters

Fine Knits has provided the Asheville community with fantastic yarns, knitting and crocheting supplies, patterns, and classes for more than 20 years. We serve everyone—from beginning knitters to experienced textile artists.

Serv

Yarns
Our buyers at Fine Knits travel all over the country to major knitting shows to learn about the best of the new yarns as they become available. Here are just a few examples of the terrific yarns we carry:
   * Tarryton Knubby Wool
   * Ika Silk/Wool Blend Light   *Ikal*
   * Fun Zone Curly
   * KnitIt Ribbon Pastels

Classes
Staff members and guest instructors work with Fine Knits to provide a variety of great classes. Here are just a few:
   * Beginners: Sassy Striped Scarf
   * Intermediate: Boxy Fall Sweater
   * Advanced: A Cardigan to Die For   *Acard*

How to Find Us
Fine Knits is located in Atherton Plaza. From Main Avenue, turn east (right if you're coming from the south, left if you're coming from the north) onto Creston Blvd. Go ½ mile, and then turn left onto Atherton St. Fine knits is in the middle of the second block, on the left.

Locate

Crystal Community College
Enrollment Comparison
Adult Continuing Education

| | Enrollment | | | |
Class	Fall	Spring	Summer Session	Annual Total
Paper Making	12	13	7	32
Pastels	15	10	12	37
Photography	6	12	16	34
Digital Photography	17	20	20	57
Pottery	18	19	14	51
Stained Glass	15	21	19	55
French 1	12	17	11	40
German 1	11	11	12	34
Computers 1	35	44	32	111
Word Processing	27	28	32	87
Business Writing	13	14	20	47
	181	**209**	**195**	**585**

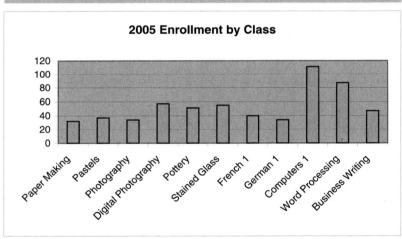

2005 Enrollment by Class

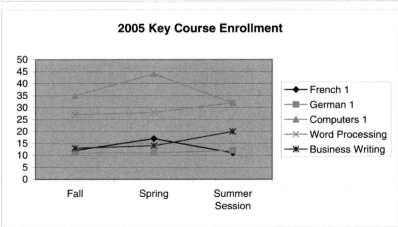

2005 Key Course Enrollment

Illustration 2

∧ *Addy*

Today's Date

Lynette Freeman
2209 Windy Trail
Asheville, NC 28804

Dear Lynette:

Thank you for agreeing to teach a class for Fine Knits next Saturday at 10 a.m. in our store. The class title and the type of yarn that will be provided by Fine Knits follow:

∧ *ACard*

∧ *Ikal*

∧ *Serv*

∧ *Locate*

Please give me a call if any questions come up as you prepare.

Best regards,

Jill Simon

Exercise 28

❖ Create Bar and Line Charts ❖ Label a Chart

Notes

Both bar charts and **line charts** identify discreet values. Each bar on a bar chart represents a single value in the series. Each point on a line chart shows a single value in the series, too, but the line connecting all the points in the series helps you better identify trends over time. Further, a line chart provides a better method of depicting series with many values; trying to cram too many data points into a bar chart makes it unattractive and even difficult to understand. Compare the relative merits of bar and line charts in this exercise.

You are working with enrollment data for Crystal Community College. Chart that data now.

Vocabulary

line chart

Directions

1. Open the **SS28** spreadsheet file.
2. Save the file as **CCCEN**.
3. Select the range E7:E17.
4. Use the chart wizard or helper to create a bar chart (column chart in Excel) of the selected range.
5. Specify the range A7:A17, which holds the class names, as the category labels.
6. Edit the chart title to read **2005 Enrollment by Class**.
7. Turn off the legend display.
8. Finish creating the chart.
9. Drag the chart to the location of your choice on the spreadsheet.
10. Resize the chart by dragging one of its corner handles.
    ✓ *If needed, click the chart to select it and display the handles. Press and hold the Shift key while you drag the corner handle to ensure that the chart retains a proportional appearance.*
11. Select the range A13:D17, which holds the enrollment figures for the non-arts courses.
12. Use the chart wizard or helper to create a line chart (with markers) of the selected range.
13. Specify that the series are in rows and specify the range B6:D6 as the category labels for the X axis..
14. Enter **2005 Key Course Enrollment** as the chart title.
15. Finish creating the chart.
16. Drag the chart to the location of your choice below the first chart on the spreadsheet.
17. Resize the chart by dragging one of its corner handles.
18. Save your changes to the spreadsheet file. The illustration on the following page shows how the spreadsheet looks with the charts.
19. Print one copy of the spreadsheet using the print settings of your choice.
20. Close the spreadsheet file.

Exercise 63

❖ Use Text Shortcuts

Notes

If you're working with a recent Word version, you may have noticed dotted purple underlines and certain buttons popping up from time to time. The dotted purple underlines and buttons provide still more shortcuts that you can use to work with text and save time with features like formatting.

The dotted purple underlines identify **smart tags**, which enable you to perform actions like adding a person's phone number or address information into the Outlook Contacts list—from within Word. (The dotted purple underlines are also called **smart tag indicators**.) To use a smart tag, move the mouse pointer over the underlined word, then click on the **Smart Tag Actions button** (it has a circled I) , then click a choice in the shortcut menu that appears.

Other buttons, namely the **Paste Options button** and the **AutoCorrect Options button**, appear when you complete a paste or copy operation. The Paste Options button appears when you paste a selection from the Office Clipboard. The AutoCorrect Options button appears when you hover the mouse pointer over a word that's been automatically corrected by Word's AutoCorrect feature. When you see one of these buttons, you can click the button to see a shortcut menu of commands.

- ✓ *As software companies update other software suites to make them more competitive with Office, you can bet that those new products will offer features similar to those covered in this exercise.*

- ✓ *Some of these features appear in other Office applications, such as Excel.*

Students can e-mail a document in to register for a class at Fine Knits yarn shop. Use smart tags and other features to work with the information in a registration document now.

Vocabulary

smart tag
smart tag indicators

Smart Tag Actions button
Paste Options button

AutoCorrect Options button

Mountain Gear
2005 Sales Results by Quarter

Product Line	Qtr 1	Qtr 2	Qtr 3	Qtr 4	Average
Footwear	$12,504.65	$13,248.09	$17,382.93	$9,389.22	13,131.22
Outerwear	$2,258.99	$4,939.39	$19,393.99	$6,549.99	8,285.59
Sportswear	$2,390.90	$11,043.46	$9,397.21	$5,373.33	7,051.23
Gear	$15,888.23	$31,845.00	$27,301.10	$12,049.30	21,770.91
Accessories	$2,393.33	$2,738.20	$4,033.97	$3,783.77	3,237.32
Total	$35,436.10	$63,814.14	$77,509.20	$37,145.61	53,476.26

Annual Total: $213,905.05

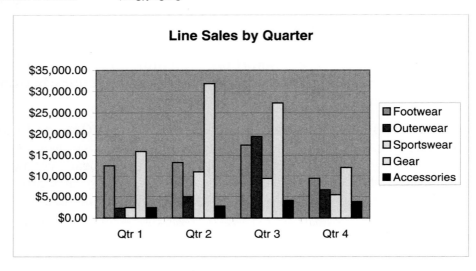

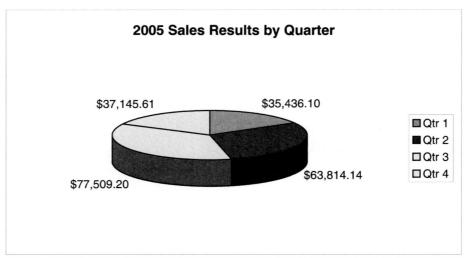

Directions

1. Open the **WP63** document file.
2. Save the file as **EREG**.
3. Move the mouse pointer over the name and address text.
4. Click the Smart Tag Actions button that appears, then click Add to Contacts.

   ✓ *Outlook must be installed for this action to work. If the Choose Profile dialog box opens at any point during the exercise, consult your instructor about which profile to choose.*

   ✓ *If you don't see any smart tags, choose Tools | AutoCorrect Options, and then click the Smart Tags tab. Make sure that the Label Text with Smart Tags option is checked, and that all the items in the Recognizers list are checked. You also can use the Recheck Document button on the Smart Tags tab to recheck the document for text that falls into any smart tag category.*

5. Notice that the phone number appears in the Business text box in the Contact window by default. Close the Contact window without saving the entry.
6. Move the mouse pointer over the desired class date.
7. Click the Smart Tag Actions button that appears, then click Show My Calendar.

   ✓ *You need to be using Microsoft Office Outlook in order to complete this step.*

8. The Outlook Calendar opens and displays the date indicated by the tagged text. Close the Outlook window.
9. In the line that reads **Type desired class date below**, delete the word **desired** and the space after it.
10. In its place, type **desirred**, with an extra **r**, and press Spacebar. Word should correct the word for you.
11. Move the mouse pointer over the corrected word, point to the blue underline that appears below the first letter, then click the AutoCorrect Options button that appears.
12. Click the first choice in the shortcut menu that appears. The word reverts to the incorrect spelling.
13. Undo the spelling change.
14. Select the company name, **Fine Knits**, at the top of the document.
15. Copy the text.
16. Position the insertion point on the last blank line in the document, and then paste the text.
17. Click the Paste Options button that appears.
18. Click the Match Destination Formatting choice in the shortcut menu.
19. Save the document changes.
20. Print one copy of the document.
21. Close the document file.

✓ Click outside a chart to deselect it and finish working with it.

9. Now select the range B10:E10.

10. Use the chart wizard or helper to create a pie chart. Choose a 3-D chart type, if available.

   ✓ A **pie chart** charts a single series. Use a pie chart to show how each value in the chart compares to the total (what proportion each value represents).

11. Specify the range B4:E4, which holds the labels Qtr 1 through Qtr 4, as the category labels. This labels each slice in the pie.

12. Enter **2005 Sales Results by Quarter** as the chart name, or specify cell A2 as the chart name (title).

   ✓ When possible, it's a good idea to specify the spreadsheet cells that hold titles and names for the chart rather than typing that information into the chart wizard or helper. That way, if you make a change in one of the cells on the spreadsheet, the chart will update automatically to reflect those changes.

13. Add a value **data label** to each pie slice. Data labels identify the value or percentage of each value in the chart.

14. Finish creating the chart.

15. Drag the chart to the location of your choice on the spreadsheet.

   ✓ To edit an existing chart in most applications, click it in the spreadsheet, then use the commands on the Chart menu that appears. In some applications, you may have to double-click the chart to edit it.

16. Save your changes to the spreadsheet file. The illustration on the following page shows how the spreadsheet looks with the charts.

17. Print one copy of the spreadsheet using the print settings of your choice.

18. Close the spreadsheet file.

Exercise 64

❖ Insert a File

Notes

So far, you've learned how to copy selections of text between open documents and to save selections for repeated use. What if you want to reuse an entire file you've already saved? You can use your word processing program's **insert file** command to insert all of the text from one file into another file.

Each of the instructors for your classes at Fine Knits has e-mailed a brief biography document. Insert each of those document files into a single document, so you'll have a one-page list with the information about each instructor.

Vocabulary

insert file

Directions

1. Create a new, blank document.
2. Create and format the heading lines (paragraphs) as shown in the illustration on the following page.
3. Press Enter twice.
4. Type the first class name as shown in the illustration, and then press Enter.
5. Insert the **WP64** file.
6. Press Enter.
7. Type the second class name shown in the illustration, and then press Enter.
8. Next insert the **WP64-2** file.
9. Press Enter.
10. Type the third class name shown in the illustration, and then press Enter.
11. Finally, insert the **WP64-3** file.
12. Inspect the document, and fix any spacing problems created by inserting the files.
13. Format the class names in bold.
14. Save the document file; name it **TEACH**.
15. Print one copy of the document.
16. Close the document.

Exercise 27

❖ Create a Bar Chart and a Pie Chart
❖ Label a Chart

Notes

Charts provide a graphic image of the data in your spreadsheet. A chart can reveal a trend or emphasize how values compare. Most spreadsheet programs offer a **chart wizard or helper** that leads you through the chart creation process. You simply specify what data to chart, pick a look for your chart, and place the chart on the spreadsheet.

The sales data spreadsheet you improved in Exercise 23 would have more impact if the data were charted. Add a bar chart and a pie chart to a version of that spreadsheet now.

Vocabulary

chart wizard or helper	legend	chart titles
bar chart	x-axis	pie chart
series	y-axis	data label

Directions

1. Open the **SS27** spreadsheet file.
2. Save the file as **MGSALES2**.
3. Select the range A4:E9.
4. Use the chart wizard or helper to create a vertical bar chart (sometimes called a column chart) of the selected range.

   ✓ A **bar chart** shows each charted value as a bar. In this case, rows 5 through 9 each hold a **series** (set) of information to be charted. The chart wizard or helper identifies each series, and assigns a particular color to all the bars in each series. The chart by default probably includes a **legend** to label which color bar represents which series, by name. The chart wizard or helper uses the labels in row 4 along the **x-axis** (bottom axis) of the chart to identify the bars for each quarter. The **y-axis** automatically includes dollar amounts.

   ✓ If your spreadsheet program calls a vertical bar chart a column chart, use the column chart type whenever this lesson instructs you to use a bar chart.

5. Specify that the series are in rows.
6. Enter **Line Sales by Quarter** as the **chart title**.
7. Finish creating the chart.
8. Drag the chart to the location of your choice below the data on the spreadsheet.

   ✓ Some spreadsheet programs only enable you to create a chart in a separate window or on a separate sheet in the spreadsheet file. Others give you the option of placing the chart as an object on the current spreadsheet or on its own sheet. If your spreadsheet program forces you to place the chart in a separate sheet or window, just use that technique to complete the exercises, and print each chart separately.

Fine Knits
Class Instructors

Beginner: Sassy Striped Scarf

∧ *Insert WP64.*

Intermediate: Boxy Fall Sweater

∧ *Insert WP64-2.*

Advanced: A Cardigan to Die For

∧ *Insert WP64-3.*

10/12/2004

	A	B	C	D	E	F	G	H	I
1	**Order Status**								
2									
3	**Client**	**Order Date**	**Order Number**	**Order Total**	**Status**	**Shipping**	**Tracking #**	**Billed**	**Notes**
36	Village Decorators	9/11/2005	AB3981	$858.99	Pending	USPS			
37	Soothing Scent Store	9/11/2005	AB3982	$940.00	Pending	USPS			
38	Reliable Goods	9/11/2005	AB3983	$684.38	Pending	FedEx			
39	Catalog Finds	9/11/2005	AB3984	$385.44	Pending	UPS			
40	Interiors by Jane	9/11/2005	AB3985	$383.99	Pending	UPS			

Page 2 of 2

Exercise 65

❖ Record a Macro ❖ Run a Macro

Notes

You may find instances where you want to repeat your actions in the word processing program, not just text. To save a sequence of actions, you create a **macro**. When you **record a macro**, your word processing program "memorizes" the steps you take. You assign a name to the macro. Then, whenever you want to repeat that sequence of steps, you **run the macro** to perform the steps.

  ✓ *Many word processing programs now include macro security features. When you open a document containing macros, the word processing program asks whether or not to enable those macros. If you need to use the macros, make sure you choose the option that leaves macros enabled. On the other hand, if you're not familiar with the person or source who created the document, you may want to disable the macros for safety.*

You want to jazz up the list of Fine Knits instructors that you created in the last exercise with a bit of formatting. Create some macros in the document to get that done and save time.

Vocabulary

macro   record a macro   run a macro

Directions

1. Open the **WP65** document file.
2. Save the file as **TEACH2**.
3. Position the insertion point just to the left of the first class name.
4. Record a macro that selects the line, applies the formatting of your choice, returns to the beginning of the line, inserts the symbol of your choice, copies the symbol, moves the insertion point to the end of the line, pastes the symbol, and right aligns the line (paragraph). Name the macro **FormatSymbolsRight**.

  ✓ *When you record a macro, the word processing program captures precise steps. This can sometimes cause tricky macro problems. For example, if you want to create a macro that performs an action and then moves to the beginning of the next paragraph, you can't use the down arrow key to move to the next paragraph. If you did, the macro would record your action as something like "press down arrow four times," instead of "move to beginning of next paragraph," so your macro would only work if the next paragraph starts exactly four lines down. In the case of this macro, you need to press the End key to move the insertion point to the end of the line. If needed, practice your macro actions before recording the macro to anticipate such problems.*

10/12/2004

Order Status

	A	B	C	D	E	F	G	H	I
1	**Order Status**								
2									
3	**Client**	**Order Date**	**Order Number**	**Order Total**	**Status**	**Shipping**	**Tracking #**	**Billed**	**Notes**
4	Taylor Gifts	9/5/2005	AB3949	$3,344.99	Shipped	UPS	UPS838390	Yes	
5	Kerry's Cottage	9/5/2005	AB3950	$293.38	Backordered	FedEx		No	Product discontinued.
6	Black Mountain Hardware	9/5/2005	AB3951	$893.33	Shipped	USPS	PS009459	Yes	
7	Jessica's Hallmark	9/5/2005	AB3952	$3,838.99	Shipped	USPS	PS009460	Yes	
8	Natural Products for You	9/5/2005	AB3953	$1,102.33	Shipped	USPS	PS009461	Yes	
9	Green Room Gifts	9/5/2005	AB3954	$1,237.33	Shipped	UPS	UPS838333	Yes	
10	Village Decorators	9/5/2005	AB3955	$227.22	Partial ship	FedEx	X1L3845967	No	Rest ships 7/9/05.
11	Soothing Scent Store	9/5/2005	AB3956	$2,933.22	Backordered	FedEx		No	
12	Reliable Goods	9/6/2005	AB3957	$283.66	Backordered	FedEx		No	
13	Catalog Finds	9/6/2005	AB3958	$17,393.99	Pending	FedEx		No	
14	Interiors by Jane	9/6/2005	AB3959	$338.22	Pending	FedEx		No	
15	Surprise by Basket	9/6/2005	AB3960	$740.00	Pending	FedEx		No	
16	Sweet Treats N More	9/6/2005	AB3961	$663.09	Pending	USPS		No	Last item in today.
17	Elegant Gifts	9/6/2005	AB3962	$295.99	Backordered	USPS		No	
18	Scents and Scentsations	9/6/2005	AB3963	$589.76	Backordered	FedEx	X1L3845993	No	
19	Fairlaine Décor	9/7/2005	AB3964	$2,049.99	Pending	UPS	UPS838333	No	
20	Interior Expressions	9/8/2005	AB3965	$1,759.99	Pending	UPS		No	
21	Taylor Gifts	9/9/2005	AB3966	$52.50	Shipped	USPS	PS009839	Yes	
22	Green Room Gifts	9/9/2005	AB3967	$354.54	Pending	FedEx			
23	Village Decorators	9/9/2005	AB3968	$987.21	Pending	UPS			
24	Soothing Scent Store	9/9/2005	AB3969	$345.00	Pending	UPS			
25	Reliable Goods	9/9/2005	AB3970	$596.00	Pending	USPS			
26	Catalog Finds	9/9/2005	AB3971	$449.00	Pending	USPS			
27	Interiors by Jane	9/9/2005	AB3972	$949.00	Pending	USPS			
28	Surprise by Basket	9/9/2005	AB3973	$4,199.00	Pending	FedEx			
29	Sweet Treats N More	9/10/2005	AB3974	$358.99	Pending	FedEx			
30	Elegant Gifts	9/10/2005	AB3975	$994.29	Pending	FedEx			
31	Scents and Scentsations	9/10/2005	AB3976	$305.03	Pending	UPS			
32	Fairlaine Décor	9/10/2005	AB3977	$558.33	Pending	FedEx			
33	Interior Expressions	9/10/2005	AB3978	$876.99	Pending	UPS			
34	Taylor Gifts	9/10/2005	AB3979	$768.22	Pending	USPS			
35	Green Room Gifts	9/10/2005	AB3980	$395.99	Pending	USPS			

Page 1 of 2

5. You can save the macro in either the document file itself, or the template file. For this exercise, save your macros in the document file.

   ✓ However, when you create your own macros to use with all your documents, you should save your macros in the default (normal) document template.

6. Remove the extra space, if any, inserted after the symbol at the end of the first line. Some word processors add this space as an automatic correction due to the punctuation mark at the end of the line.

7. Use the **FormatSymbolsRight** macro to format the next two class names in the document.

   ✓ Hint: You must place the insertion point in the right position each time you run the macro. If you don't and accidentally run the macro, you'll have to undo each of the macro's steps, which can be time consuming.

8. Position the insertion point at the beginning of the first instructor's bio. Record a macro that gives the paragraph a first line indent and 1.5 line spacing. Name the macro **MyGraf**.

9. Use the **MyGraf** macro to format the other two instructor bios.

   ✓ Notice that you can assign a shortcut key combination when you create the macro. Then, you can press that key combination to run the macro more quickly.

10. Record a macro that saves the file and displays the print preview. Name the macro **SaveView**.

11. Close the print preview.

12. Save the document file and print a copy.

13. Close the document file.

Exercise 26

❖ Add Headers ❖ Add Footers ❖ Print

Notes

As in a word processing document printout, you can include a **header** and/or **footer** to provide information on each page of the printout, such as the page number, file name, author name, or date.

You've decided you don't mind having a two-page printout of your order status spreadsheet, but you want each page to have more information, like the date it was printed. Create a header and footer for the spreadsheet you've been working with and print the spreadsheet.

Vocabulary

header   footer

Directions

1. Open the **SS26** spreadsheet file.
2. Save the file as **ORDSTAT3**. This is a copy of the spreadsheet file you printed in the last two exercises.
3. Add a header that prints the date at the right.

   ✓ *Generally, you'll find the header and footer settings along with the other page setup settings.*

   ✓ *You have to create a custom header to have the date alone.*

4. Add the **Page 1 of ?** footer. This footer numbers the pages in the printout and adds the text **Page X of Y**, where **X** is the number of the current page and **Y** is the total number of pages.
5. Choose the landscape orientation.
6. Scale or fit the printout to 1 page wide by 2 pages tall.
7. Set the top and bottom margins at **1.25"**.
8. Specify that the printout should include gridlines and row and column headings, and that rows 1 through 3 should appear as print titles.
9. Preview the printout.
10. Print the spreadsheet. The following pages illustrate how the finished printout looks in this instance. Compare your results at the end of this exercise with the finished printouts from the last two exercises.
11. Save your changes to the spreadsheet file.
12. Close the spreadsheet file.

Quiz Break 3

Circle the correct answer to each of the questions below:

T	F	1. Reading layout view can show two screens (pages) of information at once.
T	F	2. The document map shows a list of page numbers in the pane at the left.
T	F	3. You have no control over where a new page begins in a document.
T	F	4. If you turn on page numbering in a document, the page number must appear on page 1.
T	F	5. You have no control over the appearance of document headers and footers.
T	F	6. Short notes you include to yourself or other readers are called comment notes.
T	F	7. All columns in a document must have the same width.
T	F	8. When you create a table, you can specify how many rows and columns it has.
T	F	9. After you create a table, you cannot change the number of rows and columns it has.
T	F	10. Word processing programs cannot perform calculations.
T	F	11. If you want to send the same letter to multiple recipients, you have to create the letters and matching envelopes one at a time.
T	F	12. When you move or copy text, you must create a container document for it.
T	F	13. You can save a word or phrase you use repeatedly and create a repetitive text shortcut to insert it.
T	F	14. To use a document's text in another file, you must use a copy and paste operation.

Fill in your brief answers below:

1. A page break inserted by the word processing program is called a: _____

2. Use these to control the formatting for various parts of a document: _____

3. A _____ occurs when a line appears by itself at the top of a new page or column. _____

4. To divide text into multiple columns, you insert: _____

5. Tables divide information into rows and columns that form _____ where they intersect. _____

6. Press this key to move within a table: _____

7. To change the order of items in a table or list in a document, use this feature: _____

8. The _____ feature enables you to use a list of names and addresses to create letters and envelopes for multiple recipients (that is, to perform a mass mailing). _____

9. You use these to control which entries from a list are used for a mass mailing: _____

10. A collection of steps saved under a name so you can perform those steps quickly is called a: _____

10. Preview the printout one more time.
11. At this point, the preview shows that the printout lines up well on a single page.
12. Print the spreadsheet. The illustration below shows how this printout should look.

✓ *You often can print from the print preview by clicking a button named Print.*

13. Save your changes to the spreadsheet file.
14. Close the spreadsheet file.

Order Status

Client	Order Date	Order Number	Order Total	Status	Shipping	Tracking #	Billed	Notes
Taylor Gifts	9/5/2005	AB3949	$3,344.99	Shipped	UPS	UPS838390	Yes	
Kerry's Cottage	9/5/2005	AB3950	$293.38	Backordered	FedEx		No	Product discontinued.
Black Mountain Hardware	9/5/2005	AB3951	$893.33	Shipped	USPS	PS009459	Yes	
Jessica's Hallmark	9/5/2005	AB3952	$3,838.99	Shipped	USPS	PS009460	Yes	
Natural Products for You	9/5/2005	AB3953	$1,102.33	Shipped	USPS	PS009461	Yes	
Green Room Gifts	9/5/2005	AB3954	$1,237.33	Shipped	UPS	UPS838333	Yes	
Village Decorators	9/5/2005	AB3955	$227.22	Partial ship	FedEx	X1L3845967	No	Rest ships 7/9/05.
Soothing Scent Store	9/5/2005	AB3956	$2,933.22	Backordered	FedEx		No	
Reliable Goods	9/6/2005	AB3957	$283.66	Backordered	FedEx		No	
Catalog Finds	9/6/2005	AB3958	$17,393.99	Pending	FedEx		No	
Interiors by Jane	9/6/2005	AB3959	$338.22	Pending	FedEx		No	
Surprise by Basket	9/6/2005	AB3960	$740.00	Pending	FedEx		No	
Sweet Treats N More	9/6/2005	AB3961	$663.09	Pending	USPS		No	Last item in today.
Elegant Gifts	9/6/2005	AB3962	$295.99	Backordered	USPS		No	
Scents and Scentsations	9/6/2005	AB3963	$589.76	Backordered	FedEx	X1L3845993	No	
Fairlaine Décor	9/7/2005	AB3964	$2,049.99	Pending	UPS	UPS838333	No	
Interior Expressions	9/8/2005	AB3965	$1,759.99	Pending	UPS		No	
Taylor Gifts	9/9/2005	AB3966	$52.50	Shipped	USPS	PS009839	Yes	
Green Room Gifts	9/9/2005	AB3967	$354.54	Pending	FedEx			
Village Decorators	9/9/2005	AB3968	$987.21	Pending	UPS			
Soothing Scent Store	9/9/2005	AB3969	$345.00	Pending	UPS			
Reliable Goods	9/9/2005	AB3970	$596.00	Pending	USPS			
Catalog Finds	9/9/2005	AB3971	$449.00	Pending	USPS			
Interiors by Jane	9/9/2005	AB3972	$949.00	Pending	USPS			
Surprise by Basket	9/9/2005	AB3973	$4,199.00	Pending	FedEx			
Sweet Treats N More	9/10/2005	AB3974	$358.99	Pending	FedEx			
Elegant Gifts	9/10/2005	AB3975	$994.29	Pending	FedEx			
Scents and Scentsations	9/10/2005	AB3976	$305.03	Pending	UPS			
Fairlaine Décor	9/10/2005	AB3977	$558.33	Pending	FedEx			
Interior Expressions	9/10/2005	AB3978	$876.99	Pending	UPS			
Taylor Gifts	9/10/2005	AB3979	$768.22	Pending	USPS			
Green Room Gifts	9/10/2005	AB3980	$395.99	Pending	USPS			
Village Decorators	9/11/2005	AB3981	$858.99	Pending	USPS			
Soothing Scent Store	9/11/2005	AB3982	$940.00	Pending	USPS			
Reliable Goods	9/11/2005	AB3983	$684.38	Pending	FedEx			
Catalog Finds	9/11/2005	AB3984	$385.44	Pending	UPS			
Interiors by Jane	9/11/2005	AB3985	$383.99	Pending	UPS			

Circle the correct answer to each of the questions below:

1. Most word processors enable you to insert these automatically to identify sources quoted in a document:
   A. Author names.
   B. Footnotes.
   C. Endnotes.
   D. B and C only.

2. You can copy text:
   A. Within the current page.
   B. Between pages in a document.
   C. Between different documents.
   D. All of the above.

3. You can change the formatting for these table elements:
   A. Cell text, cell shading, and cell borders.
   B. Cell text.
   C. Cell borders.
   D. B and C only

4. These shortcuts can help you make edits and changes throughout a document in Word 2003
   A. Smart tags.
   B. AutoComplete Options button
   C. Paste Options button.
   D. All of the above.

5. Once you've created a data source document, you can merge its information with:
   A. A letter.
   B. Envelopes.
   C. Mailing labels.
   D. Any kind of document.

Exercise 25

❖ Shrink to Fit ❖ Preview and Print

Notes

It's a waste of paper and unattractive when one or two columns or rows in a printout bump to a separate page in the printout by themselves. Fortunately, you can use the **scaling** (shrink to fit) feature in a spreadsheet program to squeeze the print area onto one page (or a designated number of pages for a very large spreadsheet). To check your printout before you print it, use the print **preview** feature. This exercise explores both these features.

Print the LightNatural Beeswax Candles order status spreadsheet again, this time using scaling to fit it to a single landscape page.

Vocabulary

scaling (shrink to fit)   preview

Directions

1. Open the **SS25** spreadsheet file.
2. Save the file as **ORDSTAT2**.
3. Use the print preview feature to see how the spreadsheet would print by default. The default portrait orientation causes the printout to break up into two separate pages, with a lot of blank space on each page. The far right columns would be on the second page, which would make it awkward to check the data for a single order.

   ✓ *You can usually click a button or icon as a shortcut to display the preview. If your program doesn't offer such a shortcut, look for the preview command on the File menu.*

   ✓ *The print preview will offer buttons you can click to move to the next or previous page in the printout. The Page Down and Page Up keys work, as well.*

4. Close the print preview.

5. Change the page orientation to landscape.
6. Display the print preview again. Changing to landscape orientation actually increased the printout to 3 pages, with lots of blank space and awkward page breaks.

   ✓ *You often can display the print preview from the dialog box that contains page setup settings or from the print dialog box.*

7. Close the print preview.
8. Use the shrink to fit feature to size the printout to one page wide by one page tall.

   ✓ *You can use the shrink to fit feature along with a designated print area to shrink or expand the information in the print area to fill a specified number of pages.*

9. Also choose the option that centers the printed information horizontally on the page. However, don't print any gridlines, headings, or print titles in this case.

Desktop Publishing

Lessons 11-14
Exercises 1-31

Lesson 11
Working with Graphics, Rules, and Boxed Text

Lesson 12
Using Drawing Tools

Lesson 13
Adding Special Effects

Lesson 14
Working with Publisher

Illustration 2

	A	B	C	D	E	F	G	H	I
1	**Order Status**								
2									
3	**Client**	**Order Date**	**Order Number**	**Order Total**	**Status**	**Shipping**	**Tracking #**	**Billed**	**Notes**
4	Taylor Gifts	9/5/2005	AB3949	$3,344.99	Shipped	UPS	UPS838390	Yes	
5	Kerry's Cottage	9/5/2005	AB3950	$293.38	Backordered	FedEx		No	Product discontinued.
6	Black Mountain Hardware	9/5/2005	AB3951	$893.33	Shipped	USPS	PS009459	Yes	
7	Jessica's Hallmark	9/5/2005	AB3952	$3,838.99	Shipped	USPS	PS009460	Yes	
8	Natural Products for You	9/5/2005	AB3953	$1,102.33	Shipped	USPS	PS009461	Yes	
9	Green Room Gifts	9/5/2005	AB3954	$1,237.33	Shipped	UPS	UPS838333	Yes	
10	Village Decorators	9/5/2005	AB3955	$227.22	Partial ship	FedEx	X1L3845967	No	Rest ships 7/9/05.
11	Soothing Scent Store	9/5/2005	AB3956	$2,933.22	Backordered	FedEx		No	
12	Reliable Goods	9/6/2005	AB3957	$283.66	Backordered	FedEx		No	
13	Catalog Finds	9/6/2005	AB3958	$17,393.99	Pending	FedEx		No	
14	Interiors by Jane	9/6/2005	AB3959	$338.22	Pending	FedEx		No	
15	Surprise by Basket	9/6/2005	AB3960	$740.00	Pending	FedEx		No	
16	Sweet Treats N More	9/6/2005	AB3961	$663.09	Pending	USPS		No	Last item in today.
17	Elegant Gifts	9/6/2005	AB3962	$295.99	Backordered	USPS		No	
18	Scents and Scentsations	9/6/2005	AB3963	$589.76	Backordered	FedEx	X1L3845993	No	
19	Fairlaine Décor	9/7/2005	AB3964	$2,049.99	Pending	UPS	UPS838333	No	
20	Interior Expressions	9/8/2005	AB3965	$1,759.99	Pending	UPS		No	
21	Taylor Gifts	9/9/2005	AB3966	$52.50	Shipped	USPS	PS009839	Yes	
22	Green Room Gifts	9/9/2005	AB3967	$354.54	Pending	FedEx			
23	Village Decorators	9/9/2005	AB3968	$987.21	Pending	UPS			
24	Soothing Scent Store	9/9/2005	AB3969	$345.00	Pending	UPS			
25	Reliable Goods	9/9/2005	AB3970	$596.00	Pending	USPS			
26	Catalog Finds	9/9/2005	AB3971	$449.00	Pending	USPS			
27	Interiors by Jane	9/9/2005	AB3972	$949.00	Pending	USPS			
28	Surprise by Basket	9/9/2005	AB3973	$4,199.00	Pending	FedEx			
29	Sweet Treats N More	9/10/2005	AB3974	$358.99	Pending	FedEx			
30	Elegant Gifts	9/10/2005	AB3975	$994.29	Pending	FedEx			
31	Scents and Scentsations	9/10/2005	AB3976	$305.03	Pending	UPS			
32	Fairlaine Décor	9/10/2005	AB3977	$558.33	Pending	FedEx			
33	Interior Expressions	9/10/2005	AB3978	$876.99	Pending	UPS			
34	Taylor Gifts	9/10/2005	AB3979	$768.22	Pending	USPS			
35	Green Room Gifts	9/10/2005	AB3980	$395.99	Pending	USPS			
36	Village Decorators	9/11/2005	AB3981	$858.99	Pending	USPS			
37	Soothing Scent Store	9/11/2005	AB3982	$940.00	Pending	USPS			
38	Reliable Goods	9/11/2005	AB3983	$684.38	Pending	FedEx			
39	Catalog Finds	9/11/2005	AB3984	$385.44	Pending	UPS			
40	Interiors by Jane	9/11/2005	AB3985	$383.99	Pending	UPS			

Directory of Files

Exercise	File Name	Page
1	DP01	212
2	DP02, DP02-2	215
3	DP03	217
4	DP04	220
5	DP05	223
6	DP06	226
7	DP07	228
8	DP08	230
9	None	—
10	None	—
11	None	—
12	DP12	241
13	DP13	243
14	DP14	245
15	DP15	247
16	DP16	250
17	DP17	252
18	DP18	254
19	DP19	256
20	DP20	258
21	DP21	260
22	DP22	262
23	DP23	264
24	DP24	266
25	DP25	268
26	None	—
27	None	—
28	DP28	274
29	DP29	276
30	DP30	278
31	DP31, DP31-2	280

10. Now you want to print the full list. However, you also want to include the titles in rows 1 through 3. You can set up these rows as **print titles**, which print on every page or selection you print from the spreadsheet. Format the range A1:I3 (or rows 1 through 3) as print titles.

11. Set the printout to use the landscape orientation with **1"** top and bottom margins and **.5"** left and right margins, and gridlines and row and column headings.

12. Print the spreadsheet. If your instructor requires it, label and turn in a copy of the printed spreadsheet.

   ✓ *Your second printout may be four pages long. To learn how to fit printouts on paper more effectively, see the next exercise.*

13. Save your changes to the spreadsheet file.

   ✓ *Most spreadsheet programs save your page setup changes with the file. So, it pays to check the page setup before every printout, to ensure the spreadsheet will be printing with the settings you prefer.*

14. Close the spreadsheet file.

Illustration 1

	A	B	C	D	E
1	**Order Status**				
2					
3	**Client**	**Order Date**	**Order Number**	**Order Total**	**Status**
4	Taylor Gifts	9/5/2005	AB3949	$3,344.99	Shipped
5	Kerry's Cottage	9/5/2005	AB3950	$293.38	Backordered
6	Black Mountain Hardware	9/5/2005	AB3951	$893.33	Shipped
7	Jessica's Hallmark	9/5/2005	AB3952	$3,838.99	Shipped
8	Natural Products for You	9/5/2005	AB3953	$1,102.33	Shipped
9	Green Room Gifts	9/5/2005	AB3954	$1,237.33	Shipped
10	Village Decorators	9/5/2005	AB3955	$227.22	Partial ship
11	Soothing Scent Store	9/5/2005	AB3956	$2,933.22	Backordered
12	Reliable Goods	9/6/2005	AB3957	$283.66	Backordered
13	Catalog Finds	9/6/2005	AB3958	$17,393.99	Pending
14	Interiors by Jane	9/6/2005	AB3959	$338.22	Pending
15	Surprise by Basket	9/6/2005	AB3960	$740.00	Pending
16	Sweet Treats N More	9/6/2005	AB3961	$663.09	Pending
17	Elegant Gifts	9/6/2005	AB3962	$295.99	Backordered
18	Scents and Scentsations	9/6/2005	AB3963	$589.76	Backordered
19	Fairlaine Décor	9/7/2005	AB3964	$2,049.99	Pending
20	Interior Expressions	9/8/2005	AB3965	$1,759.99	Pending
21	Taylor Gifts	9/9/2005	AB3966	$52.50	Shipped

Lesson 11
Working with Graphics, Rules, and Boxed Text

Exercises 1–9

- ❖ Get started with clip art
- ❖ Enhance a document with lines, borders, and shading
- ❖ Work with text and graphics
- ❖ Create a graphic with a caption

Exercise 24

❖ Adjust Page Setup and Print Area Settings

Notes

Every spreadsheet program uses some default printing settings. Often, spreadsheets by default print information in a **portrait orientation,** with the shorter edge of the paper along the top, and don't include any **gridlines** or column or row headings (or borders) in the printout. The spreadsheet program also may decide where to insert page breaks and by default prints all the information on the spreadsheet, no matter how many pages it takes. You can control your printouts and decide whether or not a printout includes such elements as gridlines and headings. You can set up the spreadsheet to print in the **landscape orientation** (with the longer edge of the paper along the top) or designate a **print area**—the portion of the spreadsheet to print.

As the owner of LightNatural Beeswax Candles, you like to keep a close eye to ensure orders are being shipped promptly. Print an order status spreadsheet for your review now.

Vocabulary

portrait orientation
gridlines

landscape orientation
print area

print titles

Directions

1. Open the **SS24** spreadsheet file.
2. Save the file as **ORDSTAT**. The information in the spreadsheet uses numerous columns. Depending on your screen resolution, it may even have more information than you can view on the screen at once. It is also likely more information than can print on a portrait page.
3. Scroll to the right to see the full content of the far right column. You will probably want to use the landscape orientation for your printout.
4. Try printing part of the order information. Select cells A1 through E21.

5. Set the selected range as the print area. (The cells the spreadsheet program will include in the printout.)
6. Change the printout margins to **.5"** on the left and right sides.
   - ✓ *In most spreadsheet programs, you use the page setup command to access settings like the orientation, margins, and gridline settings.*
7. Specify that the printout should print with gridlines and row and column headings.
8. Print the spreadsheet. Illustration 1 on the following page shows how this printout should look.
9. Clear the print area.

Exercise 1

❖ Insert, Position, and Size Clip Art

Notes

Leading word processing programs provide a selection of **clip art**—graphic images you can add into your documents. In most cases, clip art serves as a decoration meant to make your document more interesting and attractive. You should try to select clip art images that complement the subject matter and mood of your document. For example, you wouldn't want to put animal pictures in a business document. On the other hand, you might want to use animal pictures in a poster about a zoo.

 ✓ *Microsoft Office Word 2003 offers the **Clip Organizer** to help you select and store clip art images.*

You are a member of the local Mouse Clicks computer users group. Your group has decided to hold a free workshop to teach community members basic computer skills. Add clip art to a poster for the event to help make the poster more attention getting.

Vocabulary

clip art
Clip Organizer

selection handles
anchor settings

wrap settings

Directions

1. Open the **DP01** document file.
2. Save the file as **COMPCL**.
3. Insert a clip art image that includes a computer or computer-related content.

    ✓ *If you weren't working in the page (print) layout view, your word processing program will likely change to that view when you insert clip art. You need to work in the page (print) layout view when you're working with the desktop publishing features covered in this section of the book. Otherwise, you won't be able to see the results of your changes.*

4. Size the graphic so that it's about **1.5"** tall and proportionally wide.

 ✓ *To format, resize, delete, or move a clip art image, you must select the object first by clicking it. **Selection handles** appear around the object to tell you that it's selected. To delete a selected clip art object, press the Delete key.*

 ✓ *To resize an image so that it remains proportional, drag one of the corner selection handles. To make an image taller or wider only, drag the appropriate selection handle on the side if the image.*

5. Move the image above the flyer title text and center it. Also use the Enter key to add a line of space between the clip art and the flyer title text.

Lesson 19
Print and Chart Spreadsheet Information

Exercises 24–29

❖ **Set up print options**
❖ **Work with headers and footers**
❖ **Preview a spreadsheet**
❖ **Create and label a chart**

  ✓ *In some cases, the word processing program tries to keep the clip art you insert in a specific position in relation to the text due to **anchor** or **wrap settings**. In such an instance, you need to turn off or change those anchor or wrap settings so that you can move the clip art freely and position text correctly. Top and bottom wrapping would work well for this exercise. Exercises 7 and 8 in this lesson give you more practice with changing wrapping settings, if needed.*

6. Insert another clip art image of your choice—perhaps another one with a computer theme.

  ✓ *If you have Internet access in class and your instructor allows it, you also can download new clip art from the Internet for use in this exercise. For example, in Microsoft Office 2003, you can click the Clip art on Office Online link in the Clip Art task pane or click the Clips Online button in Microsoft Clip Organizer to find and download clips. Exercise 24 in Lesson 29 provides more information about downloading clip art from the Web.*

7. Size the graphic so that it's about **1.5"** tall and proportionally wide.
8. Move the image to the bottom of the document and center it. Your finished poster should resemble the illustration on the following page.

  ✓ *You may have to press Enter after positioning the insertion point at the end of the last line in order to move the clip art into position at the bottom of the document.*

9. Save your changes to the document file.
10. Print one copy of the document.
11. Close the document file.

Exercise 23

❖ Critical Thinking

Notes

Work with functions to review your skills in this exercise.

You have created a spreadsheet summarizing quarterly sales by product line for the prior year at Mountain Gear. Enhance the spreadsheet now with needed formulas.

Vocabulary

No new vocabulary in this exercise.

Directions

1. Open the **SS23** spreadsheet file.
2. Save the file as **MGSALES**.
3. Create a range name for the sales figures for each quarter (the first range is B5:B9), naming the ranges **Qtr_1**, **Qtr_2**, and so on.

   ✓ *Notice that you can't include a space in range names, but you can use the underscore character, instead.*

4. Create a range for the sales figures for all four quarters. Name the range **All**.
5. Create a range name for the sales figures for each product line (the first range is B5:E5), assigning the product line label as the range name.
6. In each of the cells in B10:E10, enter a formula that finds the total of the values in the quarterly sales figure range above, using range names in the formulas.

   ✓ *If you try to fill a formula that uses a range name, the range name is treated as an absolute reference. It doesn't change in copies of the formula.*

7. Apply the needed currency formatting to B10:E10.
8. In each of the cells in F5:F10, enter a formula that finds the average of the values in the range of all sales figures for the line to the left (or the Total, in the case of the bottom cell). Use range names where possible.
9. Apply the needed currency formatting to F5:F10.
10. In cell B12, enter a formula that sums the values in the All range, and apply the needed currency formatting.
11. Print the spreadsheet.
12. Save your changes to the spreadsheet file.
13. Close the spreadsheet file.

FREE COMPUTER WORKSHOP
SPONSORED BY
MOUSE CLICKS COMPUTER USERS GROUP

10 a.m. – 2 p.m.
Saturday, October 22
Randall High School
Computer Lab A

Who should attend:
- Seniors who want to learn to e-mail their relatives
- Parents who want to monitor a child's computer usage
- Small business owners who want to computerize their business
- Anyone who wants to update business computer skills

This seminar is free, although donations to the Randall High School Technology Fund will be accepted. For more information, call 333-4343.

Illustration 1

	A	B	C	D	E	F	G
1	Major Manufacturing						
2	Current Job Applicant Testing Results						
3							
4	Fname	Lname	Dexterity	Computer	Dexterity Grade	Computer Grade	
5	Dan	Jones	92	67			
6	Callie	Brown	88	45			
7	Charles	Hobbs	78	88			
8	Tommy	Plemmons	56	72			
9	Mabel	Lust	95	88			
10	Karen	Kittner	90	79			
11	Mike	Parsell	88	85			
12	Chuck	Searcy	75	75			
13	Richard	Wells	78	66			
14	Ronda	Robers	80	68			
15	Chris	Norman	81	73			
16	Sarah	McCall	82	71			
17	Lane	Godsey	91	67			
18	Larry	Cook	95	60			
19	Shannon	Branch	85	50			
20							

Illustration 2

	A	B	C	D	E	F	G
1	Major Manufacturing						
2	Current Job Applicant Testing Results						
3							
4	Fname	Lname	Dexterity	Computer	Dexterity Grade	Computer Grade	
5	Dan	Jones	92	67	PASS	PASS	
6	Callie	Brown	88	45	PASS	*	
7	Charles	Hobbs	78	88	*	PASS	
8	Tommy	Plemmons	56	72	*	PASS	
9	Mabel	Lust	95	88	PASS	PASS	
10	Karen	Kittner	90	79	PASS	PASS	
11	Mike	Parsell	88	85	PASS	PASS	
12	Chuck	Searcy	75	75	*	PASS	
13	Richard	Wells	78	66	*	PASS	
14	Ronda	Robers	80	68	PASS	PASS	
15	Chris	Norman	81	73	PASS	PASS	
16	Sarah	McCall	82	71	PASS	PASS	
17	Lane	Godsey	91	67	PASS	PASS	
18	Larry	Cook	95	60	PASS	*	
19	Shannon	Branch	85	50	PASS	*	
20							

Exercise 2

❖ Insert, Position, and Size a Graphic

Notes

Digital cameras and scanners create electronic images, or **graphic** files. This equipment has dropped in price and improved in quality, so it's now becoming common to create your own **digital images** for use in documents. You can also use a drawing or painting program to create images from scratch. Or, you can **download** images from a variety of sources on the Internet. Most word processors enable you to use graphic images in a variety of formats—such as Windows bitmap (.bmp), Paintbrush (.pcx), Graphics Interchange Format (.gif), and JPEG (.jpg)—in your documents. Use this exercise to practice inserting a graphic image into your document.

You work in the HR department at Major Manufacturing. You have created an announcement for a mandatory meeting that will be placed on all employee bulletin boards. Finish the announcement now by inserting a graphic file of the company logo.

Vocabulary

graphic   digital image   download

Directions

1. Open the **DP02** document file.
2. Save the file as **EMMEET**.
3. Position the insertion point on the first blank line below the two lines at the top of the document.
4. Center that paragraph (blank line).
5. Insert the **DP02-2** graphic file. This particular file is a digital photo in the .jpg (JPEG) format, a very compact graphic file format.

   ✓ *Your word processing software uses special filters to enable it to display graphics of various types. If you try to insert the* **DP02-2** *file and get an error message, ask your lab monitor or instructor to make sure the right filter has been installed.*

   ✓ *The command for inserting a graphic image can be different from the command you used to insert clip art.*

6. Size the graphic so that it's about **1.25"** tall and proportionally wide.
7. Add a border in 3-point width in a dark blue color around the graphic. This helps lend a more finished appearance to the graphic.
8. With the graphic selected, insert at least 6 points of space before the paragraph.
9. Delete one blank line after the inserted graphic. The finished document file should look like the illustration on the following page.

Exercise 22

❖ Use IF Functions

Notes

The other important function used in many spreadsheets is the **IF** function. IF enables you to build a **logical formula**. The IF function compares the value in a cell to a test that you specify, then makes a decision as to whether the value meets the test (is true) or fails the test (is false). You specify what result the formula displays: TRUE or FALSE, YES or NO, BONUS or NO BONUS, or whatever you choose.

For example, if cell A15 in your spreadsheet contains a value, you could enter a formula in another cell that reads =IF(A15>=10,"YES","NO"). The segment A15>=10 is the logical test. The first word in quotations is the text the cell displays if the logical test evaluates to true, and the second word in quotations is the text the cell displays if the logical test evaluates to false. In this exercise, you create some IF formulas.

You work in Human Resources at Major Manufacturing. The company administers two tests to applicants for assembly and warehouse jobs: a dexterity test and a computer skills test. You have a spreadsheet that lists the raw scores, and you want to add formulas to indicate PASS or FAIL for each applicant's performance on each test. Use the IF function to create those formulas now.

Vocabulary

IF   logical formula

Directions

1. Open the **SS22** spreadsheet file.
2. Save the file as **MMGRADE**.
3. In cell E5, enter an IF formula that determines whether the value in C5 is greater than or equal to **80**. The formula should display **PASS** if the logical test is true, or * if it's false.
4. Fill the formula down through cell E19.
5. In cell F5, enter an IF formula that determines whether the value in D5 is greater than or equal to 65. The formula should display **PASS** if the logical test is true, or * if it's false.
6. Fill the formula down through cell F19.
7. Save your changes to the spreadsheet file. The illustrations on the following page compare the spreadsheet's appearance before and after your work.
8. Print one copy of the spreadsheet.
9. Close the spreadsheet file.

✓ If the dialog box for formatting the inserted graphic doesn't give you the option of adding a border, you can use the same command that you'd use to add a border to selected text. Exercises 5 and 6 in this lesson present that command.

10. Save your changes to the document file.
11. Print one copy of the document.
12. Close the document file.

Major Manufacturing
Mandatory Employee Meeting

When: 3 p.m. Wednesday, June 14, 2006

Where: Employee Café, Top Level of Building A

Why: Review of New Attendance and Time Tracking Policies

Who: Facilitated by Jan Marks, HR Manager

Attendance at this meeting is required, even for off-shift employees. If you have previously scheduled a vacation for this date, please contact Jan Marks at x2025. Refreshments will be provided.

	A	B	C	D	E	F
2	Prepared by:		Student's name			
3						
4	N/M=Not Measurable					
5						
6	Day	Precip. (in.)		Days of rain:	11	
7	1	0.61		High amount:	3.86	
8	2	0.62		Low amount:	0.1	
9	3	N/M		Daily average:	0.459167	
10	4	0.1				
11	5	N/M				
12	6	0.29				
13	7	3.86				
14	8	0.51				
15	9	N/M				
16	10	N/M				
17	11	N/M				
18	12	0.25				
19	13	0.125				
20	14	0.75				
21	15	N/M				
22	16	0.5				
23	17	0.65				
24	18	N/M				
25	19					
26	20					
27	21					
28	22					
29	23					
30	24					
31	25					
32	26					
33	27					
34	28					
35	29					
36	30					
37						

Exercise 3

❖ Import a Scanner or Digital Camera Image

Notes

As noted in the last exercise, many computer users now have either a digital camera or scanner—or both. (Scanners often are included along with new desktop computer systems.) Having a scanner or digital camera enables you to improve your business communications by providing timely, accurate images and illustrations to your colleagues and clients. In fact, in many cases such as the example shown in this exercise, an image is necessary to communicate adequately.

Many word processing programs (and other applications) enable you to **import** (or **acquire**) an image directly from a scanner or digital camera. The process varies widely depending on your application and your equipment, because your word processor may need to work with the proprietary software you received with your scanner or camera. Basically, however, you position the insertion point, start the import operation, select the scan settings or the image stored in the camera, finish inserting the image, and then size and format the image as needed in the document.

✓ *Consult your instructor to learn more about working with the software for your classroom scanner or digital camera.*

Go! Travel Consultants has arranged a special tour package to San Diego. Add a scan of a building in Balboa Park in San Diego to a promotional document about the trip.

Vocabulary

import   acquire

Directions

1. Open the **DP03** document file.
2. Save the file as **SDIEGO**.
3. Position the insertion point on the second blank line below the first full paragraph of text in the document.
4. Center that paragraph (blank line).
5. Import Illustration 1 (scan it) into the document.

   ✓ *You will find that using a custom scan gives you the greatest control over the final appearance of the image. A custom scan enables you to control such elements as the image resolution, contrast, cropping, and more.*

   ✓ *For some scanners, you may find that you get better results when scanning black and white images if you in fact scan them using a setting for color images (such as millions of colors). Sometimes, scanning a black and white image in grayscale will remove contrast and make the image appear faint or dull.*

6. In cell E6, enter a COUNT formula that finds the number of days that had measurable rain, as noted in the **RAIN** range. Again, the function counts only those cells holding values, ignoring the cells holding a notation or cells where you have not yet made an entry.

7. In cell E7, enter a MAX function formula to find the day with the highest rain amount in the **RAIN** range.

8. In cell E8, enter a MIN function formula to find the smallest rain result for any entry in the **RAIN** range.

9. In cell E9, enter an AVERAGE function formula that finds the average rainfall for the month based on the entries in the **RAIN** range.

   ✓ The AVERAGE *function sums the values in the range, counts the number of values in the range, and then performs the final average calculation.*

   ✓ *Your spreadsheet program may use slightly different names for the functions. For example, your spreadsheet program might use AVG or AVE instead of AVERAGE. If you have a problem finding any function, use your spreadsheet program's insert function feature to find the proper function name.*

10. The value in cell E9 looks too high. To test that theory, click cell E11, and enter a formula that sums all the cells in the range B7:B21, and then divides the result by 15, the number of days measured so far.

    ✓ *The result you get in Step 10 is lower than the result in cell E9. This is because the AVERAGE function used in the formula there does not factor the N/M cells into the calculation. (In other words, it divides the sum of B7:B21 by 9, the number of cells with actual values rather than 15, the total number of days measured).*

11. You need to instead use the AVERAGEA function, which will count the cells with text entries in the divisor. Edit the formula in cell E9 to change the function used to **AVERAGEA**.

12. After you change the formula, you can see that the newly-calculated result matches the test calculation in cell E11.

13. Delete the formula in cell E11.

14. Add three more entries in the **RAIN** range for the 16th through the 18th of the month: **.5**, **.65**, and **N/M**.

15. Adjust column widths as desired.

16. Save your changes to the spreadsheet file. The illustration on the following page shows how the final spreadsheet looks.

17. Print one copy of the spreadsheet.

    ✓ *Don't worry if your printout takes more than one page. In the next lesson, you'll learn techniques for controlling printouts.*

18. Close the spreadsheet file.

6. Size the scanned picture so that it's about **3"** tall and proportionally wide. The finished document file should look like Illustration 2 on the following page.

7. Save your changes to the document file.
8. Print one copy of the document.
9. Close the document file.

Illustration 1

Exercise 21

❖ Use SUM Function ❖ Use MAX Function
❖ Use MIN Function ❖ Use COUNT Function
❖ Use AVERAGE and AVERAGEA Functions

Notes

The biggest spreadsheet programs offer more than 100 different functions. Even modest spreadsheet programs offer dozens of functions. SUM, MAX, and MIN are among the most commonly used functions. This exercise introduces you to two more important functions. The **COUNT** function counts how many cells in a range contain values or formulas that calculate to values. The **AVERAGE** function calculates the average of all the values in the selected range. If a cell in the selected range holds text, then it is not considered at all in the calculation. Use the **AVERAGEA** function instead when the range to average holds some text entries, and you want each text entry to be considered a zero and used in the calculation.

The instructor is giving a meteorology lesson in one of your science courses. As part of the lesson, you are tracking daily rainfall for the month of September. You've entered your monthly measurements for part of the month in a spreadsheet, and now you need to add formulas using functions to evaluate the data, as well as making a few more data entries.

Vocabulary

COUNT	AVERAGE	AVERAGEA

Directions

1. Open the **SS21** spreadsheet file.
2. Save the file as **RAIN**.
3. Enter your name in cell C2.
4. Select the range B7:B36, which will hold all the measured rain amounts.
5. Name the range **RAIN**. Notice that not all cells in the range hold values. Some of the cells hold a notation (label entry), **N/M**.

✓ As noted in the previous exercise, in most spreadsheet applications if you use the SUM function to total a range that holds label entries or blank entries, the SUM function simply skips those entries. In other applications, such as the Works spreadsheet tool, you may need to delete the N/M entries to ensure a SUM function would total the values correctly.

Illustration 2

To: Preferred Customers
From: Go! Travel Consultants
Re: Special San Diego Package
Date: May 1, 2006

Join Go! Travel Consultants for a special tour of San Diego. Spend five days and four nights exploring the city's Old Town district and such special attractions as the San Diego Zoo and Coronado Island. Includes a day trip to lovely Balboa Park:

Basic package price includes airfare from Indianapolis, airport transfers, four nights' lodging, and meal allowance. Special excursions such as sailing tours also available by prior arrangement.

Contact Janet Mason at Go! Travel Consultants (888-777-0707) for more information. Travel must be booked by May 31, 2006.

Illustration 1

	A	B	C	D	E	F	G	H	I
1				**Major Manufacturing**					
2				6 Month Division Revenue Report					
3									
4						Hi:			
5	Estimated Costs and Taxes:			75%		Low:			
6									
7		Jan.	Feb	Mar	Apr	May	Jun	Total	
8	Household	$125,024	$245,162	$679,000	$244,000	$728,994	$485,893	$2,508,073	
9	Commercial	$568,474	$97,646	$132,654	$684,984	$321,564	$375,354	$2,180,676	
10	Eco	$32,555	$58,963	$47,222	$11,369	$47,008	$32,696	$229,813	
11	Appliance	$789,465	$654,132	$159,984	$325,469	$875,845	$847,812	$3,652,707	
12	Total								
13	Est. C & T	$0.00	$0.00	$0.00	$0.00	$0.00	$0.00	$0.00	
14									

Illustration 2

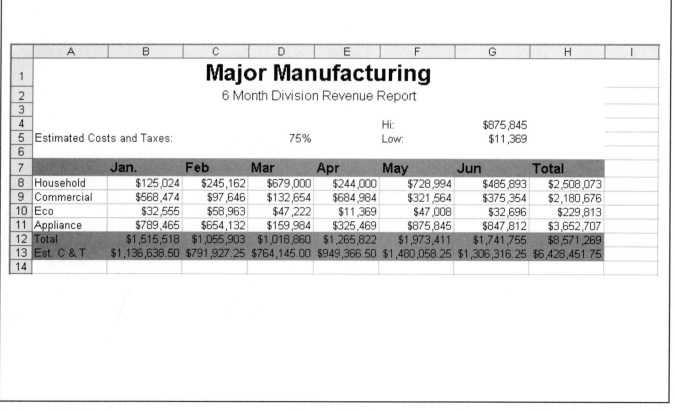

	A	B	C	D	E	F	G	H	I
1				**Major Manufacturing**					
2				6 Month Division Revenue Report					
3									
4						Hi:	$875,845		
5	Estimated Costs and Taxes:			75%		Low:	$11,369		
6									
7		Jan.	Feb	Mar	Apr	May	Jun	Total	
8	Household	$125,024	$245,162	$679,000	$244,000	$728,994	$485,893	$2,508,073	
9	Commercial	$568,474	$97,646	$132,654	$684,984	$321,564	$375,354	$2,180,676	
10	Eco	$32,555	$58,963	$47,222	$11,369	$47,008	$32,696	$229,813	
11	Appliance	$789,465	$654,132	$159,984	$325,469	$875,845	$847,812	$3,652,707	
12	Total	$1,515,518	$1,055,903	$1,018,860	$1,265,822	$1,973,411	$1,741,755	$8,571,269	
13	Est. C & T	$1,136,638.50	$791,927.25	$764,145.00	$949,366.50	$1,480,058.25	$1,306,316.25	$6,428,451.75	
14									

Exercise 4

❖ Add Borders and Rules to Set Off Text

Notes

A **border** or **rule** is a line that appears above or below a paragraph to set off information and make it easier to read. You could manually draw a line or rule, but that could create problems if you had to add or delete a lot of text in the document. Most word processing programs provide a better way to create borders or rules—by adding a border to the top or bottom of the paragraph. You can usually choose from a few different border styles and sizes, and can even apply a color to the border you select to make it more interesting.

In addition, some word processors now include a number of decorative border or **divider** graphics. These enable you to add even more variety to your document. However, you have to be careful if you add or delete text in the document, as you may have to reposition the border or divider graphic.

You are updating the letterhead for the Mountain Gear store. Enhance the letterhead document now with some rules and dividers.

Vocabulary

border   rule   divider

Directions

1. Open the **DP04** document file.
2. Save the file as **GEARL**.
3. With the insertion point in the top line, add a border above the paragraph. Choose a single line style in a 3-point width and an orange color.

   ✓ *The border formatting you select applies to all selected paragraphs, or to the paragraph that currently holds the insertion point.*

   ✓ *Notice that the borders you add by default span the full width of the page, from margin to margin, no matter what alignment the paragraph uses. When a document is divided into columns, borders span the width of the column. In some word processors, you can have the border feature*

display a line that's closer to the paragraph width by changing the paragraph indentation settings. For example, if the paragraph stops 2" from the right margin, set 2" of right indentation to make the border line shorter.

4. Click in the tag line that reads **All the Gear You Need from One Source**.
5. Add a border both above and below the paragraph. For the top border, choose a – dashed line style in a 1½-point width and a sea green color. For the bottom border, choose a triple-line style of your choice in a 3-point width and a dark red color.

8. Use the drop-down list for the name box at the left end of the formula bar to go to (select) the **JAN** range.

   ✓ *If your spreadsheet program doesn't use a feature like the name box to select a range, you can use the go to feature to find a range.*

9. Use the drop-down list for the name box at the left end of the formula bar to go to (select) the **ALL** range.

10. In cell B12, enter a SUM formula that totals the revenue values above. Use the range address B8:B11 as the argument.

    ✓ *A formula that holds a function must start with the proper symbol, like any other formula. For example, a SUM formula might look like =SUM(A1:C10) or @SUM(A1:C10).*

11. In cell C12, enter a SUM formula that totals the revenue values above. This time, use the range name, FEB, as the argument.

12. Fill the formula in cell C12 right through cell H12.

13. As you can see, this creates a problem, because most spreadsheet programs treat range names like absolute cell addresses. Click in cell E12 and review the formula in the formula bar to verify that the spreadsheet program used the same name for the fill.

14. Undo the fill.

15. Select cell B12, and fill it right through H12, instead.

16. In cell G4, enter a formula using the MAX function to find the highest value in the ALL range. Create the formula using the insert function feature in your spreadsheet program. Use the **ALL** range name as the argument.

    ✓ *The **MAX** function finds the maximum (largest) value within the range specified as the argument. The **MIN** function finds the minimum (smallest) value within the range specified as the argument.*

17. In cell G5, enter a formula using the MIN function to find the lowest revenue value in the ALL range. Create the formula using the insert function feature in your spreadsheet program. Use the **ALL** range name as the argument.

18. Format cells G4:G5 as currency with zero decimal places.

19. Save your changes to the spreadsheet file. The illustrations on the following page compare the spreadsheet's appearance before and after your work.

20. Print one copy of the spreadsheet.

    ✓ *If your instructor requires it, label and turn in a copy of the printed spreadsheet.*

21. Close the spreadsheet file.

✓ *Don't use too many different border styles within a single document. As with using too many different fonts, too many different border styles compete for attention in your design rather than complementing one another.*

6. Move the insertion point to the end of the last line in the document.
7. Press Enter.
8. Insert a decorative border or divider below the paragraph.

   ✓ *In some word processors, you can select the decorative divider (also called a horizontal line) from the same dialog box that you use to add paragraph borders. In other cases, you may need to insert the decorative divider just as you would insert a piece of clip art.*

9. If inserting the border or divider causes a second page in the document, press Backspace or delete any blank lines after the inserted border to return the document to a single page in length.
10. Change the color of all the symbols in the document to the same sea green color as the paragraph border you added earlier. The finished document should look like the illustration on the following page.
11. Save your changes to the document file.
12. Print one copy of the document.
13. Close the document file.

Exercise 20

❖ Name Ranges ❖ Use Range Names
❖ Use SUM Function ❖ Use MIN Function
❖ Use MAX Function

Notes

You can refer to a range by its range address, as in B8:C14. Or, you can identify a range by a **range name** or *cell name*, such as giving the name SALES to a range that holds sales values. After you name the range, you can use the range name to select the range or to identify the range in any formula that contains a **function**. A function performs a predefined calculation in a formula to help you create formulas more quickly. For example, the quick sum formulas you created in earlier lessons used the **SUM** function. A formula performs its calculations on **arguments** you enter between parentheses. For example, the arguments for the SUM function can be the cells you want to total or a range of cells to total. You can type a formula with a function directly into a cell, but most spreadsheet programs provide an **insert function feature** that makes it easy to select the function you need, specify arguments, and insert the function into your formula.

In this exercise, revisit the six-month revenue report you created for Major Manufacturing that you worked with in Exercise 15. In this instance, name some ranges and use those names with functions to build formulas.

Vocabulary

range name	SUM	insert function feature	MIN
function	arguments	MAX	

Directions

1. Open the **SS20** spreadsheet file.
2. Save the file as **MM6M2**.
3. Select the range B8:B11, which holds the January revenue figures.
4. Name the range **JAN**.
5. Assign range names (**FEB**, **MAR**, etc.) in the same fashion to the ranges holding the results for each of the other five months, as well as the Total results. Name that last range **TOT**.

   ✓ *Most spreadsheet programs do not treat range names as case-sensitive, so you don't have to enter the names in all caps if you prefer not to.*

6. Select the range B8:G11, which holds all the monthly revenue values.
7. Name the range **ALL**.

❧Mountain Gear☙

123 Main St.
Hot Springs, NC 28743
800-555-2222

❧All the Gear You Need from One Source☙

❧Have the gear you need to play it safe, no matter how you play!☙

Lesson 18
Use Functions and Range Names

Exercises 20–23

❖ Function basics

❖ Name spreadsheet ranges

❖ Use range names in functions

❖ Working with common functions

Exercise 5

❖ Add Borders and Shading

Notes

In addition to adding a border around a paragraph, you can add **shading**. You can also use borders and shading together, but don't overdo it. Some word processing programs even enable you to add a border around the whole page (called a **page border**). In this exercise, work with border and shading settings.

Your fellow Mouse Clicks computer users group members would like you to include borders in the poster document to emphasize certain information. Work with borders and shading in the poster now.

Vocabulary

shading   page border

Directions

1. Open the **DP05** document file.
2. Save the file as **COMPCL2**.
3. Move the insertion point to the third line of text.
4. Add a border below the paragraph. Choose a double-line style, with a 1½-point width and a light blue color.
5. Select the line that reads **Who should attend** and all of the bulleted list paragraphs.
6. Add a border around the paragraph(s). This will effectively create a box around the paragraphs. Choose a dashed-line style, with a 1½-point width and a green color.
7. Indent the left side of the **Who should attend** paragraph by .**25"**, or otherwise adjust the border so its length more closely resembles the length of the longest line in that block text. This should make the borders around the paragraphs align nicely.

8. Select the final paragraph of text at the bottom of the flyer.
9. Apply red shading with a 50% style or pattern to the paragraph.

   ✓ *The shading you select applies to all selected paragraphs, or the paragraph that currently holds the insertion point. By default, the shading usually spans the full page or column.*

   ✓ *Pattern styles named by percentage apply a mix of the selected color and white. A 50% pattern is half color and half white. A 25% pattern is 25% color and 75% white.*

   ✓ *You need to keep contrast in mind when you add shading to a paragraph. If the text uses a narrow font or a small font size, you should use very light shading. Heavier, darker text may remain readable with darker shading.*

10. Select the bottom piece of inserted clip art.

Exercise 19

❖ Critical Thinking

Notes

Finish practicing the skills you learned in this lesson now.

You work in administration at Crystal Community College. The main enrollment period for the adult continuing education fall session has just ended, so you want to finish a spreadsheet that will estimate revenue based on the number of students enrolled, class fees, and instructor fees.

Vocabulary

No new vocabulary in this exercise.

Directions

1. Open the **SS19** spreadsheet file.
2. Save the file as **CLREV**.
3. Adjust column widths as needed.
4. In cell D6, enter a formula that multiplies the first value in the **Students Enrolled** column by the **Fee** column entry.
5. Fill the formula down the column as needed.
6. In cell F6, enter a formula that subtracts the first entry in the **Instructor Fee** column from the first entry in the **Subtotal** column.
7. Fill the formula down the column as needed.
8. Since Row 8 calculates to a negative Total, delete that row.
9. Add a new label, **With Drops**, in cell G5 and adjust the column width as needed.

10. In cell G6, enter a formula that multiples the first entry in the Total column by 1 minus the Drop reduction factor entry in cell B19. Use an absolute reference to cell B19.

   ✓ *You have to subtract a percentage value from one whenever you want to use that percentage to reduce another value. In this case, the drop reduction factor reduces each total value by 5%.*

11. Fill the formula down the column as needed.
12. Enter quick sum formulas in cells B17 and D17:G17 to total the values above.
13. Apply the desired formatting, including font changes, fills, and borders, to the spreadsheet.
14. Apply additional currency formatting as needed to spruce up the spreadsheet.
15. Save your changes to the spreadsheet file.
16. Print one copy of the spreadsheet.
17. Close the spreadsheet file.

11. Add a border around the selection. Choose a single-line style, with a 3-point width and a blue color.

   ✓ *If you select a list and add a border around it, the new border should surround the entire selection, not each paragraph in the selection. If you wanted to add a border around each individual paragraph, you would have to select the first paragraph, apply the border, select the next paragraph, and so on.*

12. If your word processing program offers a page border feature, add a border around the whole page. Choose a single line style, with a 3-point width and a red color.

13. Delete spaces between paragraphs of text as needed so all the flyer text fits on a single page. The finished document file should look like the illustration on the following page.

14. Save your changes to the document file.

15. Print one copy of the document.

   ✓ *If your word processing program displays a message saying the page border is outside the printable area, continue printing. The document should print normally.*

   ✓ *Your printer may not be capable of printing all the available border styles and sizes, especially when you combine them with a color. So, you may have to experiment with different combinations to yield the results you want.*

16. Close the document file.

Exercise 18

❖ Critical Thinking

Notes

Work on your column, row, and range skills in this exercise.

Design Architects, LLC uses a simple spreadsheet to invoice clients. Work on an invoice for a particular client now.

Vocabulary

No new vocabulary in this exercise.

Directions

1. Open the **SS18** spreadsheet file.
2. Save the file as **DAINV**.
3. Enter **230** as the invoice number and the current date in the appropriate cells.
4. Move those entries from B4:B5 to C4:C5.
5. Delete column B.
6. Enter the following in cells A11:C13:

Design	175	24
Revisions	125	12
Engineering check	750	1

7. Enter a formula in cell D11 that multiplies the Rate and Quantity entries on its row.
8. Fill the formula down through cell D18.
9. Add a quick sum formula in cell D19 to total the entries above.
10. Insert a row above row 12.

11. Make the following entries in columns A through C of the new row: **Consultation, 200, 5**.
12. Copy the formula from cell D11 to D12.
13. Apply an automatic formatting selection to the range A10:D20.

   ✓ *The automatic formatting choices may make mistakes. For example, the format might fail to apply a number format or might use a column width choice you don't agree with. You can apply other formatting choices after you choose automatic formatting. Your subsequent formatting choices override the automatic formatting*

14. Apply currency formatting to cells and adjust column widths as needed.
15. Save your changes to the spreadsheet file.
16. Print one copy of the spreadsheet.
17. Close the spreadsheet file.

FREE COMPUTER WORKSHOP
SPONSORED BY
MOUSE CLICKS COMPUTER USERS GROUP

10 a.m. – 2 p.m.
Saturday, October 22
Randall High School
Computer Lab A

Who should attend:
- Seniors who want to learn to e-mail their relatives
- Parents who want to monitor a child's computer usage
- Small business owners who want to computerize their business
- Anyone who wants to update business computer skills

This seminar is free, although donations to the Randall High School Technology Fund will be accepted. For more information, call 333-4343.

9. Enter **65** in cell B6 and **73** in cell C6.
10. Select B6:C6.
11. Fill the cells to the right, D6:H6.
12. Enter a quick sum formula in cell B7 to total the cells above it.
13. Fill the formula from cell B7 to C7:H7.
14. Apply an automatic formatting selection to the range A1:H7.
15. Save your changes to the spreadsheet file. The illustrations below compare the spreadsheet's appearance before and after your work.
16. Print one copy of the spreadsheet.
17. Close the spreadsheet file.

Illustration 1

	A	B	C	D	E	F	G	H	I
1	Order Shipping Forecast								
2									
3									
4		Monday							
5	Dock 1								
6	Dock 2								
7	Total								
8									

Illustration 2

	A	B	C	D	E	F	G	H
1				Order Shipping Forecast				
2				9/14/2006				
3								
4		Monday	Tuesday	Wednesday	Thursday	Friday	Saturday	Sunday
5	Dock 1	100	112	124	136	148	160	172
6	Dock 2	65	73	81	89	97	105	113
7	Total	165	185	205	225	245	265	285
8								

Exercise 6

❖ Work More with Borders and Shading

Notes

In this exercise, resume your work with borders and shading. See how using borders and shading can create a different look. In addition, work now with **pattern** settings, which combine a color and white space to provide an interesting visual effect.

✓ *A* solid color behind a paragraph (shading) *is also called a* ***fill***. *In some word processing programs, you use one set of dialog box choices to apply a fill or shading, and another set of choices to choose a pattern and its color.*

You aren't satisfied with the look of the Mountain Gear store letterhead that you worked with in Exercise 4. Improve the letterhead document with alternate borders and shading.

Vocabulary

pattern   fill

Directions

1. Open the **DP06** document file.
2. Save the file as **GEARL2**.
3. Remove the existing borders from all paragraphs in the document.
4. Select the top five lines in the document.
5. Add a decorative single-line style border around the selection, with a 3-point size and plum color.
6. Select the tag line that reads **All the Gear You Need from One Source**.
7. Add a light green fill to the paragraph.
8. Center the bordered and shaded paragraphs at the top of the document.
9. Select the line of text at the bottom of the document.
10. Add a pattern to the selection. Choose the Dk Grid (or comparable) style, in a light green color.
11. Add a ½-point single-line border in a plum color around the selection.

12. If your word processing program offers a page border feature, add a shadow border around the whole page. Choose a single-line style, with a 2¼-point width and a gold color. Or, if your word processing program enables you to add a decorative page border, you can add a decorative border instead. The finished document file should resemble the illustration on the following page. If you compare it with your finished document from Exercise 4, you can see that using shading and patterns, along with different borders creates quite a different look for the letterhead.

    ✓ *The decorative page border feature, also called art, may be available but not installed by default. Consult your instructor if you'd like to install it and experiment with the available choices.*

13. Save your changes to the document file.

Exercise 17

❖ Fill Formulas and Series
❖ Automatic Formats

Notes

You have previously copied formulas from cell to cell in a spreadsheet. When you need to copy a formula to several adjoining cells, you can use the **fill** feature instead. The fill feature provides a quick way for you to copy information from one cell to a range of adjoining cells. You also can use the fill feature to copy a particular cell entry, or to create a **series** of numbers that follow a pattern (incrementing by 10 in a 10, 20, 30, 40... pattern, for example).

Your division's warehouse at Major Manufacturing has had some problems shipping orders for the last several weeks. Now that you've worked out the kinks, your boss has asked you to forecast the number of shipments per day for the coming week, which you expect to increase at particular number of units per day for each of the shipping docks. Use the fill and automatic formatting features to flesh out your spreadsheet.

Vocabulary

fill   series   fill handle   fill pointer

Directions

1. Open the **SS17** spreadsheet file.
2. Save the file as **SHIPFOR**.
3. Enter the date in cell A2.
4. Select cell B4, which holds the label **Monday**.
5. Fill the range C4:H4 with the remaining days of the week.

   ✓ To perform the fill, you generally drag the **fill handle** at the lower-right corner of the selected cell or range, or use a **fill pointer** to drag the lower-right corner of the range.

   ✓ In top spreadsheet programs, the fill feature has some memorized series that it can fill, generally including the months, the days of the week, and abbreviations (like Q1 or Qtr 1) for the quarters of the year. In other examples such as this one, it can make a guess about what you want to fill. If

   it guesses wrong, make the first two entries yourself, select both of them, then drag the fill handle from the selection.

6. Enter **100** in cell B5 and **112** in cell C5.
7. Select B5:C5.
8. Fill the cells to the right, D5:H5.

   ✓ When you use the fill feature to fill a series of numbers, you have to enter and select the first two entries in the series to establish the pattern (increment). You then fill from those cells. If you entered a value in one cell and then tried to fill that value, the fill feature would simply copy the value. However, you can enter a single date and use the fill feature to fill subsequent dates (daily). To fill a series of dates (such as dates spaced a week apart), you have to enter the first two dates and select them before filling.

14. Print one copy of the document.

    ✓ *If your word processing program displays a message saying the page border is outside the printable area, continue printing. The document should print normally.*

15. Close the document file.

ℰ❧Mountain Gear❦ℛ

123 Main St.

Hot Springs, NC 28743

800-555-2222

ℰ❧**All the Gear You Need from One Source**❦ℛ

ℰ❧Have the gear you need to play it safe, no matter how you play!❦ℛ

Illustration 2

	A	B	C	D	E	F	G	H
1		**Marketing Survey**						
2		**15-Nov-06**						
3								
4								
5				*Product 1*				
6		*Question 1*	*Question 2*	*Question 3*	*Question 4*	*Question 5*	*Question 6*	*Q Total*
7	*Subject 1*	$1	$7	$7	$8	$15	$12	$50
8	*Subject 2*	$3	$4	$9	$2	$3	$4	$25
9	*Subject 3*	$12	$4	$8	$10	$3	$13	$50
10	*Subject 4*	$4	$6	$6	$12	$4	$7	$39
11	*Subject 5*	$6	$9	$15	$3	$0	$14	$47
12	Q Avg	$5	$6	$9	$7	$5	$10	$42
13								
14								
15				*Product 1*				
16		*Question 1*	*Question 2*	*Question 3*	*Question 4*	*Question 5*	*Question 6*	*Q Total*
17	*Subject 1*	$1	$7	$7	$8	$15	$12	$50
18	*Subject 2*	$3	$7	$9	$2	$2	$4	$27
19	*Subject 3*	$21	$4	$8	$11	$3	$13	$60
20	*Subject 4*	$4	$0	$6	$12	$4	$7	$33
21	*Subject 5*	$6	$9	$15	$3	$0	$14	$47
22	Q Avg	$7	$5	$9	$7	$5	$10	$43

Exercise 7

❖ Wrap Text Around a Graphic ❖ Add a Caption

Notes

Another technique you can use to refine graphics in a document is to work with the **wrap settings**. The wrap settings control how text appears in relation to the graphic or clip art. You can specify that text stop above the graphic and resume after the graphic. However, the document can look much more professional if the text flows or wraps around the graphic. (You've probably seen this effect in newsletters.) Wrapping text enables you to place the graphic next to the appropriate text, making the graphic easier to identify.

For further identification, add a **caption** to the clip art or graphic. You can also set up a graphic (or clip art) to appear behind or in front of text.

You're working a bit more with the Go! Travel Consultants trip announcement from Exercise 3. By changing wrap settings for the graphic and adding a caption, you can create a better look for the announcement.

Vocabulary

wrap settings   caption

Directions

1. Open the **DP07** document file.
2. Save the file as **SDIEGO2**.
3. Select the picture object (graphic) near the middle of the document.
4. Change the wrap settings to allow for tight wrapping around the graphic.
5. Decrease the size of the graphic to about 1.75" tall and a proportional width.
6. Drag the graphic to the right until it appears at the right side of the document and its top aligns with the first paragraph of descriptive text.
7. Delete the two extra blank lines between the first and second descriptive paragraphs.

8. Select the four lines at the top of the document, and add the border of your choice.
9. Select the picture graphic again, and add a caption that reads **Visit historic Balboa Park.**

   ✓ *You may find the command for adding a caption on the Insert menu. Some word processing programs by default insert a label (or title) and number in the caption, like* **Figure 1**. *While you may not be able to avoid the label, you can add the caption, then click in the caption box, drag over the unneeded label and number, and press the Delete key to delete them. You can click in the caption box at any time to edit and format its text, or click the border of the caption box and then drag to move or resize the caption.*

✓ If you try to copy or move a selection into a range where one or more cells already contains some type of entry, your spreadsheet program should display a message warning you that you're about to overwrite existing cells. You can check what's in the range and then choose whether or not to proceed.

8. With the range A5:G12 still selected, apply the automatic formatting of your choice.
9. Add a new column to the left of Column G.

✓ Notice that the entries in cells A1:A2 recenter automatically when you add a column within the range over which you centered them.

10. Enter **Question 6** as the column heading, and enter these values down the column: **12**, **4**, **13**, **7**, and **14**.
11. Copy the formula from cell F12 to cell G12.
12. Select the range A5:H12.

13. Copy the range to A15:H22. Notice that your spreadsheet program copies some or all of the automatic formatting.

✓ If your spreadsheet program displays a blinking marquee (dashed outline) around the range you just copied, you can press Esc to clear it.

14. Change the entry in cell A15 to read **Product 2**.
15. Randomly change some entries in cells in the range B17:G21 as if you had new data to input.
16. Save your changes to the spreadsheet file. The illustrations below and on the following page compare the spreadsheet's appearance before and after your work.
17. Print one copy of the spreadsheet.
18. Close the spreadsheet file.

Illustration 1

	A	B	C	D	E	F	G
1		**Marketing Survey**					
2		**Creative Product**					
3		**1 1/2**					
4							
5		Question 1	Question 2	Question 3	Question 4	Question 5	Q Total
6	Subject 1	$1	$7	$7	$8	$15	$38
7	Subject 2	$3	$4	$9	$2	$3	$21
8	Subject 3	$12	$4	$8	$10	$3	$37
9	Subject 4	$4	$6	$6	$12	$4	$32
10	Subject 5	$6	$9	$15	$3	$0	$33
11							
12	Q Avg	$5	$6	$9	$7	$5	$32

10. Adjust the size and position of the caption box so it doesn't overlap the graphic and center the text in the caption.
11. Change the caption font to 14-point Gil Sans Ultra Bold Condensed, or a comparable font. Also remove any bolding applied by default to the caption text.
12. Change the caption box to have a light green fill.
13. Place the insertion point at the beginning of the last paragraph.
14. Press Enter.
15. Indent the paragraph **.7"** on both the left and right sides.
16. Insert a clip art graphic that looks like a background box or banner.
    - ✓ *If your word processing program doesn't provide banner clip art, choose another clip art image that might make a suitable background for a message.*
17. Change the wrap settings for the clip art to allow it to appear behind the paragraph text.
18. Resize and reposition the clip art as needed so that it appears behind the paragraph. The document should now look like the following illustration.
19. Save your changes to the document file.
20. Print one copy of the document.
21. Close the document file.

To: Preferred Customers
From: Go! Travel Consultants
Re: Special San Diego Package
Date: May 1, 2006

Join Go! Travel Consultants for a special tour of San Diego. Spend five days and four nights exploring the city's Old Town district and such special attractions as the San Diego Zoo and Coronado Island. Includes a day trip to lovely Balboa Park.

Basic package price includes airfare from Indianapolis, airport transfers, four nights' lodging, and meal allowance. Special excursions such as sailing tours also available by prior arrangement.

Visit historic Balboa Park.

Contact Janet Mason at Go! Travel Consultants (888-777-0707) for more information. Travel must be booked by May 31, 2006.

Exercise 16

❖ Copy Ranges ❖ Move Ranges
❖ Insert Columns ❖ Insert Rows
❖ Delete Columns ❖ Delete Rows
❖ Automatic Formats

Notes

Rather than copying cells one at a time, you can copy and move ranges of information. This saves time, especially if you've applied particular formatting to the range. In better spreadsheet programs, the formatting travels with the copied or moved range. Otherwise, you'd have to reformat the copied or moved range. Leading spreadsheet programs also provide formatting help via **automatic formatting** choices (called AutoFormat in Excel). You select a range in the spreadsheet, and then choose an automatic formatting choice to apply a collection of formats (including fonts, number formats, shading, and borders) to the selection.

The marketing instructor who asked you to carry out a product survey in Exercises 6 and 12 now wants you to repeat the survey for a second product, and report the results for both surveys on a single spreadsheet. You also realized that you forgot to include the results from one of the questions in the earlier spreadsheets, so you'll add those in. Use range copying, moving, and formatting—among other features—to get the job done.

Vocabulary

automatic formatting   drag and drop

Directions

1. Open the **SS16** spreadsheet file.
2. Save the file as **PRODSUR3**.
3. Delete row 2, and then delete row 10 (which used to be row 11).
4. Update the date in row 2, and change it to the dd-mmm-yy format.
5. Type **Product 1** in cell A3.
6. Select the range A3:G10.

7. Move the selected range to A5:G12.

   ✓ You can use the cut and paste commands or buttons in your spreadsheet application to perform the move. Or, you can use the **drag and drop** feature to move the selection to a new location. Drag the selection by its border, and drop the selection into place when the shaded outline reaches the right location.

Exercise 8

❖ Work with Graphics in Columns
❖ Add a Caption

Notes

When you have text formatted in multiple columns, wrapping text around graphics can look particularly dramatic. Set up a graphic for tight wrapping and position the graphic between two columns. Both columns wrap around the graphic for a truly professional look. Adjust the clip art images in a new poster design.

You are a small farmer and a member of the Haywood Organic Growers Association. Jazz up a flyer about a new farmer's market by adding clip art with a caption and some borders.

Vocabulary

No new vocabulary in this exercise.

Directions

1. Open the **DP08** document file.
2. Save the file as **FARMM**. Part of the document text uses two columns.
3. Insert an appropriate piece of clip art.
4. Change the wrap settings for the clip art to allow for square wrapping around the clip art image.
5. Resize the clip art image so it's about **2.25"** tall and proportionally wide.
6. Drag the clip art image down until the top of the image lines up with the top bullet points. Center the clip art.
   - ✓ When you first move the clip art image between the columns, the break between the columns might change and create uneven columns. You may need to adjust the clip art to get it into the right position.

7. Add a caption that reads **Support local food producers!**. Center the caption text and change it to 9 point Goudy Stout or a comparable font.
8. Resize and reposition the caption box so it fits below the clip art, with a bit of white space between the bottom of the image and the top of the caption box. Also set the wrapping for the caption text box to square.
   - ✓ When you have the caption text box selected, you typically can press an arrow key to "nudge" the box in the specified direction. You can use this technique to reposition the caption box in small increments until you're satisfied with how the text wraps around it.
9. Increase the top internal margin of the caption text box to **.1"**.

Illustration 1

	A	B	C	D	E	F	G	H
1	Major Manufacturing							
2	6 Month Division Revenue Report							
3								
4								
5	Estimated Costs and Taxes			75%				
6								
7		Jan.	Feb	Mar	Apr	May	Jun	Total
8	Household	$125,024	$245,162	$679,000	$244,000	$728,994	$485,893	
9	Commercia	$568,474	$97,646	$132,654	$684,984	$321,564	$375,354	
10	Eco	$32,555	$58,963	$47,222	$11,369	$47,008	$32,696	
11	Appliance	$789,465	$654,132	$159,984	$325,469	$875,845	$847,812	
12	Total							
13	Est. C & T							

Illustration 2

	A	B	C	D	E	F	G	H
1	Major Manufacturing							
2	6 Month Division Revenue Report							
3								
4								
5	Estimated Costs and Taxes:			75%				
6								
7		Jan.	Feb	Mar	Apr	May	Jun	Total
8	Household	$125,024	$245,162	$679,000	$244,000	$728,994	$485,893	$2,508,073
9	Commercial	$568,474	$97,646	$132,654	$684,984	$321,564	$375,354	$2,180,676
10	Eco	$32,555	$58,963	$47,222	$11,369	$47,008	$32,696	$229,813
11	Appliance	$789,465	$654,132	$159,984	$325,469	$875,845	$847,812	$3,652,707
12	Total	$1,515,518	$1,055,903	$1,018,860	$1,265,822	$1,973,411	$1,741,755	$8,571,269
13	Est. C & T	$1,136,638.50	$791,927.25	$764,145.00	$949,366.50	$1,480,058.25	$1,306,316.25	$6,428,451.75
14								

10. Add a fill to the caption box in an appropriate color, using transparency to lighten the color, if needed.
11. Add a border (or decorative divider) above the first line and below the last line on the page. The finished file should resemble the illustration below.
12. Save your changes to the document file.
13. Print one copy of the document.
14. Close the document file.

NEW BROAD STREET FARMER'S MARKET!

* Every Saturday, 8 a.m. to noon, May through September.
* In the parking lot beside the Broad Street Bakery, 222 Broad Street.

SUPPORT LOCAL FOOD PRODUCERS!

* Local organic produce.
* Locally-produced meat and dairy items.
* Delicious home baked goods.
* Live entertainment by the Blue Grass Boys.

SPONSORED BY THE HAYWOOD ORGANIC GROWERS ASSOCIATION.

Directions

1. Open the **SS15** spreadsheet file.
2. Save the file as **MM6M**.
3. Enter a quick sum formula in cell H8 to total the values to its left.
4. Copy the formula from H8 to H9, H10, and H11.

   ✓ *If your spreadsheet program doesn't automatically apply the number formats shown in the exercises in this lesson, apply the appropriate number formatting manually. Also increase column widths as needed throughout this exercise.*

   ✓ *As you're copying entries and handling other operations in recent Excel versions, a small button may pop up beside the cell selector. Click the button to see more options for completing the copy (or other) operation, or press Esc to remove the button.*

5. Enter a quick sum formula in cell B12 to total the values above it.
6. Copy the formula from B12 to each of the cells in the range C12:H12.
7. Resize the width of column A to about 12 characters, so all the division names can display.
8. In cell B13, enter a formula that calculates the costs and taxes amount for January.

   ✓ *Hint: Multiply the total by the percentage held in cell D5.*

9. Copy the formula from cell B13 to each of the cells in C13:H13. It's obvious that there's a problem, because all the copied formulas calculate to a result of $0.00.
10. Select cell B13, and change the reference to cell D5 in the formula to an absolute reference.

    ✓ *Most spreadsheet programs use dollar signs to indicate an absolute reference, as in A15. You can either type the dollar signs or select the cell address and press a shortcut key like F4 to change the reference.*

11. Recopy the formula from B13 into each of the cells from C13:H13. Because each formula now calculates by the value in cell D5, the formulas calculate correctly.
12. Click cell H8. Note that its formula reads =SUM(B8:G8).
13. Delete column G.
14. Click cell G8 (which used to be H8). The formula has changed to =SUM(B8:F8), because the relative cell references adjusted when you deleted column G.
15. Undo the column G deletion, taking note of how the values in the Total column recalculate.
16. Click cell C12. Take note of the range of the formula in the cell references.
17. Insert a new row above row 9.
18. Click cell C13, which holds the formula that used to be in C12. The range in the formula has changed due to the inserted row.
19. Undo the addition of the blank row.
20. Click cell E13. Its formula contains a relative reference to cell E12 and an absolute reference to cell D5.
21. Select A7:E12.
22. Move the selected range, which includes formulas, to A15:E20.

    ✓ *To move the range, select it, move the mouse pointer over the selection border until you see the four-arrow move pointer, and then drag the range to the new location.*

23. Click cell E13, the cell that holds the formula you looked at in Step 20. Notice that the relative reference to cell D5 didn't change, but the relative reference now refers to cell E20, rather than E12.
24. Undo the move.
25. Save your changes to the spreadsheet file. The illustrations on the following page compare the spreadsheet's appearance before and after your work.
26. Print one copy of the spreadsheet.
27. Close the spreadsheet file.

Exercise 9

❖ Critical Thinking

Notes

In this exercise, create and enhance a new document with clip art, borders, and more. Choose settings that create the look you like for your document.

You are creating the letterhead for the Haywood Organic Growers Association. Start with a new document, and build the letterhead now.

Vocabulary

No new vocabulary in this exercise.

Directions

1. Create a new document file.
2. Save the file as **FARML**.
3. Enter the group address information in the document, near the top, in any arrangement you'd like:

   Haywood Organic Growers Association
   P.O. Box 2304
   Waynesville, NC 28786
   828-555-0021

4. Near the bottom of the document, insert a tag line that reads:

   Local Growers Providing Fresh, Tasty, and Safe Food

5. Apply the alignments, fonts, font sizes, and attributes you want for the letterhead.
6. Insert at least one clip art image.
7. Resize the clip art as needed, move it to the upper-left corner of the page, and wrap the address information around it.
8. Apply borders or shading (or both) to the desired text.
9. Apply a page border. Your finished document might look like the illustration on the following page.
10. Save your changes to the document file.
11. Print one copy of the document.
12. Close the document file.

Exercise 15

❖ Copy Formulas ❖ Move Formulas
❖ Absolute Referencing
❖ Relative Referencing ❖ Insert Columns
❖ Insert Rows ❖ Delete Columns ❖ Delete Rows

Notes

Formulas you create often refer to specific cell addresses. This becomes more complicated when you think about moving or copying formulas to a new location, or inserting and deleting rows and columns. When you move a formula, the formula continues to refer to its original cells. When you copy a formula, the formula does change. Rather than referring to the original cells, it refers to cells relative to the location of the original cells. For example, say cell B8 contains the formula =B5+B6+B7. If you copy the formula from B8 to C8, you're copying the formula one cell to the right. In the copied formula, each cell address references the cell one cell to the right of the original cell (B5 becomes C5, B6 becomes C6, and B7 becomes C7).

This concept is called **relative referencing** because the cell references are relative to a location. (Similarly, if you insert a row or column that affects the address of a cell referenced in the formula, the cell reference changes in the formula.) If a formula needs to always refer to the same cell in the spreadsheet, such as the cell that holds a particular value or percentage, you should use an **absolute** (unchanging) reference. Work with relative and absolute references in this exercise.

You work in finance at Major Manufacturing, and you've been asked to report the revenue by division for the first six months of the year. As part of your report, you want to calculate (roughly) the amount of money that was used to pay costs and taxes for each month, which is typically 75% of the revenue at your company. Add the needed formulas to your spreadsheet now, copying formulas and using an absolute reference to the cell holding the 75% expense value.

Vocabulary

relative reference   absolute reference

Haywood Organic Growers Association
P.O. Box 2304
Waynesville, NC 28786
828▪555▪0021

Local Growers Providing Fresh, Tasty, and Safe Food

Illustration 2

	A	B	C	D	E	F	G	H	I
1									
2			**Mountain Gear**		**Fall Shoe Sale List**				
3					**10/6/2006**				
4									
5	**Line**		**Company**		**Gender**		**Full Price**		**Percentage Off**
6	Rox		Blazers		M		$79.99		35%
7	Rox		Blazers		F		$75.99		35%
8	Hard Hike		TopLine		M		$129.99		35%
9	Hard Hike		TopLine		F		$119.99		35%
10	Fleming		Screech		M		$99.99		25%
11	LightWing		Screech		F		$89.99		25%
12	Linda		Trail Boss		F		$72.99		20%
13	Keller		Trail Boss		M		$75.99		20%
14	Adventure		Blazers		M		$65.99		20%
15	Adventure		Blazers		F		$65.99		20%

Lesson 12
Using Drawing Tools

Exercises 10–15

- ❖ **Work with shapes**
- ❖ **Create different effects with layered shapes**
- ❖ **Enhance drawing lines with width and color**
- ❖ **Compose grouped objects**

15. Apply grid borders (both around and within the selection) in a solid medium line, formatted in a green color.
16. Add green shading to the ranges B6:B15, D6:D15, F6:F15, and H6:H15.
17. Save your changes to the spreadsheet file. The illustrations below and on the following page compare the spreadsheet's appearance before and after your formatting work.
18. Print one copy of the spreadsheet.
19. Close the spreadsheet file.

Illustration 1

	A	B	C	D	E	F	G	H	I	J
1	Mountain Gear									
2	Fall Shoe Sale List									
3	9/8/2005									
4										
5	Line		Company		Gender		Full Price		Percentage Off	
6	Rox		Blazers		M		$79.99		35%	
7	Rox		Blazers		F		$75.99		35%	
8	Hard Hike		TopLine		M		$129.99		35%	
9	Hard Hike		TopLine		F		$119.99		35%	
10	Fleming		Screech		M		$99.99		25%	
11	LightWing		Screech		F		$89.99		25%	
12	Linda		Trail Boss		F		$72.99		20%	
13	Keller		Trail Boss		M		$75.99		20%	
14	Adventure		Blazers		M		$65.99		20%	
15	Adventure		Blazers		F		$65.99		20%	

Exercise 10

❖ Create, Position, and Size Shapes
❖ Fill a Shape

Notes

While clip art images can be used for many of your needs for decorating documents, you may find reasons to draw your own **shapes**. Word processing programs (and many spreadsheet and presentation graphics programs) offer drawing tools you can use to create your own drawings. Some programs also offer tools for creating **automatic shapes**, like an arrow, star, or banner shape.

Imagine that you're taking a basic class for using a computer for graphic design. The instructor has asked you to practice drawing basic shapes with the tools in a word processing program.

Vocabulary

shapes	drawing canvas	text box	gradient
automatic shapes	object	handles	fill effect

Directions

1. Create a new, blank document.
2. Display the drawing tools in the word processing program. These tools usually occupy a single toolbar.
3. Draw the objects shown in the illustration on the following page. Some word processors automatically create a box called the **drawing canvas** to hold the drawn objects.

   ✓ An **object** is any shape you draw. Clip art images and other graphics you insert are also objects.

   ✓ A **text box** object holds text. When you place text in a text box, you can move the text box around in the document and even wrap the rest of the document text around the text box, as if the text box were a graphic.

   ✓ To draw a perfect square or circle or a straight line or arrow, press and hold the Shift key as you draw the object.

4. Fill the square and text box with the color of your choice.

   ✓ To move, format, or resize a shape (object), first click it to select it. **Handles** (small boxes) appear around the object to tell you that it's selected. Click outside the object to deselect it.

5. Fill the circle and triangle with a pattern or other fill effect.

   ✓ In some programs, you can fill an object with a **gradient** (a blend from one color to another), texture, or graphic. If your program offers this feature, you can choose a **fill effect** for the circle, triangle, or both.

6. Size each of the objects to be about **1.75"** tall and/or long.

Exercise 14

❖ Change Column Width ❖ Edit a Cell Entry
❖ Enhance a Spreadsheet with Borders and Shading

Notes

You also can use narrow columns as a formatting element in your spreadsheet. Filling a narrow column with a light color creates a subtle effect, while choosing a bold color creates a stronger dividing line.

The boot sale worksheet you created for Mountain Gear in an earlier exercise looked a little plain. Work with a version of the earlier file now to improve the formatting and update the data.

Vocabulary

No new vocabulary in this exercise.

Directions

1. Open the **SS14** spreadsheet file.
2. Save the file as **BSALE2**.
3. Update the date in cell A3 to the current date.
4. Center the entries in cells A1:A3 across columns A through I and format them in a new font of your choosing. Also increase the size to 24 points.
5. Select the range A4:I15, and increase the font size to 12.
6. Format the labels in row 5 to use the same font you chose in Step 4.
7. Increase the width of columns A, C, E, and G to about 15 characters wide.
8. Increase the column width of column I to about 21 characters wide.
9. Reduce the width of columns B, D, F, and H to about 1 character.

✓ Creating a very narrow column like this is an alternative for creating vertical dividers in a spreadsheet.

✓ If you decrease the width of a column so that one or more of its cells displays repeating # signs, this means the resized column is too narrow to display the cell contents. Fix the problem by increasing the column width or decreasing the font size.

10. Select A1:I4.
11. Apply light yellow shading.

✓ Use light shading with dark text to ensure your text remains readable.

12. Select the range A5:I5.
13. Apply light green shading.
14. Select A5:I15.

7. Move the objects into the approximate order or position shown in Illustration 2 on the following page.

    ✓ *You may have to adjust text wrapping settings for some of the objects in order to move them. Often, the wrapping setting that enables the object to be in front of the text allows the most flexibility in positioning the object. Also, if an object appears in a drawing canvas, you may need to resize that canvas to the approximate dimensions of the object by dragging the heavy black corners on the drawing canvas box border, as well as changing the text wrapping setting for the canvas area itself (rather than the object or objects within the canvas).*

8. Save the document; name it **SHAPE**.
9. Print one copy of the document.
10. Close the document.

Illustration 1

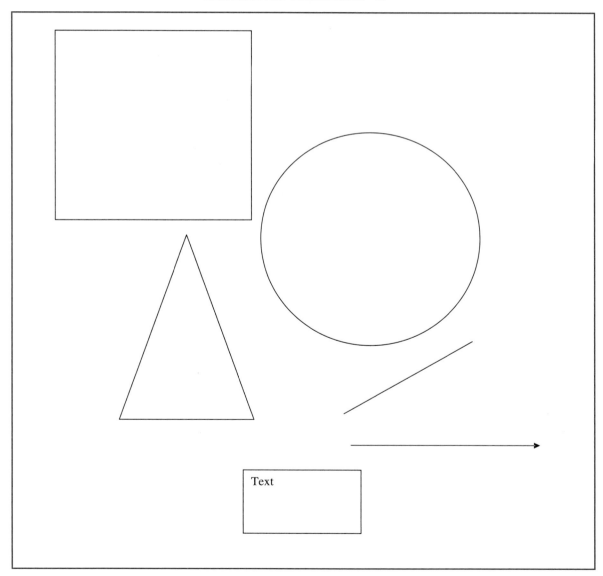

Text

Illustration 2

	A	B	C	D	E	F	G	H
1	Mike's Motors							
2	2005 Sales by Model							
3								
4								
5								
6	Model	Q1	Q2	Q3	Q4	Model Total	Model Average	
7	LE	$35,000	$48,000	$65,000	$33,000	$181,000	$45,250	
8	XL	$43,000	$66,000	$75,000	$61,000	$245,000	$61,250	
9	RX300	$73,000	$53,000	$225,000	$57,000	$408,000	$102,000	
10	F100	$27,000	$40,000	$53,000	$49,000	$169,000	$42,250	
11	F250	$75,000	$56,000	$125,000	$200,000	$456,000	$114,000	
12	Tundra	$22,000	$65,000	$45,000	$104,000	$236,000	$59,000	
13	Tahoe	$50,000	$125,000	$253,000	$75,000	$503,000	$125,750	
14								
15	Total	$325,000	$453,000	$841,000	$579,000	$2,198,000		
16	Average	$46,429	$64,714	$120,143	$82,714	$314,000		
17								

Illustration 2

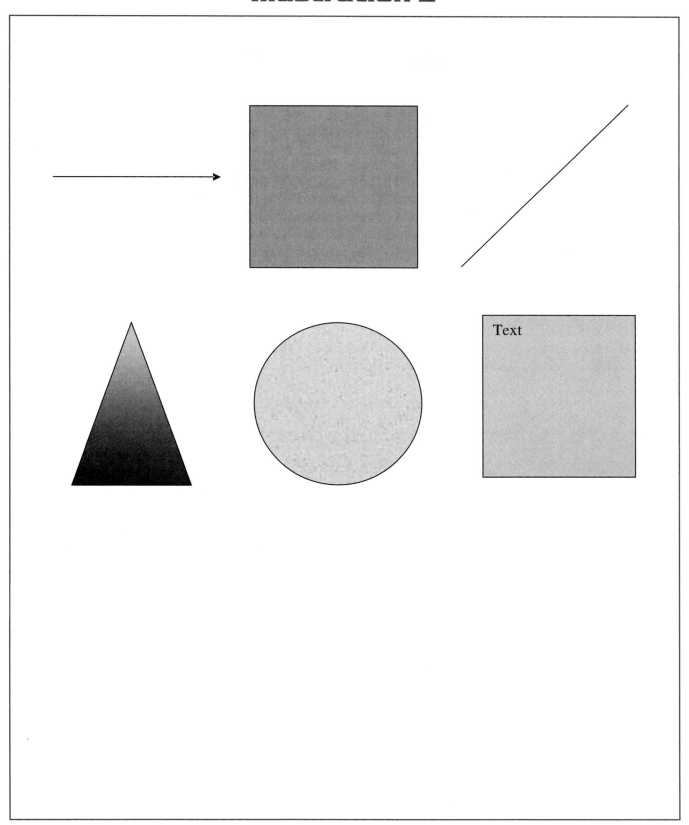

6. Select columns B through G by dragging over the column headings (column letters) at the top of the columns.
7. Resize the columns to be 12 characters wide.
8. Delete the entry in cell A3. You'll use shading to create a border effect rather than a fill character.

   ✓ *To edit a cell, you can click in the cell, click in the entry bar to make the changes you want, and then press Enter. In most cases, you can also double-click the cell, edit the cell's contents right in the cell, then press Enter to finish. To replace a cell entry completely, click the cell, type the new entry, and press Enter.*

9. Select A1:G3.
10. Apply pale blue shading.
11. Select A4:G5.
12. Apply sea green shading.
13. Select A6:G6.
14. Apply a heavy solid border in sea green to the bottom of the selection.

   ✓ *If you want to format an entire row or column, select the row or column first.*

   ✓ *If you apply a border to more than one side of the selection, keep in mind that the border will go around the selected range, not each cell in the range.*

15. Change the entry in cell D7 to **65,000**.
16. Change the entry in cell B13 to **50,000**.
17. Change the entry in cell E10 to **49,000**.
18. Save your changes to the spreadsheet file. The illustrations below and on the following page compare the spreadsheet's appearance before and after your formatting work.
19. Print one copy of the spreadsheet.

   ✓ *If your instructor requires it, label and turn in a copy of the printed spreadsheet.*

20. Close the spreadsheet file.

Illustration 1

	A	B	C	D	E	F	G	H
1		**Mike's Motors**						
2		**2005 Sales by Model**						
3	@@@@@@@@@@@@@@@@@@@@@@@@@							
4								
5								
6	Model	Q1	Q2	Q3	Q4	Model Total	Model Average	
7	LE	$35,000	$48,000	$27,000	$33,000	$143,000	$35,750	
8	XL	$43,000	$66,000	$75,000	$61,000	$245,000	$61,250	
9	RX300	$73,000	$53,000	$225,000	$57,000	$408,000	$102,000	
10	F100	$27,000	$40,000	$53,000	$40,000	$160,000	$40,000	
11	F250	$75,000	$56,000	$125,000	$200,000	$456,000	$114,000	
12	Tundra	$22,000	$65,000	$45,000	$104,000	$236,000	$59,000	
13	Tahoe	$75,000	$125,000	$253,000	$75,000	$528,000	$132,000	
14								
15	**Total**	$350,000	$453,000	$803,000	$570,000	#########		
16	**Average**	$50,000	$64,714	$114,714	$81,429	$310,857		
17								

Exercise 11

❖ Layer Shapes ❖ Change Line Width and Color

Notes

A simple shape may not create the effect you want. You can create more interesting images by layering several of the shapes you draw. You control the layering order by using the **Bring Forward** and **Send Backward** commands, which each move the selected object moves one "layer" forward or backward. Use the **Bring to Front** and **Send to Back** commands to move the selected object to the top or bottom of the stack of objects.

You are preparing graphic objects for newsletters for various clients. Create the objects by layering shapes and clip art, and working with object fills and lines.

Vocabulary

Bring Forward	Send Backward	Bring to Front	Send to Back

Directions

1. Create a new, blank document.
2. Display the drawing tools in the word processing program, if needed.
3. Draw the objects shown in Illustration 1 on the following page. (Use the AutoShapes button in Word 2003 to add special shapes.) Also insert the clip art objects shown.
   - ✓ You can also layer clip art and graphic images with shapes you draw.
   - ✓ If your word processing program doesn't show a shape or clip art image shown in this exercise, use a similar shape or image.
4. Format the objects with fills and lines as shown in the illustration.
   - ✓ To create a shape that looks solid, format the shape to use no line. When you want a text box to blend in with another object, you should format the text box to use the same fill color as the other object and no line. In some cases, you also can choose No Fill so the text box background is transparent.

5. Change the wrapping settings for the clip art objects so you can move them around as desired.
6. Move, resize, and layer the objects as shown in Illustration 2.
   - ✓ When you resize a text box, your word processing program may not resize the font you've applied to the text in the text box. You can select the text and apply a new, appropriate font.
   - ✓ Placing a clip art or graphic image in front of a patterned rectangle creates a "framed" appearance for the image.
7. Save the document; name it **GRAPHICS**.
8. Print one copy of the document.
9. Close the document.

Exercise 13

❖ Change Column Width ❖ Edit a Cell Entry
❖ Enhance a Spreadsheet with Borders and Shading

Notes

While the importance of a spreadsheet program is its ability to calculate efficiently, you also want your spreadsheets to look attractive. In this exercise, you adjust the **column widths** for columns so that all entries in the columns are readable. You also can apply **borders and shading** to highlight key cells or improve the spreadsheet's overall appearance. To finish "polishing" the spreadsheet, you can edit the entries in a few cells to ensure the information is as accurate as possible.

You're working again here with the car sales spreadsheet for Mike's Motors from Exercise 8. Add formatting to enhance the spreadsheet appearance, and update a few entries to reflect new sales data that you've received.

Vocabulary

column width   borders and shading

Directions

1. Open the **SS13** spreadsheet file.
2. Save the file as **CSALES2**.
   - ✓ *Cell F15 displays only pound signs. That's because the formula results are too wide to display in the column based on the current column width. You will fix that problem shortly.*
3. Select the range A6:G16, and increase the font size to 12.
   - ✓ *Notice that some entries in column A appear cut off at the right. This is because a label entry can't overlap any cell to the right that holds a cell entry. You can resize the column to fix this problem.*
4. Format all the other labels in column A and row 6 to use the Bodoni MT Black font.

5. Increase the width of column A to about 12 characters wide. The column A entries no longer spill over the column B entries.
   - ✓ *You can use a column width command in your spreadsheet program to enter a precise width for the column. You can also drag the right column border to resize the column. (Or, select multiple columns first, then drag one right border to resize all the columns.) Finally, you can double-click the right column border to size the column to the width of the largest entry in the column; be careful with this feature, though, because you may end up with a column that's wider than you expected.*

Illustration 1

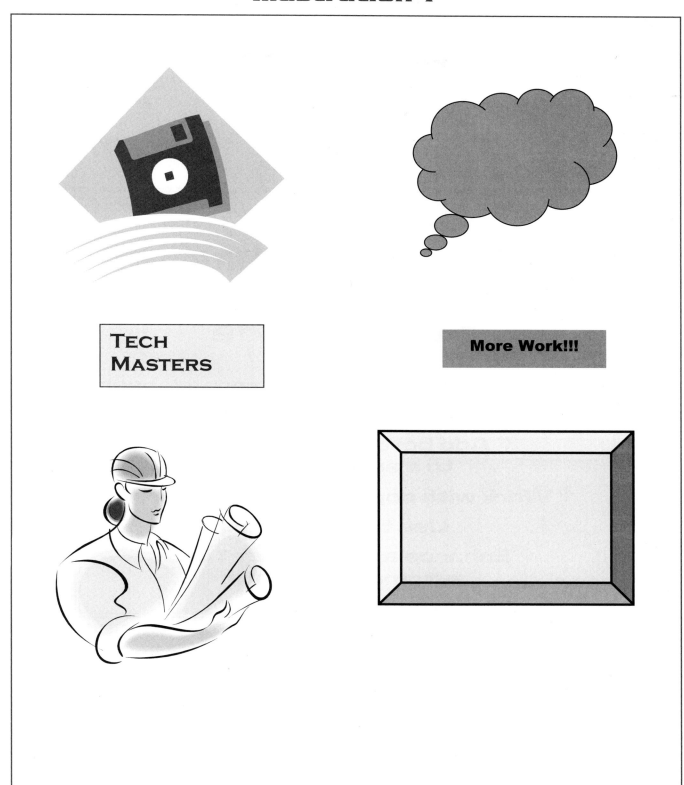

Lesson 17
Copy Formulas; Additional Spreadsheet Enhancements

Exercises 13–19

❖ **Adjust column width in a spreadsheet**

❖ **Add and remove columns and rows**

❖ **Add borders and shading to a spreadsheet**

❖ **Work with copy and move features**

❖ **Use the fill feature**

❖ **Enhance a spreadsheet with automatic formats**

Illustration 2

Exercise 12

❖ Critical Thinking

Notes

This last practice session again calls on you to create formulas and add formatting.

You're going to take another look at the survey data spreadsheet you created in Exercise 6, adding some calculations and formulas to make the data more meaningful and attractive.

Vocabulary

No new vocabulary in this exercise.

Directions

1. Open the **SS12** spreadsheet file.
2. Save the file as **PRODSUR2**.
3. Add a new column of quick sum formulas to total the amounts entered for each subject. Enter **Q Total** as the label above the new formulas and center the label.
4. Add a new row of formulas to average the responses to each question above in row 12, as well as the overall total. Enter **Q Avg** as the label to the left of the new formulas.
5. Format the formula results cells in row 12 as currency with zero decimal places.

6. Format the spreadsheet titles and date in the font of your choice in 20-point size. Center them across the range that spans the width of the spreadsheet entries.
7. Format the date in cell A3 to use the m/dd format.
8. Format the labels throughout the spreadsheet in the font and size of your choice.
9. Save your changes to the spreadsheet file.
10. Print one copy of the spreadsheet.
11. Close the spreadsheet file.

Exercise 12

❖ Group and Upgroup Objects

Notes

You can arrange and layer a number of shapes and objects. But if you try to move them, your careful arrangement will get out of order. You can temporarily combine multiple objects by **grouping** them. Then you can move the group as a single unit. If you need to apply new formatting, you can **ungroup** the objects and work with them individually.

You will be helping other team members at work put together word processing documents that will ultimately be published to the Web. In particular, you are in charge of designing graphical items to appear on the pages. Work with grouping and ungrouping as you refine a few objects now.

Vocabulary

group	grid	nudge
ungroup	snap to grid	

Directions

1. Open the **DP12** document file.
2. Save the file as **WEBG**.
3. Display the drawing tools in the word processing program, if needed.
4. Move and layer the individual objects into the positions shown in the illustration on the following page.

   ✓ *If your objects won't line up the way you want them to, your word processing program may be using a layout **grid**. Turn off the **snap to grid** feature to gain more control over object positioning. Your word processing program also may offer commands for aligning multiple objects. For example, you may be able to select a few objects and center them so they all align to the same center point or to **nudge** an object to move it slightly in one direction.*

   ✓ *Some programs enable you to Shift+click multiple objects and then align them. For example, Word offers a variety of alignment commands on the Align or Distribute submenu of the Draw menu on the Drawing toolbar. Using some of these commands could greatly help you align the rings of the bullseye graphic, for example.*

5. Group each set of objects.

   ✓ *To select multiple objects to group them, click the first object. Press and hold the Shift key, and click the other objects. Handles appear around all the selected objects. Then choose the group command (Draw|Group from the Drawing toolbar in Word 2003).*

6. Drag each of the grouped objects to the location of your choice.

Exercise 11

❖ Critical Thinking

Notes

You should now feel fairly comfortable with using formulas, formatting, and number formats. In this exercise, supply the formulas and formatting for a spreadsheet.

The project estimate worksheet you created for Design Architects isn't yet complete. Work on a version of that file now to add needed formulas and formatting.

Vocabulary

No new vocabulary in this exercise.

Directions

1. Open the **SS11** spreadsheet file.
2. Save the file as **DAPROJ2**.
3. Enter your name and update the date in cells C8 and C6.
4. Add a formula in each cell in the range E15:E17 that multiplies the **Hours** entry by the **Rate** entry on the same row.
5. Enter a formula in cell E18 that totals the calculated values in the three cells above.

   ✓ *You can use the method of your choice to enter sum formulas, using the quick sum method when you prefer.*

6. Add a formula in each cell in the range E22:E23 that multiplies the **Items** entry by the **Rate** entry on the same row.
7. Enter a formula in cell E24 that totals the calculated values in the two cells above.
8. Enter a formula in cell E26 that totals the two subtotal values.

9. Format the spreadsheet title cells in the font of your choice in 16-point size.
10. Format all other labels in bold.
11. Center the labels in cells A13 and A20 across all five columns of spreadsheet content, and apply the same font you chose in Step 9.
12. Format the label in cell B26 with wrap text alignment.
13. Format all the cells under the **Rate** labels with currency number format and zero decimal places.
14. Formal all the cells under the **Total** labels with the currency number format using a dollar sign, thousands comma, and two decimal places.
15. Save your changes to the spreadsheet file.
16. Print one copy of the spreadsheet.
17. Close the spreadsheet file.

7. Ungroup the **Garden Pro** object.
8. Move the text box from the top of the object.
9. Move the text box back into position on the banner object.
10. Regroup the **Garden Pro** object.
11. Save your changes to the document file.
12. Print one copy of the document.
13. Close the document.

Summer
Fun

Garden
Pro

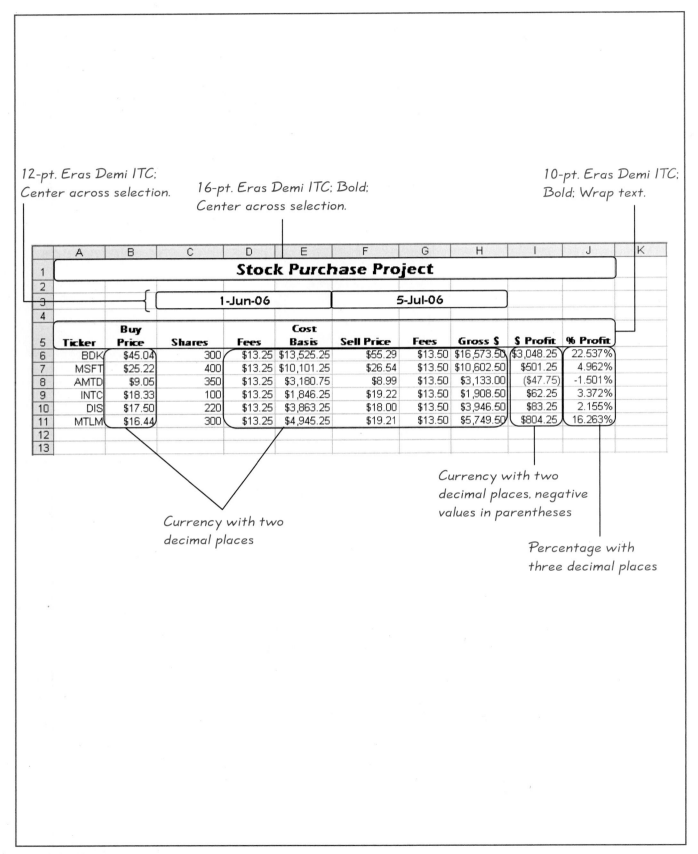

12-pt. Eras Demi ITC;
Center across selection.

16-pt. Eras Demi ITC; Bold;
Center across selection.

10-pt. Eras Demi ITC;
Bold; Wrap text.

	A	B	C	D	E	F	G	H	I	J	K
1				Stock Purchase Project							
2											
3				1-Jun-06			5-Jul-06				
4											
5	Ticker	Buy Price	Shares	Fees	Cost Basis	Sell Price	Fees	Gross $	$ Profit	% Profit	
6	BDK	$45.04	300	$13.25	$13,525.25	$55.29	$13.50	$16,573.50	$3,048.25	22.537%	
7	MSFT	$25.22	400	$13.25	$10,101.25	$26.54	$13.50	$10,602.50	$501.25	4.962%	
8	AMTD	$9.05	350	$13.25	$3,180.75	$8.99	$13.50	$3,133.00	($47.75)	-1.501%	
9	INTC	$18.33	100	$13.25	$1,846.25	$19.22	$13.50	$1,908.50	$62.25	3.372%	
10	DIS	$17.50	220	$13.25	$3,863.25	$18.00	$13.50	$3,946.50	$83.25	2.155%	
11	MTLM	$16.44	300	$13.25	$4,945.25	$19.21	$13.50	$5,749.50	$804.25	16.263%	
12											
13											

Currency with two
decimal places

Currency with two
decimal places, negative
values in parentheses

Percentage with
three decimal places

Exercise 13

❖ Copy Objects ❖ Group Objects
❖ Ungroup Objects

Notes

After you build a more complex object group or design formatting that you want to reuse, you can copy either the individual object or the group, to save time.

You want to develop a graphic divider object for use in various types of documents. Try copying, grouping, and ungrouping objects to create interesting effects in your divider.

Vocabulary

flip   rotate

Directions

1. Open the **DP13** document file.
2. Save the file as **DIVIDE**.
3. Display the drawing tools in the word processing program, if needed.
4. Move and layer the individual objects into the positions shown in Illustration 1 on the following page.
5. Group the objects.
6. Copy the grouped object, and paste seven copies of it.

   ✓ *Once you make one copy of any selection, whether it's text or an object, you can paste as many copies of the object as you want.*

   ✓ *Most word processing programs include commands that let you **flip** and **rotate** objects. For example, you can make a copy of an object and flip the copy horizontally to create a mirror image of the original object.*

7. Drag the grouped objects to position them as shown in Illustration 2. As you can see from this illustration, you're creating a row of shapes to form the decorative divider.
8. Ungroup every other grouped object.
9. Move the green dots on the ungrouped objects to the upper quadrants of the circle.
10. Regroup the objects. The finished design should look like Illustration 3.

    ✓ *If you want to copy your design, you would select each of the grouped objects, and group all of them into a single unit. Grouping enables you to construct much more complex objects.*

11. Save your changes to the document file.
12. Print one copy of the document.
13. Close the document.

5. In each cell in the range H6:H11 under the **Gross $** label, enter a formula that multiplies the **Shares** entry by the **Sell Price** entry, and then deducts the value in the second **Fees** column.

   ✓ *In this case, you deduct the fee, because it reduces the proceeds of the stock sale.*

6. In cells I6:I11 under the **$ Profit** label, enter formulas that subtract each calculated **Cost Basis** result (E6:E11) from the calculated **Gross $** result (H6:H11) on the same row.

   ✓ *You can wait until this point to format the values in your spreadsheet, if you want. Then it's easier to see the difference that displaying different numbers of decimal places makes. Also, some entries would be clearer with currency formatting.*

7. In cells J6:J11 under the **% Profit** label, enter formulas that divide each calculated **$ Profit** result (I6:I11) by the calculated **Cost Basis** result (E6:E11) on the same row.

   ✓ *The preceding step may sound backward, but that's the correct way to make the calculation. "One number is a percentage of the other." Insert the division operator in place of the word "of" in that statement.*

   ✓ *Some spreadsheet programs also offer a fraction number format, so you could display the decimal portions of stock prices (or other types of entries) as fractions. If you apply the fraction number format to a cell holding 8.125, the cell would then display 8 1/8. You also might see special formats for ZIP Codes, phone numbers, and formats.*

   ✓ *If a formula calculates several decimal places but you apply a number format with fewer decimal places (such as two), your spreadsheet program rounds the number for display purposes only. The formula result will still store all its decimal place values to ensure accuracy in all spreadsheet calculations.*

8. Format the date entries in cells C3 and F3 with the dd-mmm-yy format.

9. Save your changes to the spreadsheet file.

   ✓ *Don't worry if some of your columns aren't wide enough. You'll learn how to change column widths in the next lesson.*

10. Print one copy of the spreadsheet.
11. Close the spreadsheet file.

Illustration 1

Illustration 2

Illustration 3

Exercise 21

❖ Reverse Text ❖ Letter Spacing

Notes

Normally, your document presents black (or colored) text on a light background. **Reverse** text (or a reverse treatment) places white or nearly white text on a black or nearly black background. Because reverse text is more difficult to print and read, you should use it sparingly in your documents. You may need to adjust the **letter spacing** (character spacing) in a selection. By adding more spacing between letters, you can give the text an expanded or extended appearance. Using less letter spacing makes text look compact. Extreme letter spacing settings make text difficult to read, so be careful when using these formatting options.

You are a small farmer and a member of the Haywood Organic Growers Association. Use some reverse text and letter spacing changes to improve a flyer about a new farmer's market that you worked with previously.

Vocabulary

reverse   letter spacing   kerning

Directions

1. Open the **DP21** document file.
2. Save the file as **FARMM2**.
3. Select the two title lines at the top of the document.
4. Add dark red shading behind the selected paragraphs.
5. Change the text color for the selected text to white.
6. Increase (expand) the letter spacing by 3 points.

   ✓ *Your word processing program may also offer a **kerning** feature. Kerning adjusts the spacing between certain pairs of letters to make them look better when printed. For example, in the word **WAY**, the kerning feature reduces the amount of space between the capital W and capital A, because these letters have complementary shapes.*

7. Click outside the selected text so you can see the results of your changes.
8. Select the paragraph at the bottom of the document and apply the same treatment: dark red shading behind the paragraph, change the text to white, and increase the letter spacing by 3 points.
9. Click at the beginning of the paragraph and press Enter once to extend the shaded area above the text. The finished document should resemble the illustration on the following page.
10. Save your changes to the document file.
11. Print one copy of the document. Close the document.

	A	B	C	D
1	Three Month Budget			
2	September-November			
3				
4		Sept.	Oct.	Nov.
5	Meals	75	85	70
6	Cell Ph.	45	45	45
7	Books	250	25	25
8	Clothing	300	50	50
9	Sum			

NEW BROAD STREET FARMER'S MARKET!

SUPPORT LOCAL FOOD PRODUCERS!

❋ Every Saturday, 8 a.m. to noon, May through September.

❋ In the parking lot beside the Broad Street Bakery, 222 Broad Street.

❋ Local organic produce.

❋ Locally-produced meat and dairy items.

❋ Delicious home baked goods.

❋ Live entertainment by the Blue Grass Boys.

SPONSORED BY THE HAYWOOD ORGANIC GROWERS ASSOCIATION.

Exercise 2

❖ Enter Labels ❖ Enter Values
❖ Make Simple Corrections
❖ Save and Close a File

Notes

Each cell in a spreadsheet file can hold a single **cell entry**. You can enter a **value** (numeric entry), **date**, or **label** (text entry) in a cell. To make a cell entry, click a cell, type your entry, and press Enter. To change a cell entry, first **select** the cell. Then, type a new entry or click in the formula bar and use normal editing keys to make your changes. Press Enter to complete your changes. Most spreadsheet programs include a **clear** command that enables you to delete the entry in a cell.

Your parents have asked you to put together a budget for the spending money you'll need for the first few months of school. Develop the basic budget spreadsheet now, and practice updating it so you can use it for whatever timeframe you prefer.

Vocabulary

cell entry   date   select
value   label   clear

Directions

1. Start your spreadsheet program.
2. In the blank spreadsheet file that appears, make the entries shown in the illustration on the following page.

   ✓ *Labels align left in a cell by default. Values and dates align right in a cell. Spreadsheets can generally tell when you're using a label that includes numbers and will apply the correct formatting.*

   ✓ *When you make an entry and press Enter, the cell selector always moves one cell in a default direction, either right, left, down, or up. Most spreadsheet programs allow you to change this default direction to one of your choice.*

   ✓ *When you make an entry, you can click on another cell to complete the entry instead of pressing the Enter key. Pressing an arrow key also completes the entry.*

3. Replace the example label in cell A2 with **December-February.**
4. Change the entries in cells B4:D4 to **Dec.**, **Jan.**, and **Feb.**.
5. Change the cell A9 entry to **Total**.
6. Save the spreadsheet file; name it **BUDGET**.
7. Close the spreadsheet file.

Exercise 22

❖ Reverse Text ❖ Letter Spacing

Notes

Work again with reverse text and letter spacing formatting in this exercise.

Also update the Haywood Organic Growers Association letterhead with reverse text.

Vocabulary

No new vocabulary in this exercise.

Directions

1. Open the **DP22** document file.
2. Save the file as **FARML2**.
3. Select the name, address, and phone lines at the top of the document.
4. Change the shading behind the paragraphs to green and change the text color to light green.
5. Increase the letter spacing by 2 points.
6. Change the wrapping for the clip art object so that it appears in front of the text. Resize the object so it's about one inch high and proportionally wide. Also add a green fill and center the object.
7. Center the address lines.
8. Click at the beginning of the first address line (the company name) and press Enter several times to expand the shaded area until the text starts below the clip art. The top of the letterhead should now resemble the illustration on the following page, with the clip art object background blending with the shading.
9. Delete a few blank lines in the body of the document so that it returns to a single page in length.
10. Select the shaded paragraph at the bottom of the document.
11. Change the shading to green and the text color to light green. The finished document should resemble the illustration on the following page.
12. Save your changes to the document file.
13. Print one copy of the document.
14. Close the document.

Formula bar
or entry bar

Highlighted
column

Column letters

Task pane

Cell selector around
the active cell

Mouse pointer

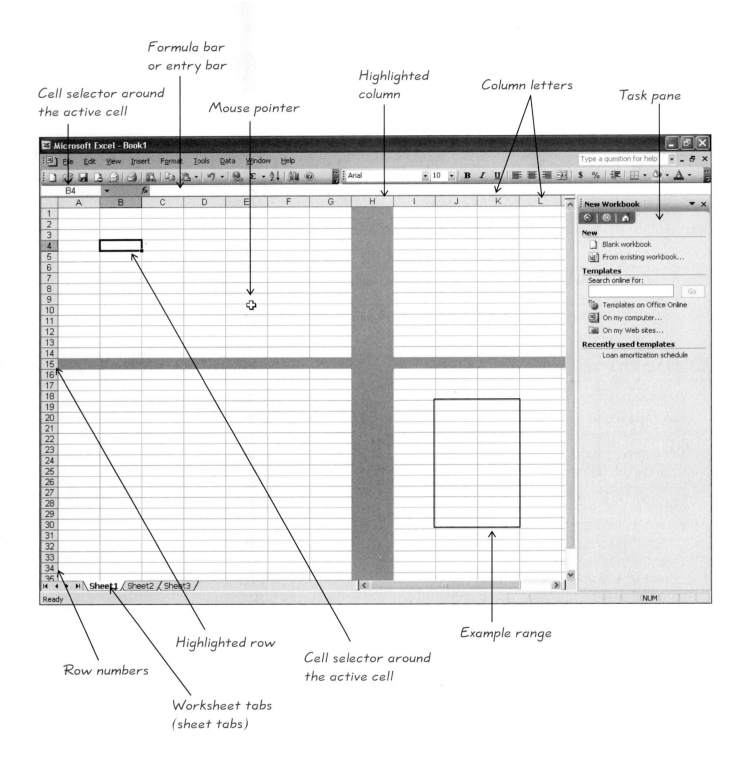

Highlighted row

Example range

Row numbers

Cell selector around
the active cell

Worksheet tabs
(sheet tabs)

Haywood Organic Growers Association
P.O. Box 2304
Waynesville, NC 28786
828▪555▪0021

Local Growers Providing Fresh, Tasty, and Safe Food

3. Use the arrow keys (or any shortcut of your choice) to move the cell selector to the following cells, one at a time:
   - E16
   - L21
   - AI125
   - CK395
   - A1

   ✓ Here are reminders of a couple of shortcuts: press Ctrl+Home to move the cell selector back to cell A1 on the current worksheet; to move to a cell on the current worksheet, enter the cell address in the name box and press Enter.

   ✓ Scrolling the spreadsheet changes what portion of the spreadsheet you see on-screen, but does not move the cell selector. So, after you scroll with a scroll bar, click a cell to move the cell selector to the displayed area.

4. If your spreadsheet file holds multiple worksheets, move the cell selector to the following cells, one at a time:
   - Sheet2!L360
   - Sheet3!F10
   - Sheet1!A1
5. Select these ranges in order:
   - row 35
   - Column M
   - C8:I30
   - DZ113:EF128
   - I1101:AB1115
   - B4:D13
6. Move the cell selector back to cell A1.
7. Close the file without saving changes.
8. Exit the spreadsheet program.

Exercise 23

❖ Pull Quotes

Notes

When you want to highlight a statement included in your document, you can set it up as a **pull quote**. A pull quote is a specially formatted text box object that contains a copy of selected text from the document. Pull quotes work well in newsletters, letters, and other sales documents.

Your history instructor allows you some latitude in formatting your reports. In this case, add a pull quote to a report about Thomas Jefferson to highlight a key statement in the report.

Vocabulary

pull quote

Directions

1. Open the **DP23** document file.
2. Save the file as **JEFF3**.
3. In the first paragraph, select the text that reads **Jefferson framed powerful political ideas in accessible, graceful language.**
4. Copy the selected text.
5. Deselect the text.
   - ✓ *If you fail to deselect the text, some word processing programs automatically cut it out of the main document and place it in the text box. In this example, you want the pull quote to repeat the text, instead.*
6. Insert a text box to hold the pull quote.
7. Paste the copied text into the text box.
   - ✓ *For more casual documents or when you're not repeating a direct quote, the pull quote doesn't have to repeat the text verbatim. It can paraphrase information found elsewhere in the text.*
8. Format the text in the text box in 12-point Arial Black. Center the text.
9. Size the text box so it can hold all the text in a wide format, about **2"** wide and **1.5"** tall. (If needed, drag corners of the drawing canvas to make it the same size as the text box.)
10. Wrap text around the text box (or drawing canvas).
11. Position the text box near the center right of the document, so its top approximately aligns with the first bullet in the bulleted list.
12. Increase the top internal margin of the text box to approximately **.15"**, to better vertically center the text in the box.
13. Add light shading to the text box. The finished document should resemble the illustration on the following page.
14. Save your changes to the document file.
15. Print one copy of the document.
16. Close the document.

Exercise 1

❖ Explore the Spreadsheet ❖ Make Selections

Notes

You can use a **spreadsheet** program to organize information in **cells** formed by intersecting lettered **columns** and numbered **rows**. A cell's column letter and row number form the **cell address**—a name like C3 that you use to refer to that cell. The **cell selector**, a heavy black outline, surrounds the **active (current) cell**, and the cell address for that cell appears in the **name box** or address box at the far left below the toolbar. A block of adjoining cells is called a **range**; in most spreadsheet programs, the **range address** consists of the cell address for the upper-left cell, a colon, and the cell address for the lower-right cell, as in C3:G10.

In the top three spreadsheet programs, each spreadsheet file (called a *workbook* or *notebook* file in some programs) may hold multiple individual **worksheets**, each of which has its own **worksheet tab**. To identify a cell on a particular worksheet, you add (in most programs) the sheet name plus an exclamation point before the cell address, as in *Sheet*2!F15.

You've just installed a new spreadsheet program on your computer, and you want to take the time to become familiar with the program and moving around in it.

Vocabulary

spreadsheet	row	active (current) cell	range address
cell	cell address	name box	worksheet
column	cell selector	range	worksheet tab
			task pane

Directions

1. Start the spreadsheet program, if needed.

   ✓ *The illustration on page 289 shows Microsoft Office Excel 2003. When you start your spreadsheet program, it automatically opens a blank spreadsheet file. Note that we've highlighted a row and a column for illustrative purposes; these would not be highlighted in your new, blank spreadsheet file.*

2. In Excel 2003, click the Close (X) button in the upper-right corner of the **task pane** window to close it.

   ✓ *You can close the task pane any time you no longer need it on-screen. It will reopen when you choose certain commands. Or, you can choose View | Task Pane to open and close the task pane as needed. Illustrations in this book will not show the task pane unless it's needed for an exercise.*

Thomas Jefferson:
Author of Our Independence

Despite his human flaws and foibles, Thomas Jefferson influenced the government of our country perhaps more than any other political figure. In writing the Declaration of Independence, Jefferson framed powerful political ideas in accessible, graceful language. Jefferson dedicated his life to applying those ideas to build a lasting government for the United States of America.

After a brief stint with a tutor at his family home, Jefferson was sent to live with other instructors who provide a classical education of studies in Greek, Latin, history, literature, geography, and natural science. Moving on to William and Mary College in Williamsburg, Virginia, Jefferson developed an interest in the law. He studied law for five years. In 1767, he began practicing law in Virginia while maintaining his primary source of income from his family's plantation.

Jefferson's focus on political matters developed soon after. He served in the Virginia Burgess, applying his leadership to the following matters:

- The Townshend Acts
- Committee of Correspondence
- The Richmond Convention

> **Jefferson framed powerful political ideas in accessible, graceful language.**

Jefferson's experience with the Burgess made him a key figure as the Continental Congress formed to fight the British Government's oppression of the colonies. In 1775, Jefferson was among the drafters of a document explaining why the colonies were making a stand against Britain.

In 1776, after Jefferson had become a fully-elected delegate to the Congress, he joined a committee of five congressman whose mission it was to draft a declaration that explained a resolution that the colonies should be free and independent. The committee members asked Jefferson to create the first draft of the declaration, which he later corrected along with John Adams and Benjamin Franklin.

The document incorporated ideas of European philosophers like John Locke, including notions such as government by consent and the natural rights of the individual. The original draft even denounced slavery and the slave trade, although that language was removed as a result of debate.

On July 2, 1776, Congress passed the resolution declaring the colonies independent. After debate and correction by the full body, the Declaration of Independence was formally adopted by Congress on July 4, 1776. The document was distributed throughout the colonies, so that inhabitants would know that America was a free nation.

While Jefferson went on to make many other contributions to the United States of American, including serving as its third president, he will be perhaps remembered most and most fondly for writing the Declaration of Independence.

Lesson 15
Create, Save, and Exit a Spreadsheet

Exercises 1–6

❖ **Create a spreadsheet**
❖ **Move within a spreadsheet**
❖ **Enter information in a spreadsheet**
❖ **Print a spreadsheet**
❖ **Save and close a spreadsheet file**

Exercise 24

❖ Pull Quotes

Notes

Pull quotes need not be limited to highlighting existing document content. You also can use a pull quote to highlight other information, such as a quote from a satisfied customer or the terms of a special offer.

Update the StyleTique Salon's price list now to include a pull quote about monthly specials.

Vocabulary

No new vocabulary in this exercise.

Directions

1. Open the **DP24** document file.
2. Save the file as **SALONPR2**.
3. Insert a text box to hold the pull quote.
4. Enter the following text in the text box:
   Ask about our monthly specials!
   Lou
5. Format the text in the text box in 18-point Gigi. Bold and center the text.
6. Size the text box so it's a bit more than **1.5"** square—big enough to hold all the pull quote text. (If needed, drag corners of the drawing canvas to make it the same size as the text box.)
7. Position the text box at the bottom of the center "column," which lists the available services.
8. Remove the text box border.
9. Select the pull quote text, and use paragraph formatting to apply a 3-point blue border above and below the pull quote text.
10. Add a 3-point blue border to the top and bottom boundaries of the page. The finished document should resemble the illustration on the following page.
11. Save your changes to the document file.
12. Print one copy of the document.
13. Close the document.

Directory of Files

Exercise	File Name	Page
1	None	—
2	None	—
3	None	—
4	None	—
5	None	—
6	None	—
7	SS07	300
8	SS08	302
9	SS09	305
10	SS10	307
11	SS11	310
12	SS12	311
13	SS13	313
14	SS14	316
15	SS15	320
16	SS16	322
17	SS17	325
18	SS18	327
19	SS19	328
20	SS20	330
21	SS21	333
22	SS22	336
23	SS23	338
24	SS24	340
25	SS25	343
26	SS26	345
27	SS27	348
28	SS28	351
29	SS29	353

styleTique Salon

Services and Pricing

Hair

Wash and cut	$25.00
Wash, cut, style	$30.00
Highlights	$35.00 and up
Full color	$30.00 and up

Skin

Facial, ½ hour	$45.00
Facial, 1 hour	$60.00
Mild glycolic peel	$75.00
Paraffin treatment, hands	$15.00
Paraffin treatment, feet	$20.00

Waxing

Half leg	$25.00
Full leg	$45.00
Brow	$10.00
Lip	$8.00

Ask about our
monthly
specials!
Lou

Lessons 15-19
Exercises 1-29

Lesson 15
Create, Save, and Exit a Spreadsheet

Lesson 16
Use Formulas; Spreadsheet Enhancements

Lesson 17
Copy Formulas; Additional Spreadsheet Enhancements

Lesson 18
Use Functions and Range Names

Lesson 19
Print and Chart Spreadsheet Information

Exercise 25

❖ Critical Thinking

Notes

Create and apply desktop publishing formatting to a new document on your own in this exercise.

Design Architects, LLC wants you to apply a new design to the firm's brochure.

Vocabulary

No new vocabulary in this exercise.

Directions

1. Open the **DP25** document file.
2. Save the file as **DA2**.
3. Format the document using any combination of the special text effects covered in this lesson: text design objects, drop caps, watermarks, reverse text, letter spacing, and pull quotes. Feel free to use any other formatting techniques you prefer, as well.
4. Save the document.
5. Print one copy of the document.
6. Close the document.

Circle the correct answer to each of the questions below:
1. Decorative and dividing lines you add into a document are called:
    A. Lines.
    B. Rules.
    C. Horizontal lines.
    D. All of the above.

2. When you use shading with a paragraph of text, you have to be make sure there's enough _____ for the text to print well and be readable:
    A. Lightness.
    B. Brightness.
    C. Boldness.
    D. Contrast.

3. Use these tools to create shapes in a document in most word processing programs:
    A. Paint tools.
    B. Pen tools.
    C. Drawing tools.
    D. Dot tools.

4. To control a shape's size and location, select the shape and then:
    A. Drag handles or a border with the mouse.
    B. Press the Space Bar.
    C. Press the F2 key.
    D. None of the above.

5. When you want to control the layering of clip art, shapes, and other objects, use this command:
    A. Bring Forward.
    B. Bring to Front.
    C. Send Backward.
    D. All of the above.

6. When you want to add text from a Word document into publisher, you:
    A. Retype it.
    B. Copy and paste it.
    C. Import it.
    D. Revise it.

Lesson 14
Working with Publisher

Exercises 26–31

❖ **Create a Quick Publication with text and a graphic**

❖ **Create a new publication from a template**

❖ **Change publication design, colors, and fonts**

❖ **Insert a design gallery object**

❖ **Adjust borders and fills**

❖ **Use a document from Word as a story**

Quiz Break 4

Circle the correct answer to each of the questions below:

T	F	1. You don't have to change any settings to be able to position clip art as desired.
T	F	2. You can resize a clip art image as needed.
T	F	3. Many word processing programs today work directly with your digital camera and scanner and the software powering those devices.
T	F	4. When you add a caption for a clip art image, you have no control over the caption's appearance.
T	F	5. You can only add one shape per document page.
T	F	6. You can control the fill and line style and color for many types of objects.
T	F	7. You can create more complex designs and nice effects by layering multiple objects.
T	F	8. Press and hold the Shift key, and then click various objects, to select multiple objects.
T	F	9. A drop capital is an oversized letter, usually found at the beginning of a heading or paragraph, that you create for emphasis.
T	F	10. You cannot drag a drop capital to change its position.
T	F	11. Depending on your word processing program, you insert a watermark in the header view, on the background, or as a regular object formatted with enhanced brightness and less contrast.
T	F	12. Pull quotes should never repeat text already in the document.

Fill in your brief answers below:

1. You can add _____ and _____ to enhance the appearance of a paragraph or page. _____

2. The formatting that controls whether a clip art image or other object appears in front of or behind text, or whether text abuts it is called: _____

3. The type of shape or object (such as a star or sun) that you can easily create with a special tool or command is called: _____

4. You _____ and _____ objects to lock them together as a single object or split them back into individual objects. _____

5. A type of fill that fades from one color to another is called a: _____

6. A special decorative text object is called: _____

7. The setting for formatting an object as a watermark may be called this: _____

8. When you create light text on a dark paragraph fill, it's called: _____

9. In Publisher, you can use a _____ or a _____ to establish your document's design. _____

10. In Publisher, placing each _____ in an individual text box enables you to have a great deal of flexibility in formatting and editing the text. _____

Exercise 26

❖ **Create a Quick Publication**
❖ **Add text to a placeholder**
❖ **Add a graphic to a placeholder**

Notes

Microsoft Office 2003 Professional Edition includes the Publisher 2003 program. Publisher offers greater desktop publishing and design capabilities than Word. So, if you want to create designer-quality publications in less time, Publisher is a great tool.

To create a basic flyer in Publisher, all you need to do is choose a **Quick Publication**. Each Quick Publication features an attractive, colorful design and placeholders for text and a graphic. All you have to do is **place** your own text or graphic in the placeholders to have a finished publication.

You have sailed your own boat for years and have been awarded all the certifications you need to teach others to sail, too. Create a flyer for your first sailing class now using a Quick Publication in Publisher.

Vocabulary

Quick Publication   place

Directions

1. Start Publisher, if needed. Or, if Publisher is already running, choose **File|New** to open the New Publication task pane at the left.
2. Display the available **Quick Publication** designs from the **Publications for Print** category.
3. Choose the **Scallops** Quick Publication design.
   - ✓ *If the Personal Information dialog box appears, click Cancel to continue.*
4. Apply the **Large picture in the middle** layout.

5. Select the Heading placeholder, and type **Learn to Sail!**
   - ✓ *Notice how Publisher automatically resizes the text to fit the placeholder, not vice versa. That's one reason why it's so easy to use a Quick Publication for your document.*
6. Replace the picture in the graphic placeholder with a clip art graphic of a sailboat.
   - ✓ *Right-click the picture, point to Change Picture, and then click Clip Art to get started. Once you've found the desired clip art, click it to add it into the placeholder.*

Learn to Sail!

Saturdays in June

10 a.m.—2p.m.

Marlowe Marina

Certified Instructor

Certifications Earned:

Keelboat Sailing Certified

Coastal Cruising Certified

Coastal Navigation Certified

Learn to Sail!
555-7878

Learn to Sail!
555-7878

Learn to Sail!
555-7878

Learn to Sail!
555-7878

Learn to Sail!
555-7878

Learn to Sail!
555-7878

Learn to Sail!
555-7878

Learn to Sail!
555-7878

Learn to Sail!
555-7878

Learn to Sail!
555-7878

Learn to Sail!
555-7878

Learn to Sail!
555-7878

Learn to Sail!
555-7878

7. Select the text in the bottom placeholder and type:
   Saturdays in June
   10 a.m.-2 p.m.
   Marlowe Marina
   Certified Instructor
   Call 555-7878.
8. Save the file as **SAILFLY**. The finished document should resemble the illustration below.

   ✓ *Your publication may use a different color scheme. Exercise 28 will explain how to work with color schemes.*

9. Print one copy of the document. (Continue the print job if you see a message telling you that the margins are outside the printable area.)
10. Close the document.

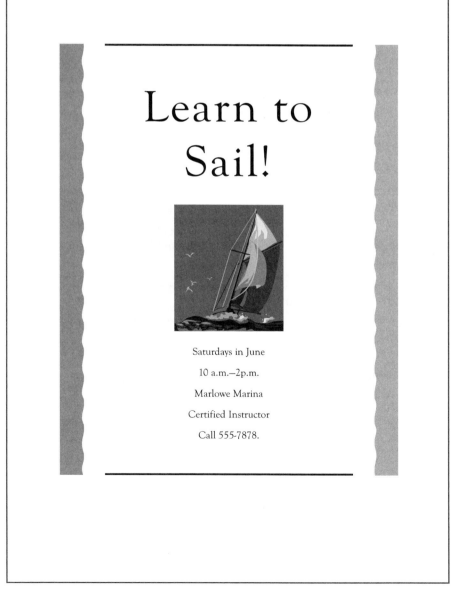

Exercise 31

❖ Place a Word Document as a Story
❖ Edit a Story in Word

Notes

If you have text that you've already saved in a Word document file, you don't have to retype that information into your Publisher document. You can instead copy the text as a **story** in your Publisher document. Create a new text box to hold the story you insert. Placing individual stories in separate text boxes enables you to better control where text appears in the document.

Finish your sailing class flyer by inserting a story that lists your sailing certifications. Use Word to update that information, too.

Vocabulary

story

Directions

1. Open the **DP31** document file.
2. Save the file as **SAILFLY5**.
3. Insert a new text box and position it approximately in the lower-left corner of the existing bottom text box. Make it about **3½"** wide and **1"** tall.
4. Start the Word application, and open the **DP31-2** file.
5. Select all file's contents, and copy the selection.
6. Exit Word, closing the document without saving any changes.
7. Switch back to the **SAILFLY5** document in Publisher, if needed.
8. Select the text box you created in Step 3.
9. Paste the copied text using the formatting in Publisher.
10. You want to add a heading to the story contents, so open the story for editing in Word.

   ✓ *Right-click the text box, point to Change Text, and click Edit Story in Microsoft Word.*

11. Add a new line that reads **Certifications Earned:** above the existing text.
12. Close the temporary document and return to the Publisher document.

   ✓ *Use the File | Close & Return to (document) command.*

13. Select the new story heading in the text box, increase its size to 10 point, and add boldface. The finished document should resemble the illustration on the following page.
14. Save your changes to the document file.
15. Print one copy of the document.
16. Close the document.

Exercise 27

❖ Use a Template ❖ Add Text and Graphics

Notes

In addition to the Quick Publications, Publisher offers dozens of designs for numerous publication types, including banners, business cards, envelopes, gift certificates, invitations, letterhead, and newsletters. As with a Quick Publication, templates provide text placeholders, design elements, and in some cases, placeholders for graphics.

Use a Publisher template to create a business card for your new role as sailing instructor.

Vocabulary

No new vocabulary in this exercise.

Directions

1. Start Publisher, if needed. Or, if Publisher is already running, choose **File|New** to open the New Publication task pane at the left.
2. Display the available **Business Cards** designs from the **Publications for Print** category.
3. Choose the **Scallops** design.
   - ✓ *Publisher also helps you create consistent-looking documents for your organization by offering the same or similar designs for a variety of publications.*
   - ✓ *By default, Publisher will plug in the information from the Primary Business personal information set in the Personal Information dialog box. For this exercise, you can simply replace any inserted information. However, if you want to save your actual personal information in Publisher, choose Edit|Personal Information.*
4. Click in the top text placeholder, the Organization Name, and type **Safe Sailing, LLC**.

   - ✓ *If clicking a placeholder doesn't select the text so that you can replace it, drag over the text before you begin typing.*
   - ✓ *If you hover the mouse pointer over a text box or placeholder, a pop-up tip will identify what information you should enter in the box.*

5. Click in the next placeholder, Personal Name, and type your name.
6. Click in the Job Title placeholder, and type **Sailing Instructor**.
7. Click in the Address placeholder, and type:
   Keelboat Sailing Certified
   Coastal Cruising Certified
   Coastal Navigation Certified
8. Click in the last placeholder, Phone/Fax/E-mail, and type **555-7878**.
9. Ungroup the logo graphic and Organization placeholders at the lower right. Click Yes when prompted to confirm the change.

Learn to Sail!

Saturdays in June

10 a.m.—2p.m.

Marlowe Marina

Certified Instructor

Learn to Sail!
555-7878

Learn to Sail!
555-7878

Learn to Sail!
555-7878

Learn to Sail!
555-7878

Learn to Sail!
555-7878

Learn to Sail!
555-7878

Learn to Sail!
555-7878

Learn to Sail!
555-7878

Learn to Sail!
555-7878

Learn to Sail!
555-7878

Learn to Sail!
555-7878

Learn to Sail!
555-7878

Learn to Sail!
555-7878

10. Replace the logo graphic placeholder with the sailboat clip art you inserted in the flyer in Exercise 26.
11. Select the clip art only and resize it to make it larger. Re-center it over the Organization placeholder.
12. Click the word Organization in the placeholder, and type **Learn to Sail!** to replace the original text. The finished business card should look like the illustration below.

   ✓ *Your publication may use a different color scheme. Exercise 28 will explain how to work with color schemes.*

13. Save the file as **SAILCRD**.
14. Save your changes to the document file. Do not save changes to the Primary Business personal information set.
15. Print one copy of the document.
16. Close the document.

Safe Sailing, LLC

Student's Name
Sailing Instructor

Keelboat Sailing Certified
Coastal Cruising Certified
Coastal Navigation Certified

555-7878

Learn to Sail!

Exercise 30

❖ Work with Borders ❖ Work with Fills

Notes

Publisher offers the same ability to uses borders and fills as a typical word processing program. Even a simple border or fill can improve the appeal of a design.

Continue enhancing your sailing class flyer by working with borders and fills.

Vocabulary

No new vocabulary in this exercise.

Directions

1. Open the **DP30** document file.
2. Save the file as **SAILFLY4**.
3. Select the top text box that holds the **Learn to Sail!** text.
4. Use the Format Text Box dialog box to apply the **Accent 3** color from the color scheme as a fill for the text box.
5. Left align the text in the smaller text box, and increase the font size to 16 point.
6. Increase the size of the sailing picture clip art until it's about **2"** high and proportionally wide.
7. Add a 3-point border (line) in the **Accent 2** color from the color scheme around the clip art.
8. Select the phone tear-off object at the bottom of the document.
9. Use the Format Object text box to apply the **Accent 3** color as a fill. Your finished document should resemble the illustration on the following page.
10. Save your changes to the document file.
11. Print one copy of the document.
12. Close the document.

Exercise 28

❖ Change Publication Design
❖ Change Color Scheme ❖ Change Font Scheme

Notes

Publisher makes it easy to change the appearance of any publication. With only a mouse click or two, you can apply a whole new **publication design**, **color scheme**, or **font scheme**.

You've decided you want to change the appearance of the sailing class flyer you created earlier (in Exercise 26). Change the flyer's design, colors, and fonts now.

Vocabulary

publication design   color scheme   font scheme

Directions

1. Open the **DP28** document file.
2. Save the file as **SAILFLY2**.
3. Display the Publication Designs task pane.
4. Apply the **Quadrant Quick Publication** design.
5. Display the Color Schemes task pane.
6. Apply the **Reef** color scheme.
7. Display the Font Schemes task pane.
8. Apply the **Punch** font scheme.
9. Display the Quick Publication Options task pane.
10. Apply the **Small picture in the middle** layout to finish the publication. The illustration on the following page shows the finished document.
11. Save your changes to the document file.
12. Print one copy of the document.
13. Close the document.

Learn to Sail!

Saturdays in June

10 a.m.—2p.m.

Marlowe Marina

Certified Instructor

Learn to Sail!
555-7878

Learn to Sail!
555-7878

Learn to Sail!
555-7878

Learn to Sail!
555-7878

Learn to Sail!
555-7878

Learn to Sail!
555-7878

Learn to Sail!
555-7878

Learn to Sail!
555-7878

Learn to Sail!
555-7878

Learn to Sail!
555-7878

Learn to Sail!
555-7878

Learn to Sail!
555-7878

Learn to Sail!
555-7878

Learn
to Sail!

Saturdays in June

10 a.m.—2p.m.

Marlowe Marina

Certified Instructor

Call 555-7878.

Exercise 29

❖ Add a Design Gallery Object

Notes

In the past, if you wanted to include a special element in a document—such as a coupon, ad, or specially-designed border—you had to build the element yourself out of various drawing and text objects. Publisher saves you many steps and a lot of time by offering a Design Gallery with predesigned objects for you to insert. The available **Design Gallery objects** include coupons, ads, attention getters, phone number tear-offs, reply forms, and a variety of other elements that you can choose to complete a document.

Add a phone number tear-off to the sailing class flyer now, so that interested persons will be able to tear-off your phone number.

Vocabulary

Design Gallery object

Directions

1. Open the **DP29** document file.
2. Save the file as **SAILFLY3**.
3. Open the Design Gallery.
   ✓ *You have to choose Insert│Design Gallery Object.*
4. Choose the Phone Tear-Off category.
5. Insert the **Phone Tear-Off** object.
6. Drag the tear-off object down and place its bottom border on the bottom edge of the page.
7. Increase the width of the tear-off so that it's as wide as the page.
   ✓ *Publisher automatically increases the number of tear-off tags when you make the tear-off wider.*
8. Resize the black outline box and the green border along the left side so they align with the top of the phone tear-off object.

9. Select the text in one of the tear-off tags.
10. Type:
    Learn to Sail!
    555-7878
11. Click in one of the other tear-off tags. Publisher automatically updates all of the tags to use the text that you typed.
12. In the large text box, delete the line that reads **Call 555-7878**. The finished document should resemble the illustration on the following page.
13. Save the document.
14. Print one copy of the document. (Continue the print job if you see a message telling you that the margins are outside the printable area.)
15. Close the document.

Index